Shojo Beat

O·TO·MEN

Story & Art by
Aya Kanno

Volume
SIXTEEN

OTOMEN Characters & Story

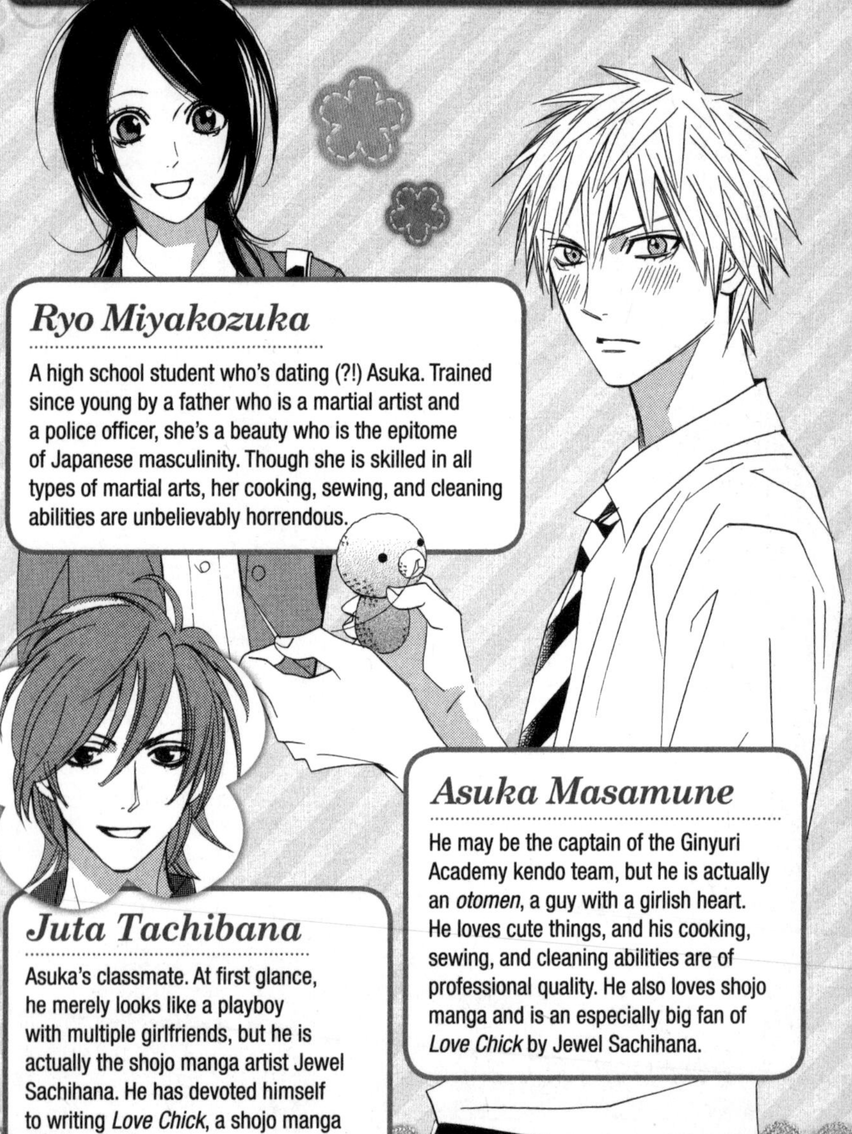

Ryo Miyakozuka

A high school student who's dating (?!) Asuka. Trained since young by a father who is a martial artist and a police officer, she's a beauty who is the epitome of Japanese masculinity. Though she is skilled in all types of martial arts, her cooking, sewing, and cleaning abilities are unbelievably horrendous.

Asuka Masamune

He may be the captain of the Ginyuri Academy kendo team, but he is actually an *otomen*, a guy with a girlish heart. He loves cute things, and his cooking, sewing, and cleaning abilities are of professional quality. He also loves shojo manga and is an especially big fan of *Love Chick* by Jewel Sachihana.

Juta Tachibana

Asuka's classmate. At first glance, he merely looks like a playboy with multiple girlfriends, but he is actually the shojo manga artist Jewel Sachihana. He has devoted himself to writing *Love Chick*, a shojo manga based on Asuka and Ryo's relationship.

STORY

Asuka and his friends attend the summer festival. Yamato lies to an old classmate about having a girlfriend, and Ryo unwittingly goes on a double date with him. Unfortunately, a group of rough guys start harassing them. Yamato distracts them by saying that he's actually a girl. Ryo tells him that he looked cool doing that, and Yamato starts having feelings for Ryo. He doesn't think his feelings are going to lead anywhere, but Juta urges him on, telling him that love is a battle.

RYO IS IN DANGER!

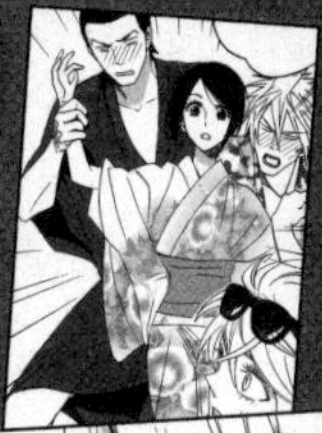

USING CUTENESS AND THE POWER OF DELUSION AS A WEAPON…

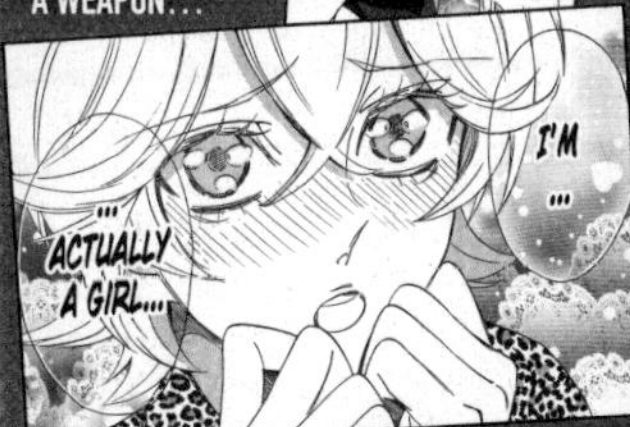
I'M ...
... ACTUALLY A GIRL...

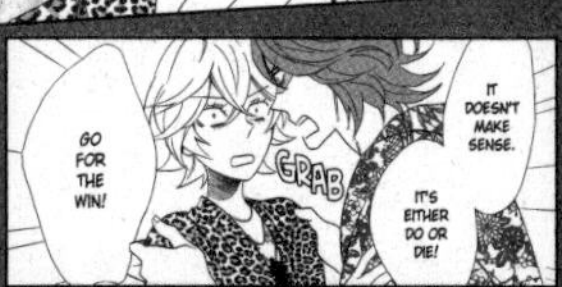
IT DOESN'T MAKE SENSE.
IT'S EITHER DO OR DIE!
GRAB
GO FOR THE WIN!

JUTA SENSEI GIVES A LECTURE ON LOVE!

OTHER OTOMEN

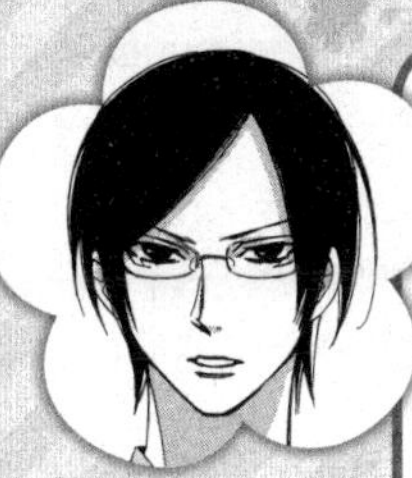

Hajime Tonomine

The captain of the Kinbara High School kendo team, he considers Asuka his sworn rival. He is actually an *otomen* who is good with cosmetics.

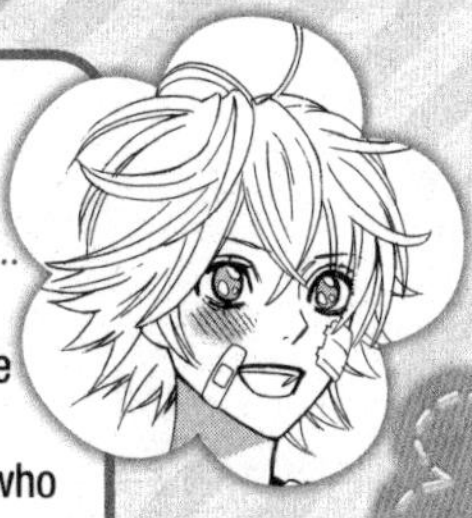

Yamato Ariake

He is younger than Asuka and looks like a cute girl. He is a delusional *otomen* who admires manliness.

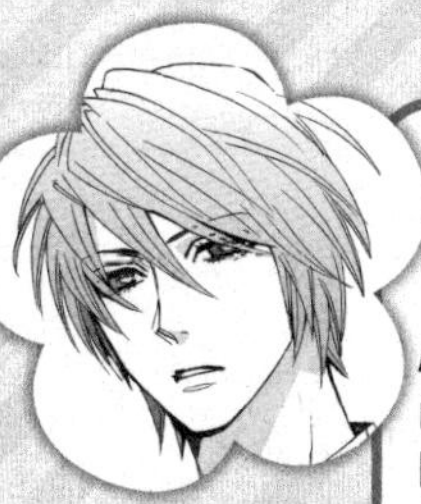

Kitora Kurokawa

Asuka's classmate. A man who is captivated by the beauty of flowers. He is an obsessed *otomen* who wants to cover the world in flowers.

OTOMEN
volume 16
CONTENTS

OTOMEN 05

GLOSSARY 192

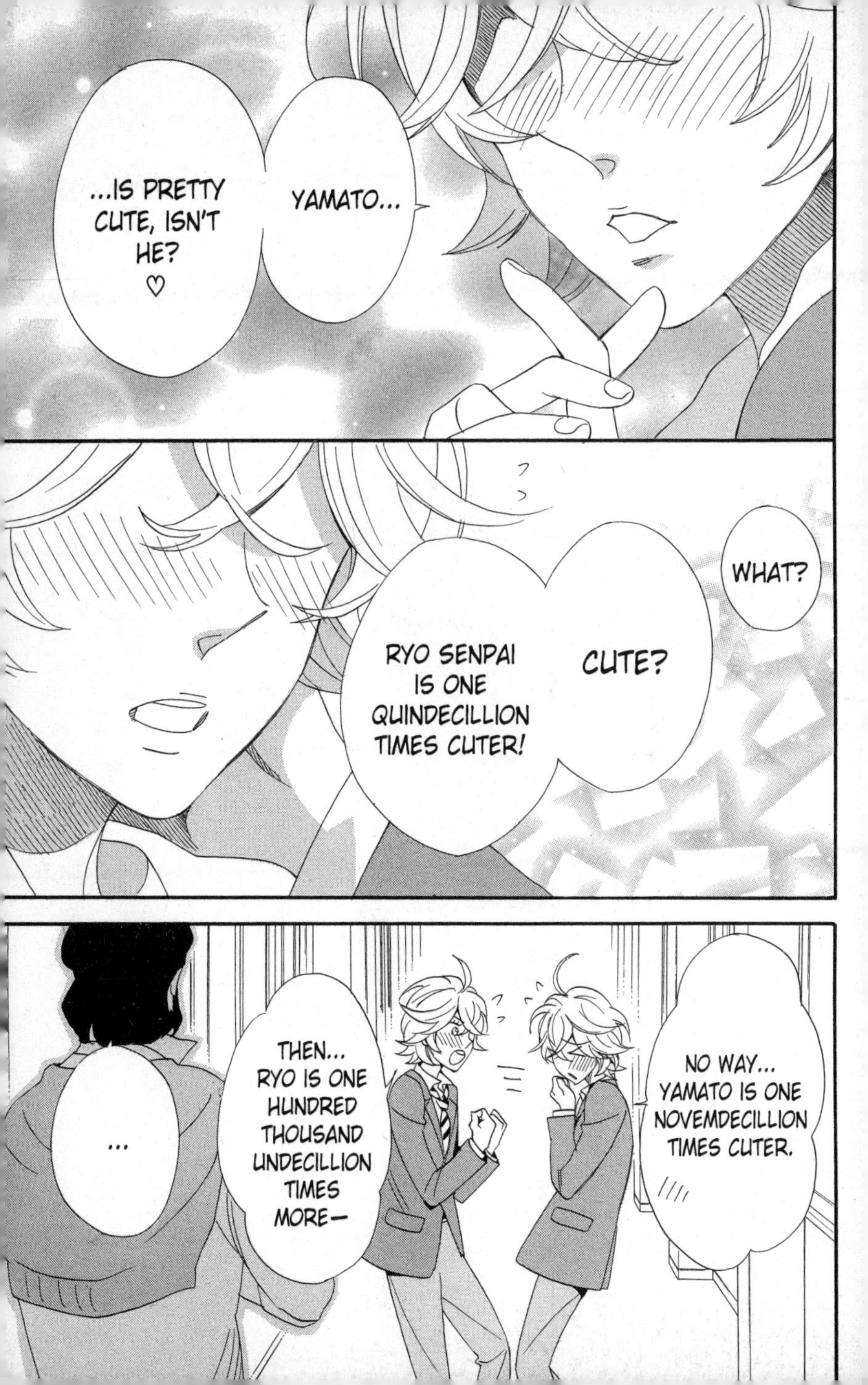
YAMATO...
...IS PRETTY CUTE, ISN'T HE? ♡
WHAT?
CUTE?
RYO SENPAI IS ONE QUINDECILLION TIMES CUTER!
NO WAY... YAMATO IS ONE NOVEMDECILLION TIMES CUTER.
THEN... RYO IS ONE HUNDRED THOUSAND UNDECILLION TIMES MORE—
...

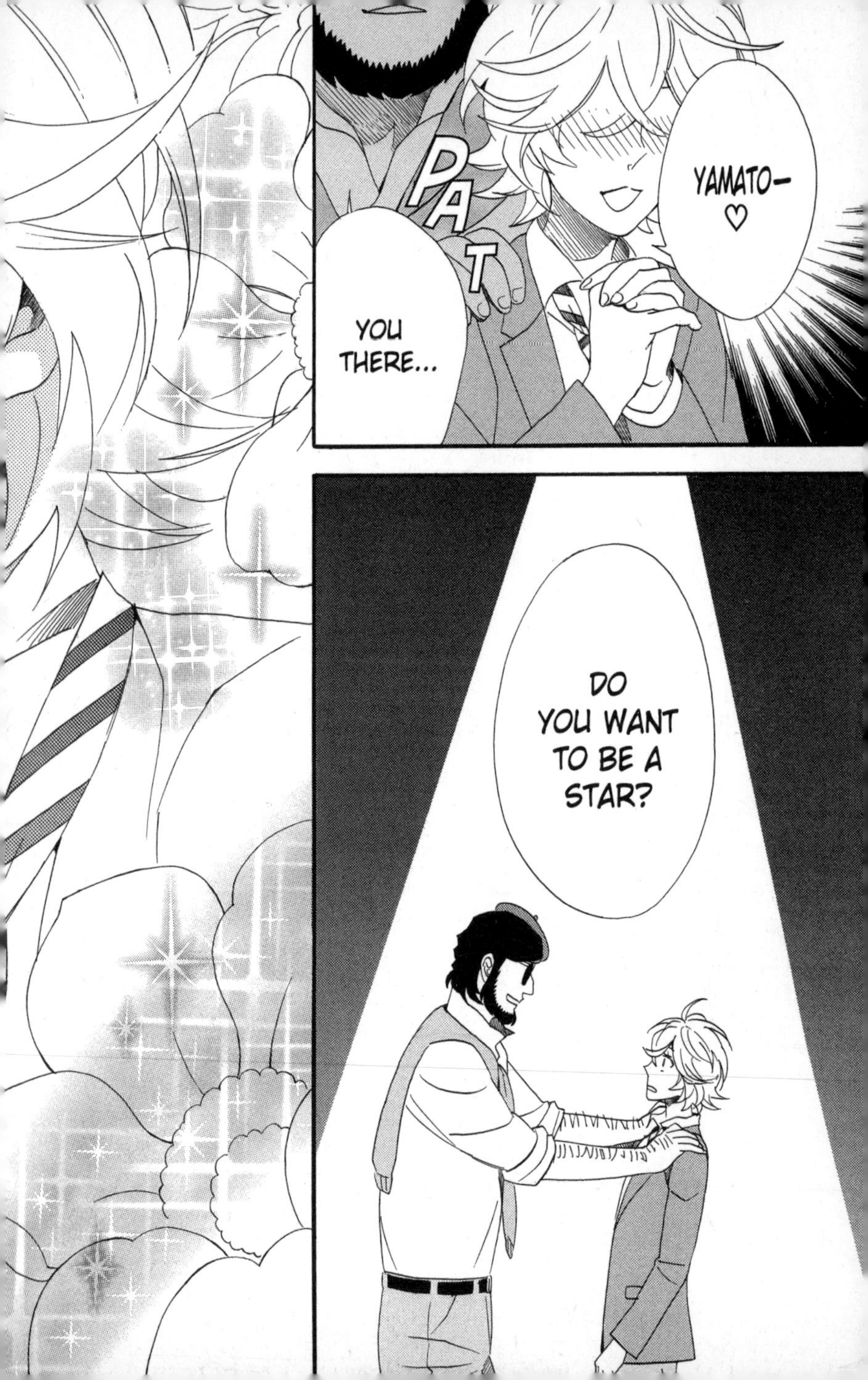
YAMATO-♡
PAT
YOU THERE...
DO YOU WANT TO BE A STAR?

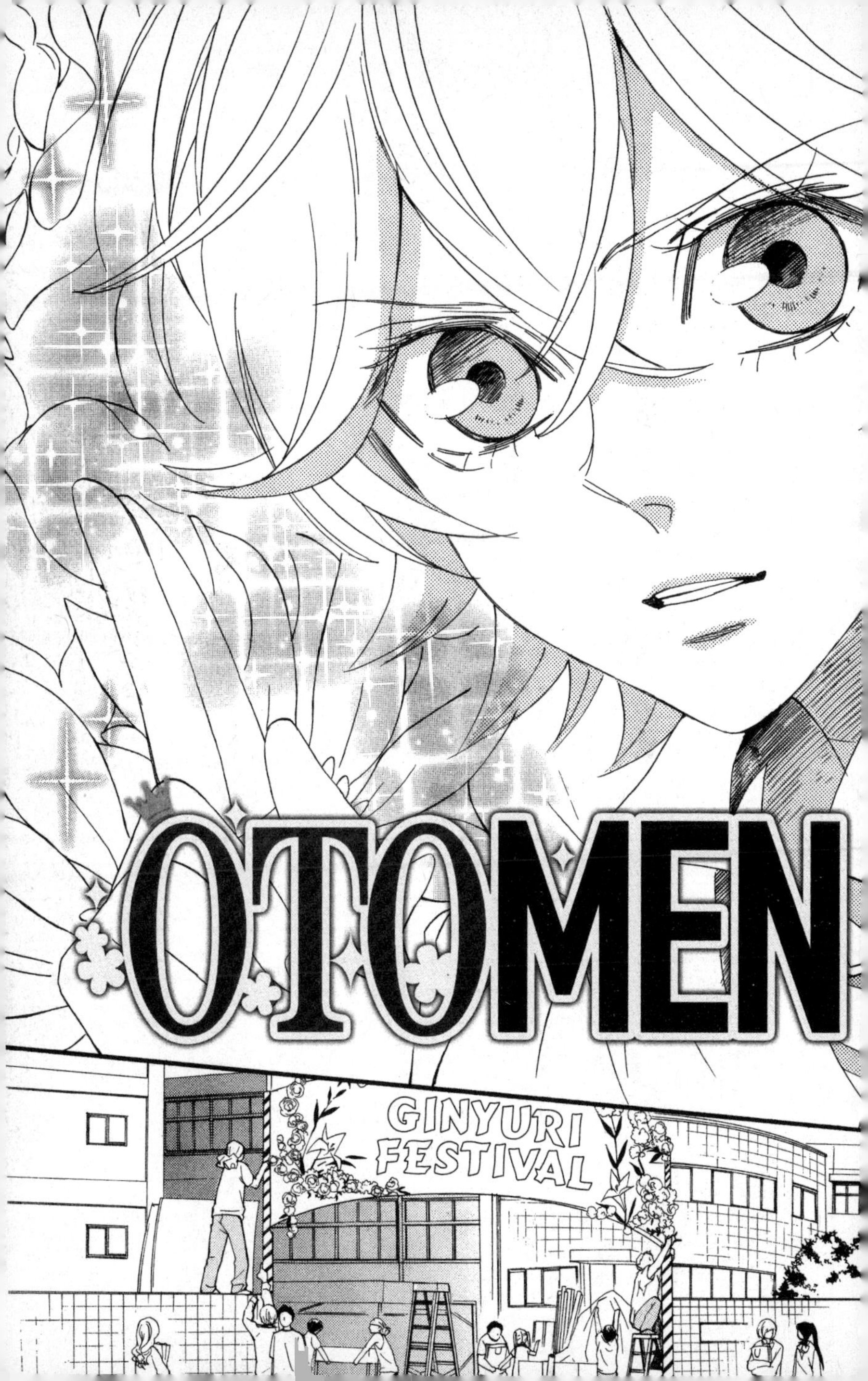
OTOMEN
GINYURI
FESTIVAL

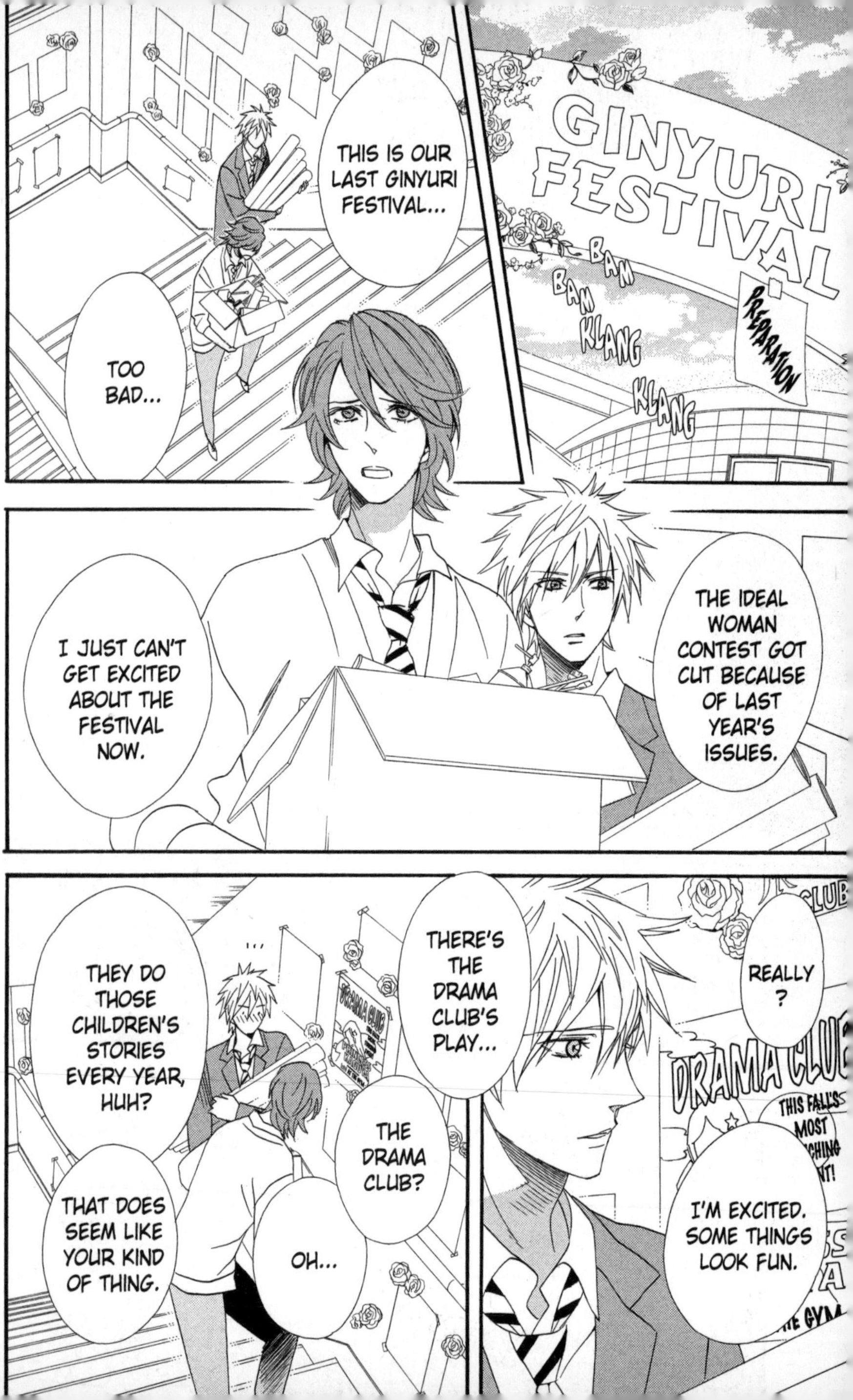
GINYURI FESTIVAL
PREPARATION
BAM
BAM
KLANG
KLANG
THIS IS OUR LAST GINYURI FESTIVAL...
TOO BAD...
THE IDEAL WOMAN CONTEST GOT CUT BECAUSE OF LAST YEAR'S ISSUES.
I JUST CAN'T GET EXCITED ABOUT THE FESTIVAL NOW.
REALLY?
DRAMA CLUB
THIS FALL'S MOST
I'M EXCITED. SOME THINGS LOOK FUN.
THERE'S THE DRAMA CLUB'S PLAY...
THE DRAMA CLUB?
THEY DO THOSE CHILDREN'S STORIES EVERY YEAR, HUH?
...
OH...
THAT DOES SEEM LIKE YOUR KIND OF THING.

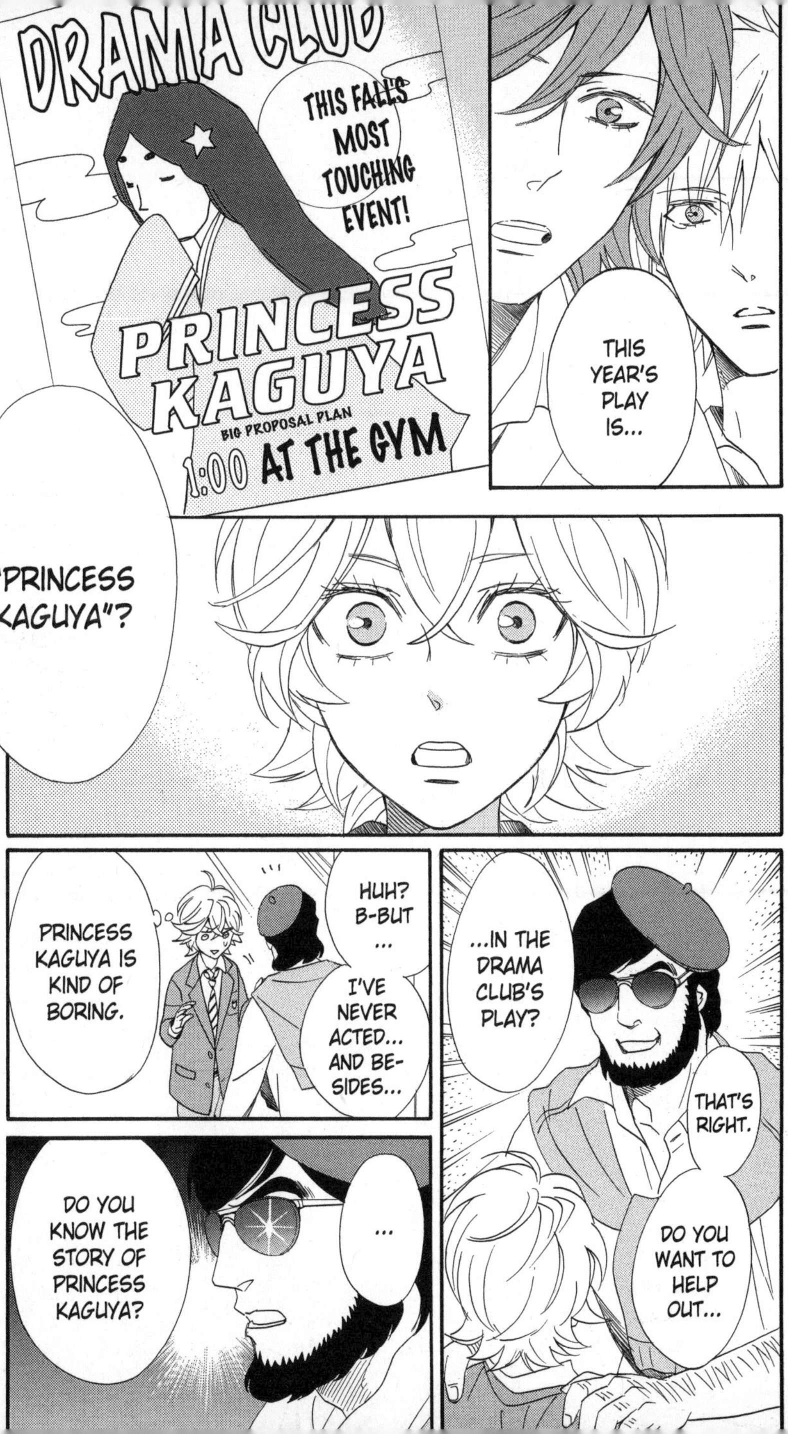
THIS YEAR'S PLAY IS...
DRAMA CLUB
THIS FALL'S MOST TOUCHING EVENT!
PRINCESS KAGUYA
BIG PROPOSAL PLAN
1:00 AT THE GYM
"PRINCESS KAGUYA"?
THAT'S RIGHT.
DO YOU WANT TO HELP OUT...
...IN THE DRAMA CLUB'S PLAY?
HUH? B-BUT ...
I'VE NEVER ACTED... AND BE-SIDES...
PRINCESS KAGUYA IS KIND OF BORING.
...
DO YOU KNOW THE STORY OF PRINCESS KAGUYA?

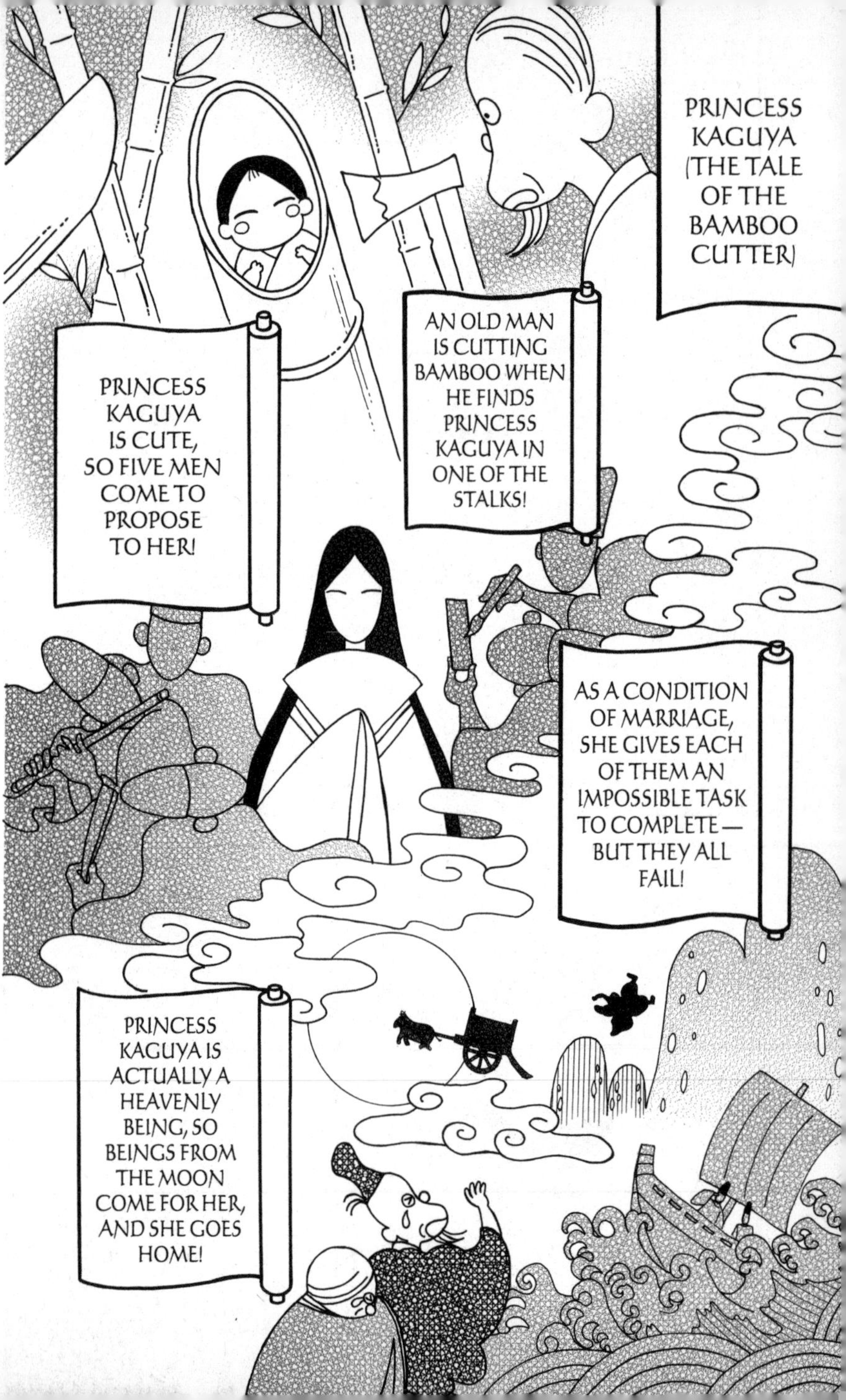
PRINCESS KAGUYA (THE TALE OF THE BAMBOO CUTTER)
AN OLD MAN IS CUTTING BAMBOO WHEN HE FINDS PRINCESS KAGUYA IN ONE OF THE STALKS!
PRINCESS KAGUYA IS CUTE, SO FIVE MEN COME TO PROPOSE TO HER!
AS A CONDITION OF MARRIAGE, SHE GIVES EACH OF THEM AN IMPOSSIBLE TASK TO COMPLETE— BUT THEY ALL FAIL!
PRINCESS KAGUYA IS ACTUALLY A HEAVENLY BEING, SO BEINGS FROM THE MOON COME FOR HER, AND SHE GOES HOME!

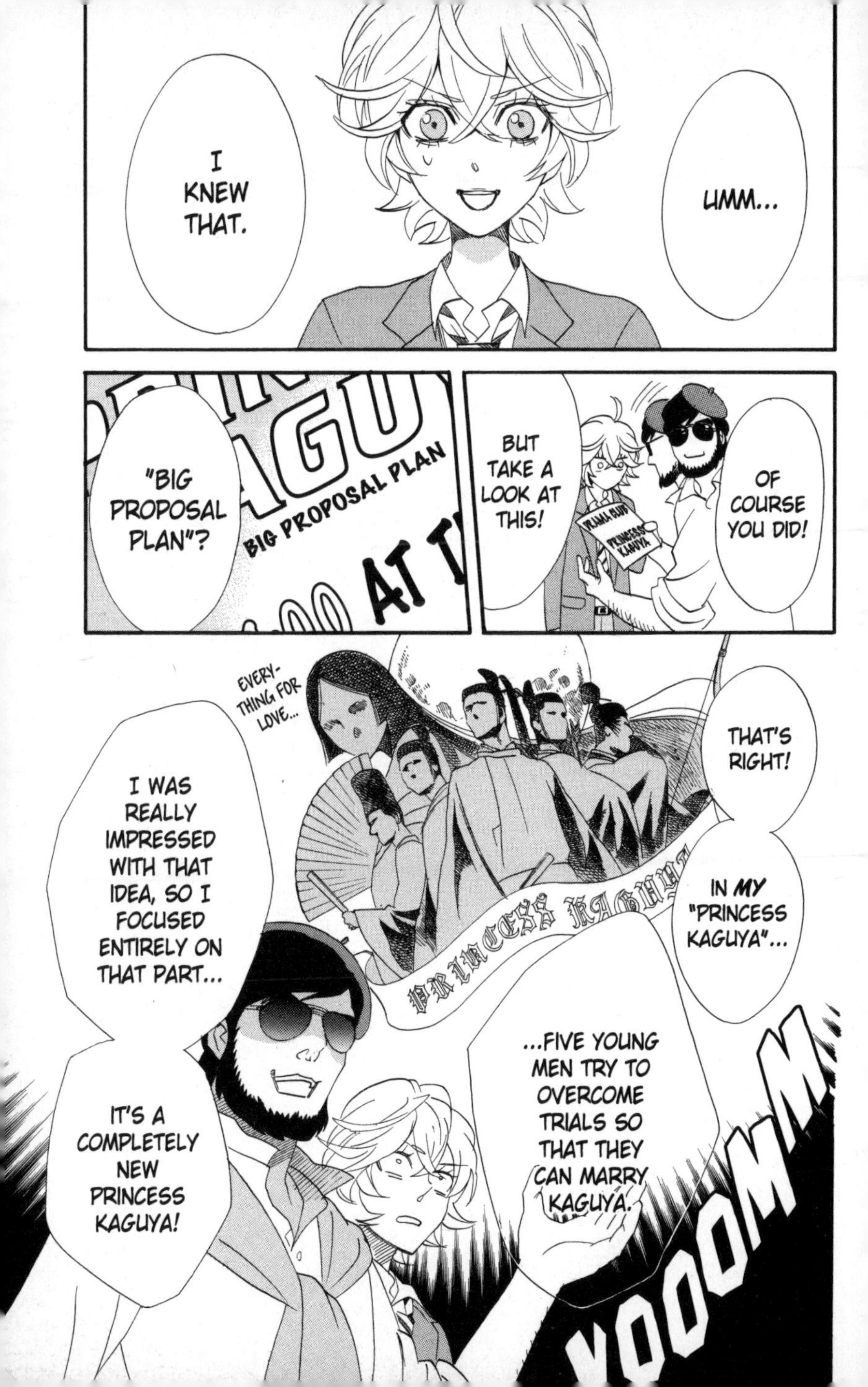
UMM...
I KNEW THAT.
OF COURSE YOU DID!
BUT TAKE A LOOK AT THIS!
DRAMA CLUB
PRINCESS KAGUYA
BIG PROPOSAL PLAN
"BIG PROPOSAL PLAN"?
THAT'S RIGHT!
IN *MY* "PRINCESS KAGUYA"...
EVERY-THING FOR LOVE...
PRINCESS KAGUYA
I WAS REALLY IMPRESSED WITH THAT IDEA, SO I FOCUSED ENTIRELY ON THAT PART...
...FIVE YOUNG MEN TRY TO OVERCOME TRIALS SO THAT THEY CAN MARRY KAGUYA.
IT'S A COMPLETELY NEW PRINCESS KAGUYA!
VOOOMM

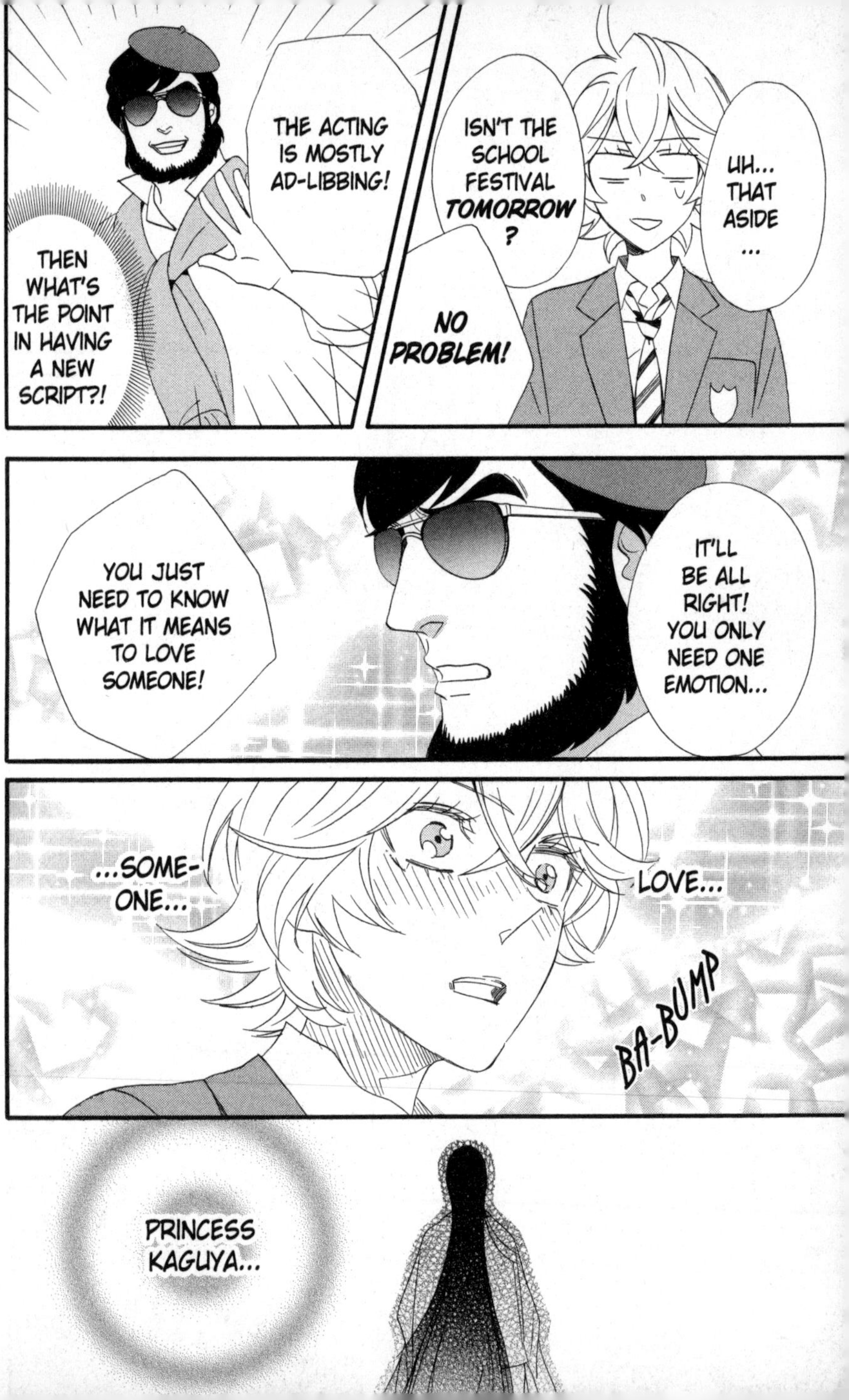
UH... THAT ASIDE...
ISN'T THE SCHOOL FESTIVAL TOMORROW?
NO PROBLEM!
THE ACTING IS MOSTLY AD-LIBBING!
THEN WHAT'S THE POINT IN HAVING A NEW SCRIPT?!
IT'LL BE ALL RIGHT! YOU ONLY NEED ONE EMOTION...
YOU JUST NEED TO KNOW WHAT IT MEANS TO LOVE SOMEONE!
LOVE...
BA-BUMP
...SOME-ONE...
PRINCESS KAGUYA...

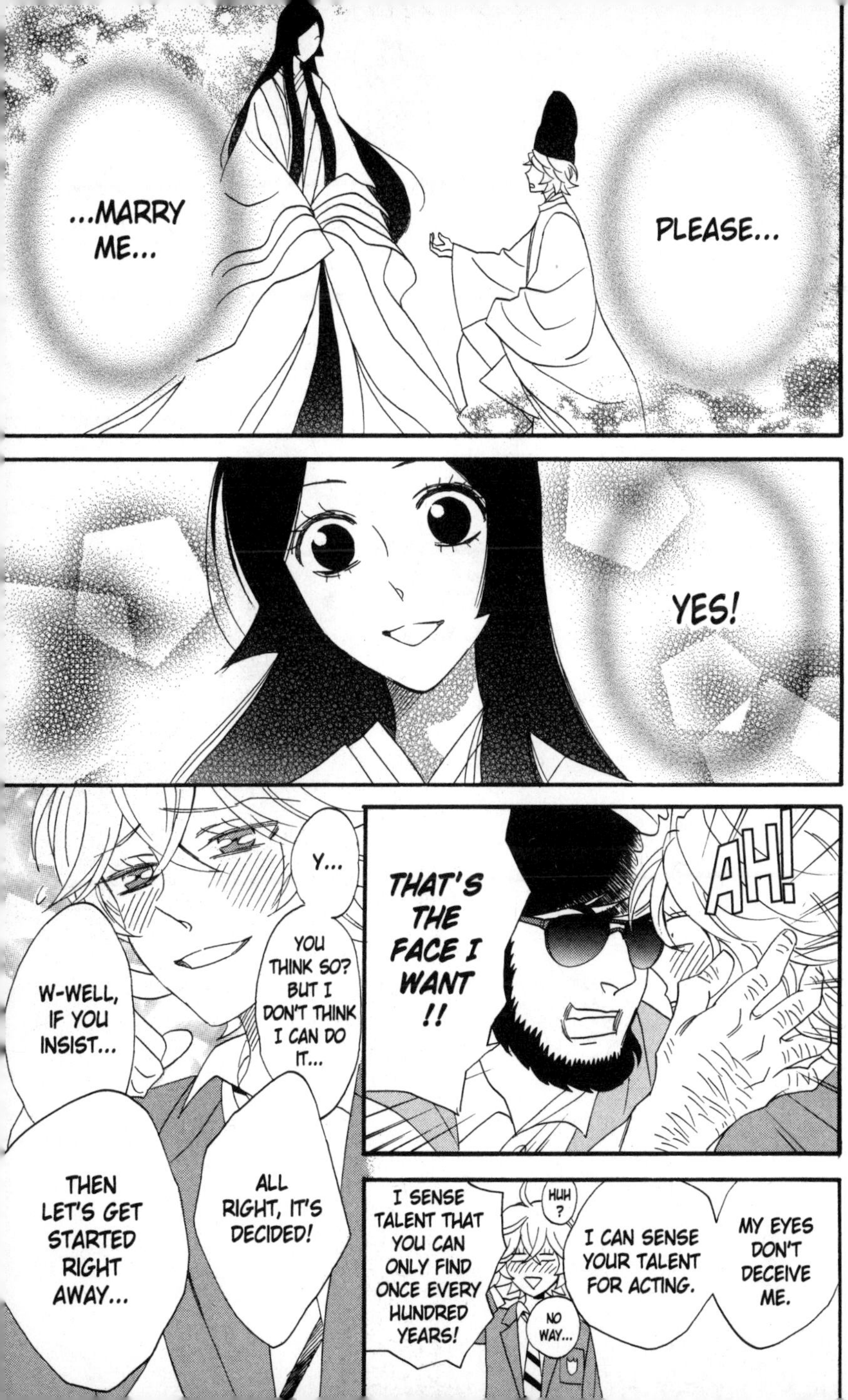
PLEASE...
...MARRY ME...
YES!
AH!
THAT'S THE FACE I WANT!!
MY EYES DON'T DECEIVE ME.
I CAN SENSE YOUR TALENT FOR ACTING.
HUH?
I SENSE TALENT THAT YOU CAN ONLY FIND ONCE EVERY HUNDRED YEARS!
NO WAY...
Y...
YOU THINK SO? BUT I DON'T THINK I CAN DO IT...
W-WELL, IF YOU INSIST...
ALL RIGHT, IT'S DECIDED!
THEN LET'S GET STARTED RIGHT AWAY...

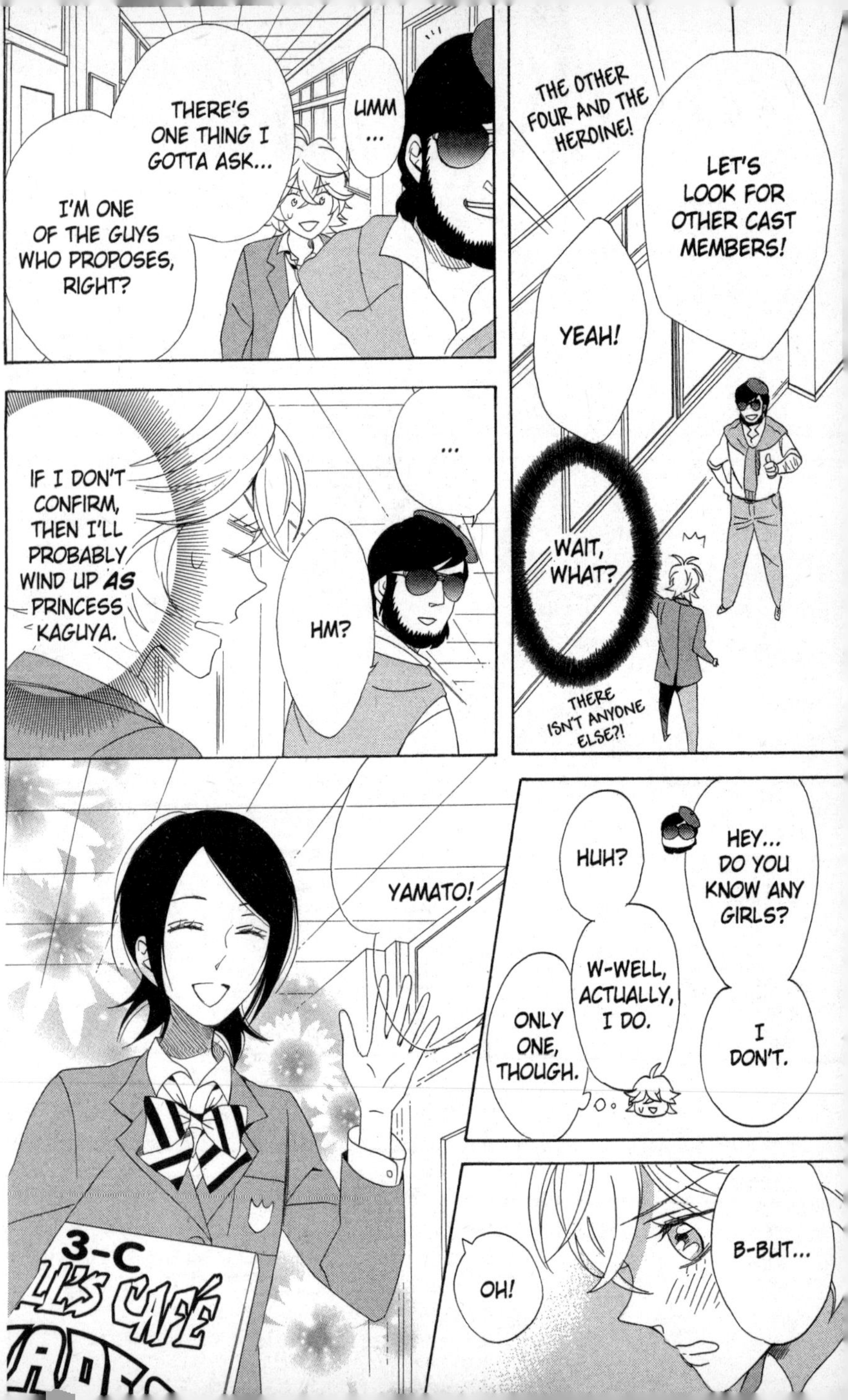

LET'S LOOK FOR OTHER CAST MEMBERS!
THE OTHER FOUR AND THE HEROINE!
YEAH!
WAIT, WHAT?
THERE ISN'T ANYONE ELSE?!
UMM ...
THERE'S ONE THING I GOTTA ASK...
I'M ONE OF THE GUYS WHO PROPOSES, RIGHT?
...
HM?
IF I DON'T CONFIRM, THEN I'LL PROBABLY WIND UP AS PRINCESS KAGUYA.
HEY... DO YOU KNOW ANY GIRLS?
HUH?
I DON'T.
W-WELL, ACTUALLY, I DO.
ONLY ONE, THOUGH.
B-BUT...
OH!
YAMATO!
3-C

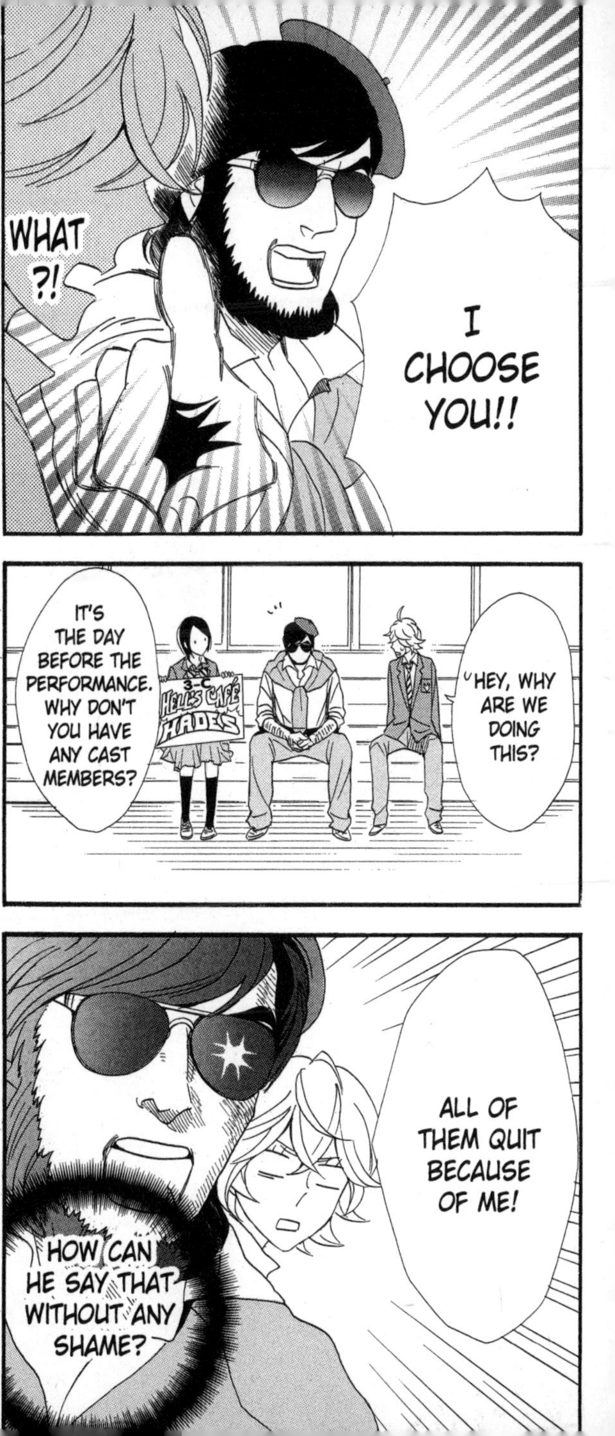
I CHOOSE YOU!!
WHAT ?!
HEY, WHY ARE WE DOING THIS?
IT'S THE DAY BEFORE THE PERFORMANCE. WHY DON'T YOU HAVE ANY CAST MEMBERS?
3-C HELL'S CAFÉ HADES
ALL OF THEM QUIT BECAUSE OF ME!
HOW CAN HE SAY THAT WITHOUT ANY SHAME?

Hello, this is volume 16!

Yamato's turn continues from the last volume.

It's a Yamato festival.

It's very easy to draw Yamato. (When he first appeared, I think I mentioned that it was difficult to move him around, but that's not true anymore.) I kind of got carried away with this story. Yes.

It was fun. *Ha ha.*

Furthermore, because of the director, this story became rather absurd.

The director was also very easy to move. Or rather, he's the kind of character I like.

I tried to avoid making too many jokes. (And yet, he still turned out this way.)

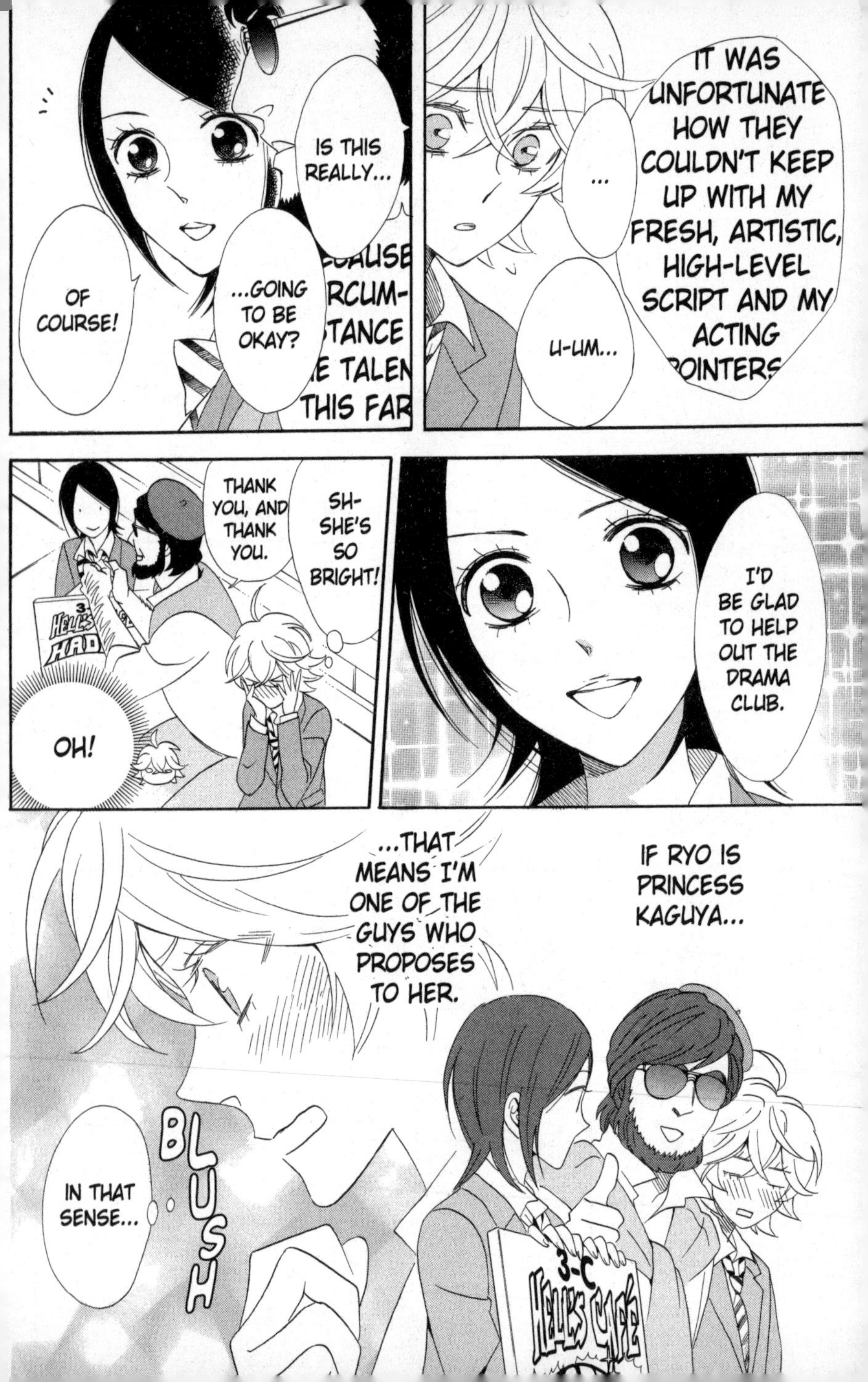
IT WAS UNFORTUNATE HOW THEY COULDN'T KEEP UP WITH MY FRESH, ARTISTIC, HIGH-LEVEL SCRIPT AND MY ACTING POINTERS
...
U-UM...
IS THIS REALLY...
...GOING TO BE OKAY?
OF COURSE!
I'D BE GLAD TO HELP OUT THE DRAMA CLUB.
SH-SHE'S SO BRIGHT!
THANK YOU, AND THANK YOU.
OH!
IF RYO IS PRINCESS KAGUYA...
...THAT MEANS I'M ONE OF THE GUYS WHO PROPOSES TO HER.
IN THAT SENSE...
BLUSH
3-C HELL'S CAFE

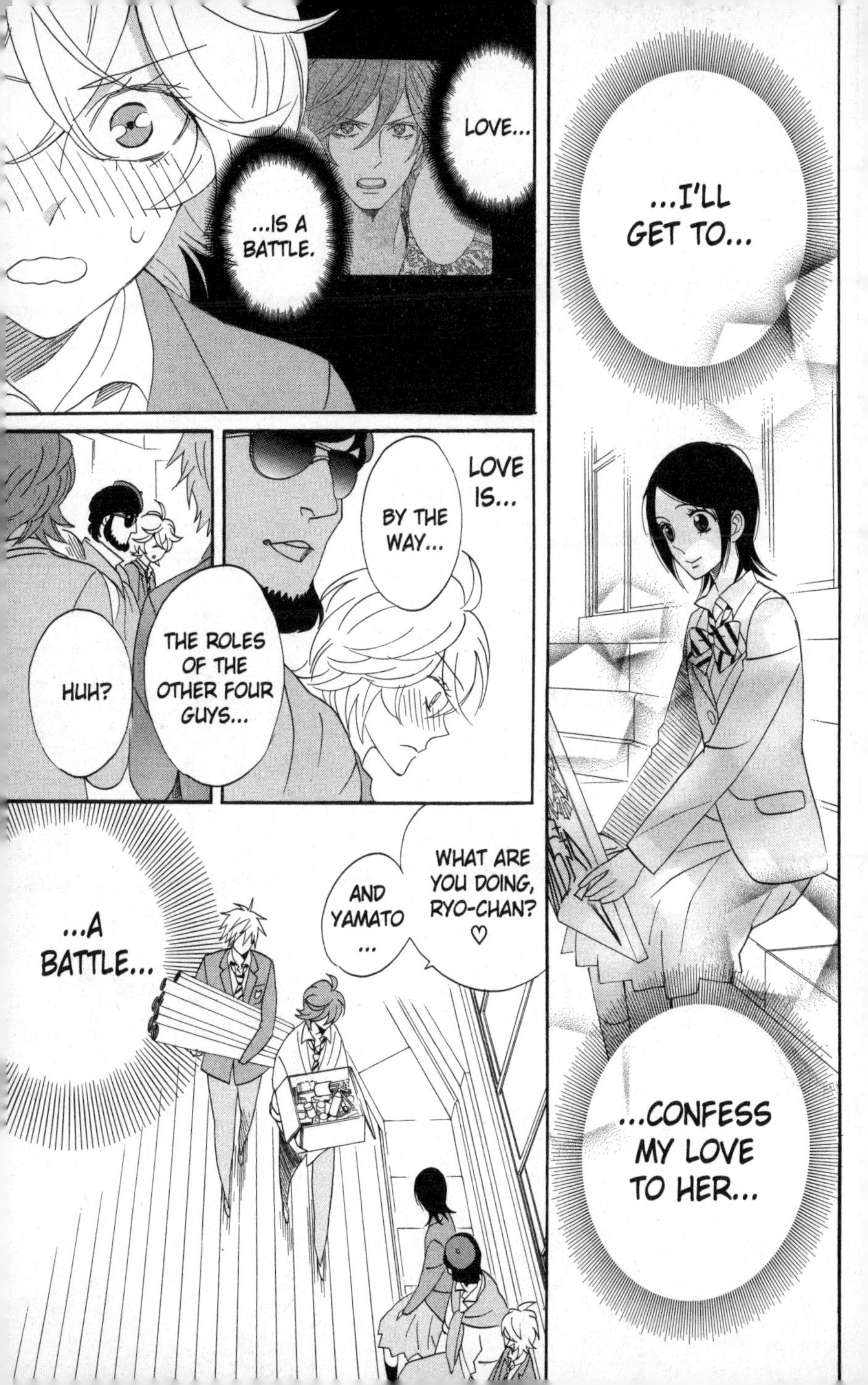
...I'LL GET TO...
...CONFESS MY LOVE TO HER...
LOVE...
...IS A BATTLE.
LOVE IS...
BY THE WAY...
THE ROLES OF THE OTHER FOUR GUYS...
HUH?
WHAT ARE YOU DOING, RYO-CHAN? ♡
AND YAMATO ...
...A BATTLE...

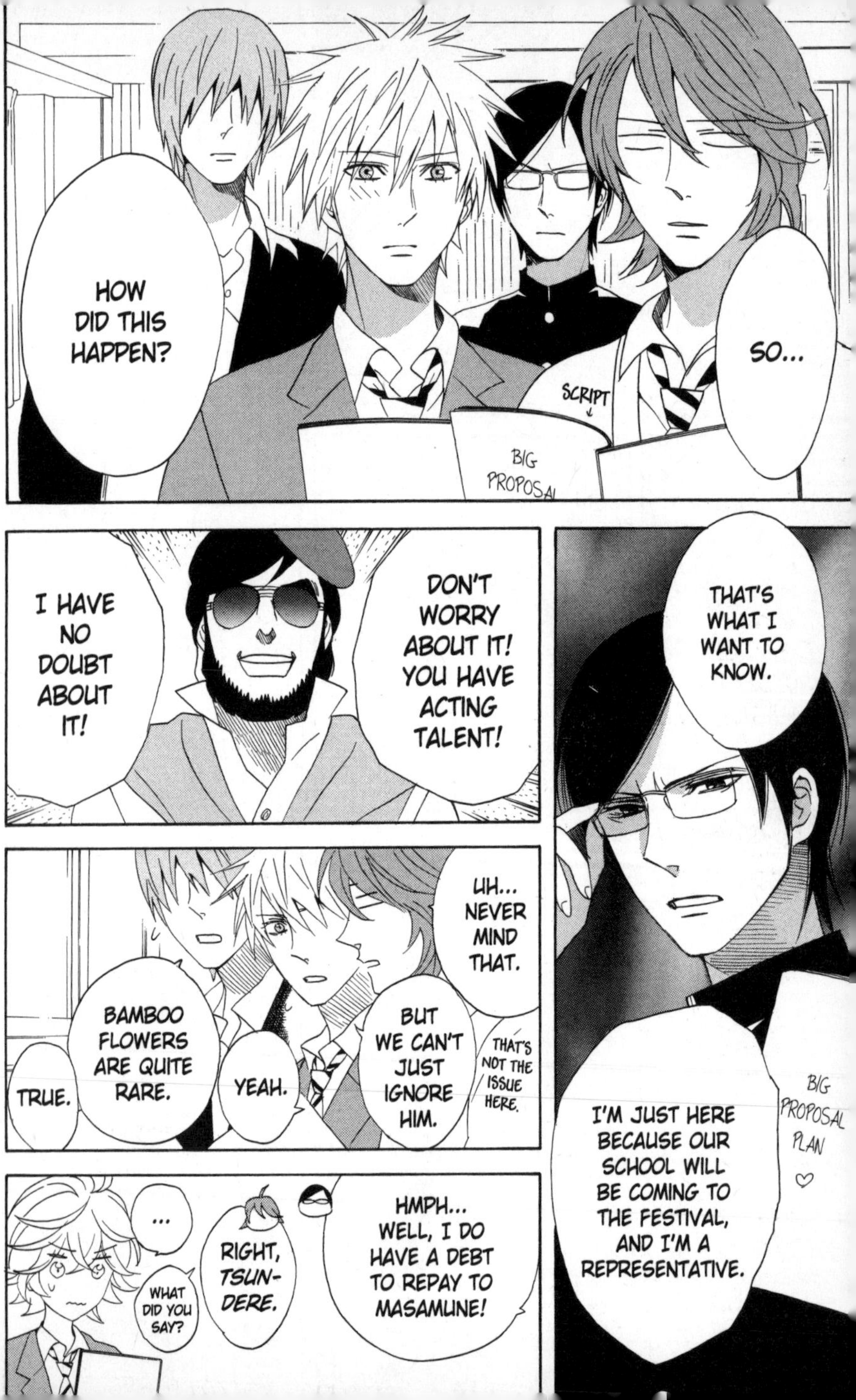
SO...
SCRIPT
BIG PROPOSAL
HOW DID THIS HAPPEN?
THAT'S WHAT I WANT TO KNOW.
I'M JUST HERE BECAUSE OUR SCHOOL WILL BE COMING TO THE FESTIVAL, AND I'M A REPRESENTATIVE.
BIG PROPOSAL PLAN ♡
DON'T WORRY ABOUT IT! YOU HAVE ACTING TALENT!
I HAVE NO DOUBT ABOUT IT!
UH... NEVER MIND THAT.
THAT'S NOT THE ISSUE HERE.
BUT WE CAN'T JUST IGNORE HIM.
YEAH.
BAMBOO FLOWERS ARE QUITE RARE.
TRUE.
HMPH... WELL, I DO HAVE A DEBT TO REPAY TO MASAMUNE!
RIGHT, TSUNDERE.
...
WHAT DID YOU SAY?

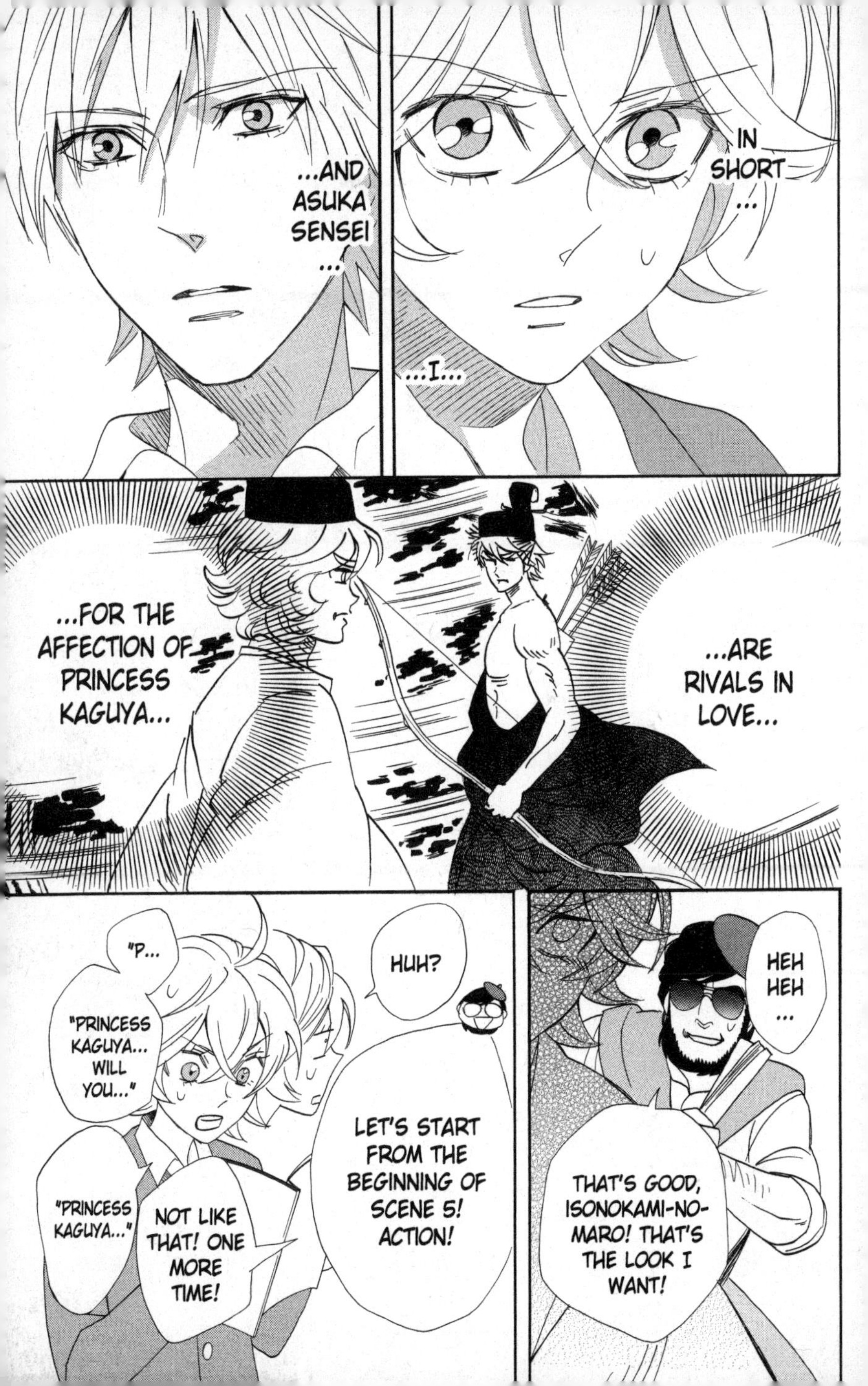
IN SHORT...
...I...
...AND ASUKA SENSEI...
...ARE RIVALS IN LOVE...
...FOR THE AFFECTION OF PRINCESS KAGUYA...
HEH HEH...
THAT'S GOOD, ISONOKAMI-NO-MARO! THAT'S THE LOOK I WANT!
HUH?
LET'S START FROM THE BEGINNING OF SCENE 5! ACTION!
"P...
"PRINCESS KAGUYA... WILL YOU..."
NOT LIKE THAT! ONE MORE TIME!
"PRINCESS KAGUYA..."

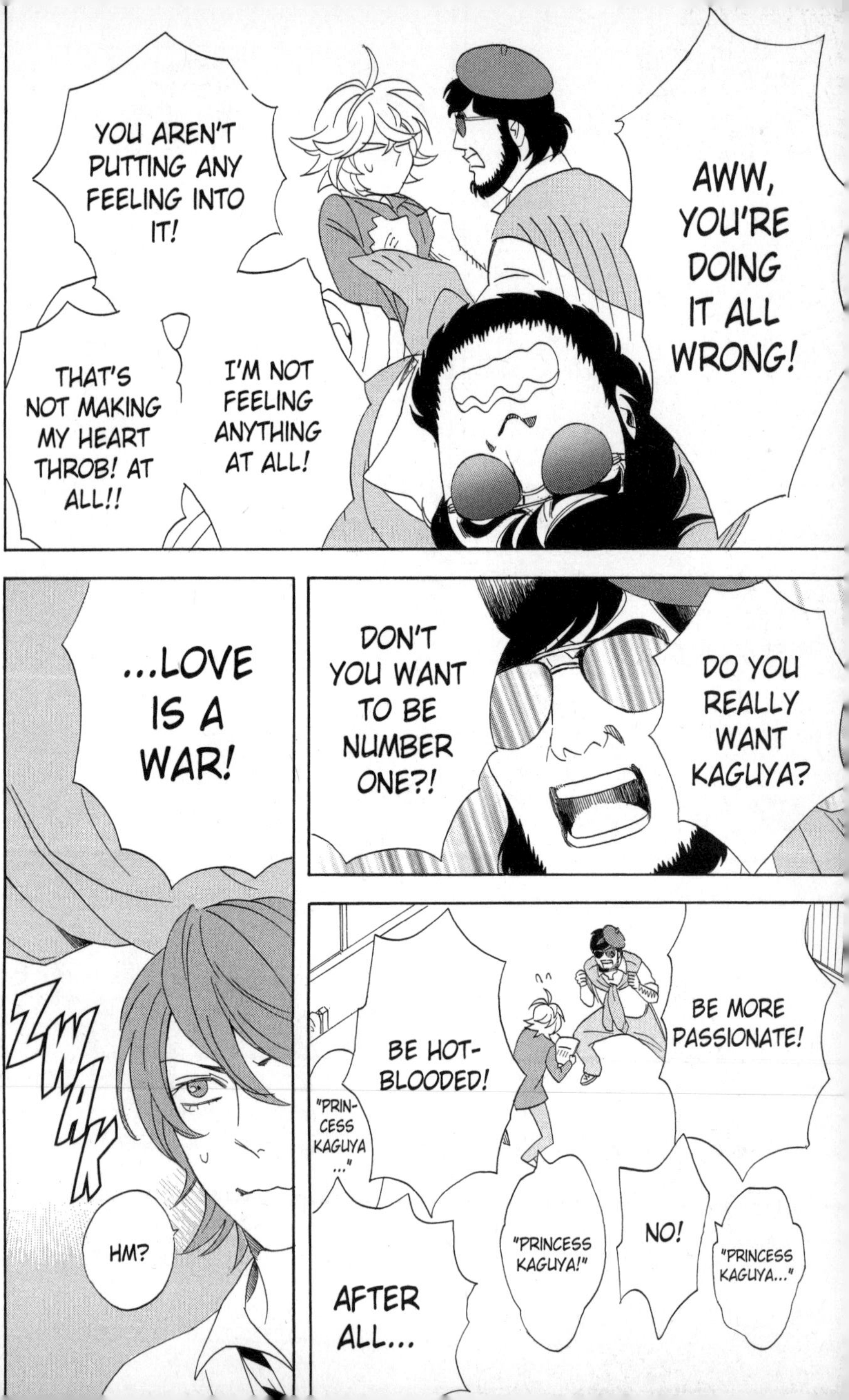
AWW, YOU'RE DOING IT ALL WRONG!
YOU AREN'T PUTTING ANY FEELING INTO IT!
I'M NOT FEELING ANYTHING AT ALL!
THAT'S NOT MAKING MY HEART THROB! AT ALL!!
DO YOU REALLY WANT KAGUYA?
DON'T YOU WANT TO BE NUMBER ONE?!
BE MORE PASSIONATE!
BE HOT-BLOODED!
"PRINCESS KAGUYA..."
NO!
"PRINCESS KAGUYA!"
"PRIN-CESS KAGUYA..."
AFTER ALL...
...LOVE IS A WAR!
ZWAK
HM?

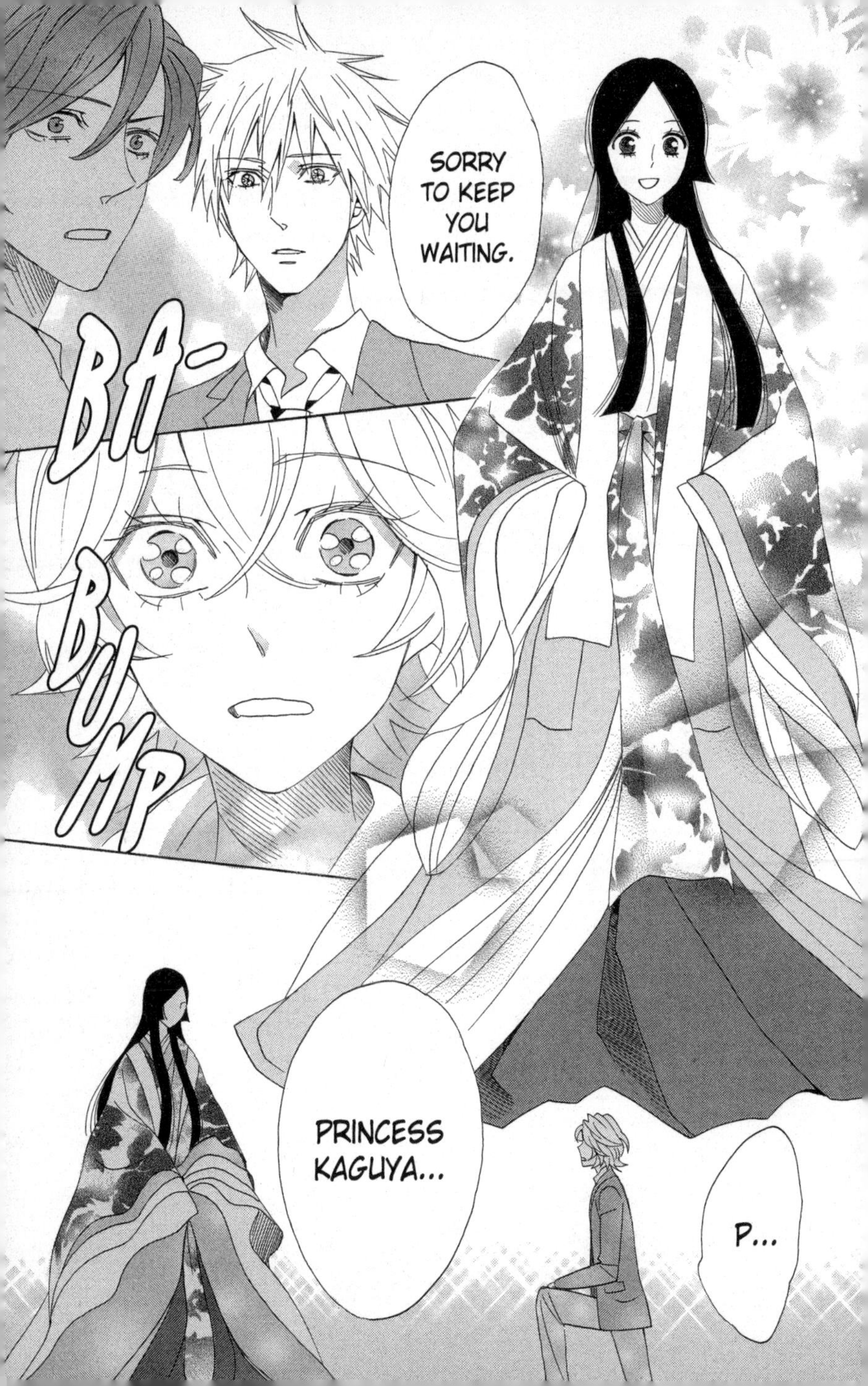
SORRY TO KEEP YOU WAITING.
BA-BUMP
P...
PRINCESS KAGUYA...

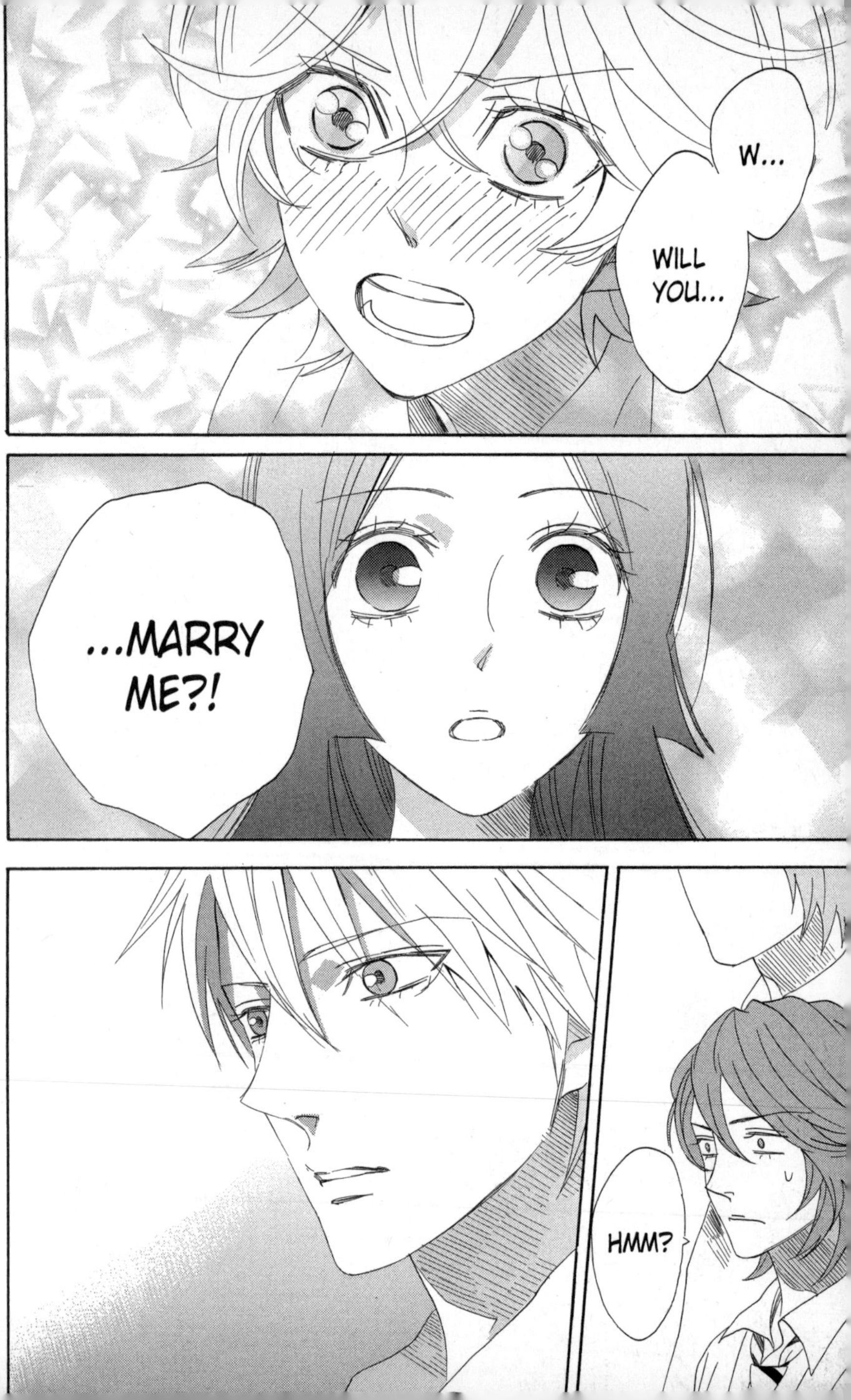
W...
WILL YOU...
...MARRY ME?!
HMM?

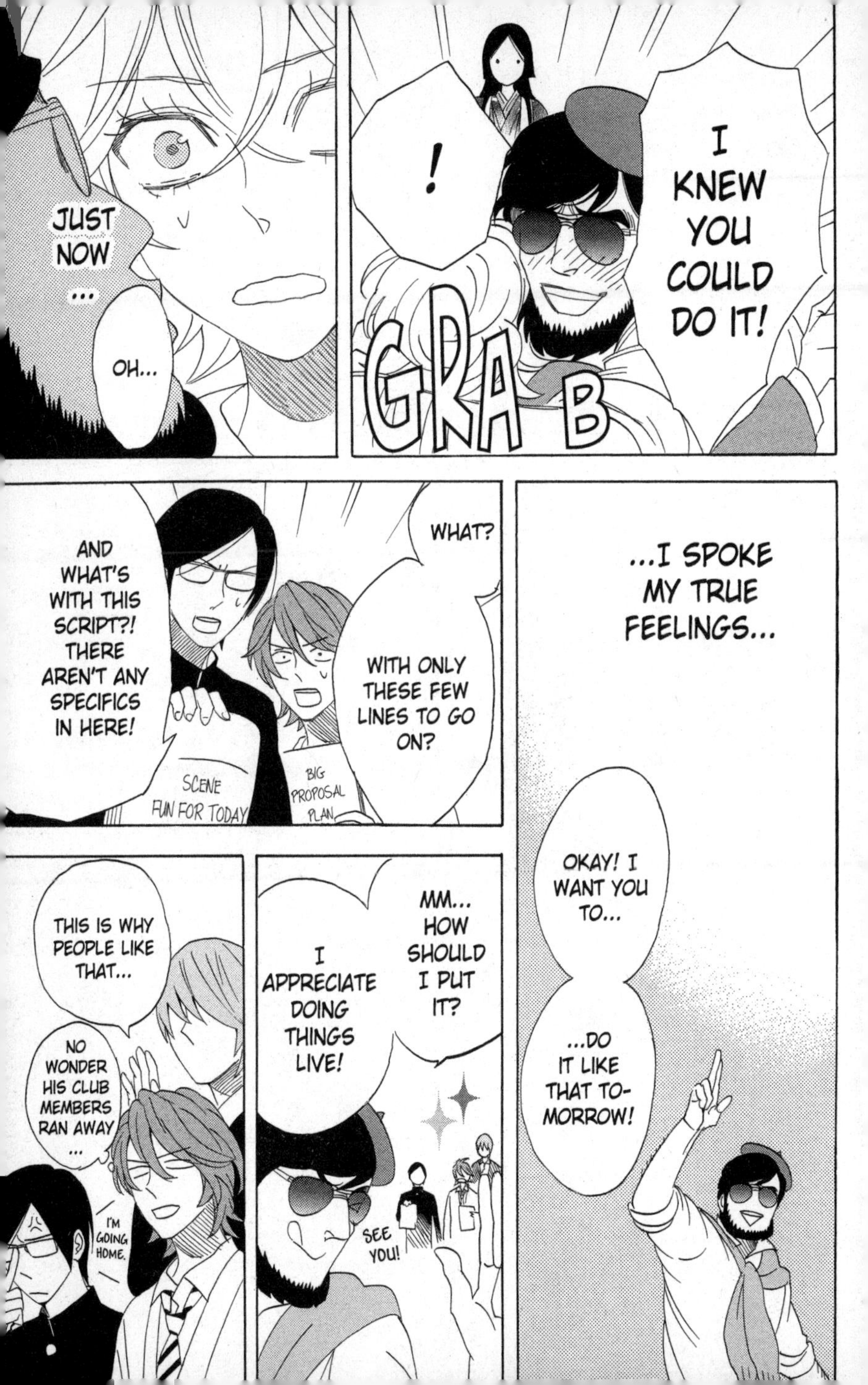
I KNEW YOU COULD DO IT!
!
GRAB
JUST NOW ...
OH...
...I SPOKE MY TRUE FEELINGS...
OKAY! I WANT YOU TO...
...DO IT LIKE THAT TO-MORROW!
WHAT?
WITH ONLY THESE FEW LINES TO GO ON?
AND WHAT'S WITH THIS SCRIPT?! THERE AREN'T ANY SPECIFICS IN HERE!
BIG PROPOSAL PLAN
SCENE RUN FOR TODAY
MM... HOW SHOULD I PUT IT?
I APPRECIATE DOING THINGS LIVE!
SEE YOU!
THIS IS WHY PEOPLE LIKE THAT...
NO WONDER HIS CLUB MEMBERS RAN AWAY ...
I'M GOING HOME.

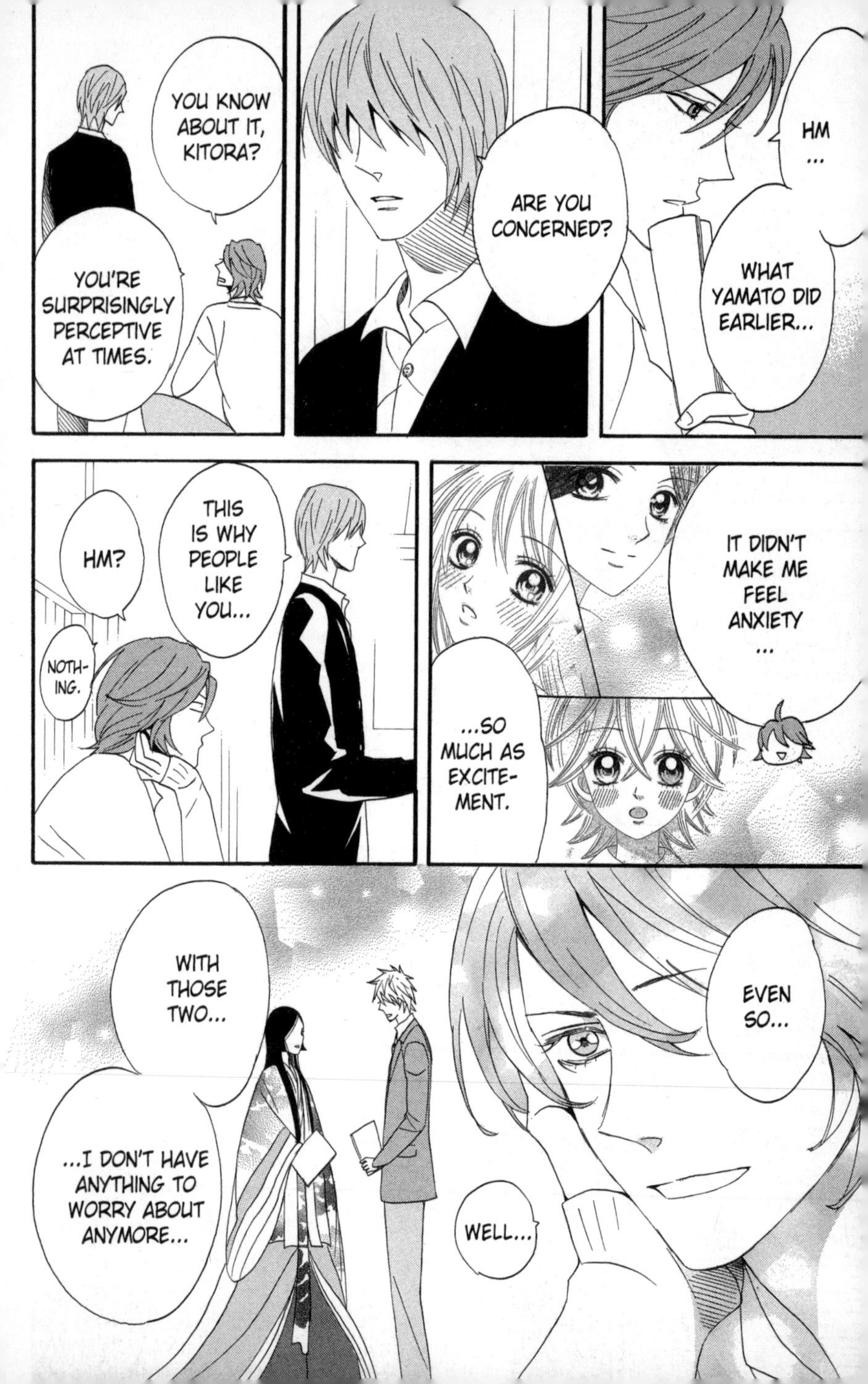
HM ...
WHAT YAMATO DID EARLIER...
ARE YOU CONCERNED?
YOU KNOW ABOUT IT, KITORA?
YOU'RE SURPRISINGLY PERCEPTIVE AT TIMES.
IT DIDN'T MAKE ME FEEL ANXIETY ...
...SO MUCH AS EXCITEMENT.
THIS IS WHY PEOPLE LIKE YOU...
HM?
NOTHING.
EVEN SO...
WELL...
WITH THOSE TWO...
...I DON'T HAVE ANYTHING TO WORRY ABOUT ANYMORE...

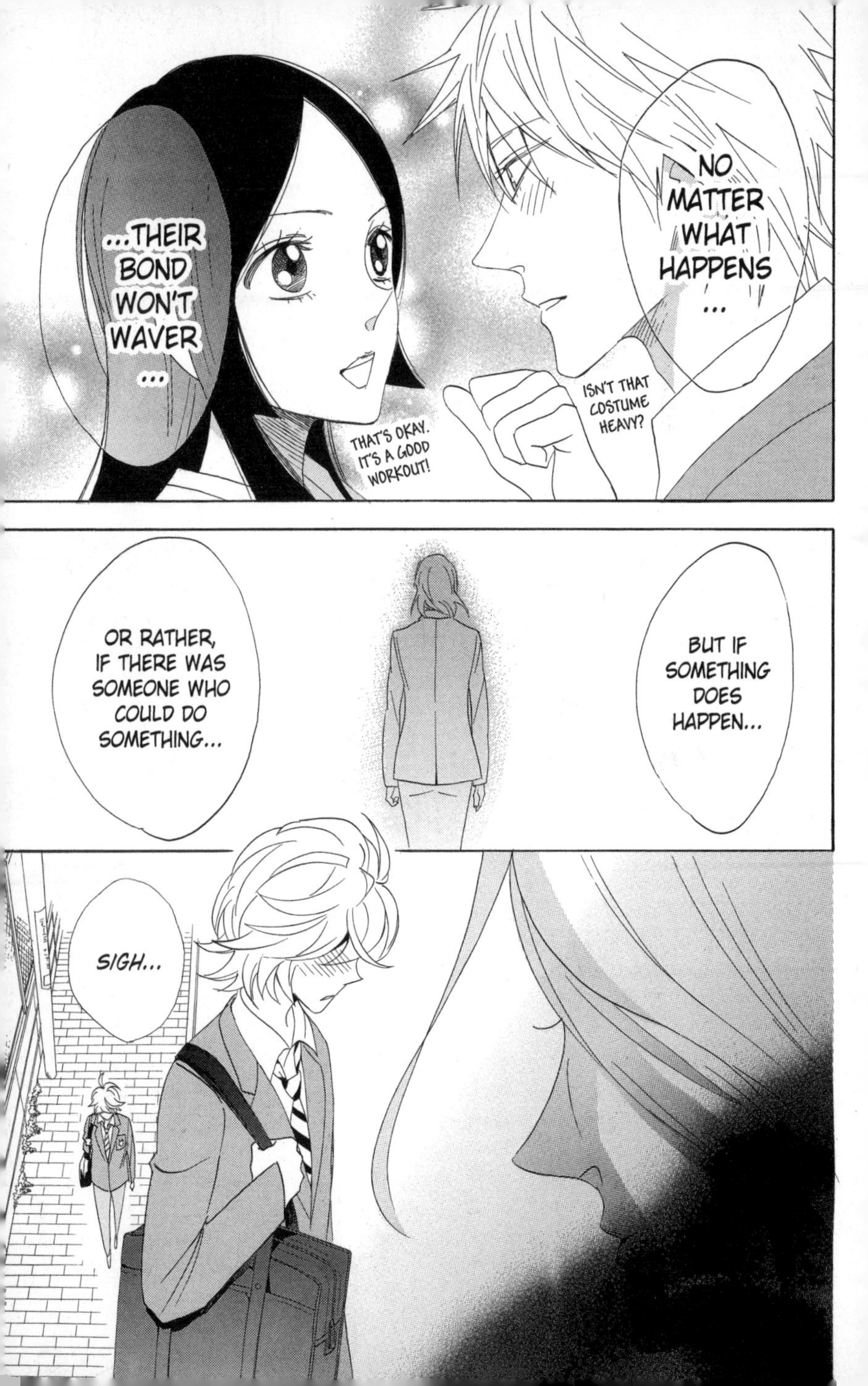
NO MATTER WHAT HAPPENS...
...THEIR BOND WON'T WAVER...
ISN'T THAT COSTUME HEAVY?
THAT'S OKAY. IT'S A GOOD WORKOUT!
BUT IF SOMETHING DOES HAPPEN...
OR RATHER, IF THERE WAS SOMEONE WHO COULD DO SOMETHING...
SIGH...

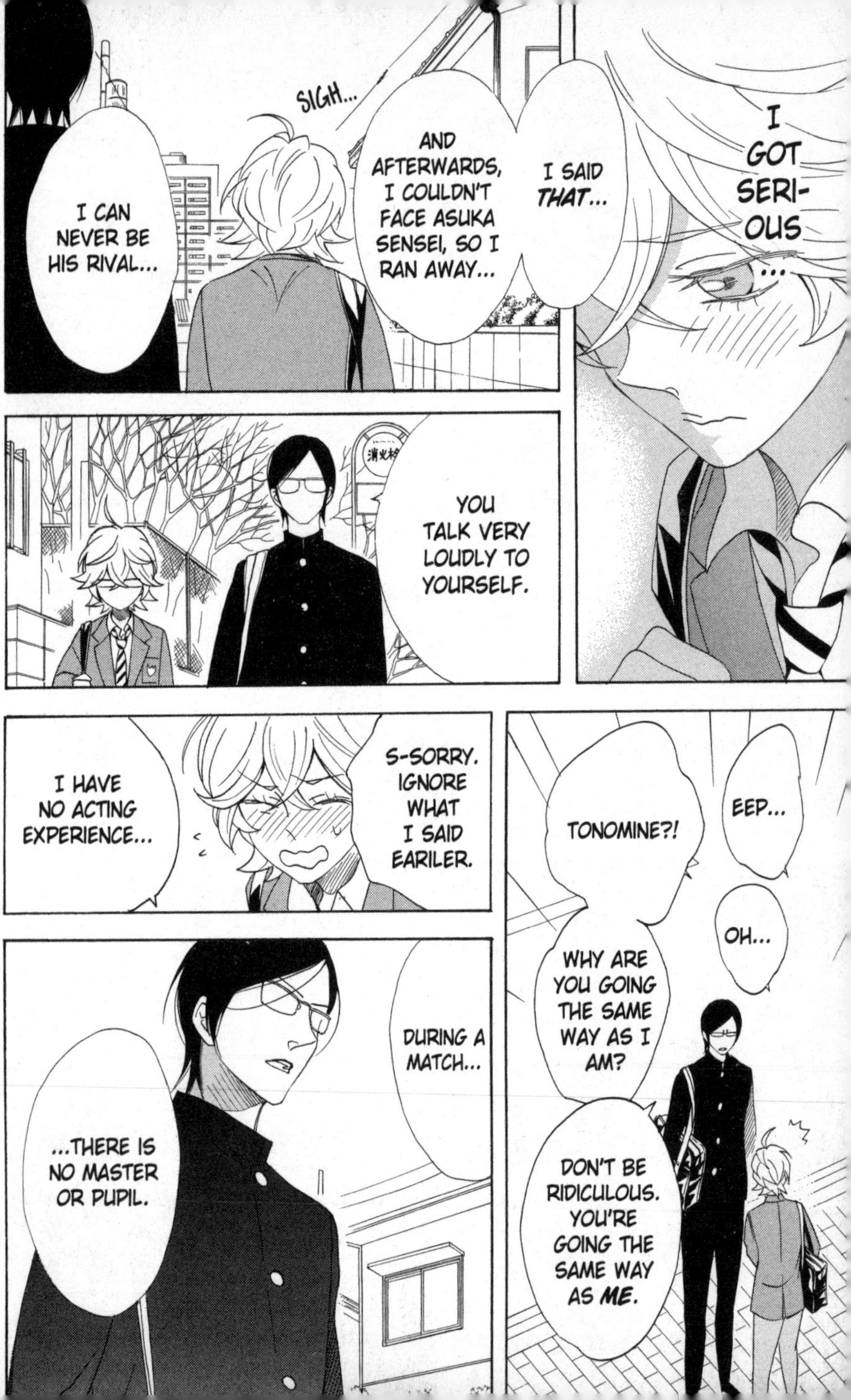
I GOT SERIOUS...
I SAID THAT...
AND AFTERWARDS, I COULDN'T FACE ASUKA SENSEI, SO I RAN AWAY...
SIGH...
I CAN NEVER BE HIS RIVAL...
YOU TALK VERY LOUDLY TO YOURSELF.
EEP...
TONOMINE?!
OH...
WHY ARE YOU GOING THE SAME WAY AS I AM?
DON'T BE RIDICULOUS. YOU'RE GOING THE SAME WAY AS ME.
S-SORRY. IGNORE WHAT I SAID EARILER.
I HAVE NO ACTING EXPERIENCE...
DURING A MATCH...
...THERE IS NO MASTER OR PUPIL.

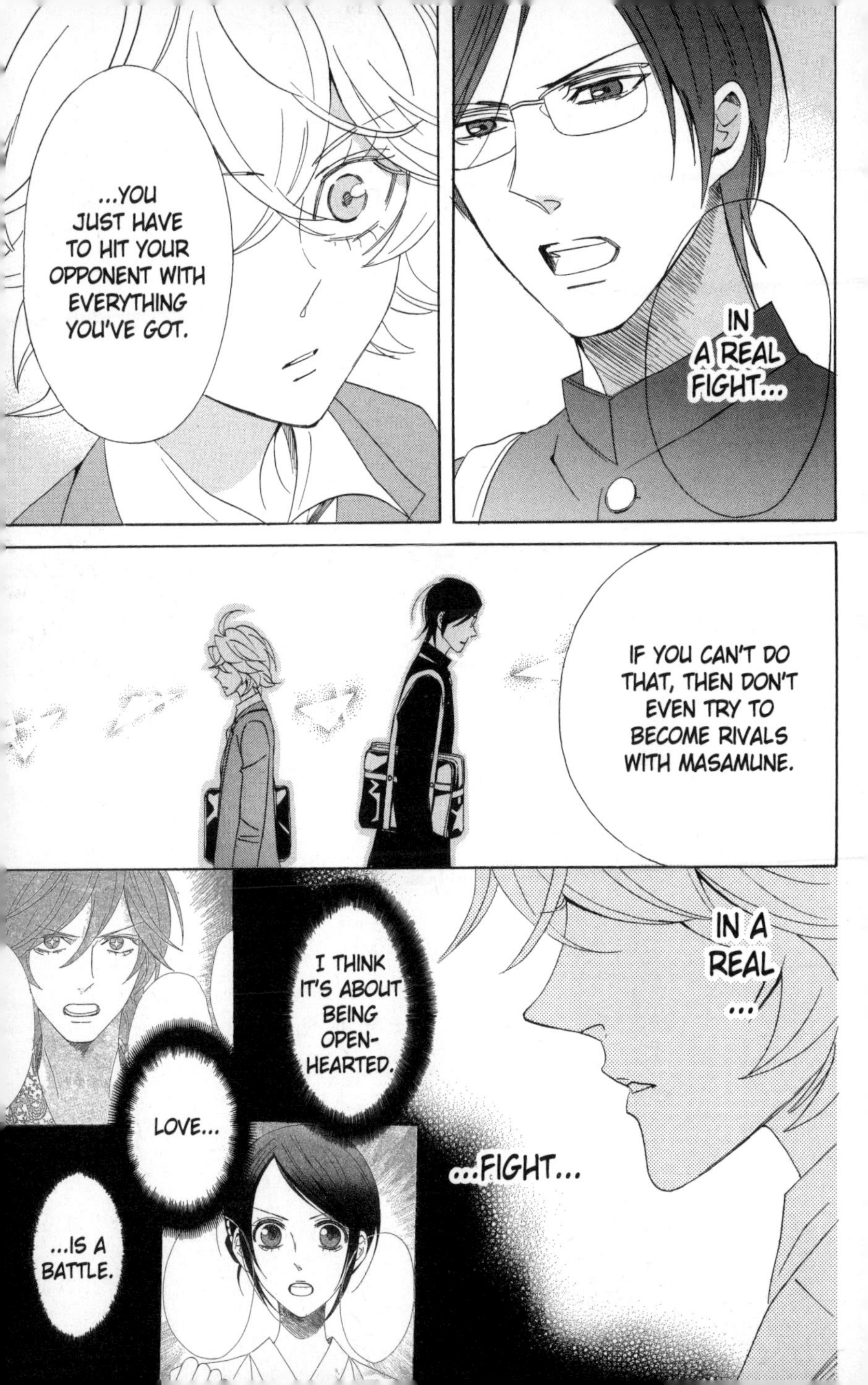
IN A REAL FIGHT...
...YOU JUST HAVE TO HIT YOUR OPPONENT WITH EVERYTHING YOU'VE GOT.
IF YOU CAN'T DO THAT, THEN DON'T EVEN TRY TO BECOME RIVALS WITH MASAMUNE.
IN A REAL...
...FIGHT...
I THINK IT'S ABOUT BEING OPEN-HEARTED.
LOVE...
...IS A BATTLE.

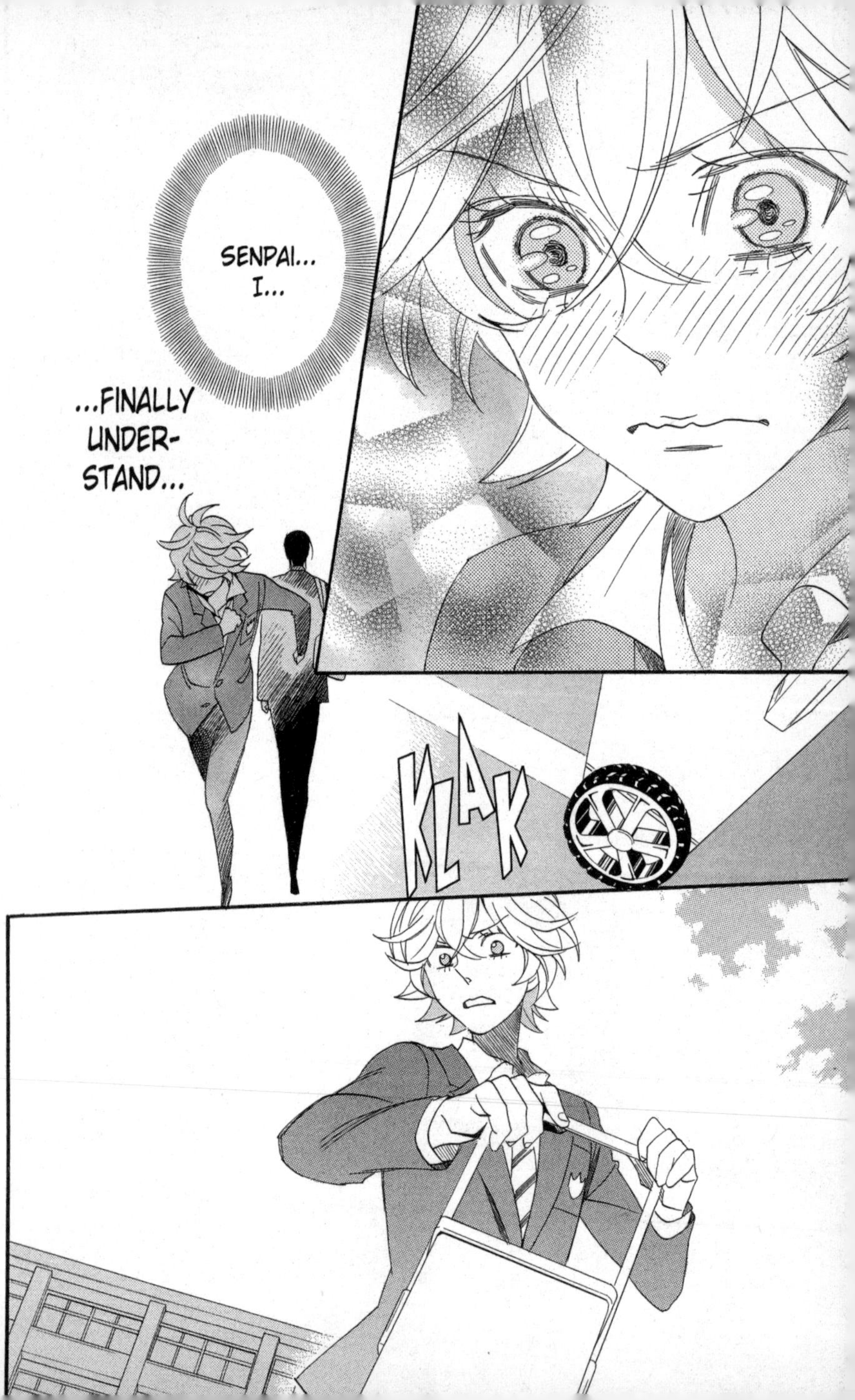
SENPAI... I...
...FINALLY UNDER-STAND...
KLAK

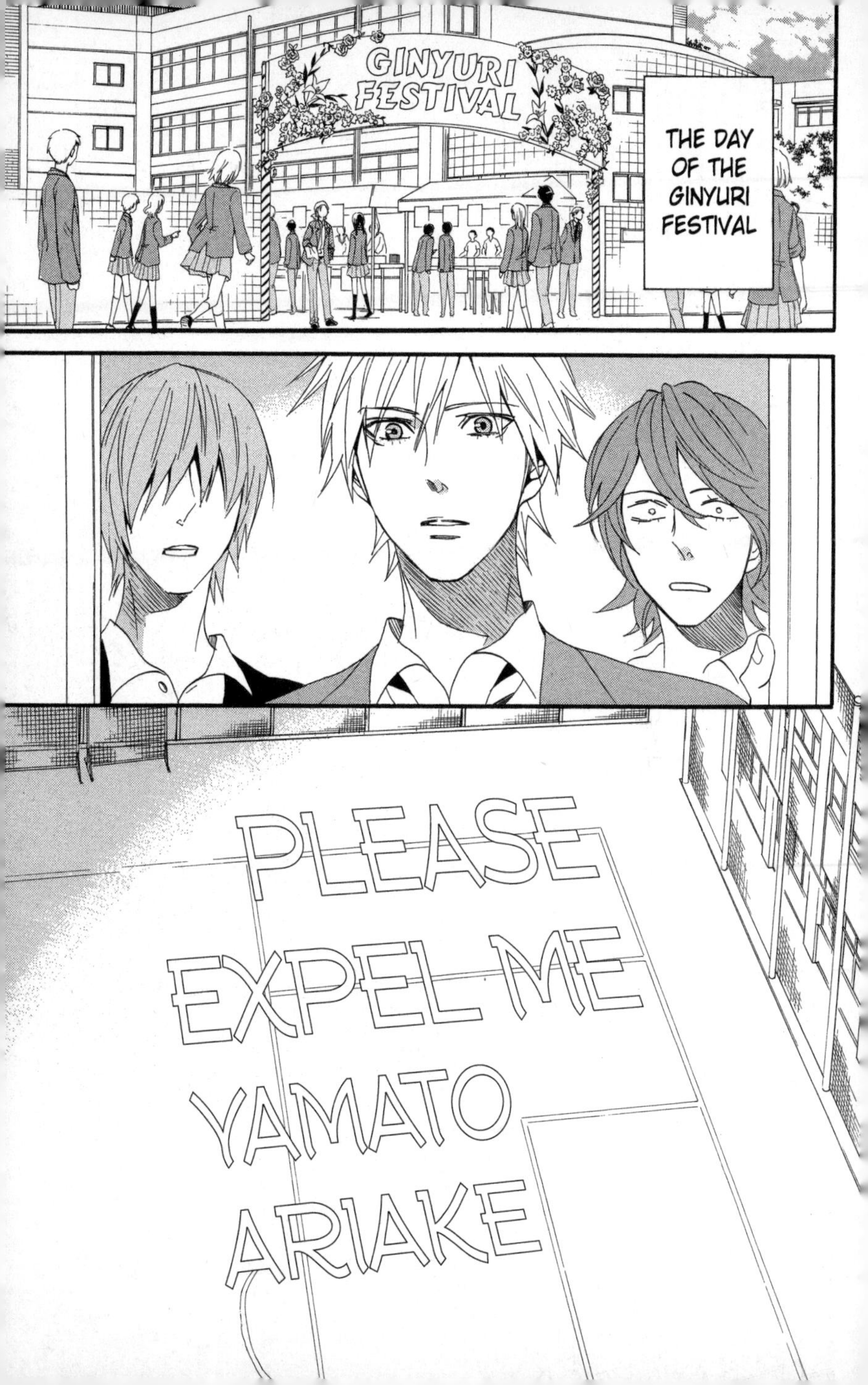
GINYURI FESTIVAL
THE DAY OF THE GINYURI FESTIVAL
PLEASE EXPEL ME
YAMATO ARIAKE

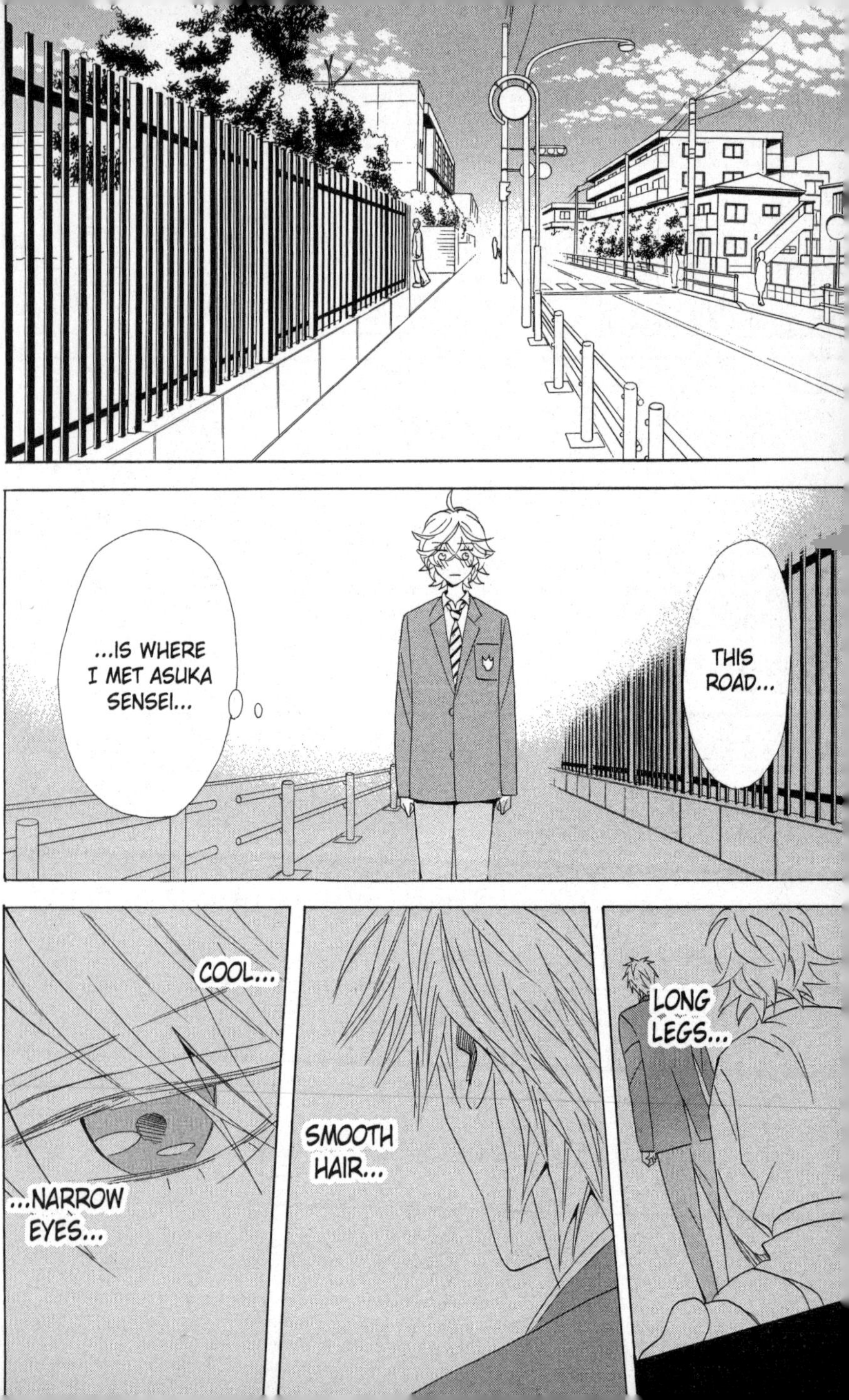
THIS ROAD...
...IS WHERE I MET ASUKA SENSEI...
LONG LEGS...
SMOOTH HAIR...
COOL...
...NARROW EYES...

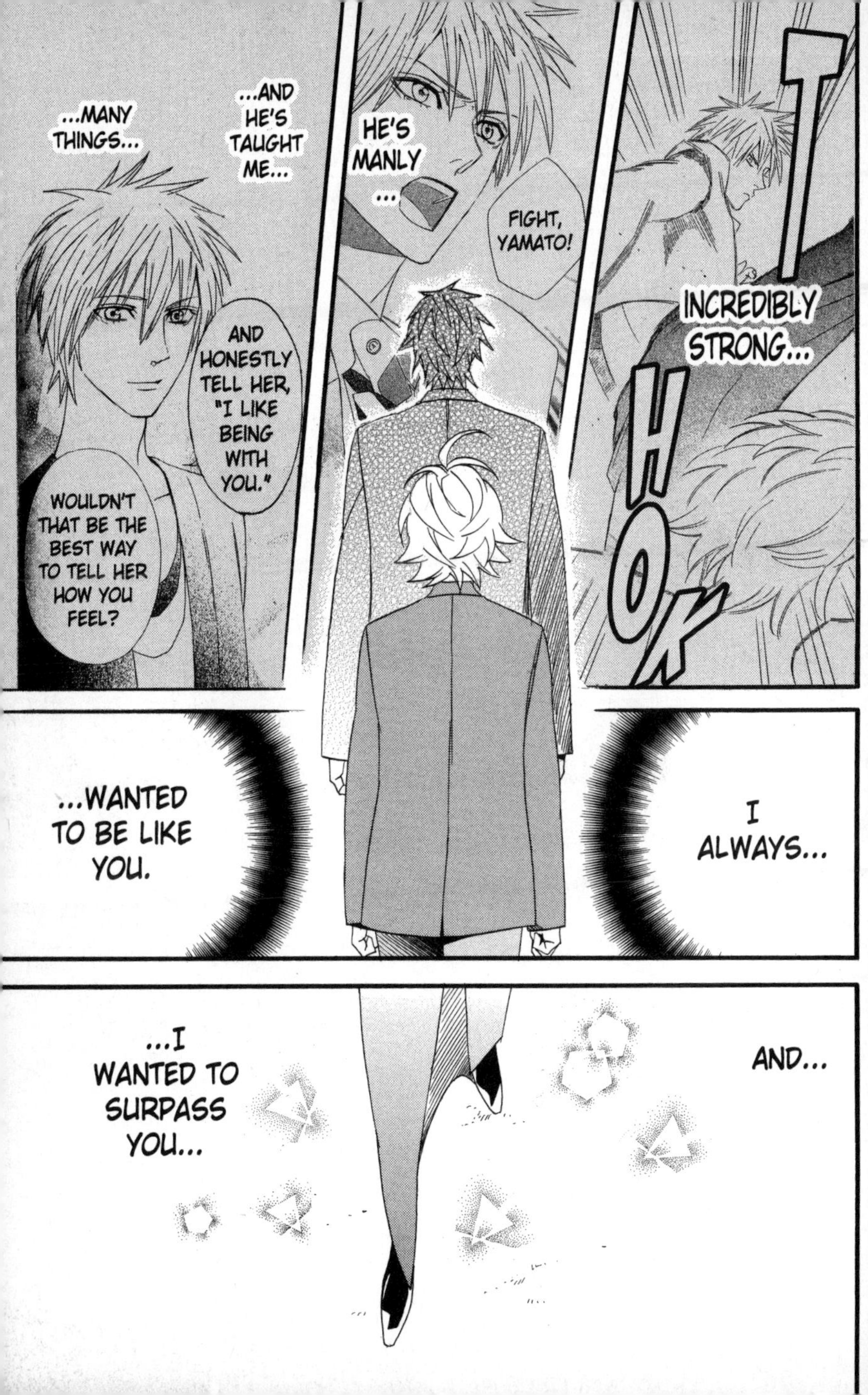

THOK
INCREDIBLY STRONG...
HE'S MANLY ...
FIGHT, YAMATO!
...AND HE'S TAUGHT ME...
...MANY THINGS...
AND HONESTLY TELL HER, "I LIKE BEING WITH YOU."
WOULDN'T THAT BE THE BEST WAY TO TELL HER HOW YOU FEEL?
I ALWAYS...
...WANTED TO BE LIKE YOU.
AND...
...I WANTED TO SURPASS YOU...

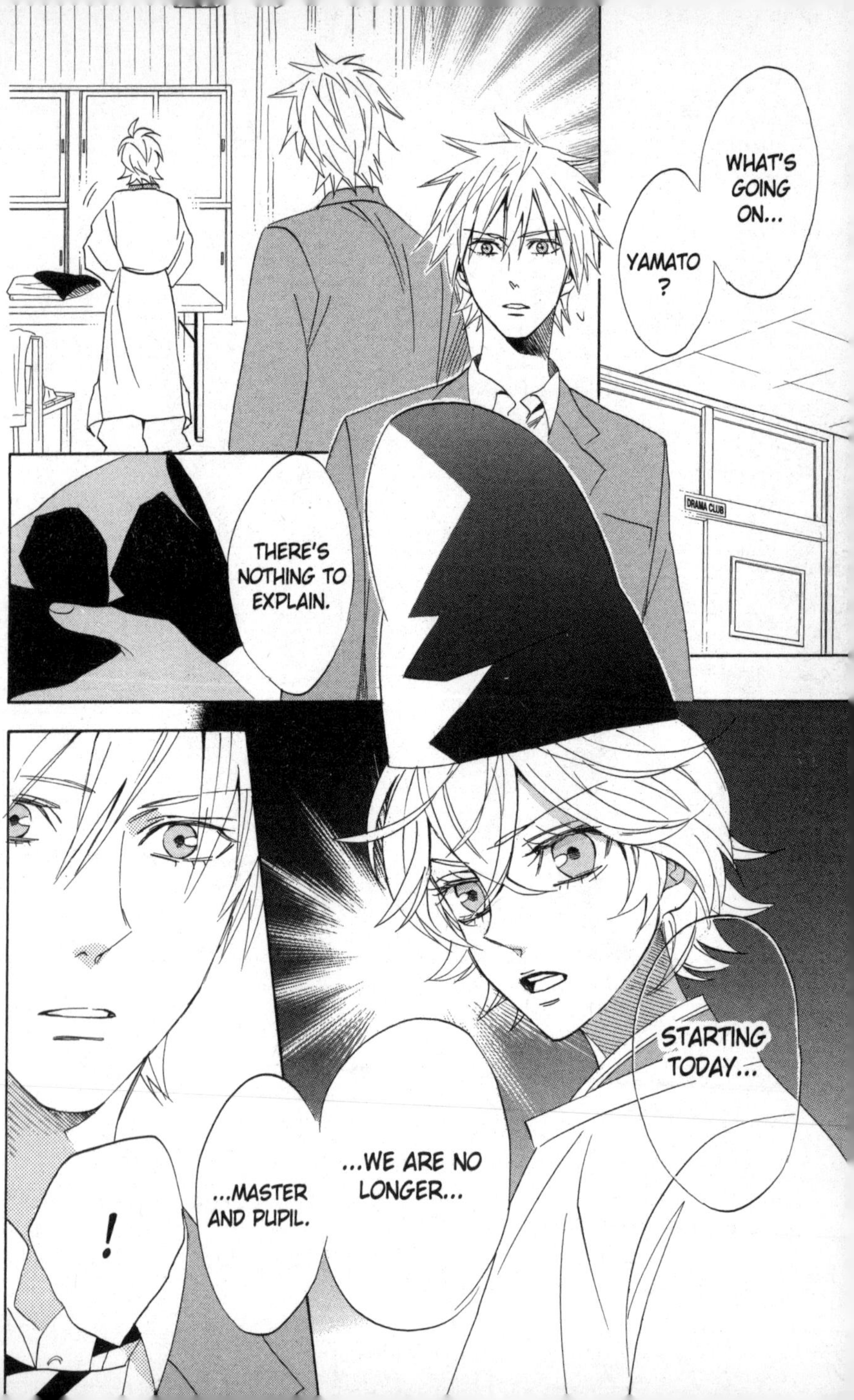
WHAT'S GOING ON...
YAMATO?
DRAMA CLUB
THERE'S NOTHING TO EXPLAIN.
STARTING TODAY...
...WE ARE NO LONGER...
...MASTER AND PUPIL.
!

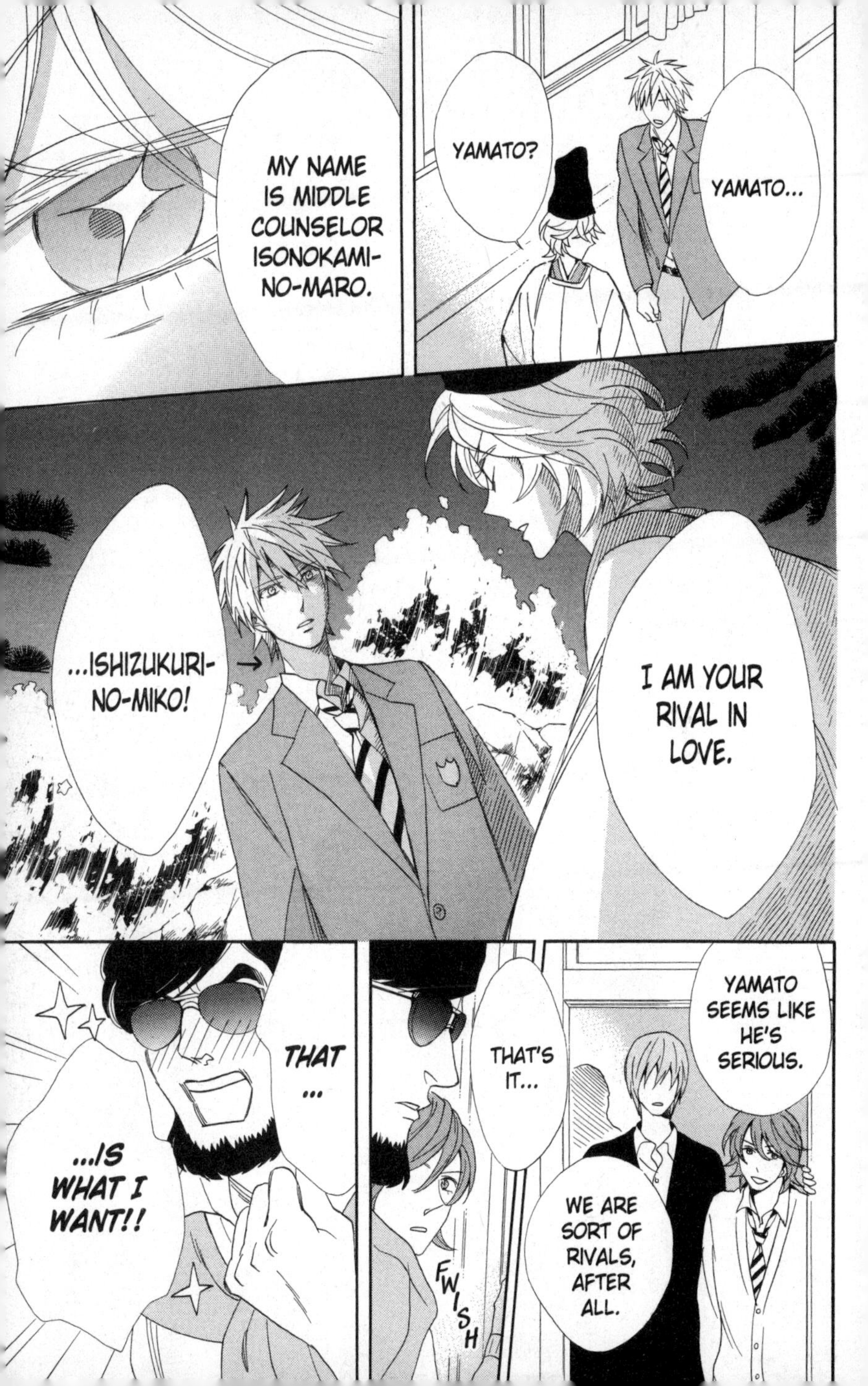
YAMATO...
YAMATO?
MY NAME IS MIDDLE COUNSELOR ISONOKAMI-NO-MARO.
I AM YOUR RIVAL IN LOVE.
...ISHIZUKURI-NO-MIKO!
YAMATO SEEMS LIKE HE'S SERIOUS.
WE ARE SORT OF RIVALS, AFTER ALL.
THAT'S IT...
FWISH
THAT ...
...IS WHAT I WANT!!

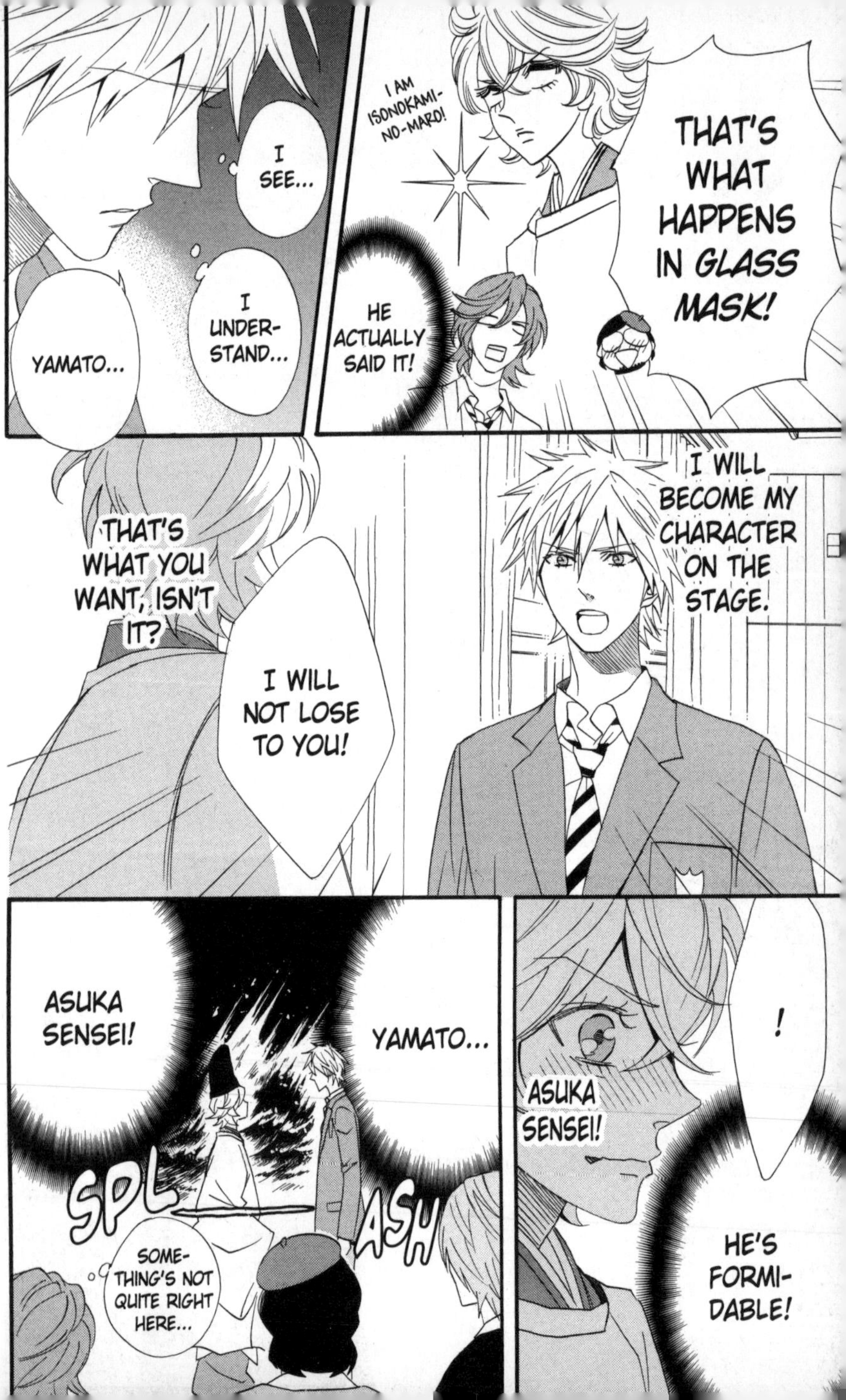
I AM ISONOKAMI-NO-MARO!
THAT'S WHAT HAPPENS IN *GLASS MASK!*
HE ACTUALLY SAID IT!
I SEE...
I UNDERSTAND...
YAMATO...
I WILL BECOME MY CHARACTER ON THE STAGE.
I WILL NOT LOSE TO YOU!
THAT'S WHAT YOU WANT, ISN'T IT?
!
ASUKA SENSEI!
HE'S FORMIDABLE!
YAMATO...
ASUKA SENSEI!
SPLASH
SOMETHING'S NOT QUITE RIGHT HERE...

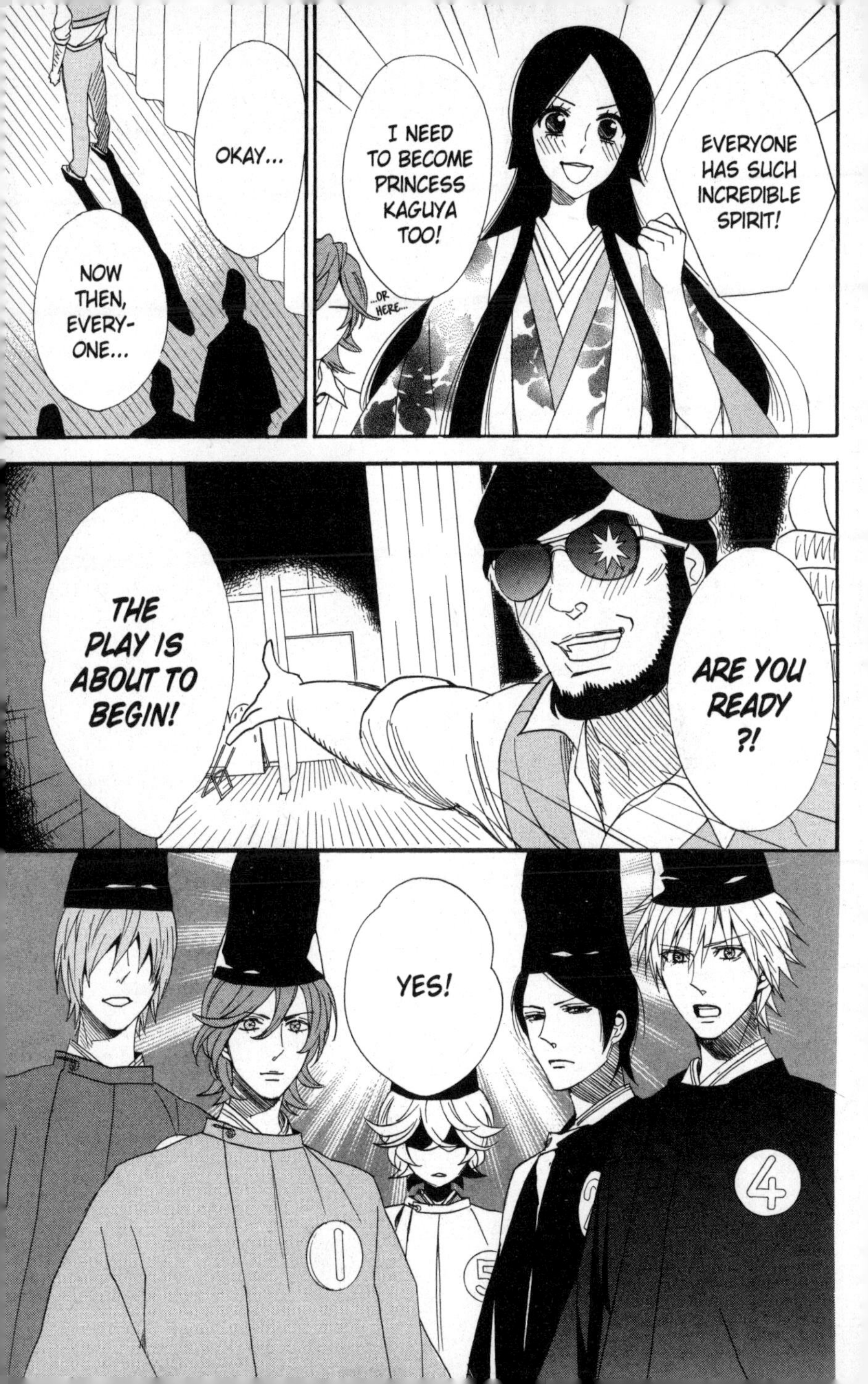
EVERYONE HAS SUCH INCREDIBLE SPIRIT!
I NEED TO BECOME PRINCESS KAGUYA TOO!
...OR HERE...
OKAY...
NOW THEN, EVERY-ONE...
ARE YOU READY?!
THE PLAY IS ABOUT TO BEGIN!
YES!

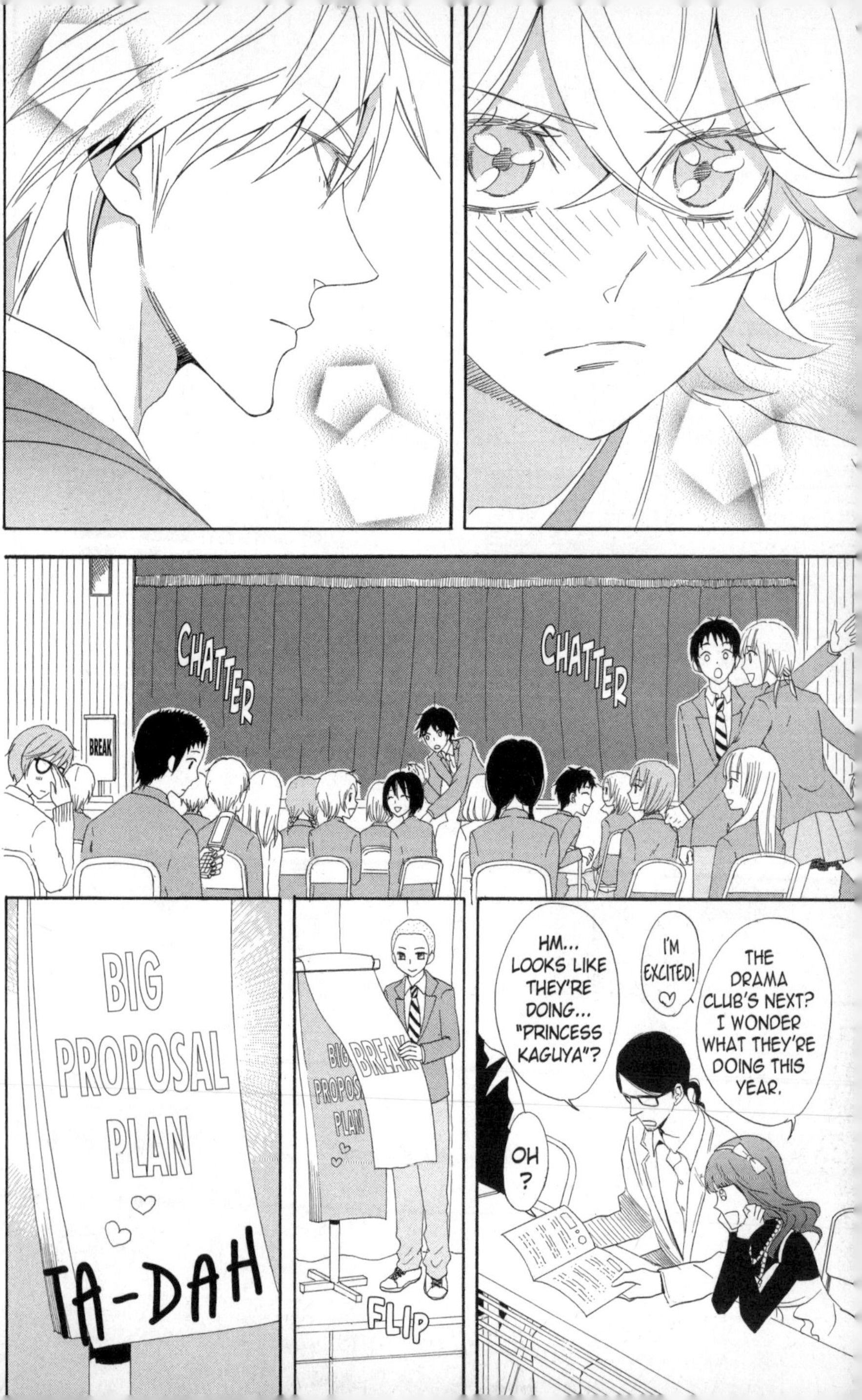

CHATTER
CHATTER
BREAK
THE DRAMA CLUB'S NEXT? I WONDER WHAT THEY'RE DOING THIS YEAR.
I'M EXCITED! ♡
HM... LOOKS LIKE THEY'RE DOING... "PRINCESS KAGUYA"?
OH?
BREAK
BIG PROPOSAL PLAN ♡
FLIP
BIG PROPOSAL PLAN ♡ ♡
TA-DAH

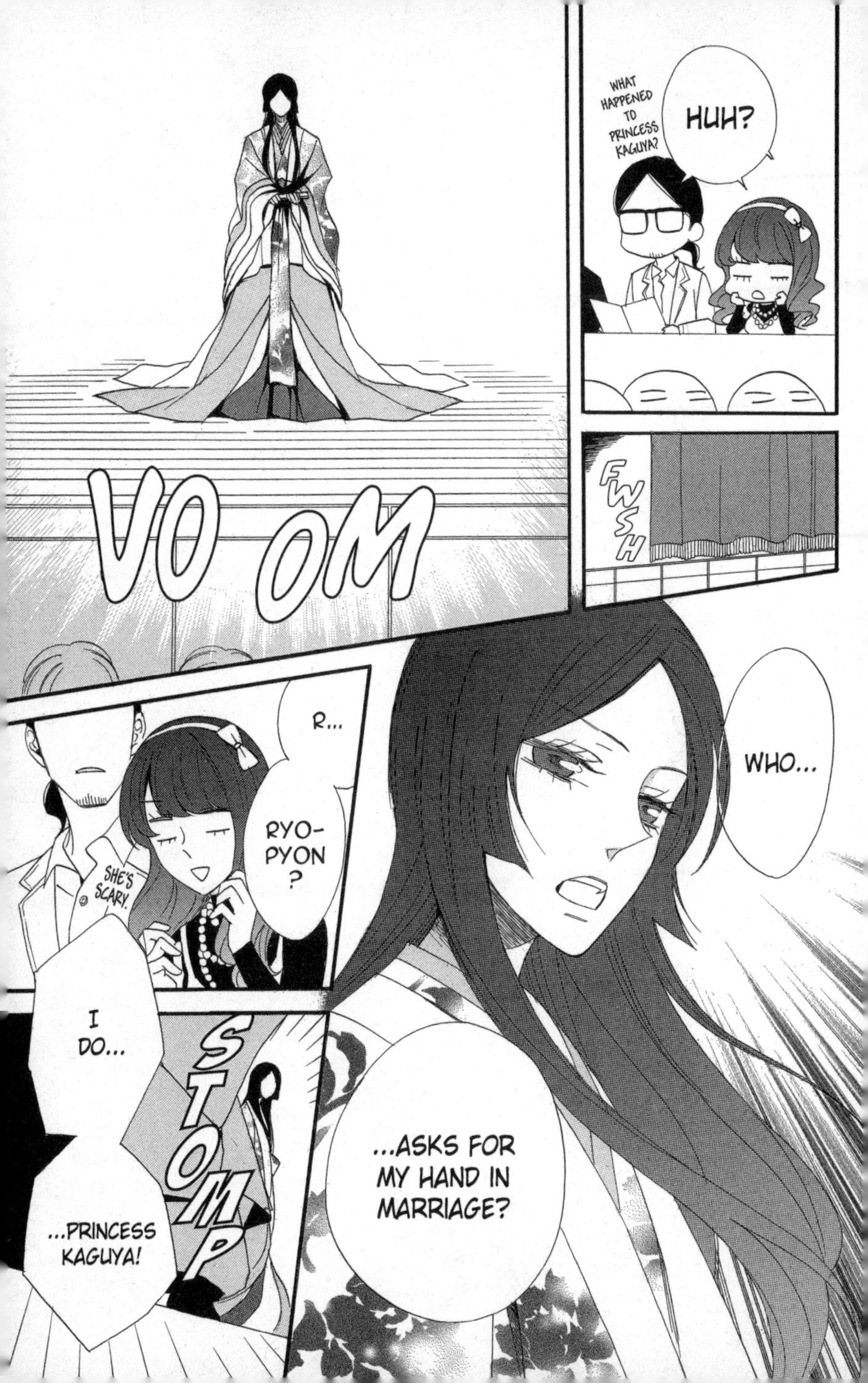
HUH?
WHAT HAPPENED TO PRINCESS KAGUYA?
FWSH
VO OM
WHO...
...ASKS FOR MY HAND IN MARRIAGE?
R...
RYO-PYON?
SHE'S SCARY.
I DO...
STOMP
...PRINCESS KAGUYA!

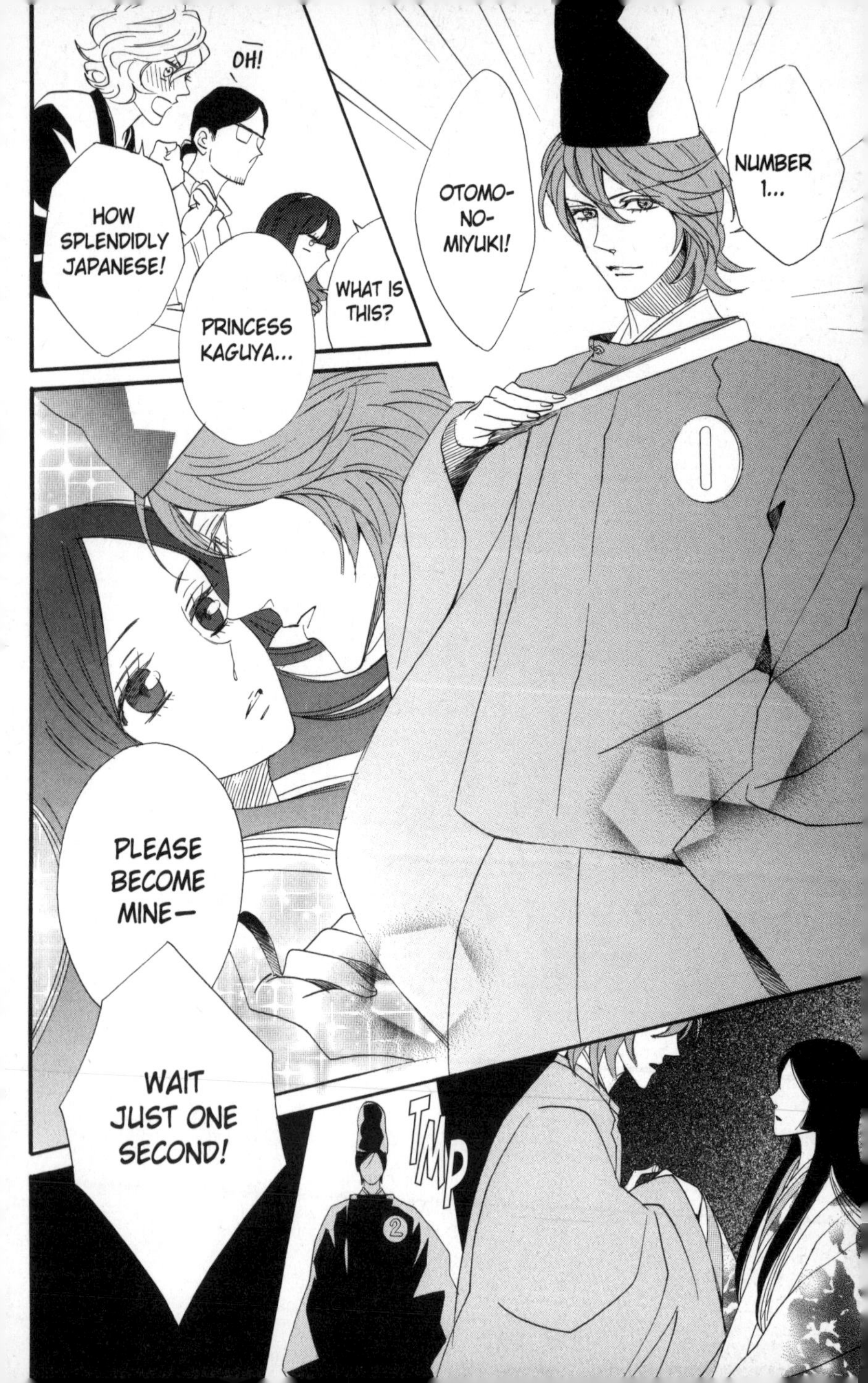
NUMBER 1...
OTOMO-NO-MIYUKI!
OH!
WHAT IS THIS?
HOW SPLENDIDLY JAPANESE!
PRINCESS KAGUYA...
PLEASE BECOME MINE—
TMP
WAIT JUST ONE SECOND!

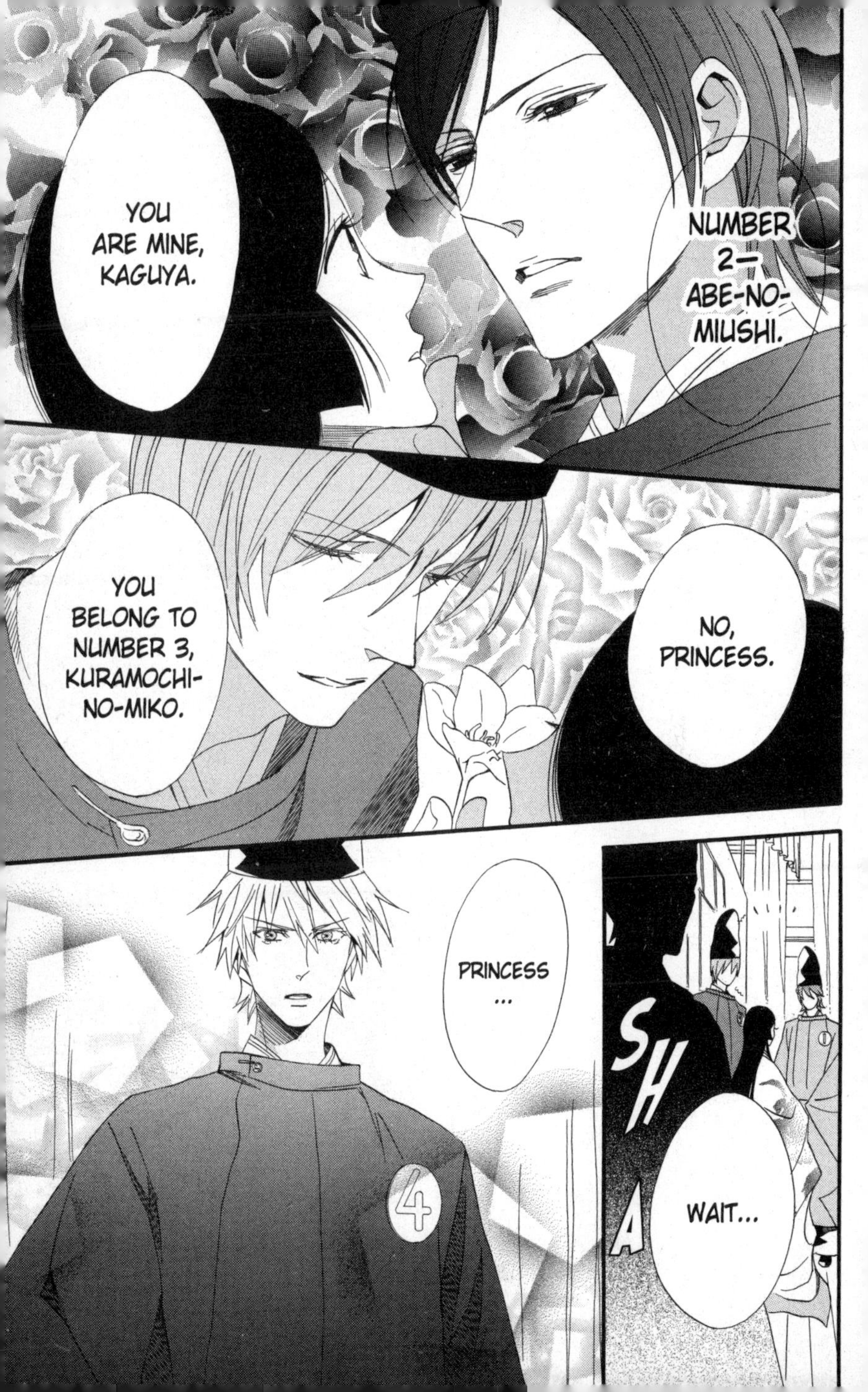
NUMBER 2—ABE-NO-MIUSHI.
YOU ARE MINE, KAGUYA.
NO, PRINCESS.
YOU BELONG TO NUMBER 3, KURAMOCHI-NO-MIKO.
SHA
WAIT...
PRINCESS ...

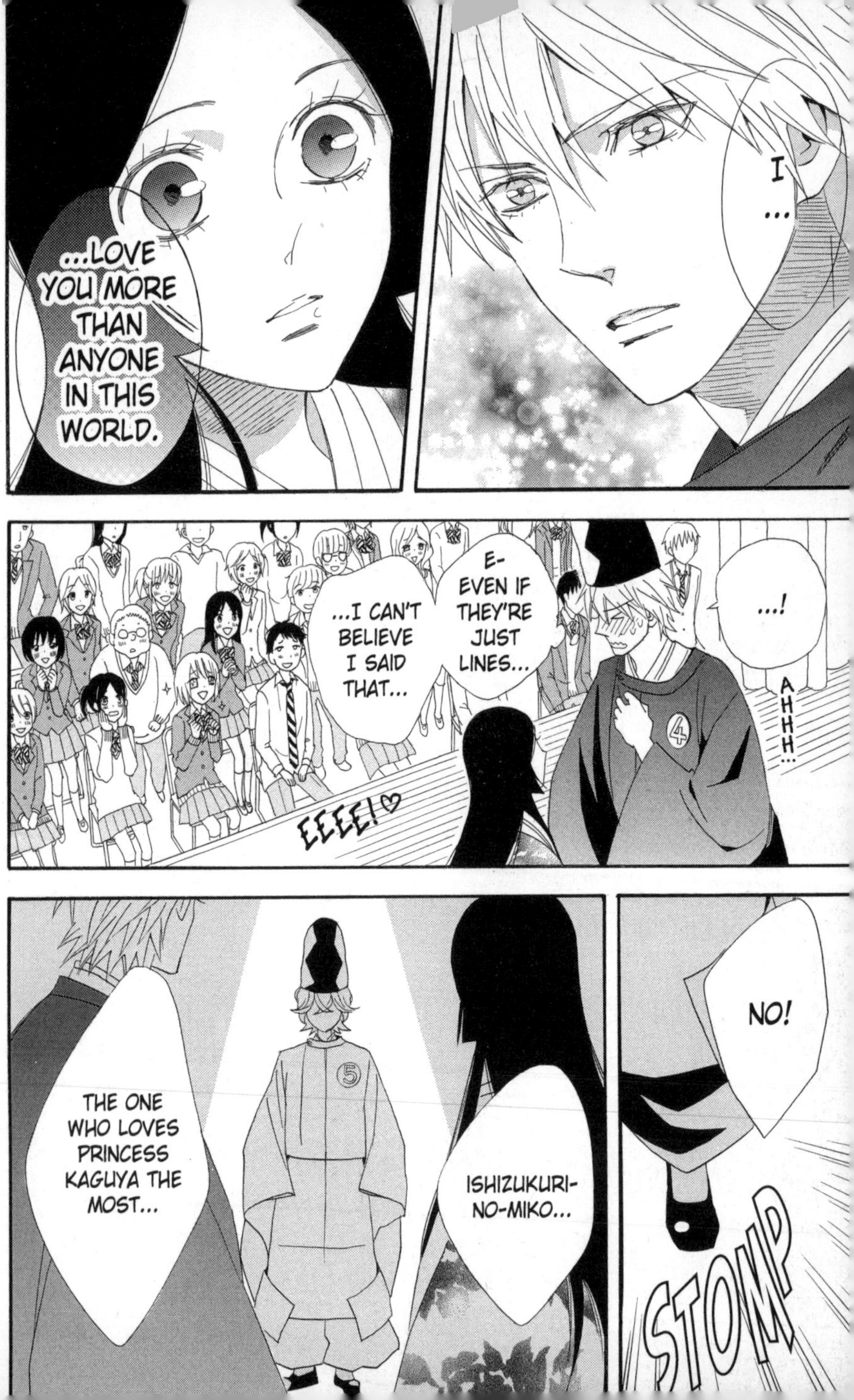
I ...
...LOVE YOU MORE THAN ANYONE IN THIS WORLD.
...!
AHHH...
E- EVEN IF THEY'RE JUST LINES...
...I CAN'T BELIEVE I SAID THAT...
EEEE! ♡
NO!
STOMP
THE ONE WHO LOVES PRINCESS KAGUYA THE MOST...
ISHIZUKURI-NO-MIKO...

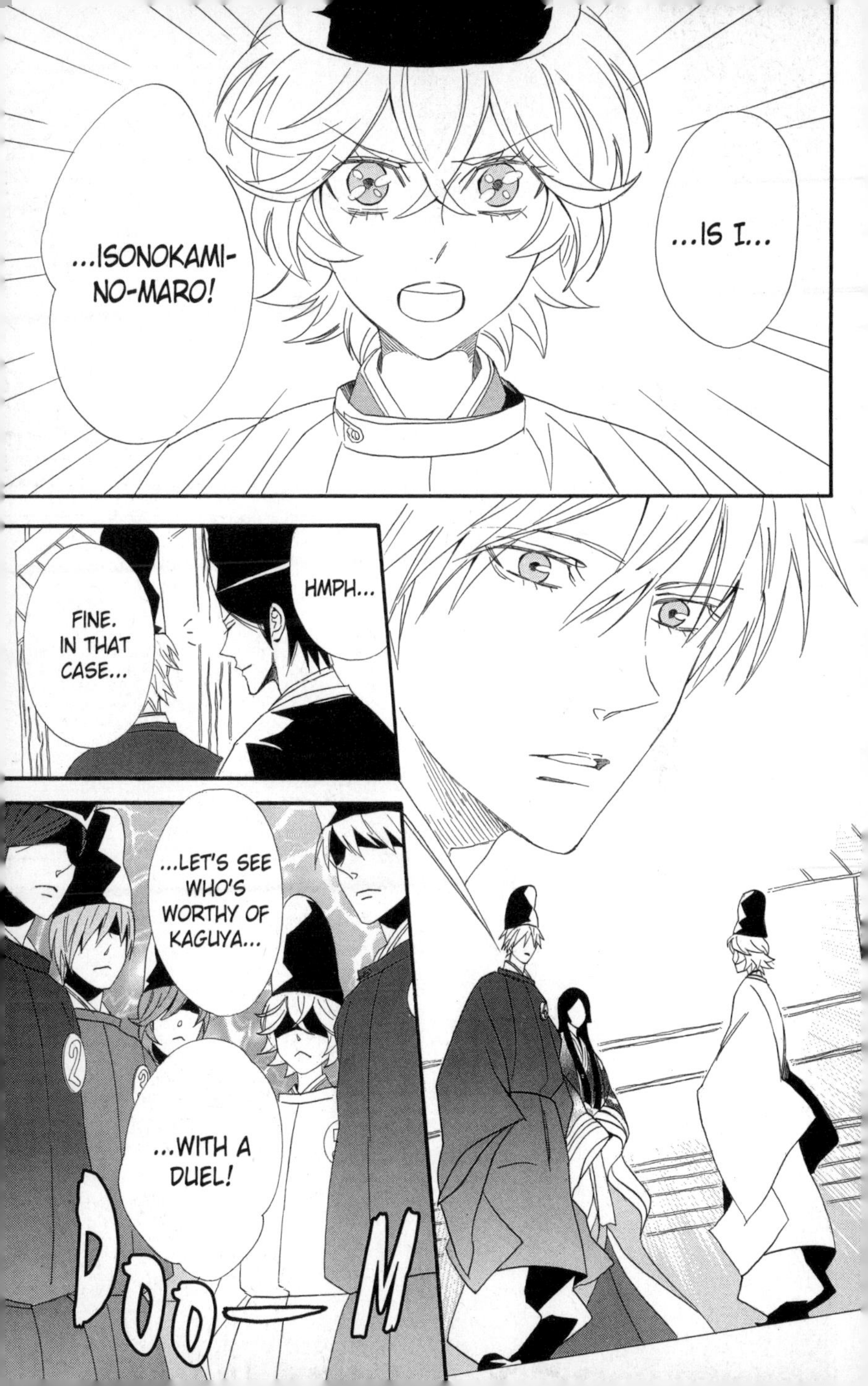
...IS I...
...ISONOKAMI-NO-MARO!
HMPH...
FINE. IN THAT CASE...
...LET'S SEE WHO'S WORTHY OF KAGUYA...
...WITH A DUEL!
DOO—M

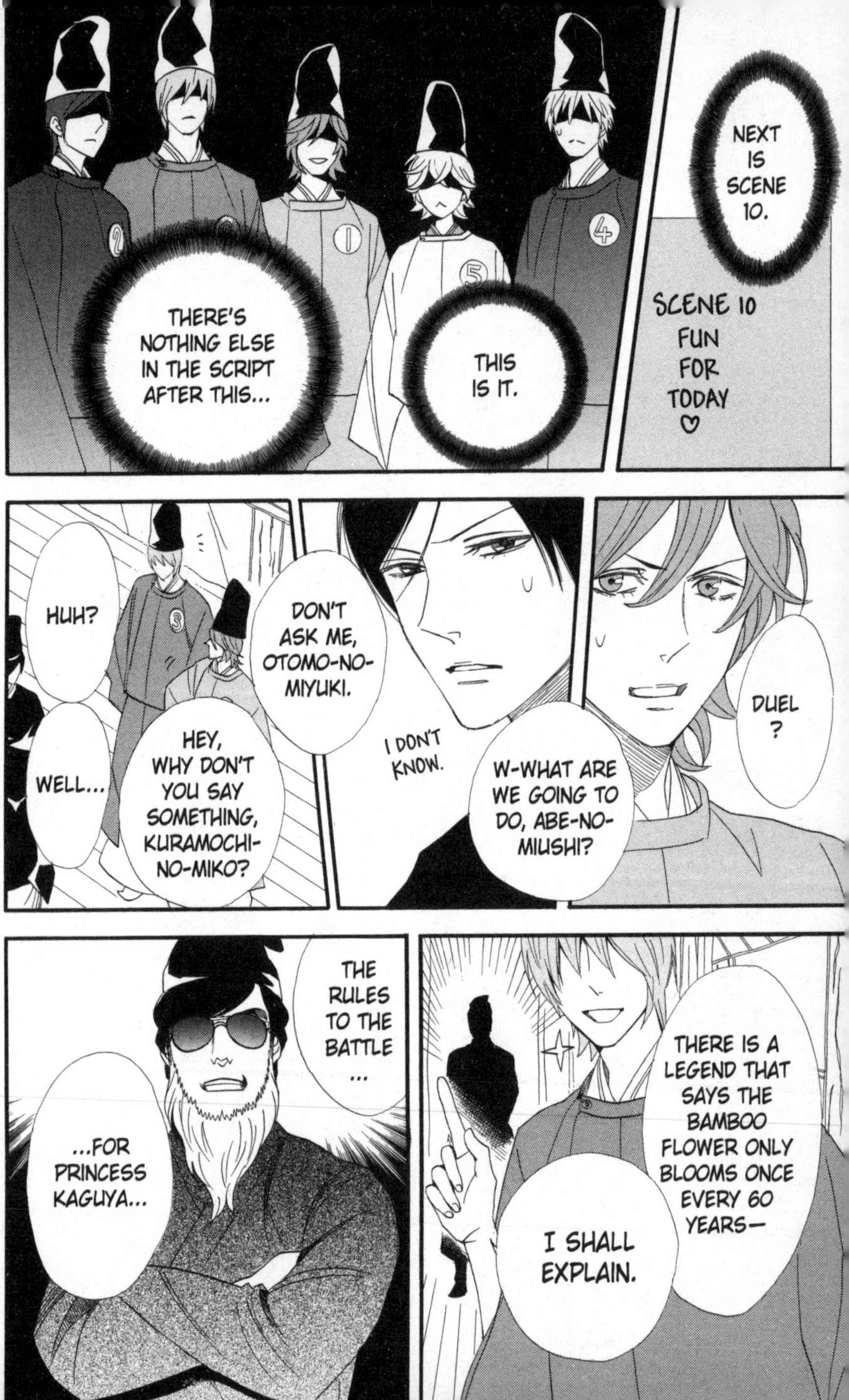
NEXT IS SCENE 10.
SCENE 10 FUN FOR TODAY ♡
THERE'S NOTHING ELSE IN THE SCRIPT AFTER THIS...
THIS IS IT.
DUEL ?
W-WHAT ARE WE GOING TO DO, ABE-NO-MIUSHI?
DON'T ASK ME, OTOMO-NO-MIYUKI.
I DON'T KNOW.
HUH?
HEY, WHY DON'T YOU SAY SOMETHING, KURAMOCHI-NO-MIKO?
WELL...
THERE IS A LEGEND THAT SAYS THE BAMBOO FLOWER ONLY BLOOMS ONCE EVERY 60 YEARS—
I SHALL EXPLAIN.
THE RULES TO THE BATTLE ...
...FOR PRINCESS KAGUYA...

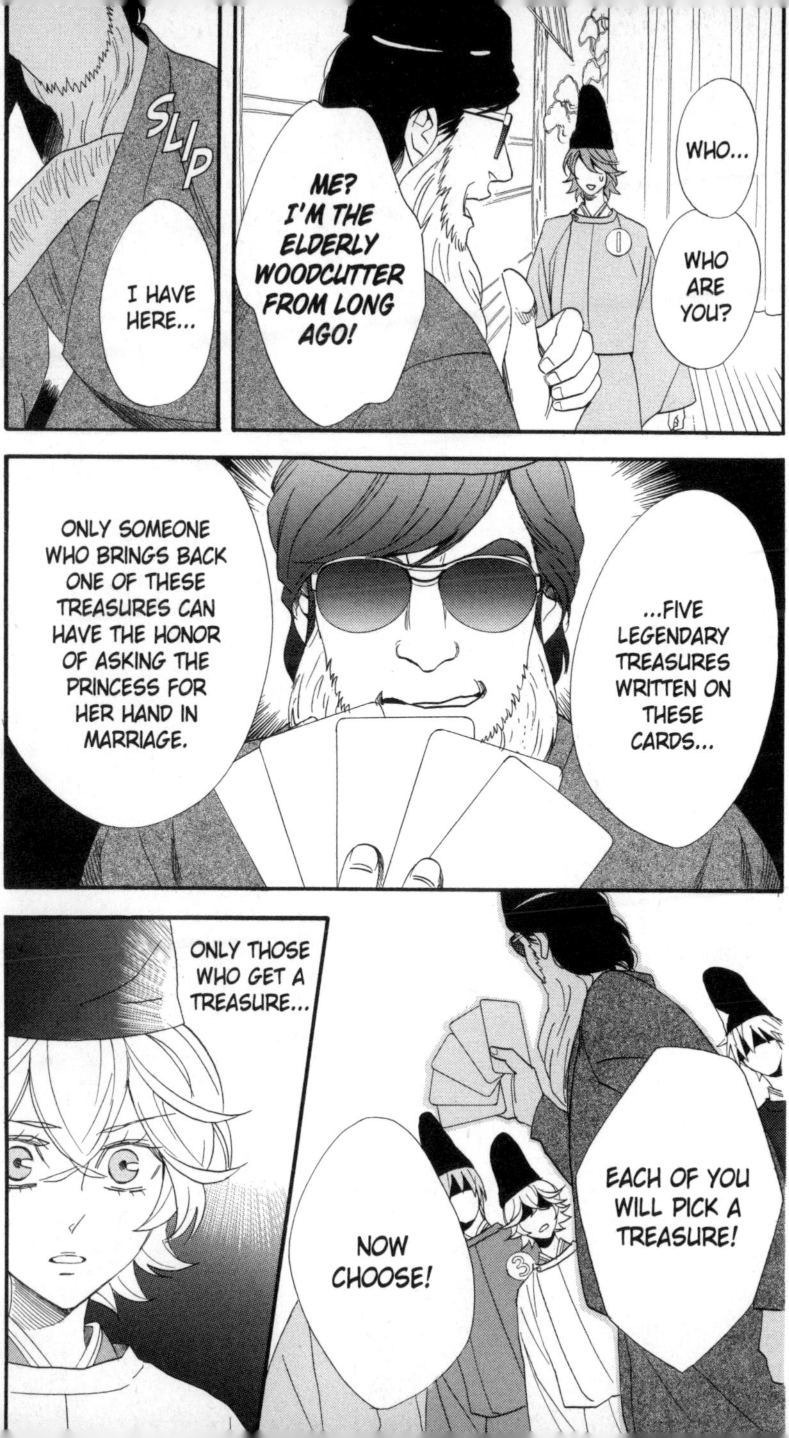
WHO...
WHO ARE YOU?
ME? I'M THE ELDERLY WOODCUTTER FROM LONG AGO!
SLIP
I HAVE HERE...
...FIVE LEGENDARY TREASURES WRITTEN ON THESE CARDS...
ONLY SOMEONE WHO BRINGS BACK ONE OF THESE TREASURES CAN HAVE THE HONOR OF ASKING THE PRINCESS FOR HER HAND IN MARRIAGE.
EACH OF YOU WILL PICK A TREASURE!
NOW CHOOSE!
ONLY THOSE WHO GET A TREASURE...

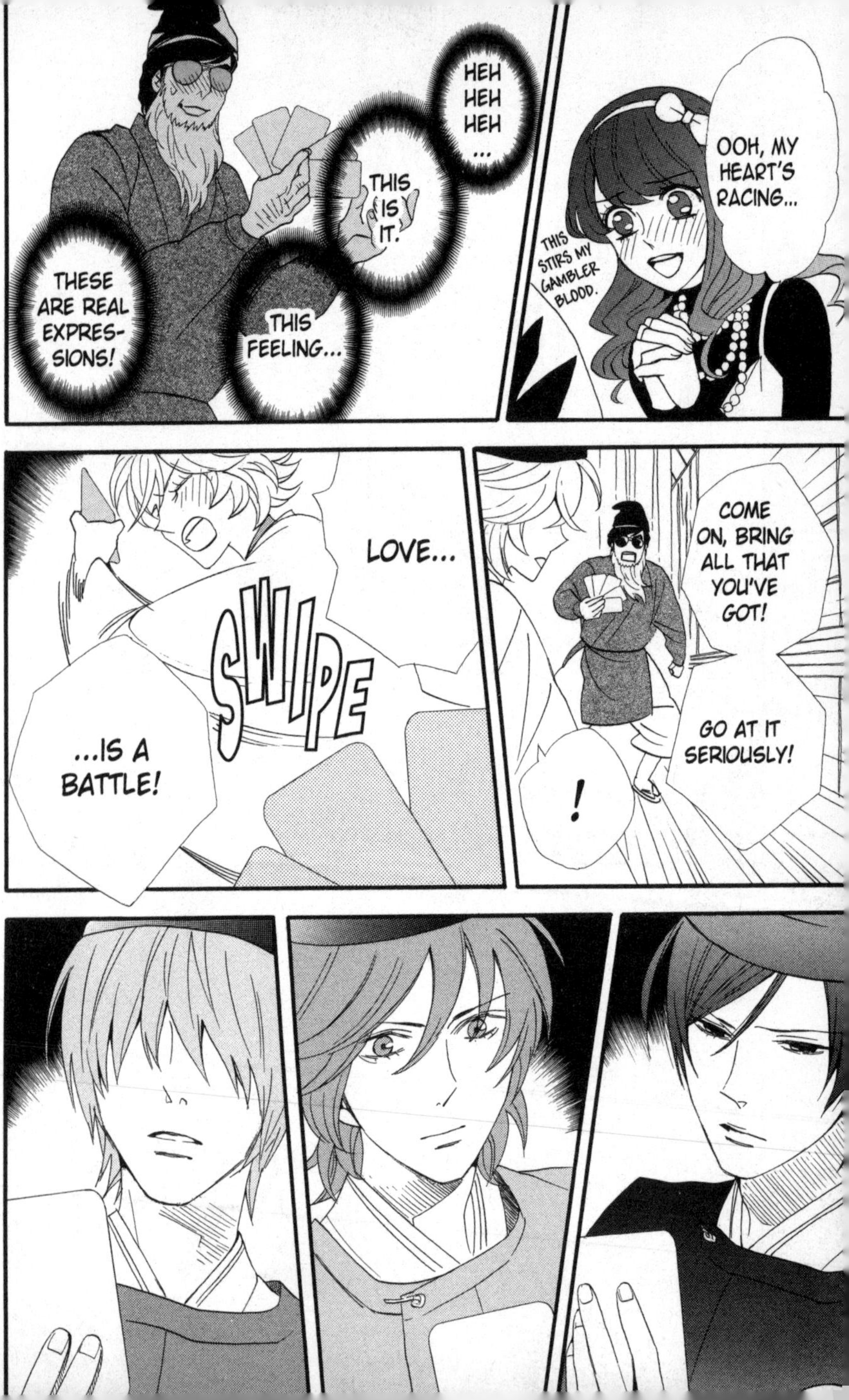
OOH, MY HEART'S RACING...
THIS STIRS MY GAMBLER BLOOD.
HEH HEH HEH ...
THIS IS IT.
THIS FEELING...
THESE ARE REAL EXPRES-SIONS!
COME ON, BRING ALL THAT YOU'VE GOT!
GO AT IT SERIOUSLY!
!
LOVE...
SWIPE
...IS A BATTLE!

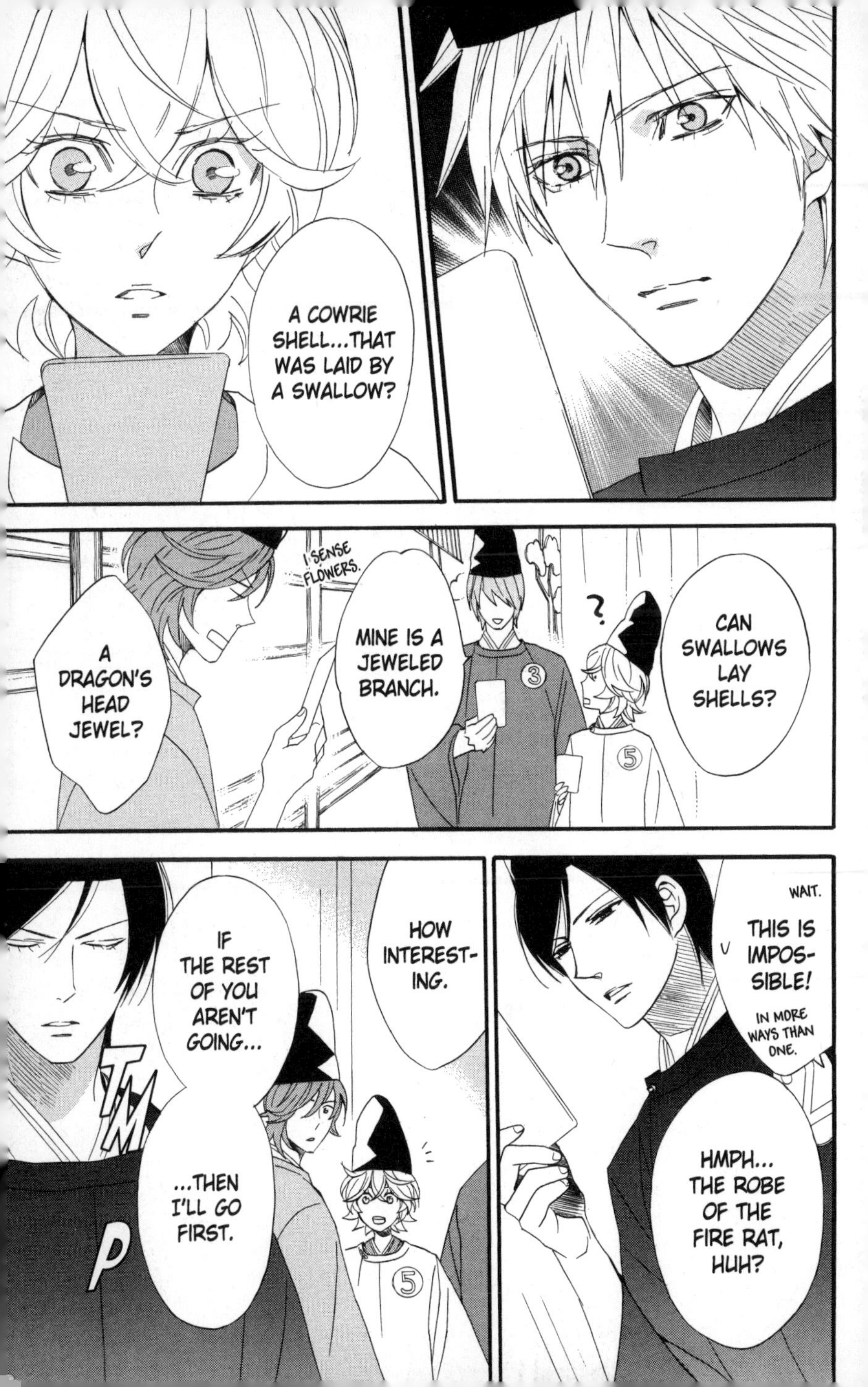
A COWRIE SHELL...THAT WAS LAID BY A SWALLOW?
CAN SWALLOWS LAY SHELLS?
?
MINE IS A JEWELED BRANCH.
I SENSE FLOWERS.
A DRAGON'S HEAD JEWEL?
WAIT.
THIS IS IMPOS-SIBLE!
IN MORE WAYS THAN ONE.
HMPH... THE ROBE OF THE FIRE RAT, HUH?
HOW INTEREST-ING.
IF THE REST OF YOU AREN'T GOING...
TMP
...THEN I'LL GO FIRST.

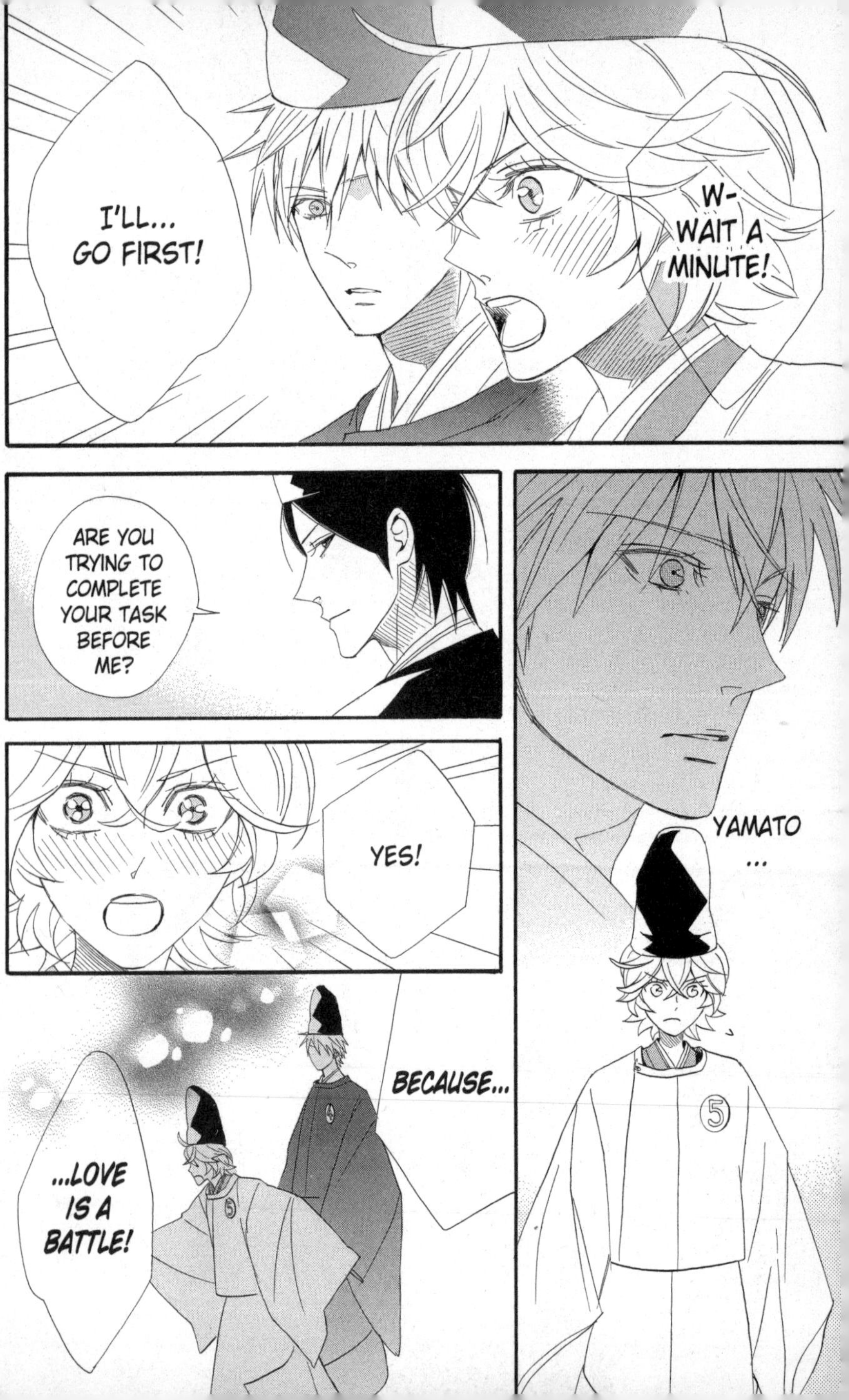
W- WAIT A MINUTE!
I'LL... GO FIRST!
YAMATO ...
ARE YOU TRYING TO COMPLETE YOUR TASK BEFORE ME?
YES!
BECAUSE...
...LOVE IS A BATTLE!

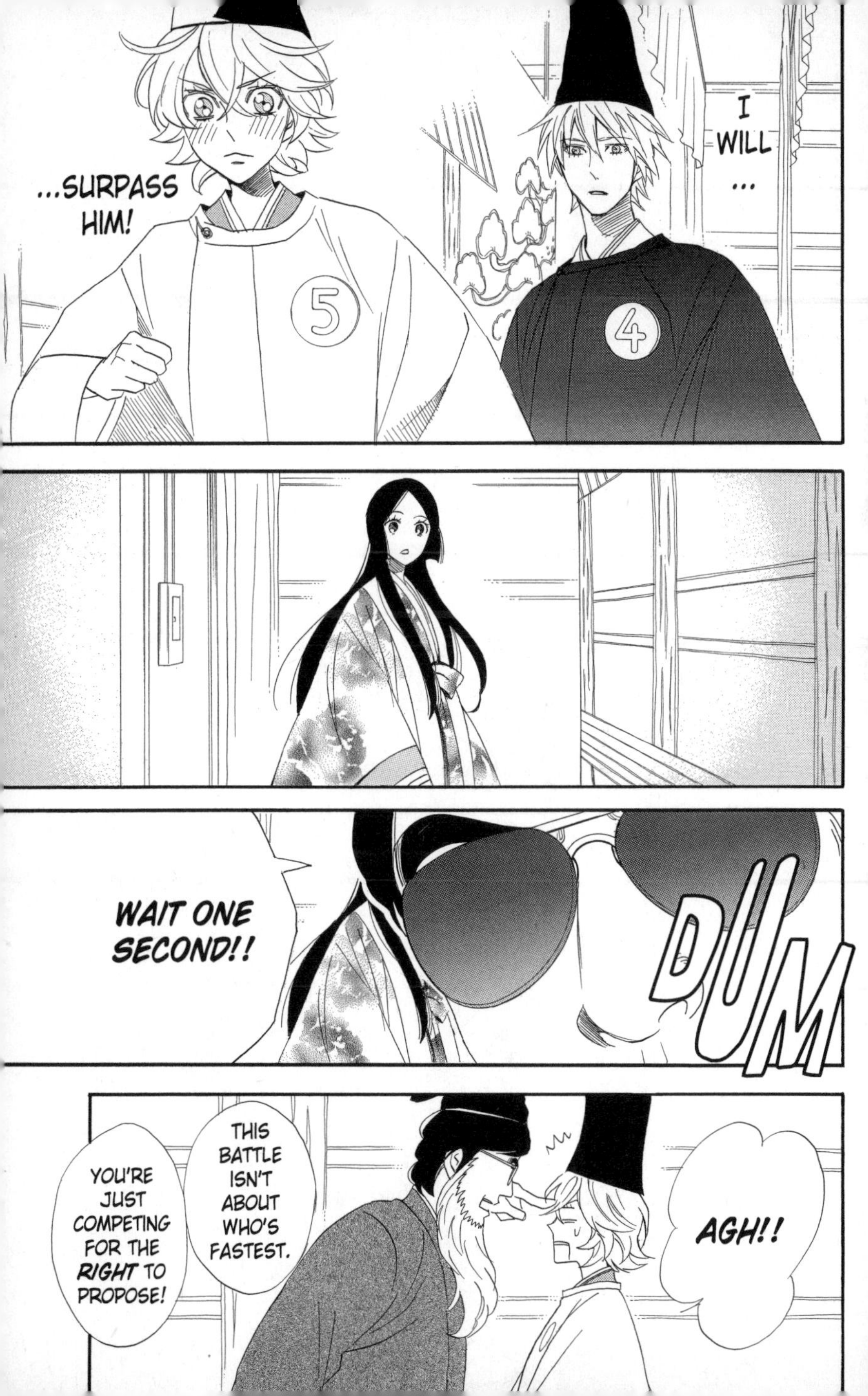
I WILL ...
...SURPASS HIM!
DUM
WAIT ONE SECOND!!
AGH!!
THIS BATTLE ISN'T ABOUT WHO'S FASTEST.
YOU'RE JUST COMPETING FOR THE *RIGHT* TO PROPOSE!

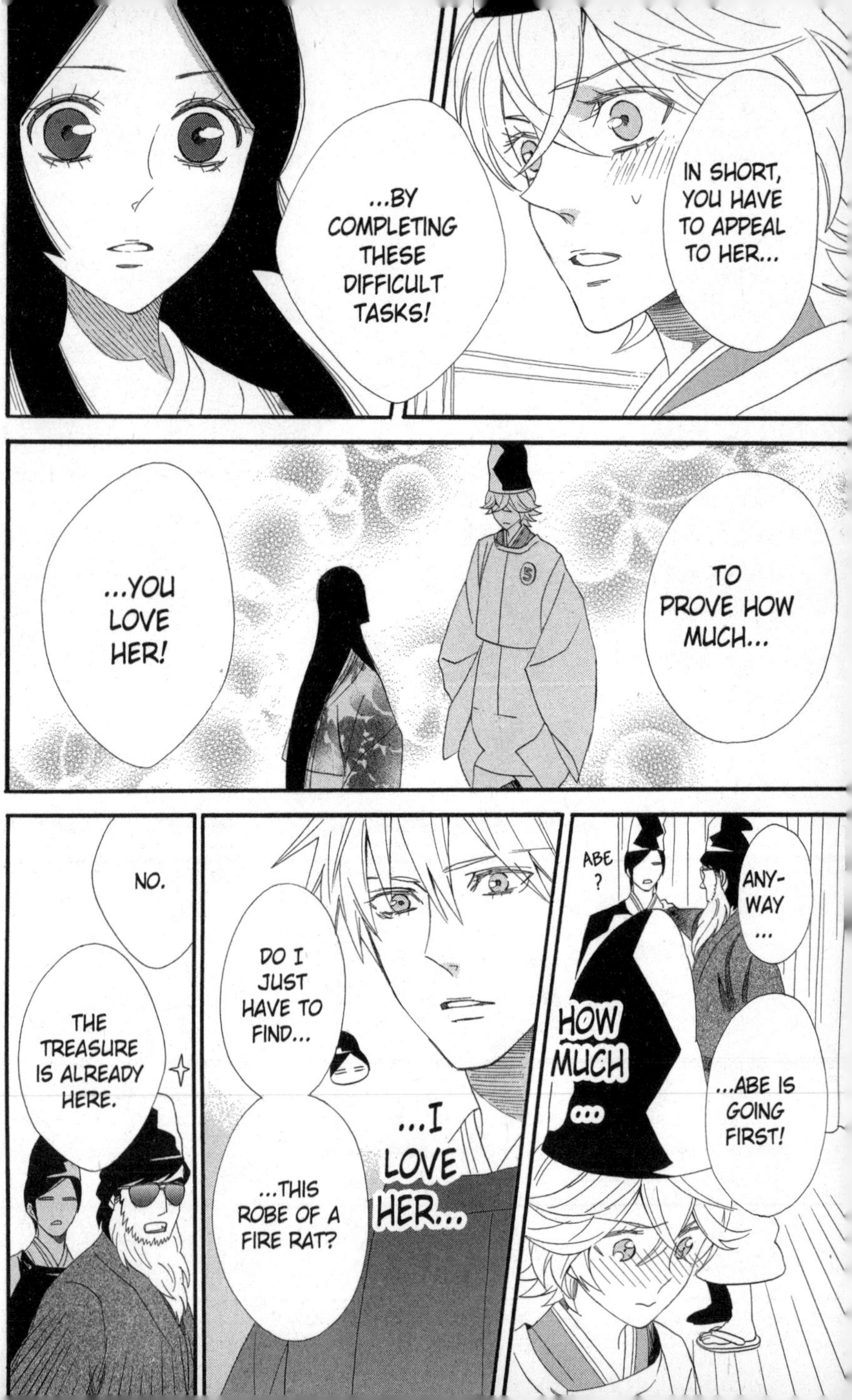
IN SHORT, YOU HAVE TO APPEAL TO HER...
...BY COMPLETING THESE DIFFICULT TASKS!
TO PROVE HOW MUCH...
...YOU LOVE HER!
ANY-WAY...
ABE?
...ABE IS GOING FIRST!
HOW MUCH...
DO I JUST HAVE TO FIND...
...I LOVE HER...
...THIS ROBE OF A FIRE RAT?
NO.
THE TREASURE IS ALREADY HERE.

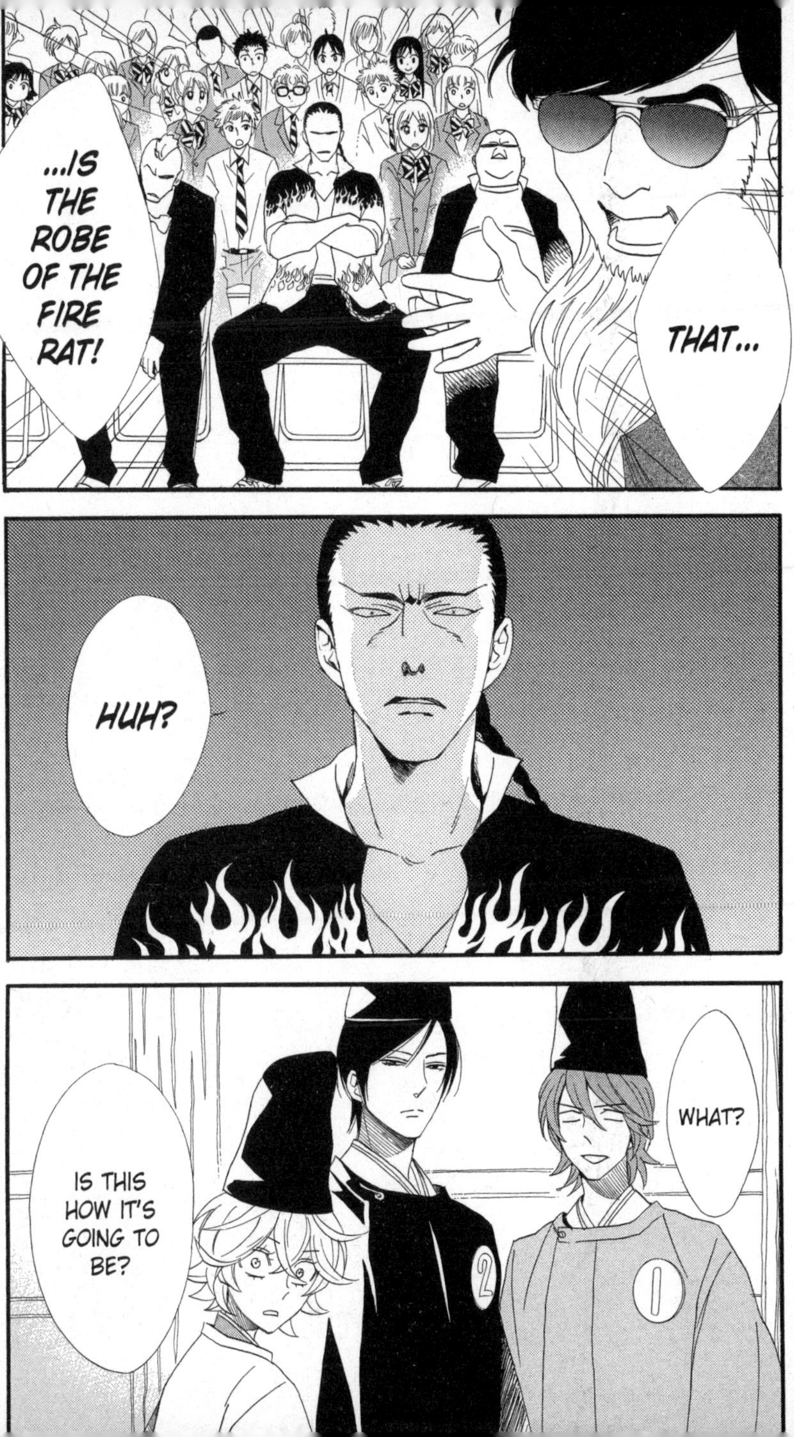
THAT...
...IS THE ROBE OF THE FIRE RAT!
HUH?
WHAT?
IS THIS HOW IT'S GOING TO BE?

OTOMEN

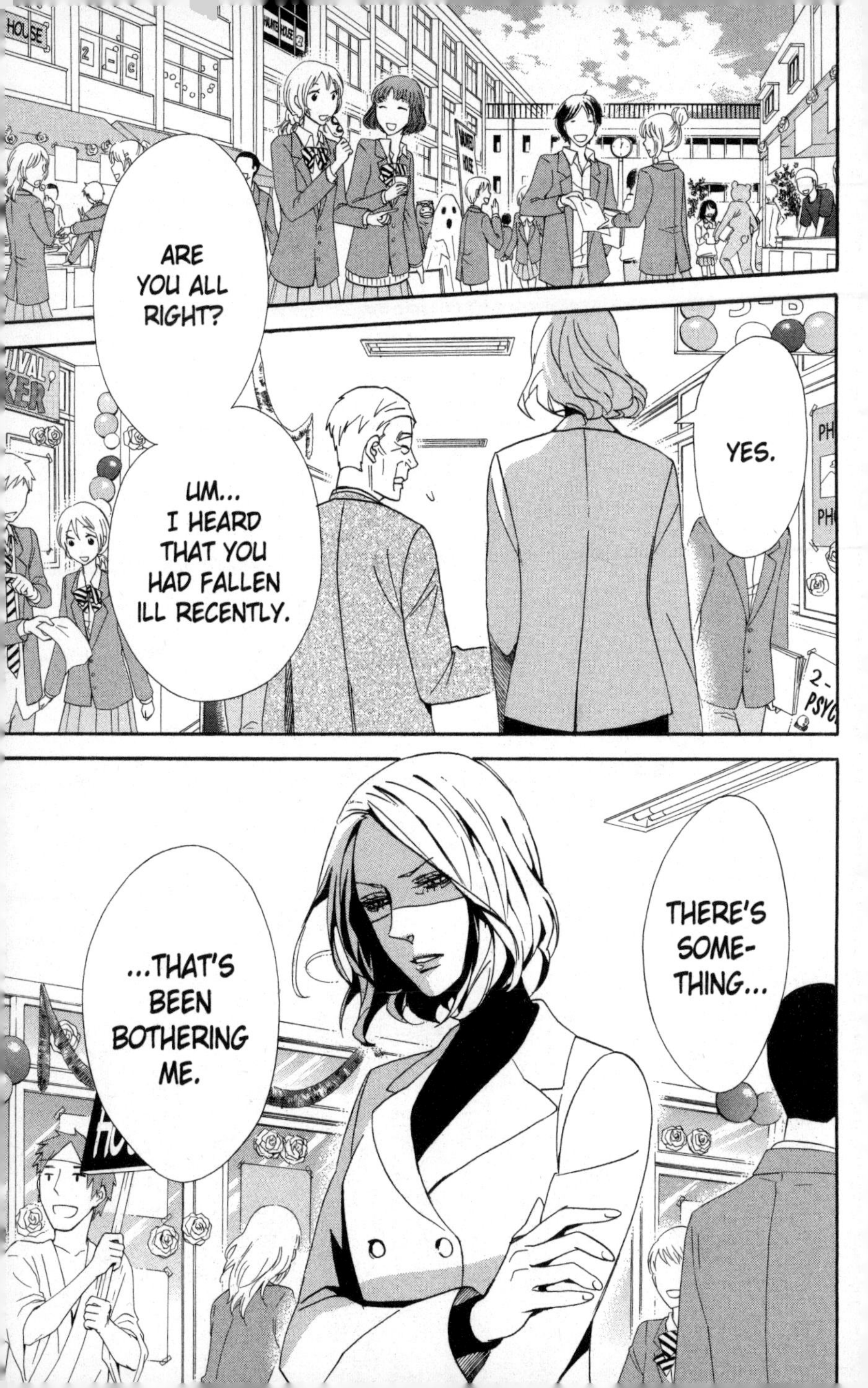
ARE YOU ALL RIGHT?
YES.
UM... I HEARD THAT YOU HAD FALLEN ILL RECENTLY.
THERE'S SOME-THING...
...THAT'S BEEN BOTHERING ME.

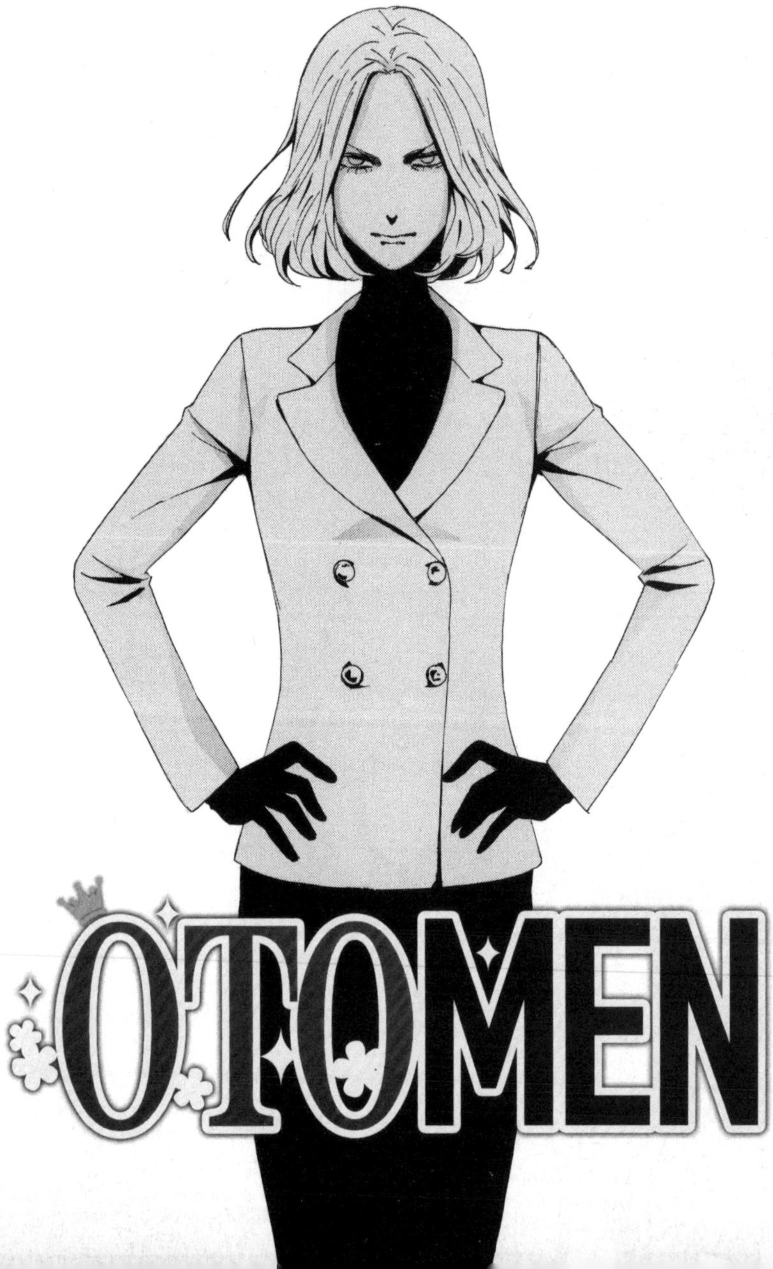
OTOMEN

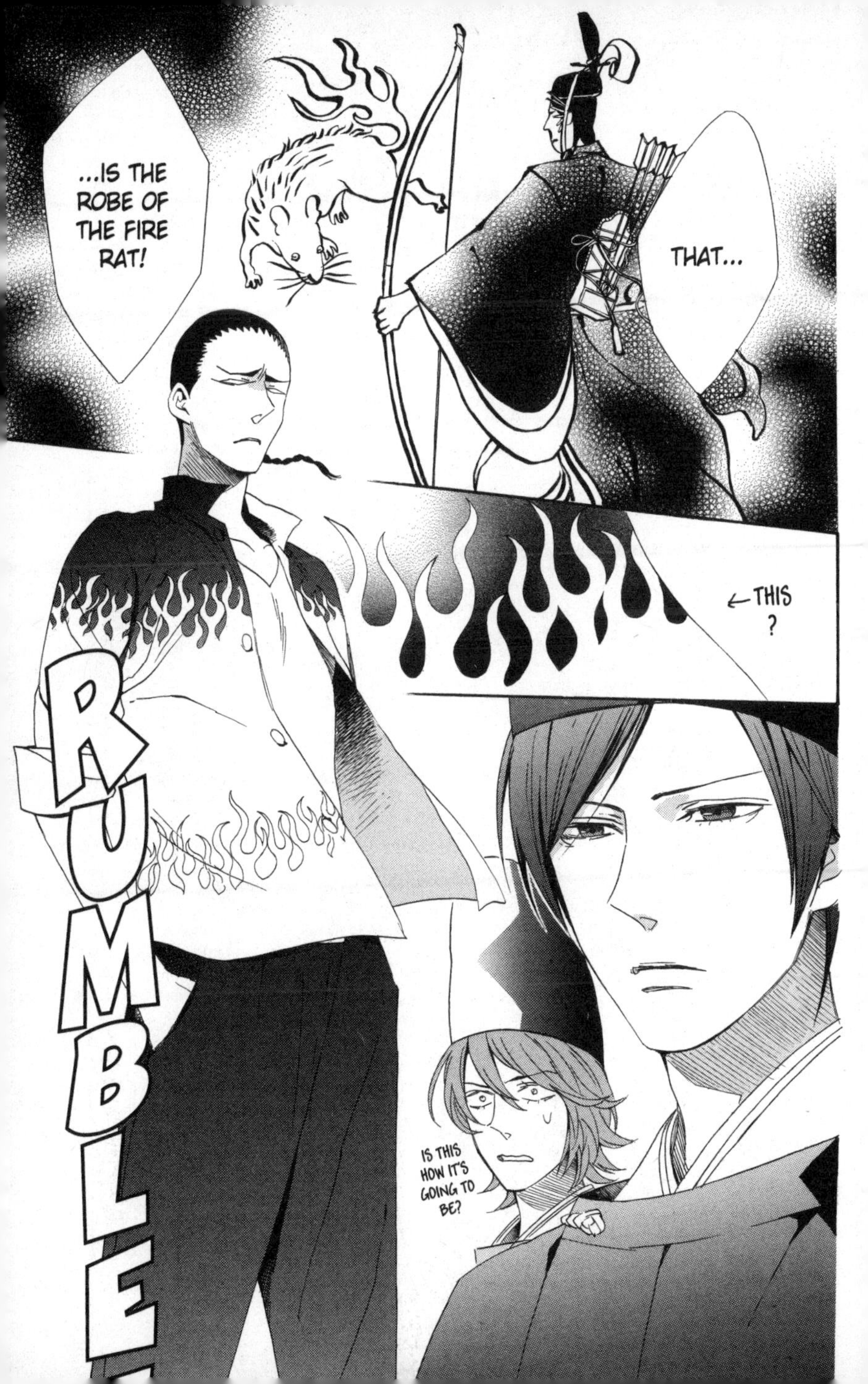
THAT...
...IS THE ROBE OF THE FIRE RAT!
← THIS ?
IS THIS HOW IT'S GOING TO BE?
RUMBLE

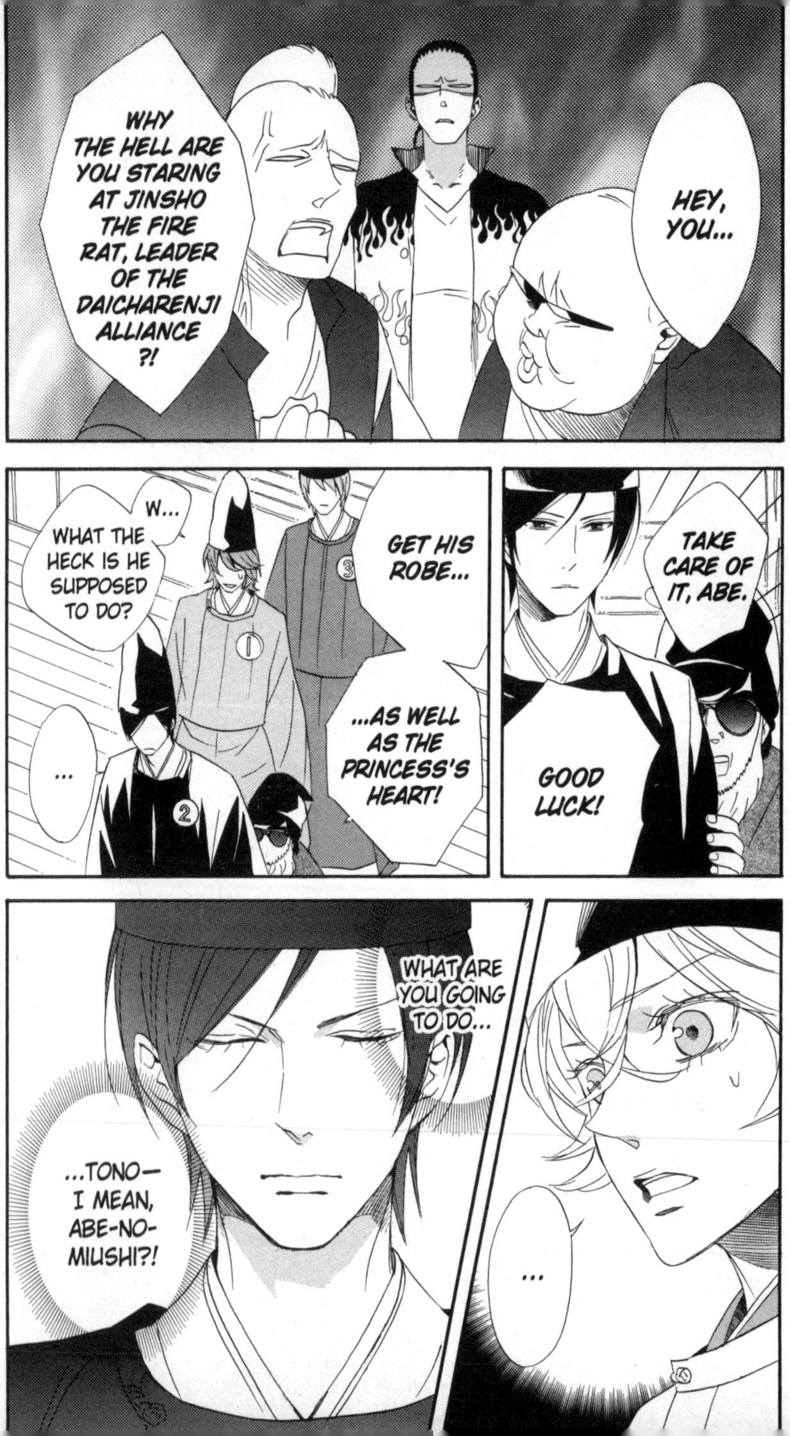
HEY, YOU...
WHY THE HELL ARE YOU STARING AT JINSHO THE FIRE RAT, LEADER OF THE DAICHARENJI ALLIANCE ?!
TAKE CARE OF IT, ABE.
GOOD LUCK!
GET HIS ROBE...
...AS WELL AS THE PRINCESS'S HEART!
W...
WHAT THE HECK IS HE SUPPOSED TO DO?
...
...
WHAT ARE YOU GOING TO DO...
...TONO— I MEAN, ABE-NO-MIUSHI?!

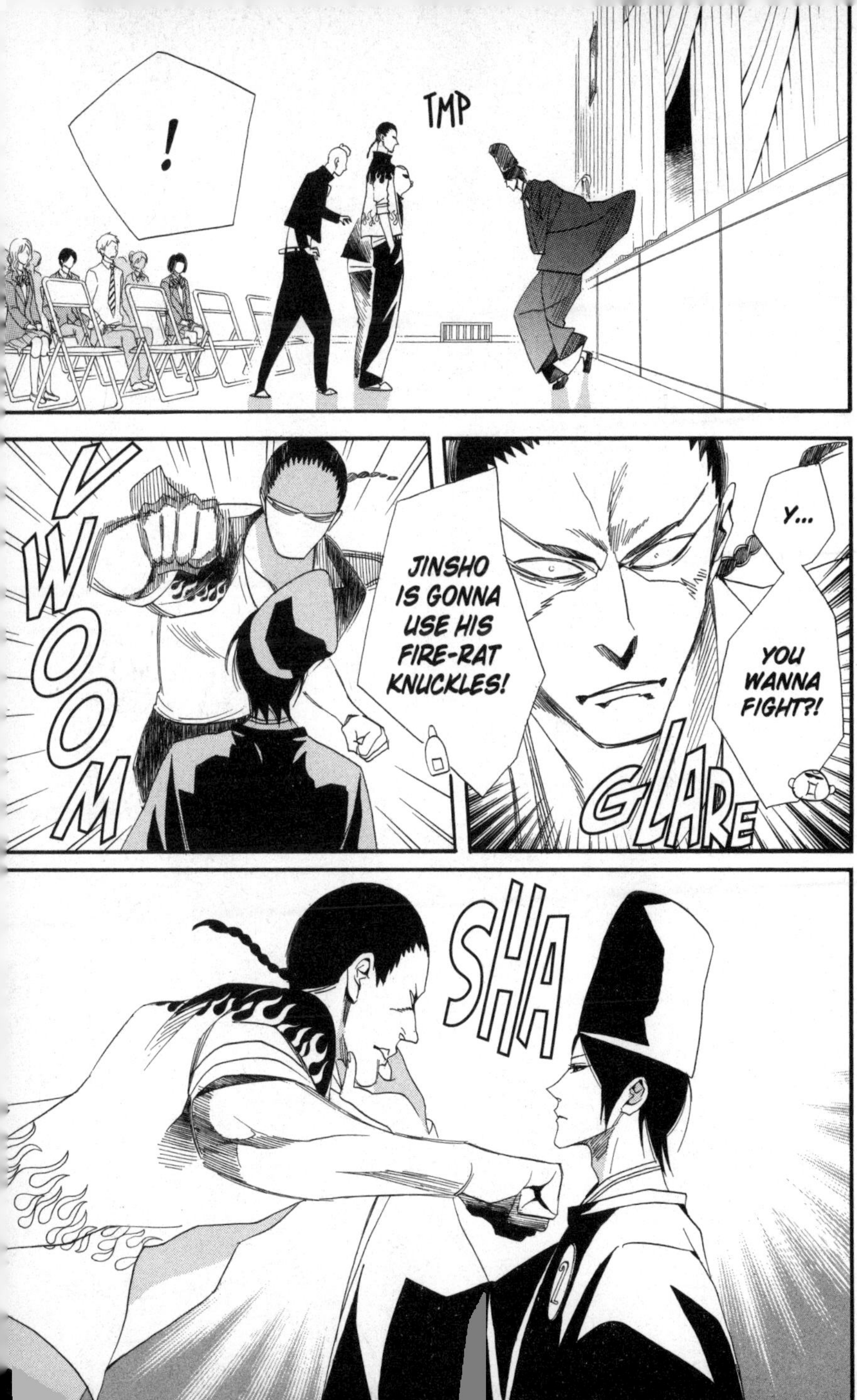
TMP
!
Y...
YOU WANNA FIGHT?!
GLARE
JINSHO IS GONNA USE HIS FIRE-RAT KNUCKLES!
VWOOOM
SHA

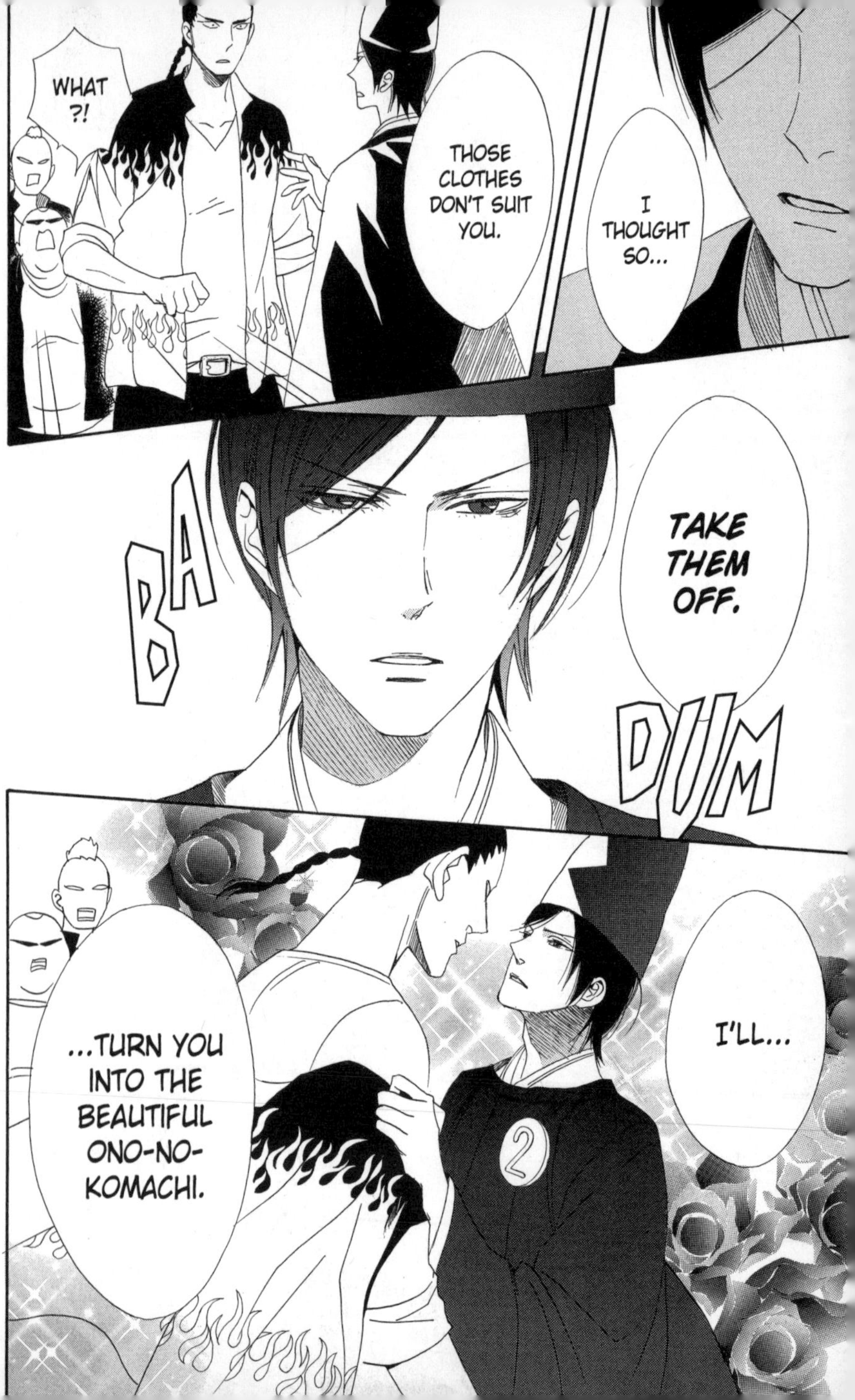
I THOUGHT SO...
THOSE CLOTHES DON'T SUIT YOU.
WHAT?!
TAKE THEM OFF.
BA
DUM
I'LL...
...TURN YOU INTO THE BEAUTIFUL ONO-NO-KOMACHI.

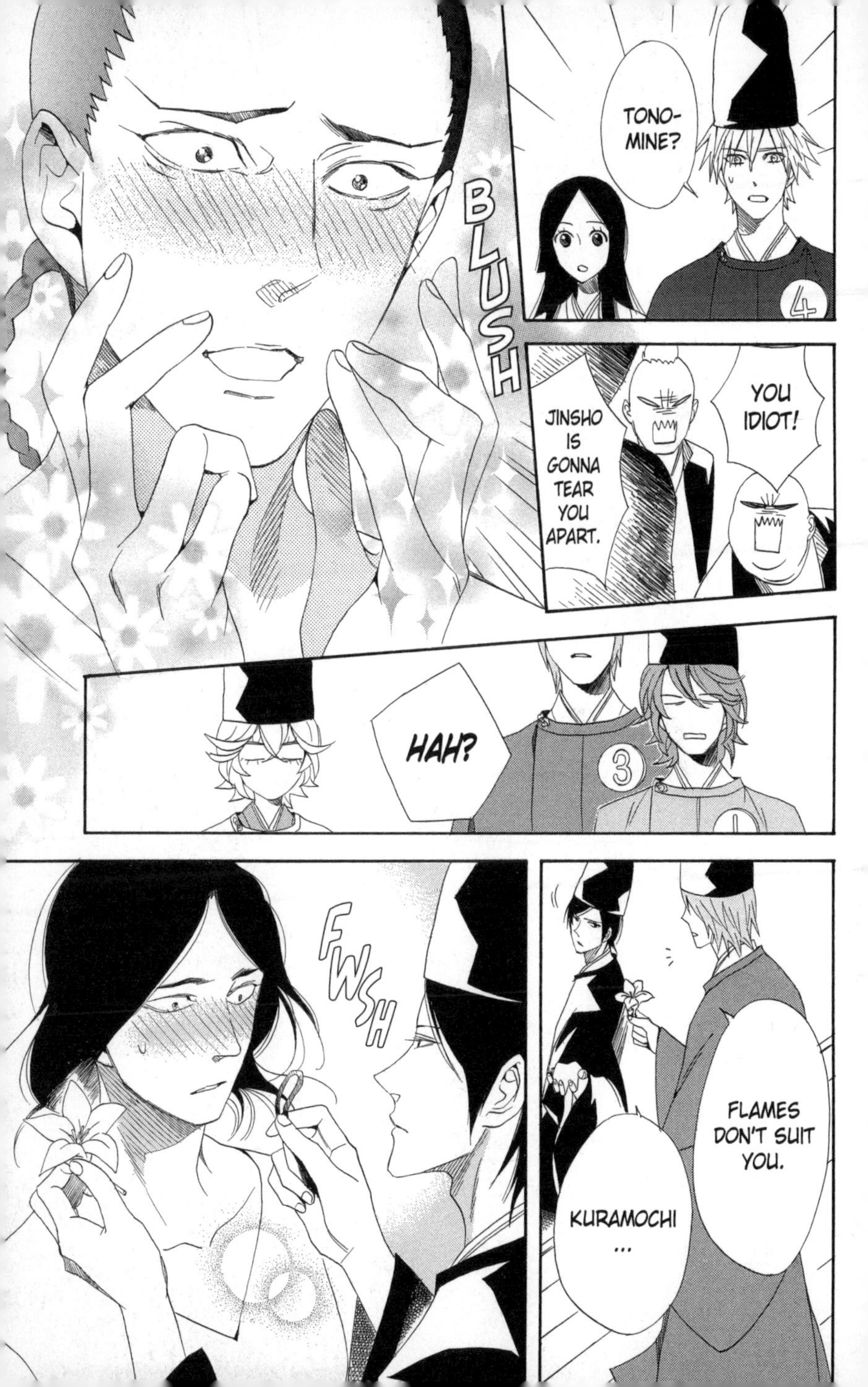
TONO-MINE?
YOU IDIOT!
JINSHO IS GONNA TEAR YOU APART.
BLUSH
HAH?
FLAMES DON'T SUIT YOU.
KURAMOCHI ...
FWSH

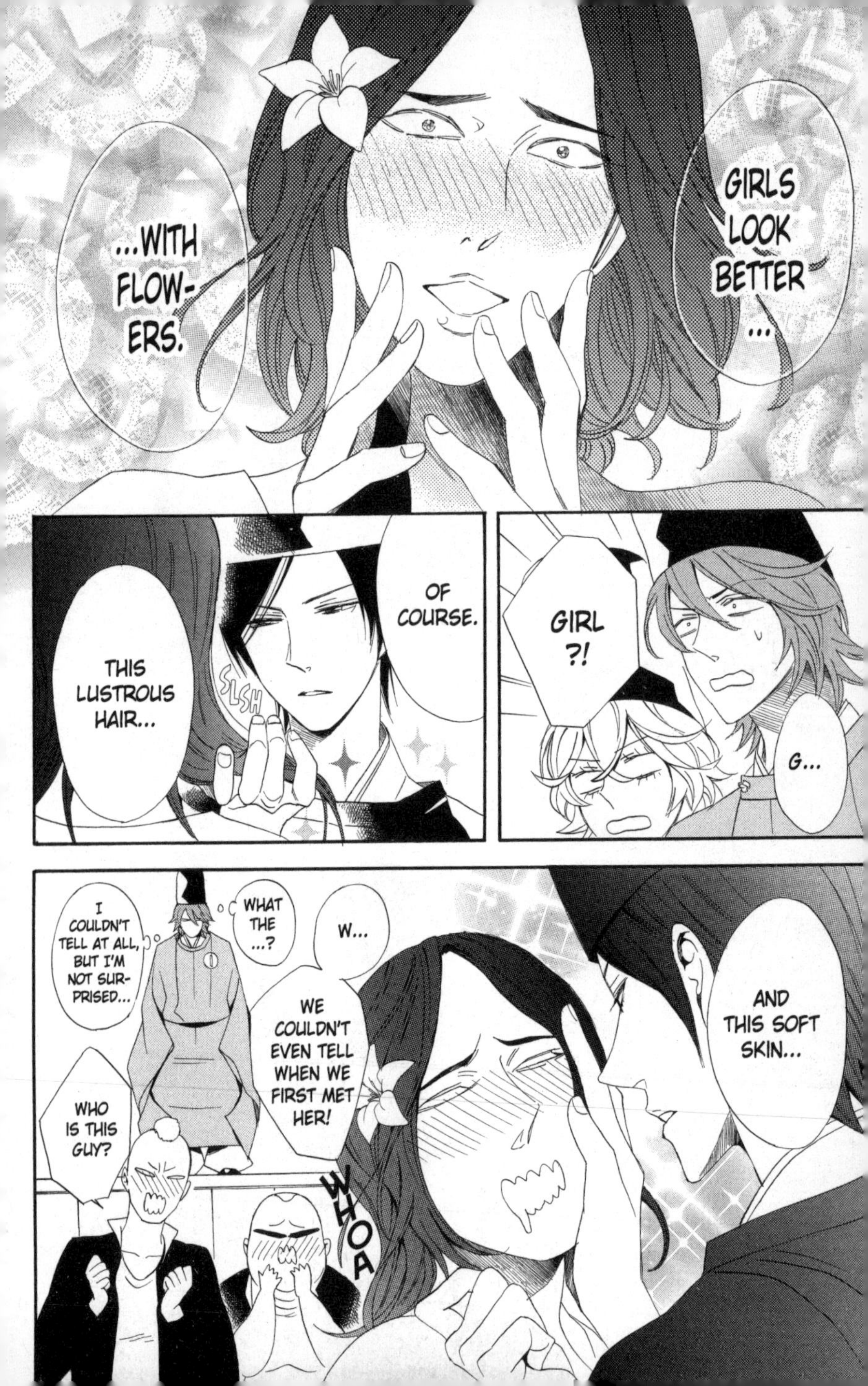
GIRLS LOOK BETTER...
...WITH FLOWERS.
GIRL?!
G...
OF COURSE.
THIS LUSTROUS HAIR...
SLSH
AND THIS SOFT SKIN...
W...
WHAT THE ...?
I COULDN'T TELL AT ALL, BUT I'M NOT SURPRISED...
WE COULDN'T EVEN TELL WHEN WE FIRST MET HER!
WHOA
WHO IS THIS GUY?

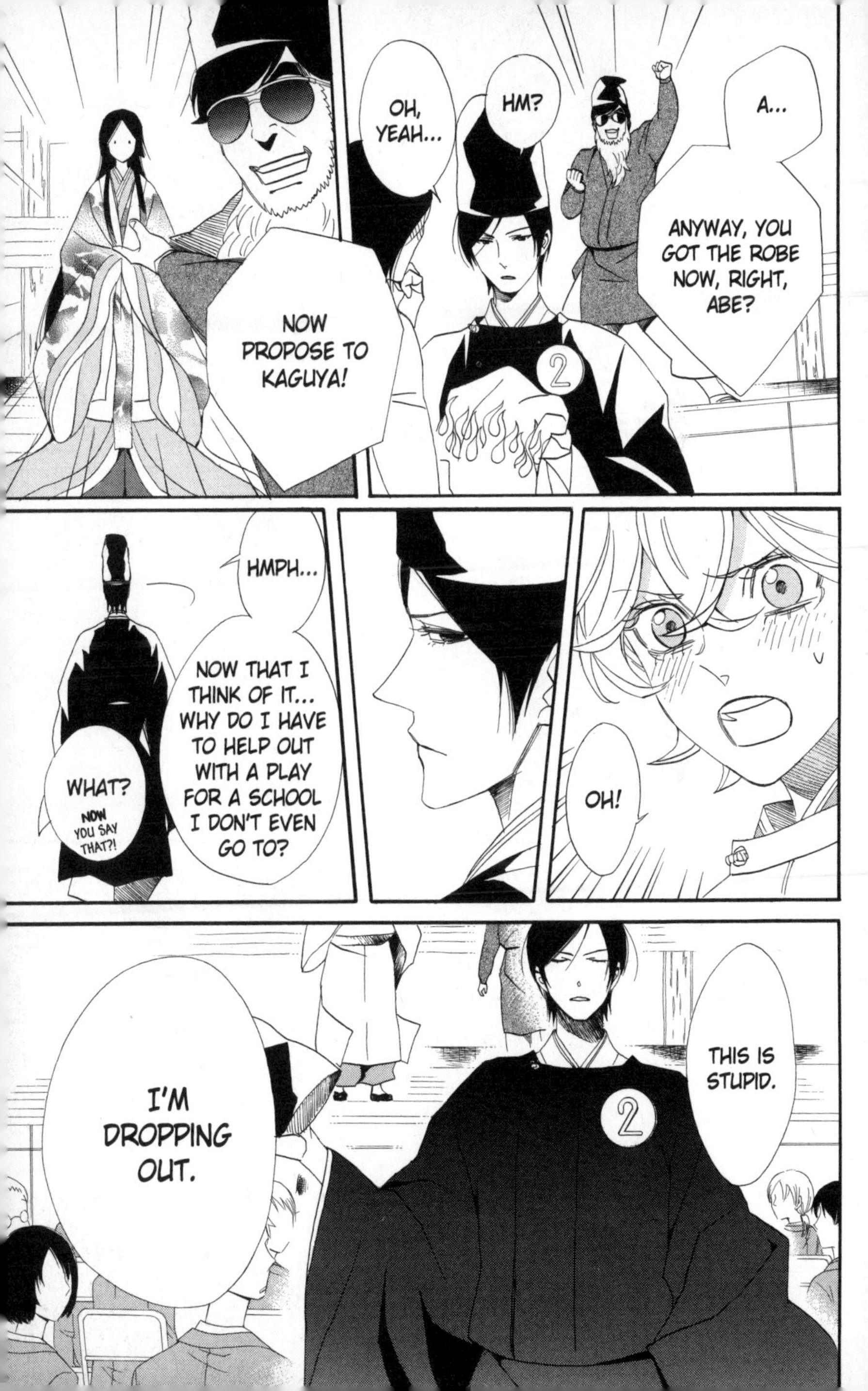
A...
ANYWAY, YOU GOT THE ROBE NOW, RIGHT, ABE?
HM?
OH, YEAH...
NOW PROPOSE TO KAGUYA!
OH!
HMPH...
NOW THAT I THINK OF IT... WHY DO I HAVE TO HELP OUT WITH A PLAY FOR A SCHOOL I DON'T EVEN GO TO?
WHAT? NOW YOU SAY THAT?!
THIS IS STUPID.
I'M DROPPING OUT.

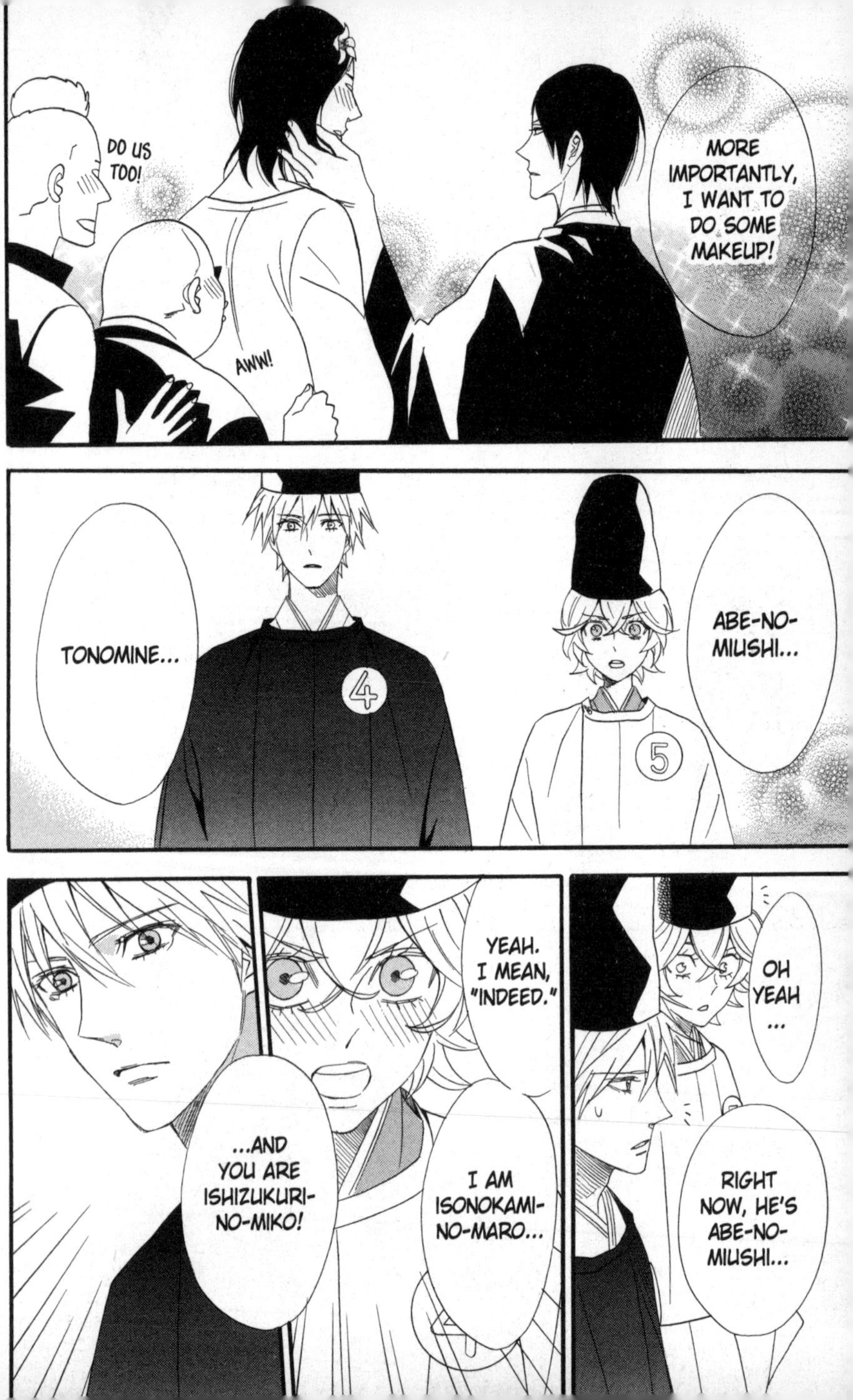
MORE IMPORTANTLY, I WANT TO DO SOME MAKEUP!
DO US TOO!
AWW!
ABE-NO-MIUSHI...
TONOMINE...
OH YEAH ...
RIGHT NOW, HE'S ABE-NO-MIUSHI...
YEAH. I MEAN, "INDEED."
I AM ISONOKAMI-NO-MARO...
...AND YOU ARE ISHIZUKURI-NO-MIKO!

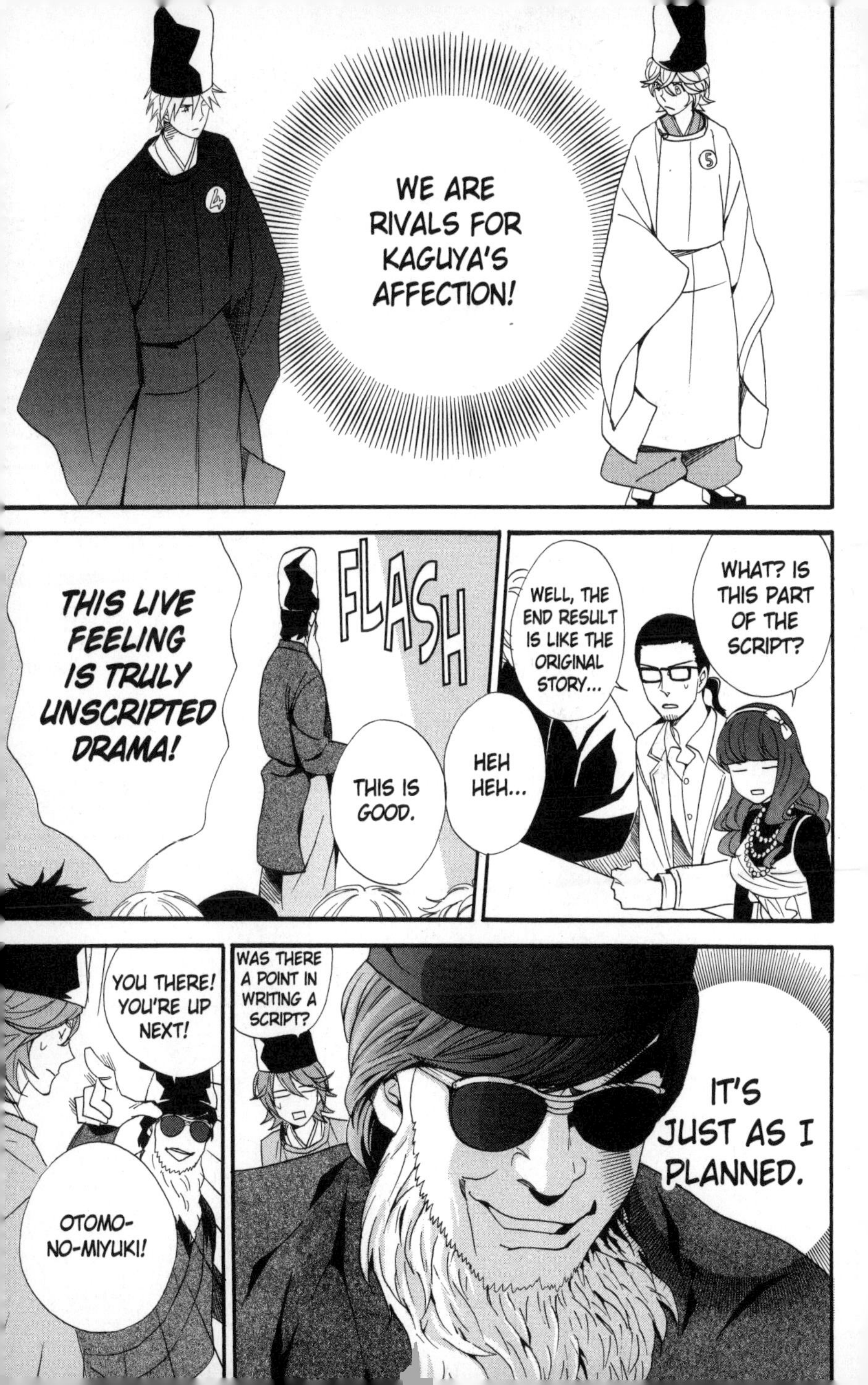
WE ARE RIVALS FOR KAGUYA'S AFFECTION!
WHAT? IS THIS PART OF THE SCRIPT?
WELL, THE END RESULT IS LIKE THE ORIGINAL STORY...
FLASH
HEH HEH...
THIS IS GOOD.
THIS LIVE FEELING IS TRULY UNSCRIPTED DRAMA!
WAS THERE A POINT IN WRITING A SCRIPT?
IT'S JUST AS I PLANNED.
YOU THERE! YOU'RE UP NEXT!
OTOMO-NO-MIYUKI!

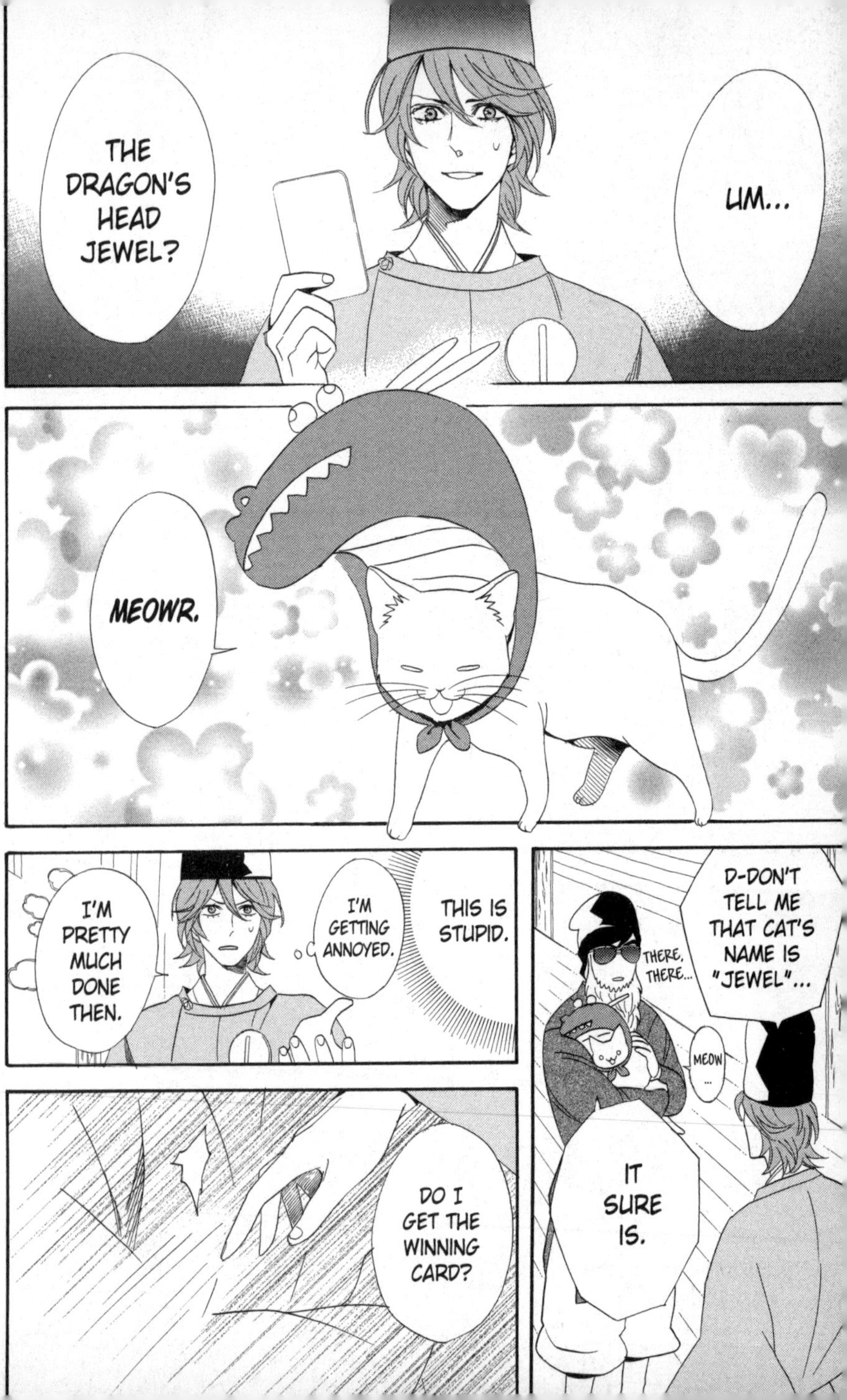
UM...
THE DRAGON'S HEAD JEWEL?
MEOWR.
D-DON'T TELL ME THAT CAT'S NAME IS "JEWEL"...
THERE, THERE...
MEOW ...
IT SURE IS.
THIS IS STUPID.
I'M GETTING ANNOYED.
I'M PRETTY MUCH DONE THEN.
DO I GET THE WINNING CARD?

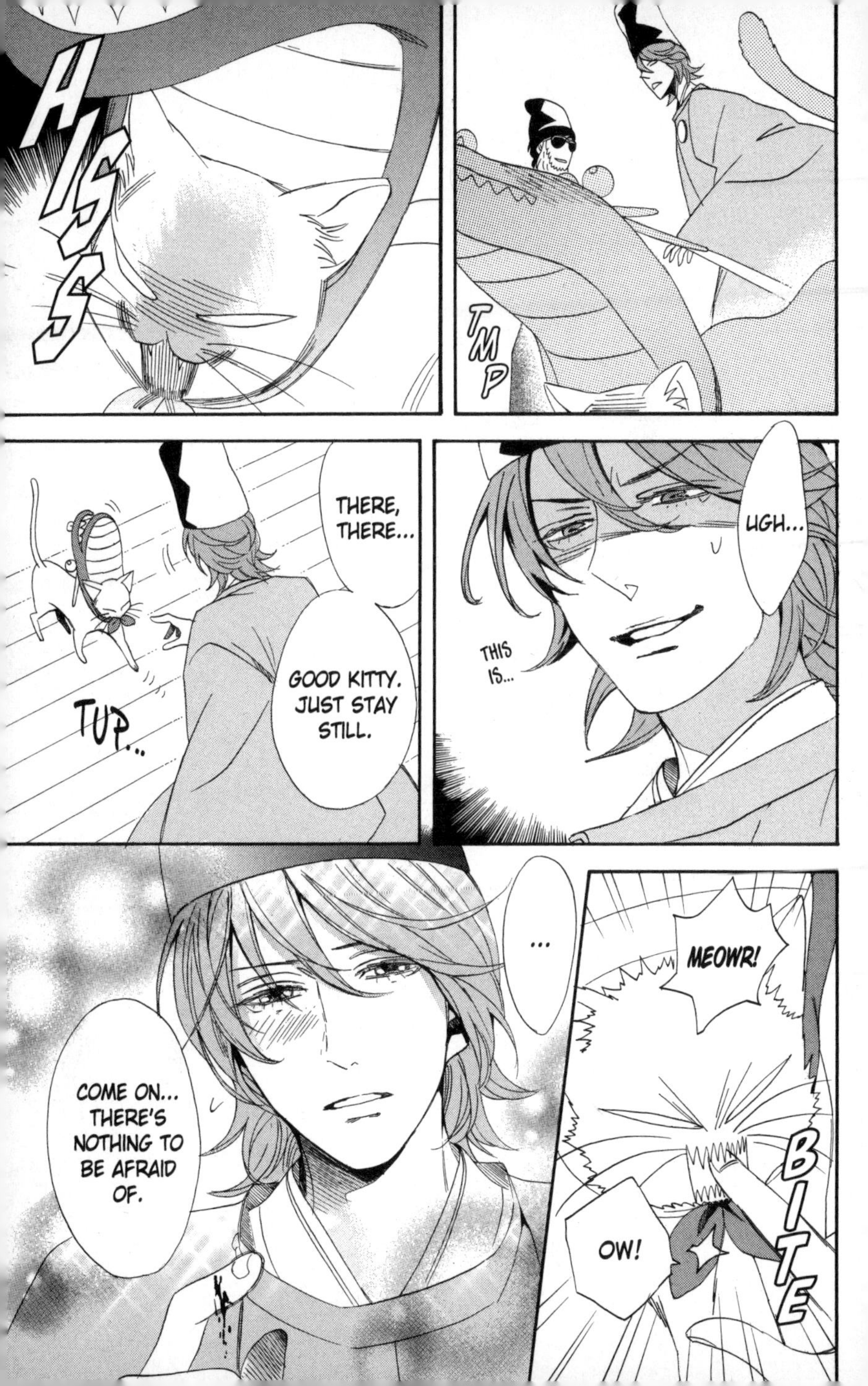
TMP
HISS
UGH...
THIS IS...
THERE, THERE...
GOOD KITTY. JUST STAY STILL.
TUP...
MEOWR!
BITE
OW!
...
COME ON... THERE'S NOTHING TO BE AFRAID OF.

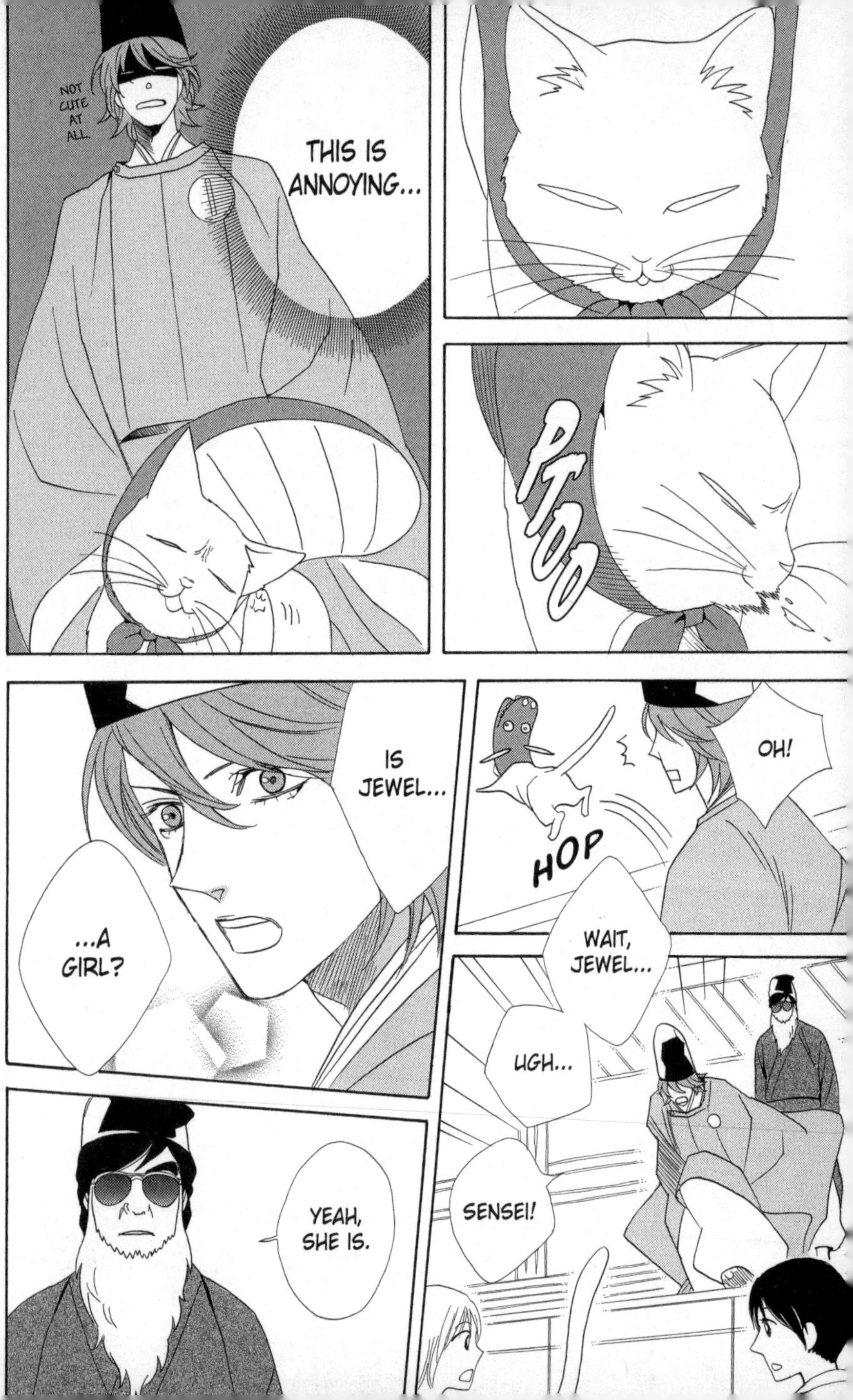
PTOOO
THIS IS ANNOYING...
NOT CUTE AT ALL.
OH!
HOP
IS JEWEL...
...A GIRL?
WAIT, JEWEL...
UGH...
SENSEI!
YEAH, SHE IS.

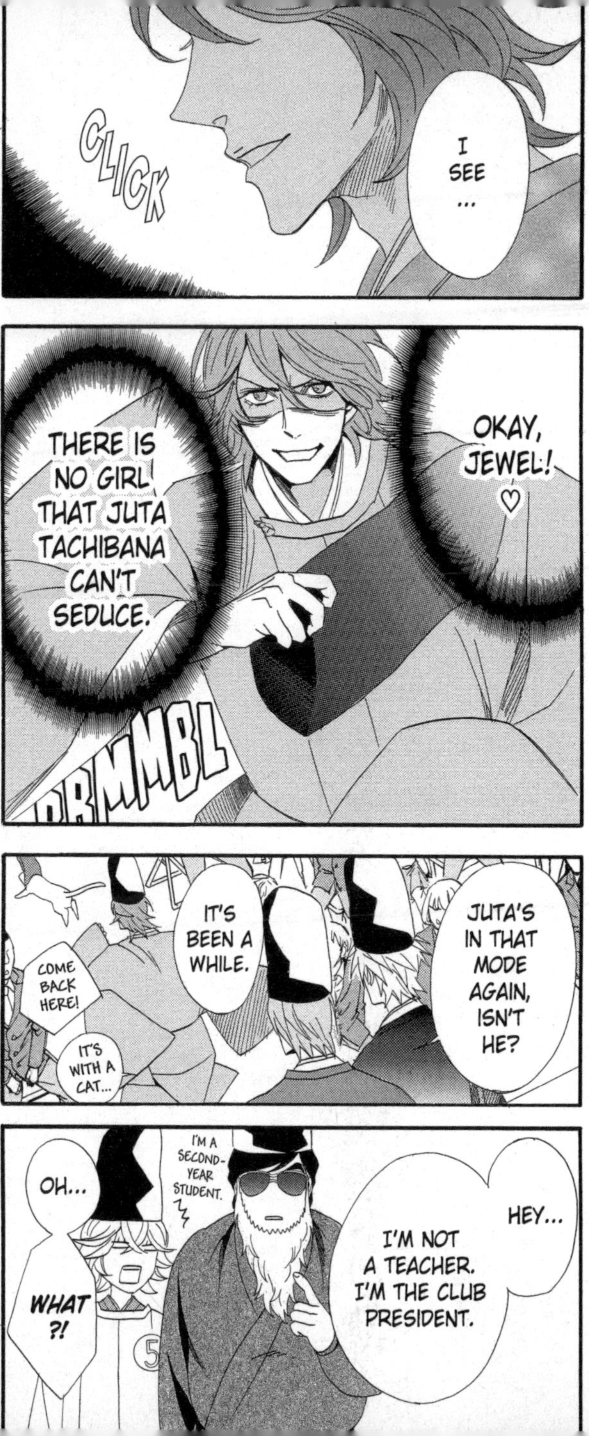
I SEE...
CLICK
OKAY, JEWEL! ♡
THERE IS NO GIRL THAT JUTA TACHIBANA CAN'T SEDUCE.
DRMMBL
JUTA'S IN THAT MODE AGAIN, ISN'T HE?
IT'S BEEN A WHILE.
COME BACK HERE!
IT'S WITH A CAT...
HEY...
I'M NOT A TEACHER. I'M THE CLUB PRESIDENT.
I'M A SECOND-YEAR STUDENT.
OH...
WHAT?!

About the cover... This volume's cover is unusual for *Otomen*. It's goth! I tried to make it dark. Asuka's mother is there, after all.

Kiyomi is *Otomen's* only dark character. In the story, she's the enemy, or rather, the person you're supposed to hate, but because of that, she is a character who is essential to *Otomen*.

Despite all her talk about men being masculine and women being feminine, Kiyomi is incredibly manly.

It was very fun to draw dark faces. It gives it a homey feel. *Ha ha.*

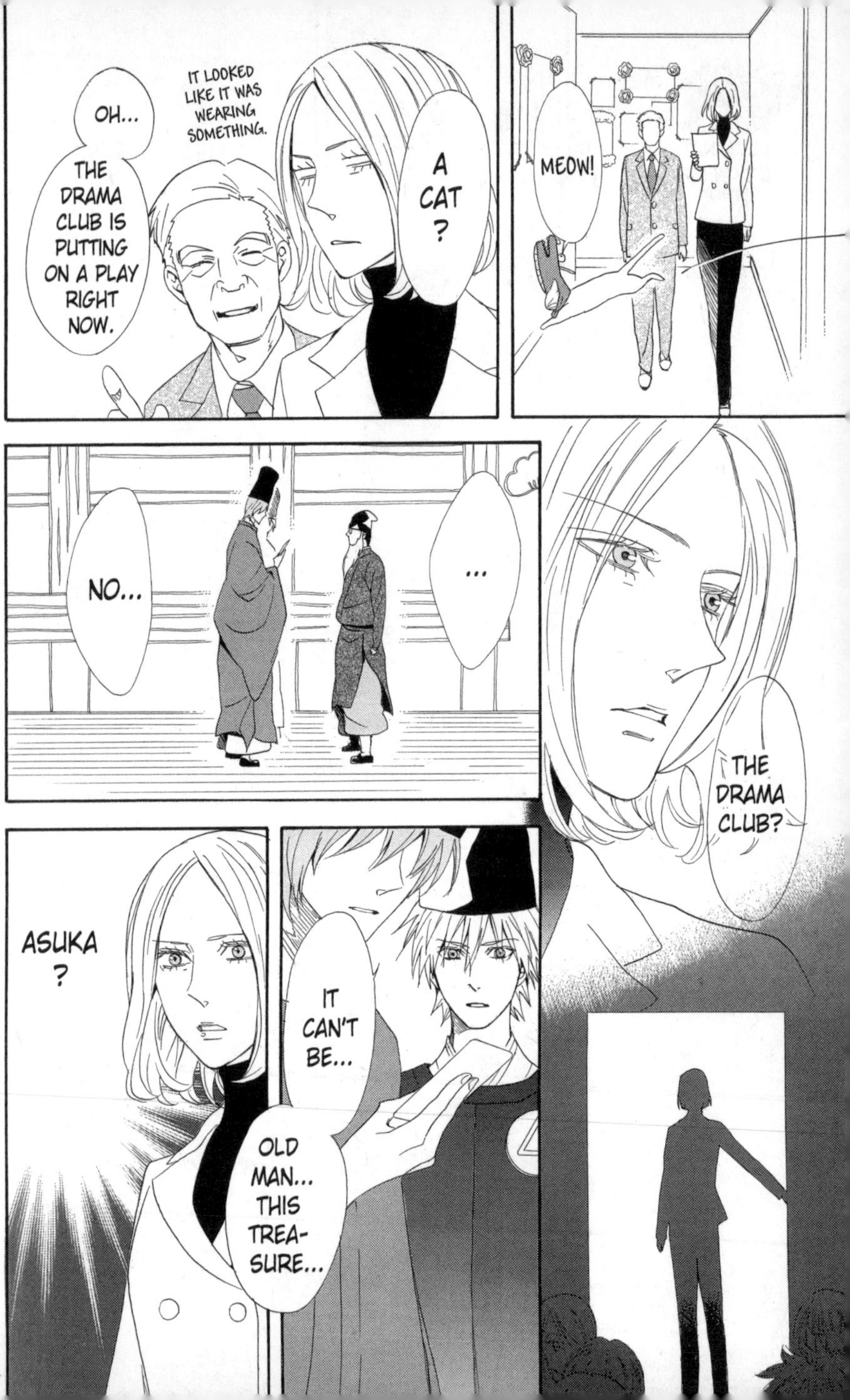
MEOW!
A CAT?
IT LOOKED LIKE IT WAS WEARING SOMETHING.
OH...
THE DRAMA CLUB IS PUTTING ON A PLAY RIGHT NOW.
THE DRAMA CLUB?
...
NO...
IT CAN'T BE...
OLD MAN... THIS TREA-SURE...
ASUKA?

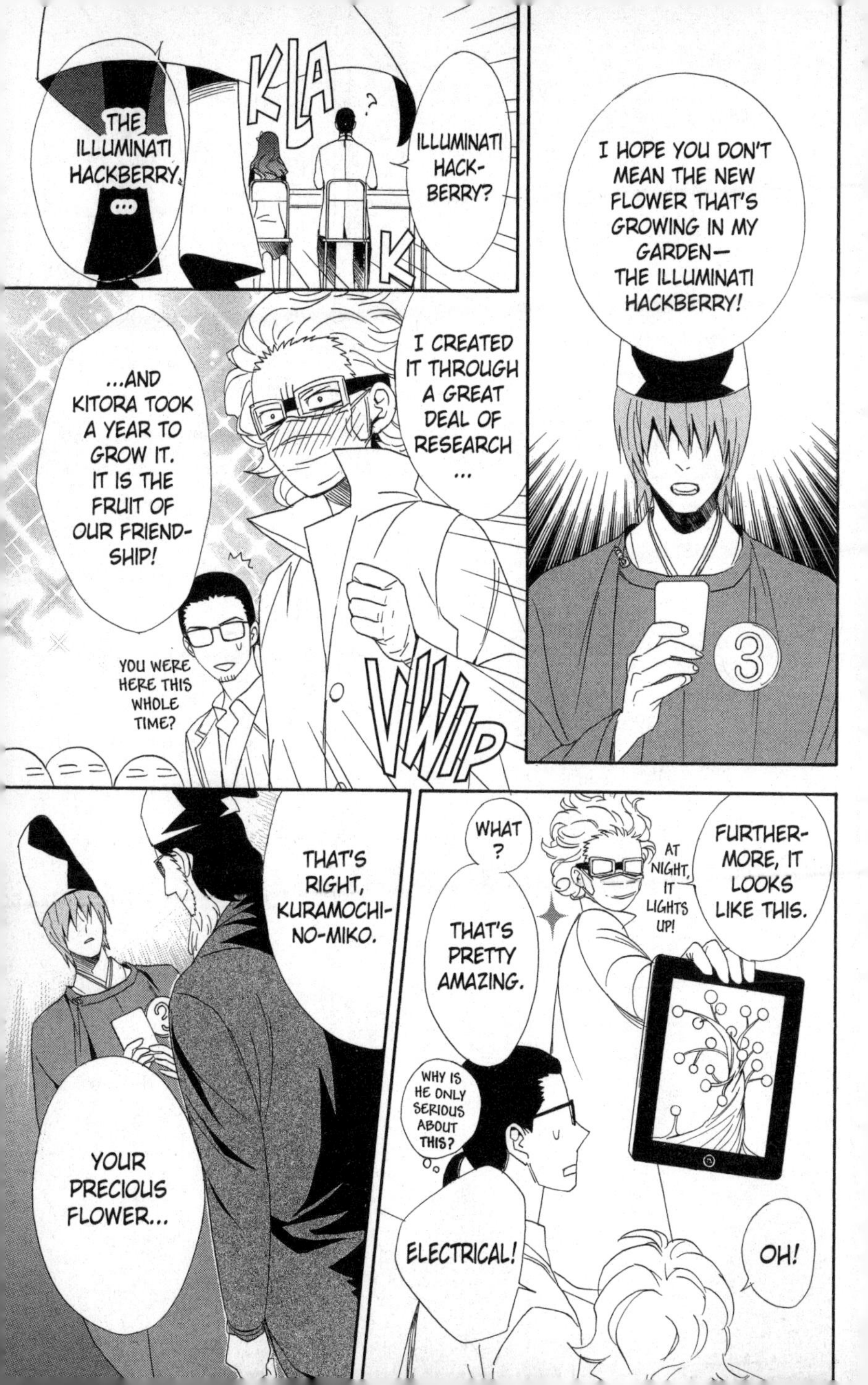
I HOPE YOU DON'T MEAN THE NEW FLOWER THAT'S GROWING IN MY GARDEN—THE ILLUMINATI HACKBERRY!
ILLUMINATI HACK-BERRY?
KLAK
THE ILLUMINATI HACKBERRY.
...
I CREATED IT THROUGH A GREAT DEAL OF RESEARCH...
...AND KITORA TOOK A YEAR TO GROW IT. IT IS THE FRUIT OF OUR FRIEND-SHIP!
VWIP
YOU WERE HERE THIS WHOLE TIME?
FURTHER-MORE, IT LOOKS LIKE THIS.
AT NIGHT, IT LIGHTS UP!
WHAT?
THAT'S PRETTY AMAZING.
WHY IS HE ONLY SERIOUS ABOUT THIS?
OH!
ELECTRICAL!
THAT'S RIGHT, KURAMOCHI-NO-MIKO.
YOUR PRECIOUS FLOWER...

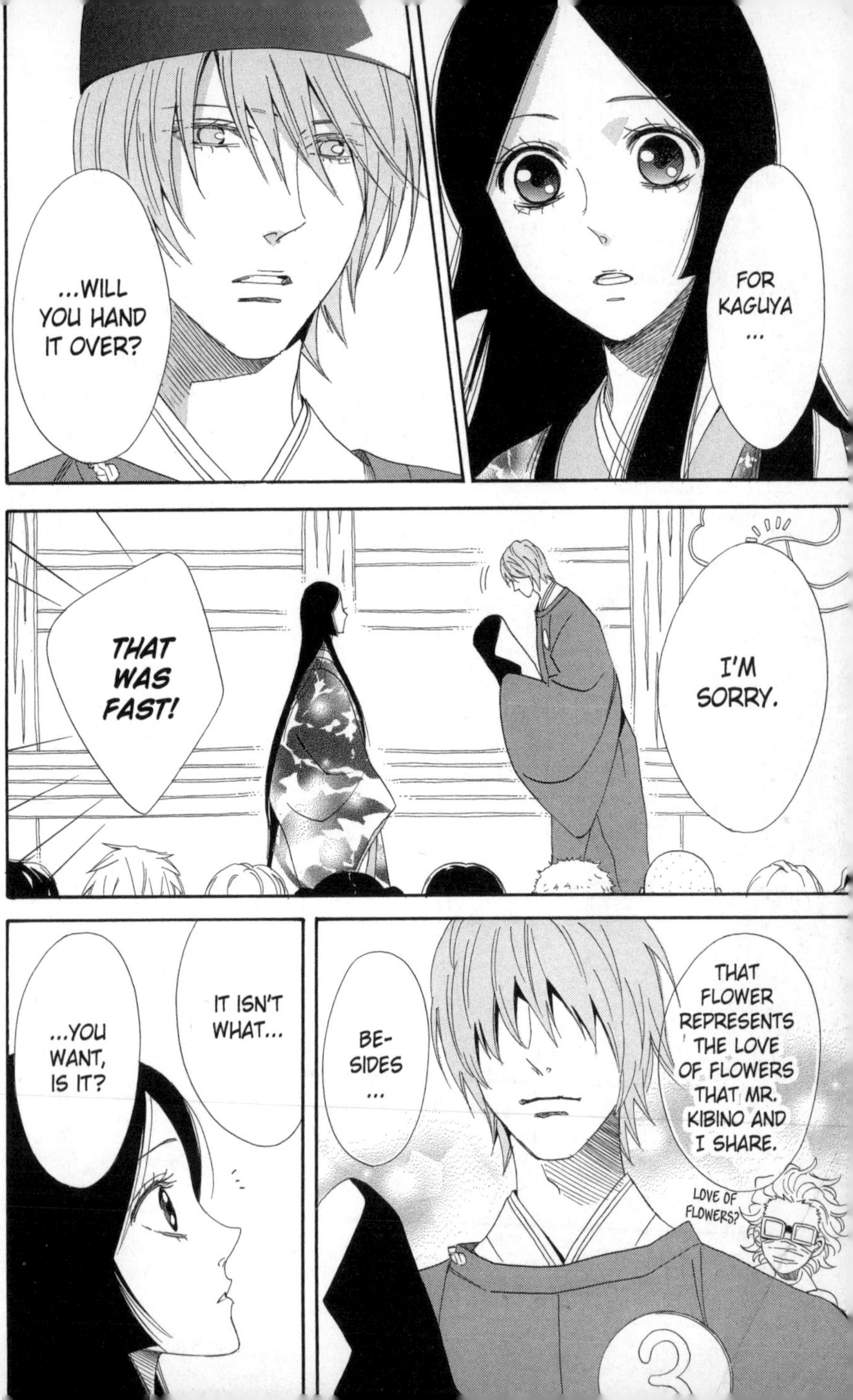
FOR KAGUYA ...
...WILL YOU HAND IT OVER?
I'M SORRY.
THAT WAS FAST!
THAT FLOWER REPRESENTS THE LOVE OF FLOWERS THAT MR. KIBINO AND I SHARE.
BE-SIDES ...
LOVE OF FLOWERS?
IT ISN'T WHAT...
...YOU WANT, IS IT?

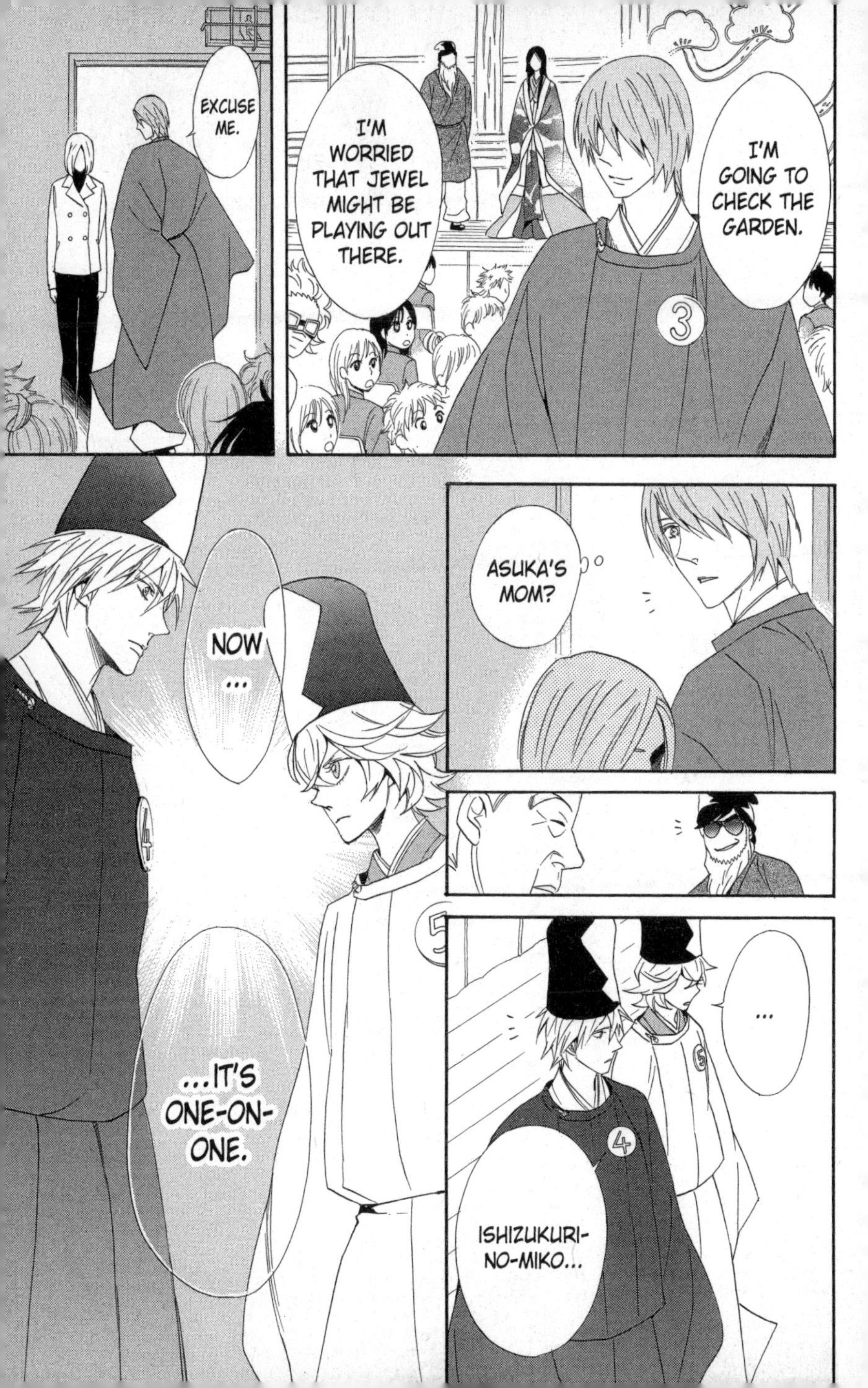
I'M GOING TO CHECK THE GARDEN.
I'M WORRIED THAT JEWEL MIGHT BE PLAYING OUT THERE.
EXCUSE ME.
ASUKA'S MOM?
...
ISHIZUKURI-NO-MIKO...
NOW...
...IT'S ONE-ON-ONE.

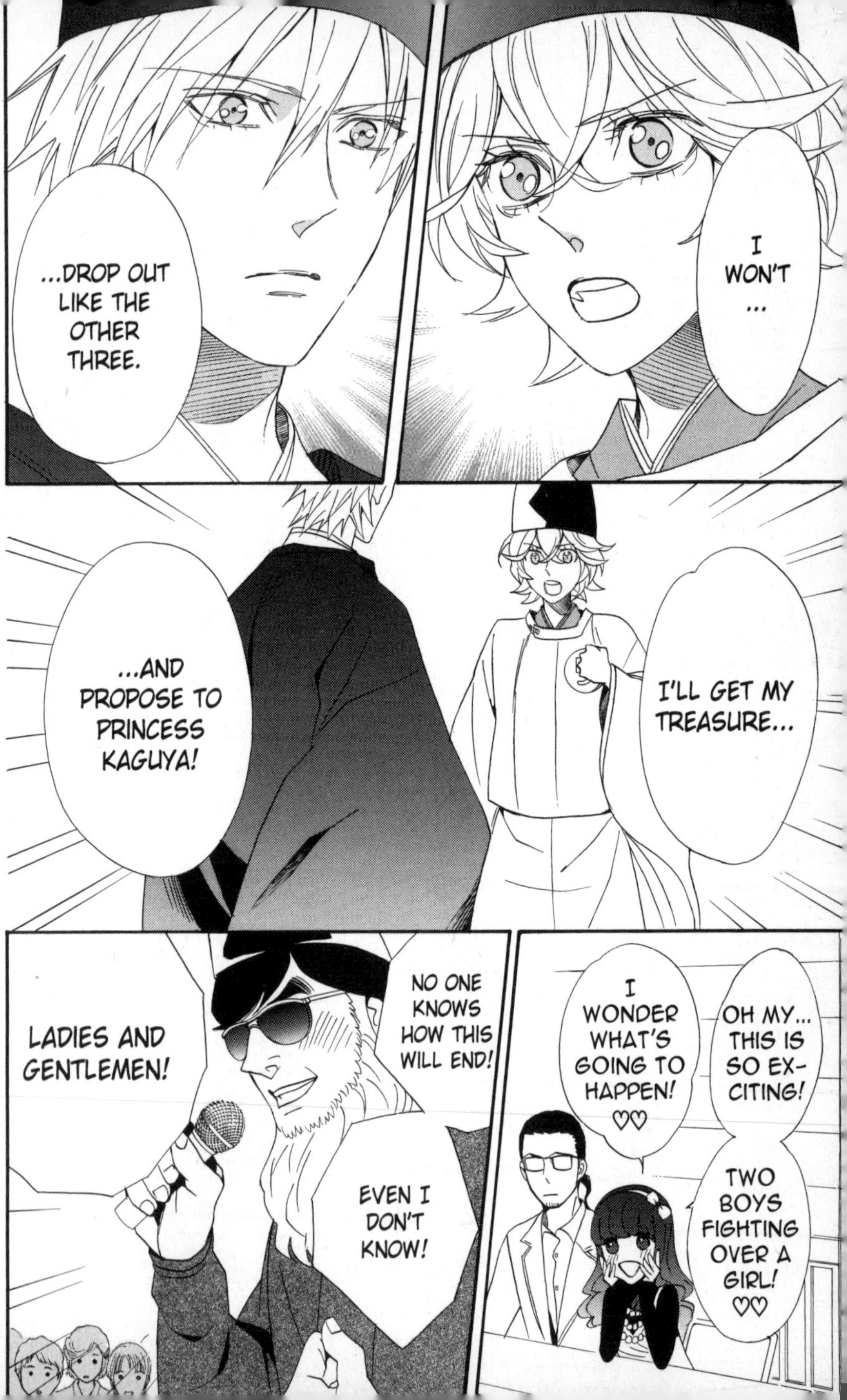
I WON'T ...
...DROP OUT LIKE THE OTHER THREE.
I'LL GET MY TREASURE...
...AND PROPOSE TO PRINCESS KAGUYA!
OH MY... THIS IS SO EX-CITING!
I WONDER WHAT'S GOING TO HAPPEN! ♡♡
TWO BOYS FIGHTING OVER A GIRL! ♡♡
LADIES AND GENTLEMEN!
NO ONE KNOWS HOW THIS WILL END!
EVEN I DON'T KNOW!

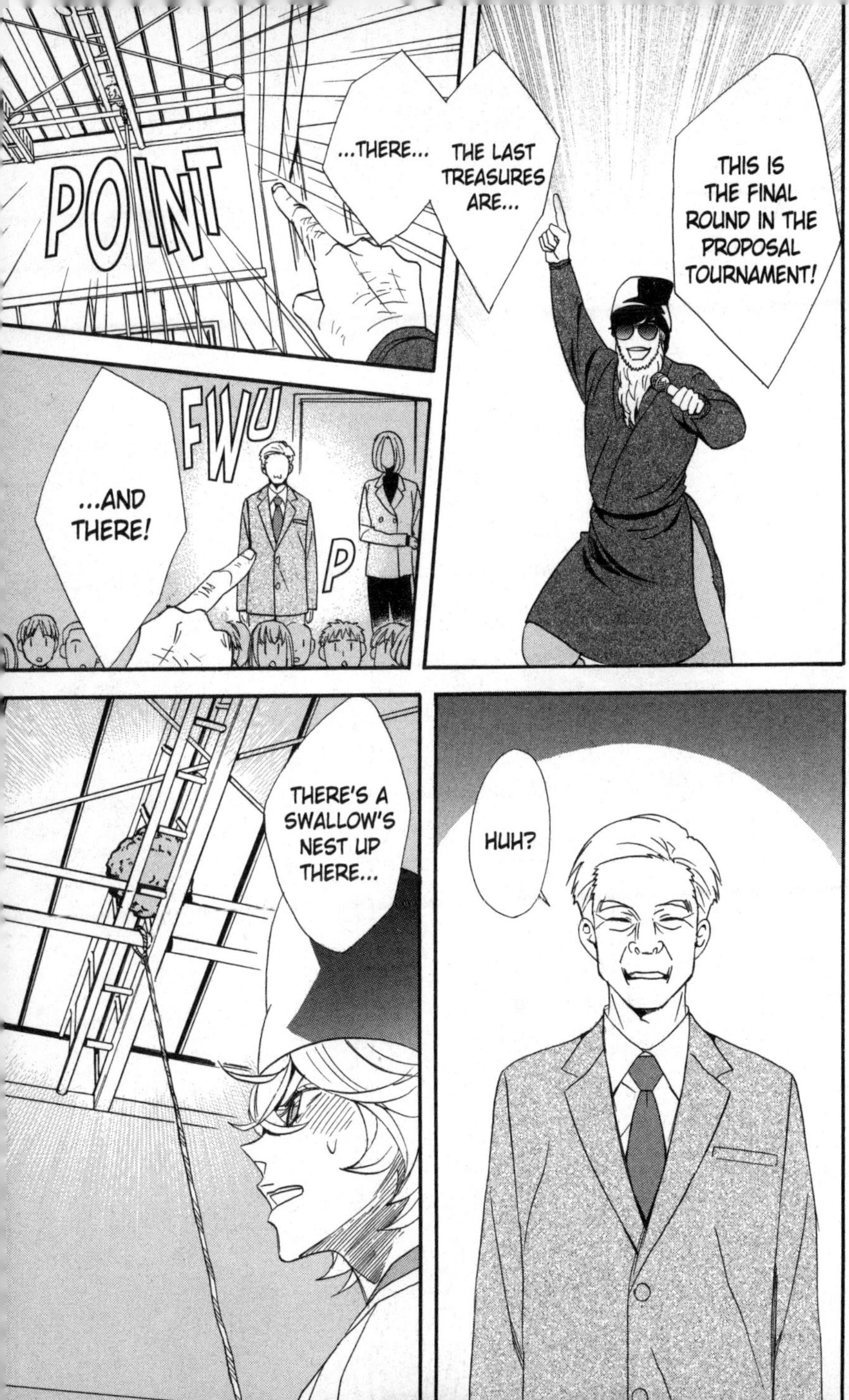
THIS IS THE FINAL ROUND IN THE PROPOSAL TOURNAMENT!
THE LAST TREASURES ARE...
...THERE...
POINT
FWU
P
...AND THERE!
HUH?
THERE'S A SWALLOW'S NEST UP THERE...

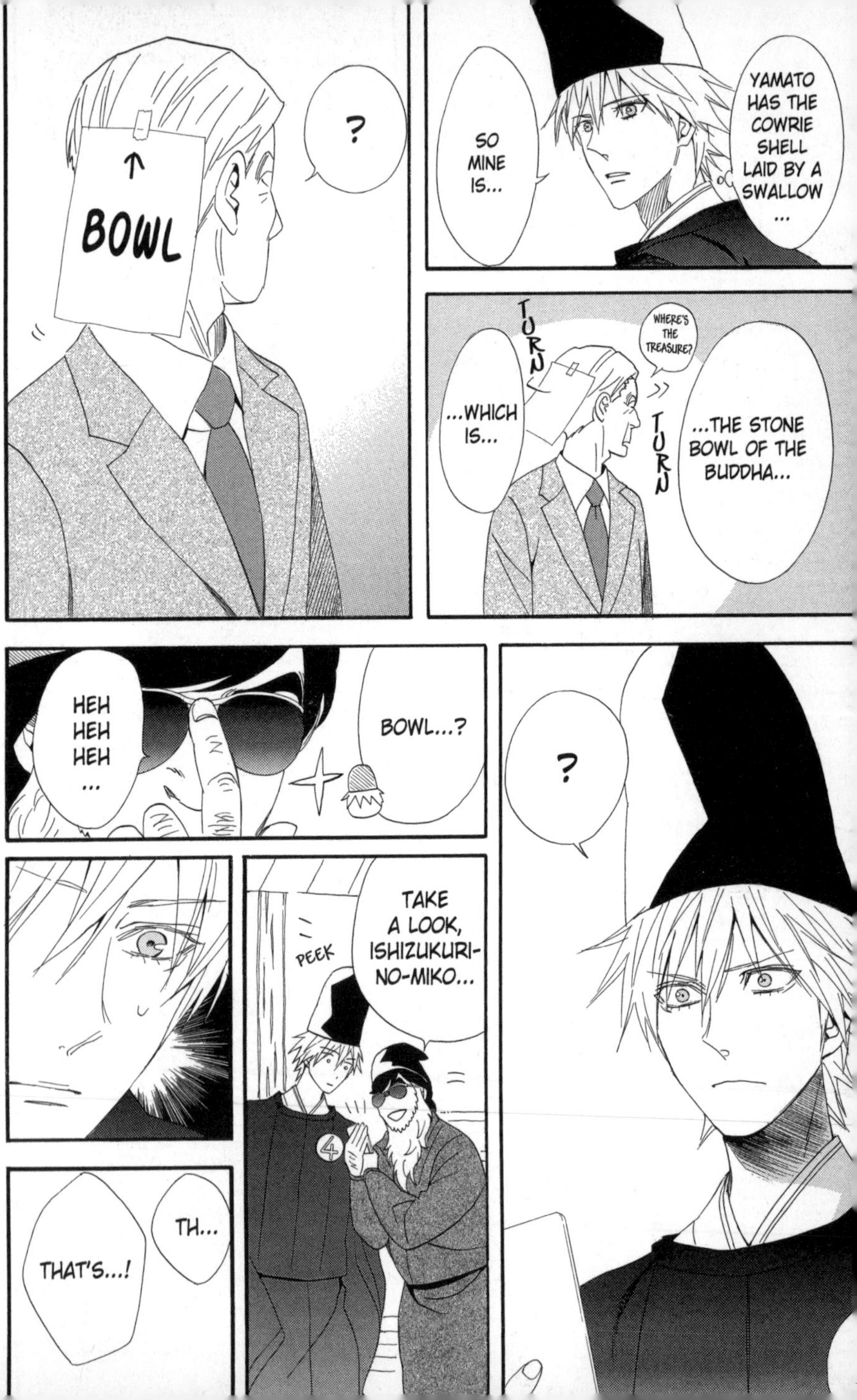
YAMATO HAS THE COWRIE SHELL LAID BY A SWALLOW...
SO MINE IS...
...THE STONE BOWL OF THE BUDDHA...
TURN
WHERE'S THE TREASURE?
...WHICH IS...
TURN
↑
BOWL
?
?
BOWL...?
HEH HEH HEH...
TAKE A LOOK, ISHIZUKURI-NO-MIKO...
PEEK
TH...
THAT'S...!

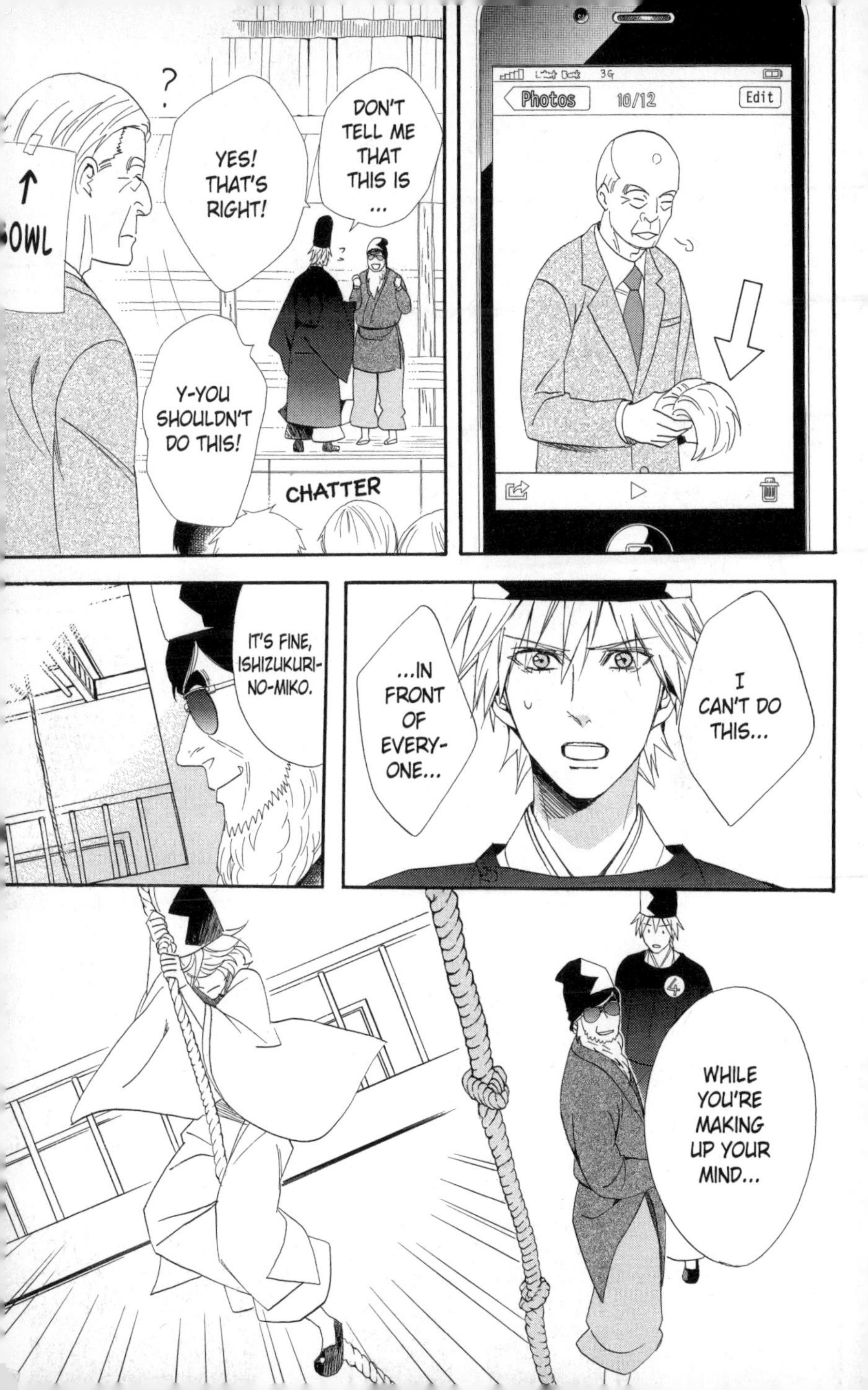
3G
Photos
10/12
Edit
DON'T TELL ME THAT THIS IS ...
?
YES! THAT'S RIGHT!
Y-YOU SHOULDN'T DO THIS!
CHATTER
OWL
I CAN'T DO THIS...
...IN FRONT OF EVERYONE...
IT'S FINE, ISHIZUKURI-NO-MIKO.
WHILE YOU'RE MAKING UP YOUR MIND...

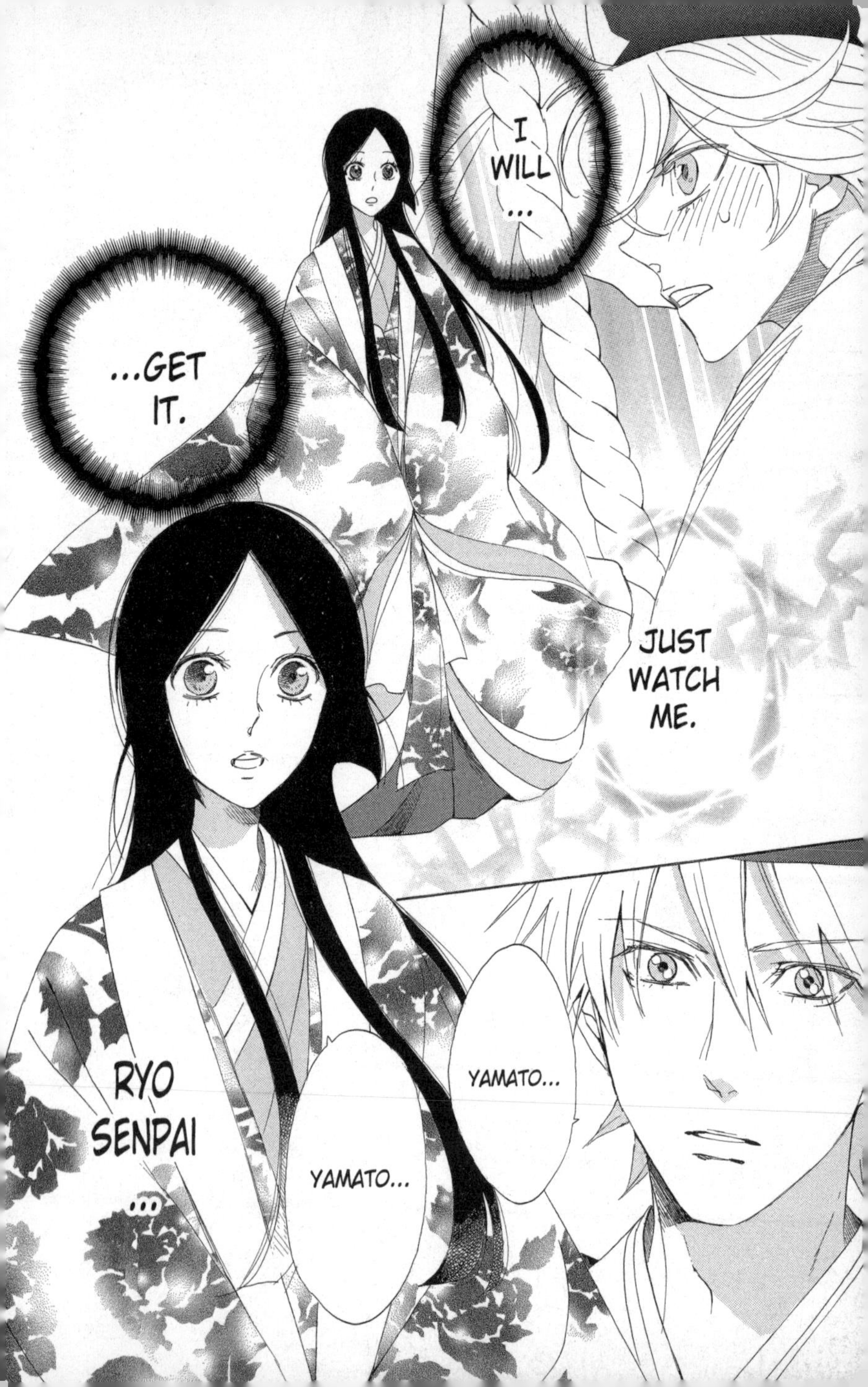
I WILL...
...GET IT.
JUST WATCH ME.
YAMATO...
YAMATO...
RYO SENPAI...

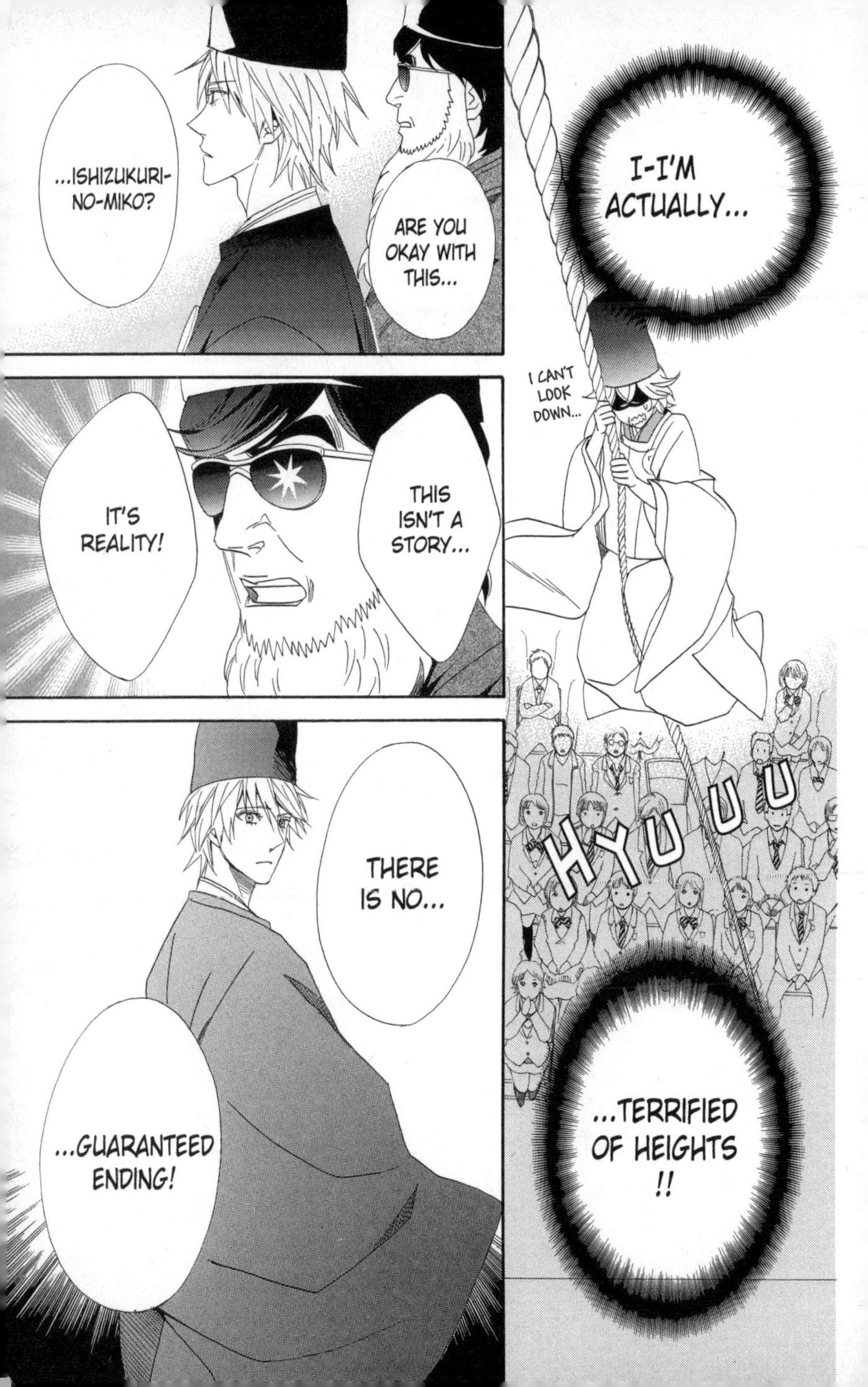
I-I'M ACTUALLY...
I CAN'T LOOK DOWN...
HYUUU
...TERRIFIED OF HEIGHTS !!
ARE YOU OKAY WITH THIS...
...ISHIZUKURI-NO-MIKO?
THIS ISN'T A STORY...
IT'S REALITY!
THERE IS NO...
...GUARANTEED ENDING!

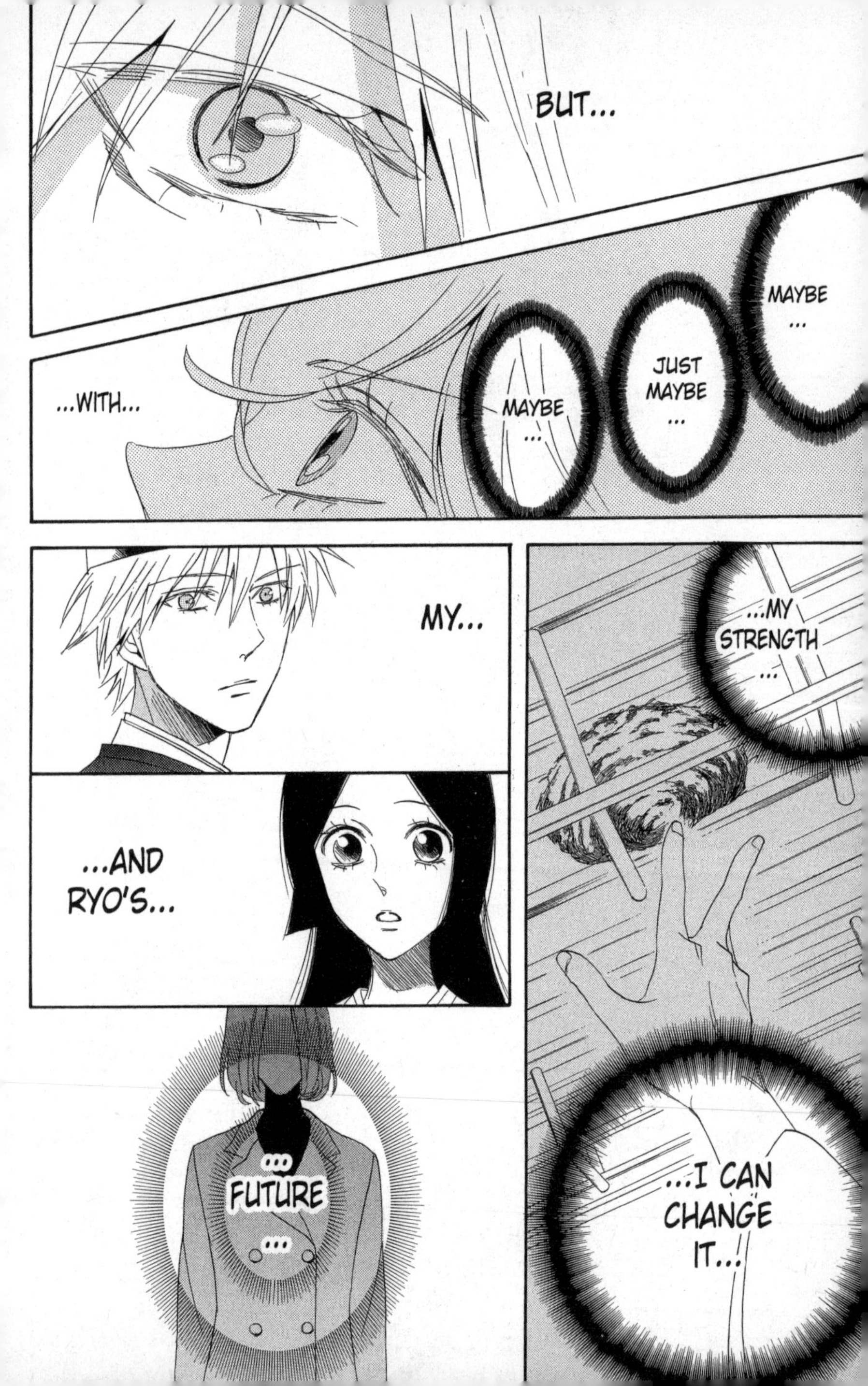
BUT...
MAYBE ...
JUST MAYBE ...
MAYBE ...
...WITH...
...MY STRENGTH ...
...I CAN CHANGE IT...
MY...
...AND RYO'S...
... FUTURE ...

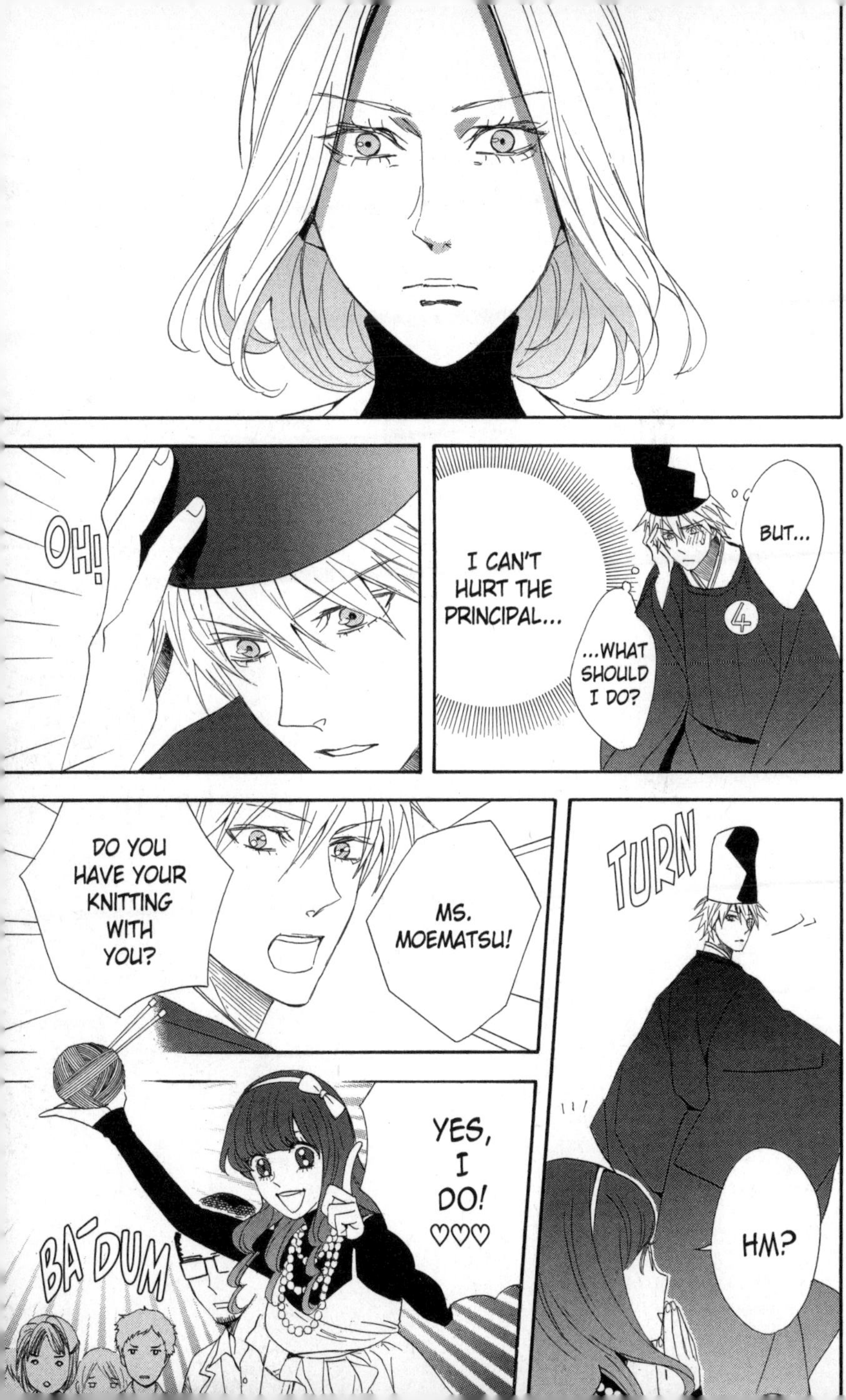
I CAN'T HURT THE PRINCIPAL...
BUT...
...WHAT SHOULD I DO?
OH!
TURN
HM?
MS. MOEMATSU!
DO YOU HAVE YOUR KNITTING WITH YOU?
YES, I DO! ♡♡♡
BA-DUM

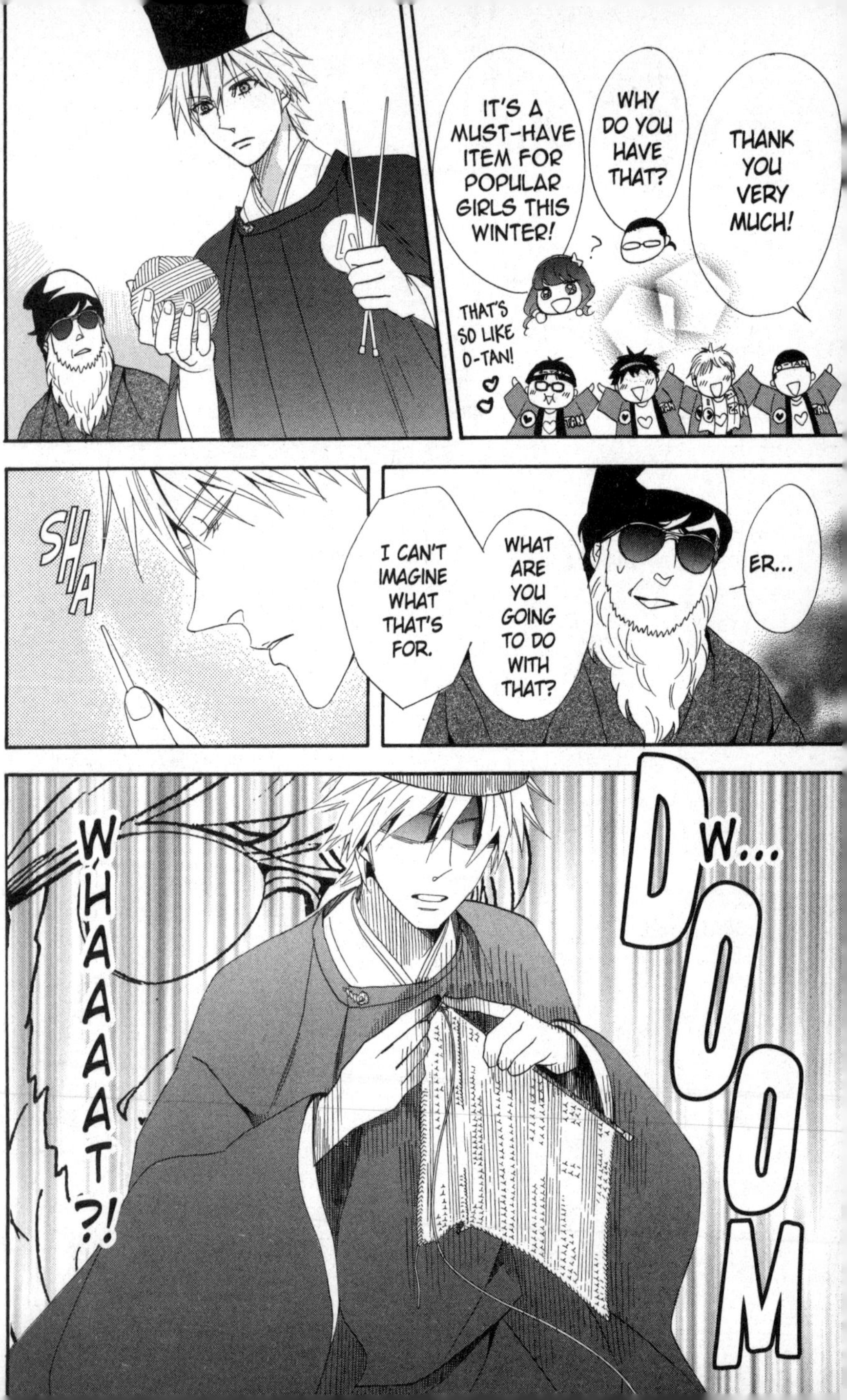
THANK YOU VERY MUCH!
WHY DO YOU HAVE THAT?
IT'S A MUST-HAVE ITEM FOR POPULAR GIRLS THIS WINTER!
THAT'S SO LIKE O-TAN!
ER...
WHAT ARE YOU GOING TO DO WITH THAT?
I CAN'T IMAGINE WHAT THAT'S FOR.
SHA
DW... DOOOM
WHAAAAAT?!

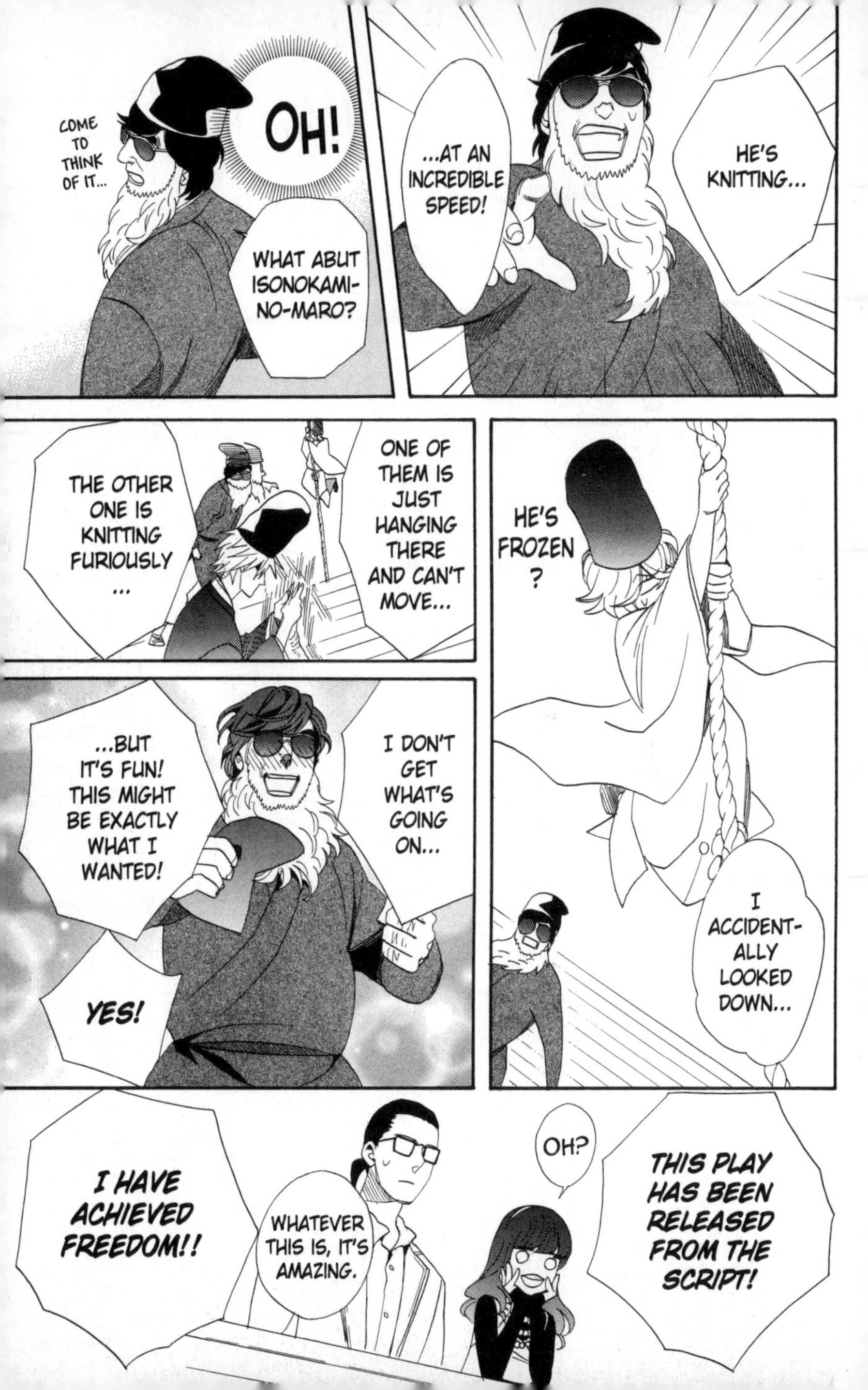
HE'S KNITTING...
...AT AN INCREDIBLE SPEED!
OH!
COME TO THINK OF IT...
WHAT ABUT ISONOKAMI-NO-MARO?
HE'S FROZEN ?
I ACCIDENT-ALLY LOOKED DOWN...
ONE OF THEM IS JUST HANGING THERE AND CAN'T MOVE...
THE OTHER ONE IS KNITTING FURIOUSLY ...
I DON'T GET WHAT'S GOING ON...
...BUT IT'S FUN! THIS MIGHT BE EXACTLY WHAT I WANTED!
YES!
THIS PLAY HAS BEEN RELEASED FROM THE SCRIPT!
OH?
WHATEVER THIS IS, IT'S AMAZING.
I HAVE ACHIEVED FREEDOM!!

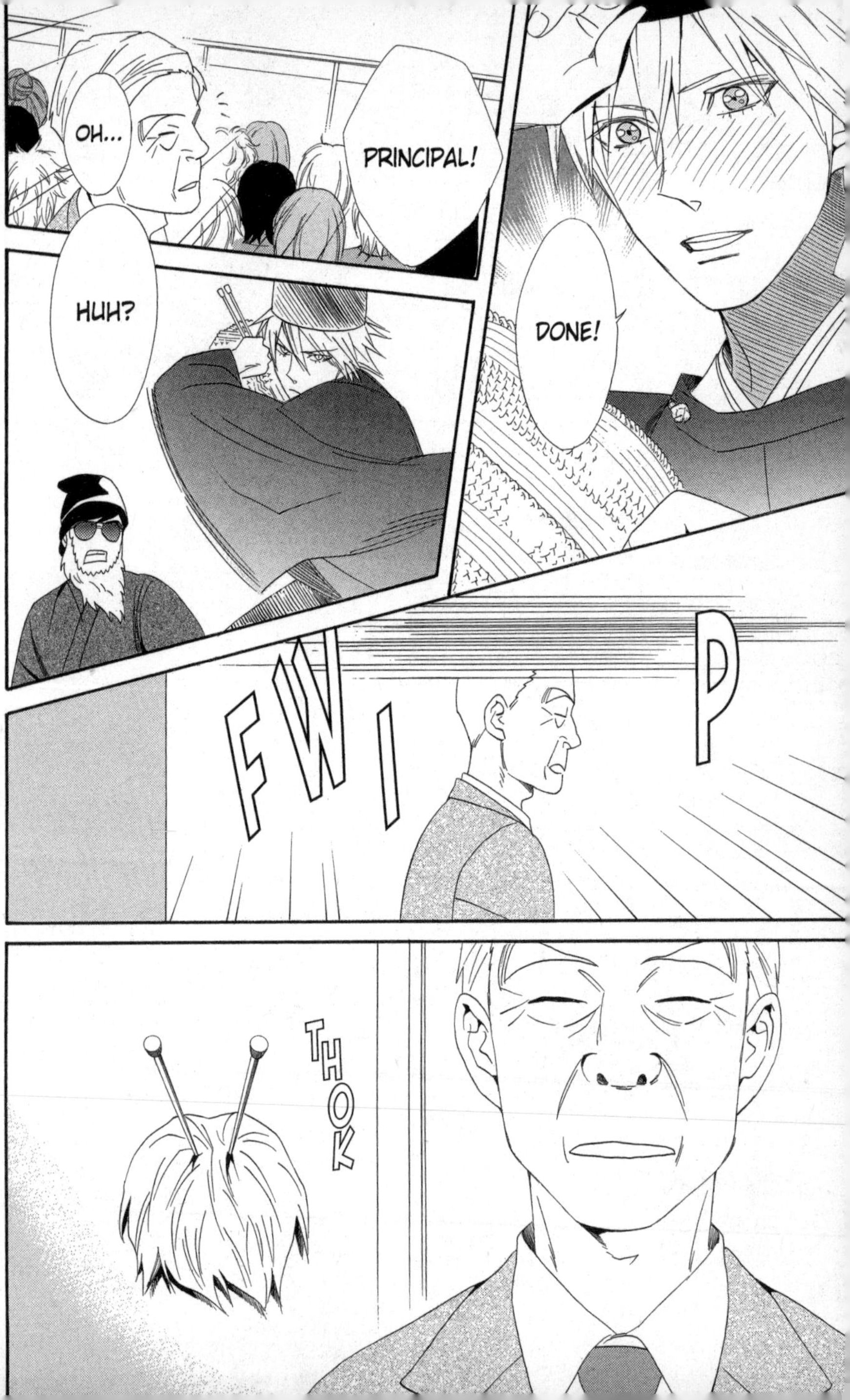
DONE!
PRINCIPAL!
OH...
HUH?
FWIP
THOK

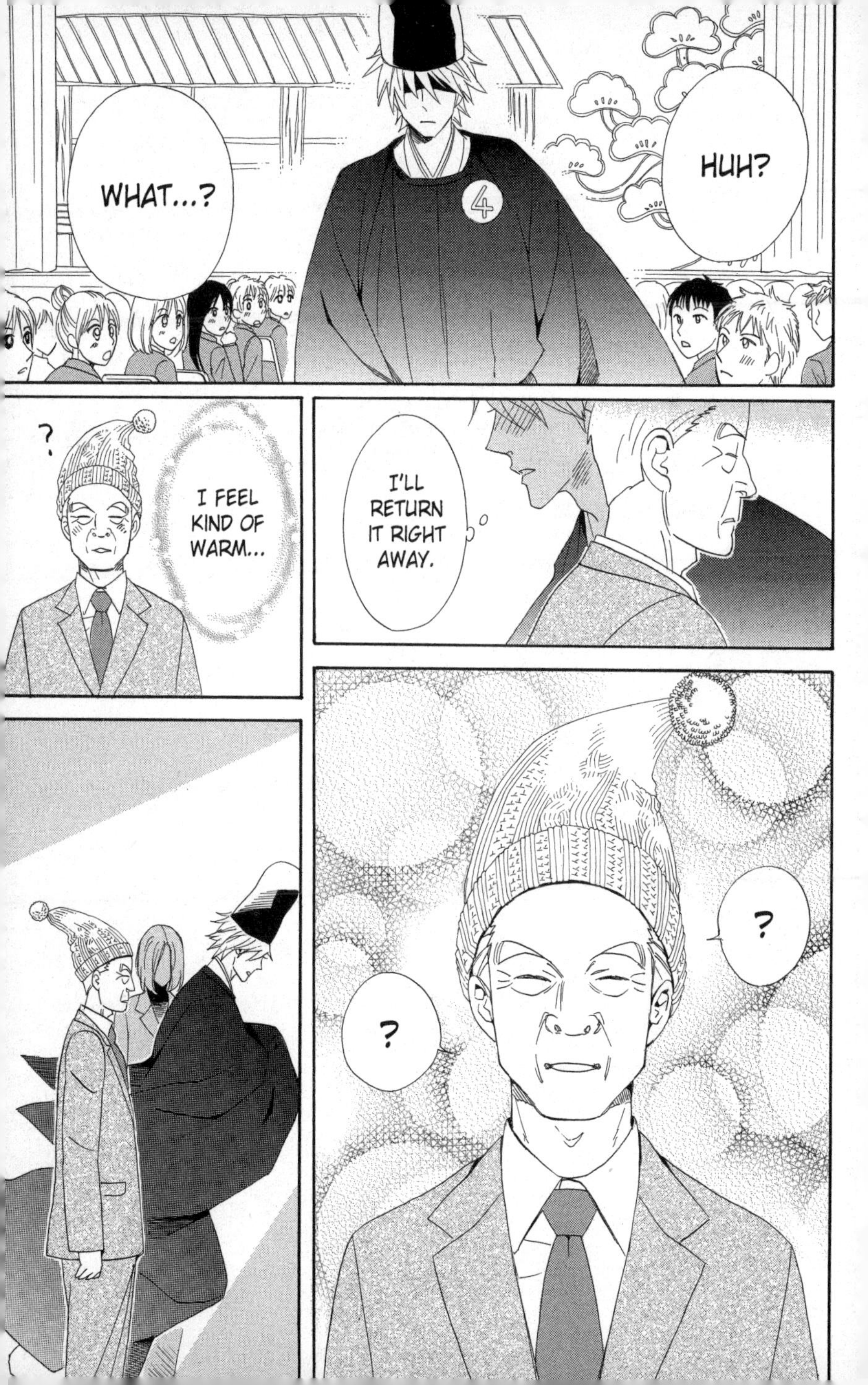
HUH?
WHAT...?
I'LL RETURN IT RIGHT AWAY.
?
I FEEL KIND OF WARM...
?
?

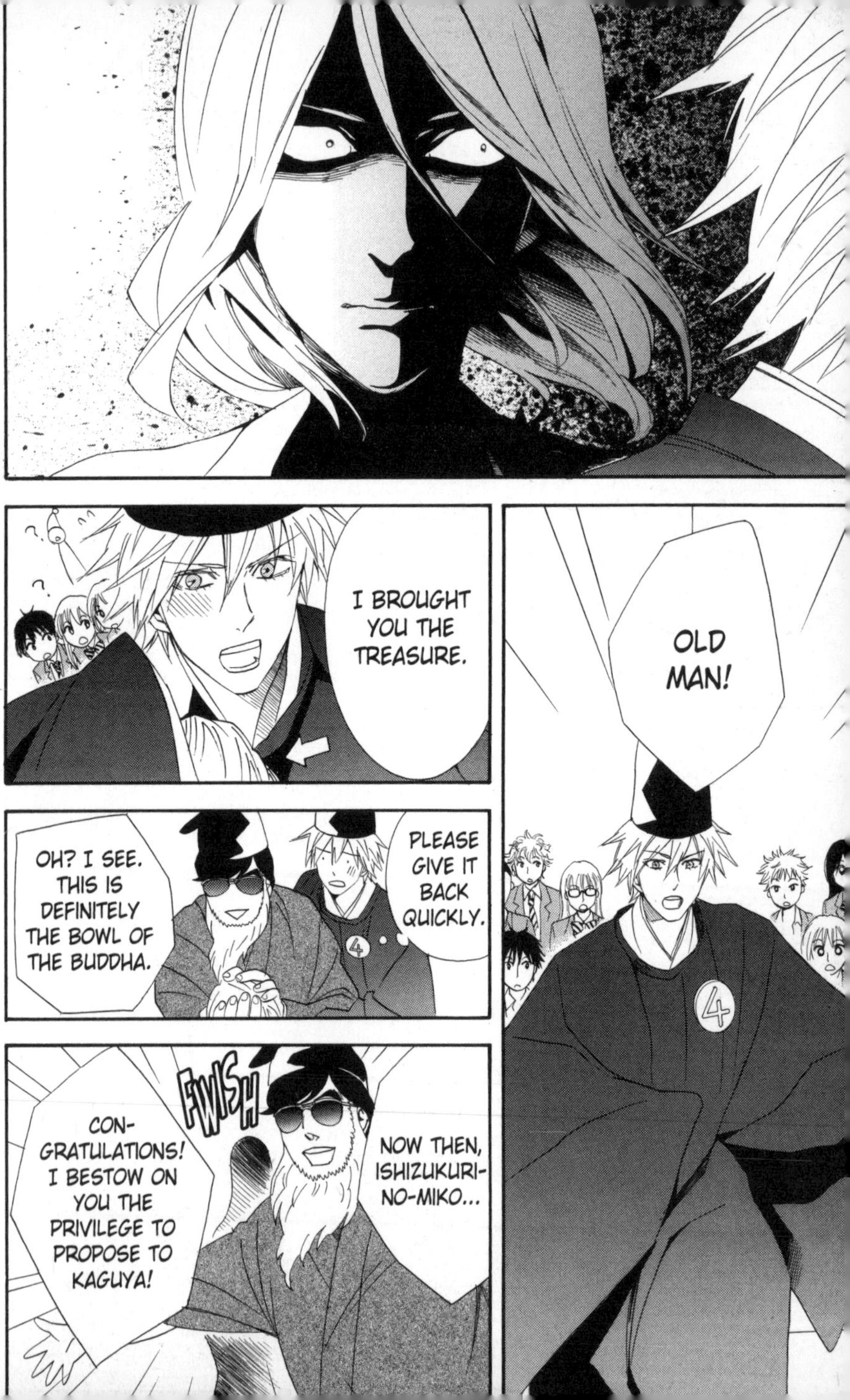
OLD MAN!
I BROUGHT YOU THE TREASURE.
PLEASE GIVE IT BACK QUICKLY.
OH? I SEE. THIS IS DEFINITELY THE BOWL OF THE BUDDHA.
NOW THEN, ISHIZUKURI-NO-MIKO...
FWISH
CON-GRATULATIONS! I BESTOW ON YOU THE PRIVILEGE TO PROPOSE TO KAGUYA!

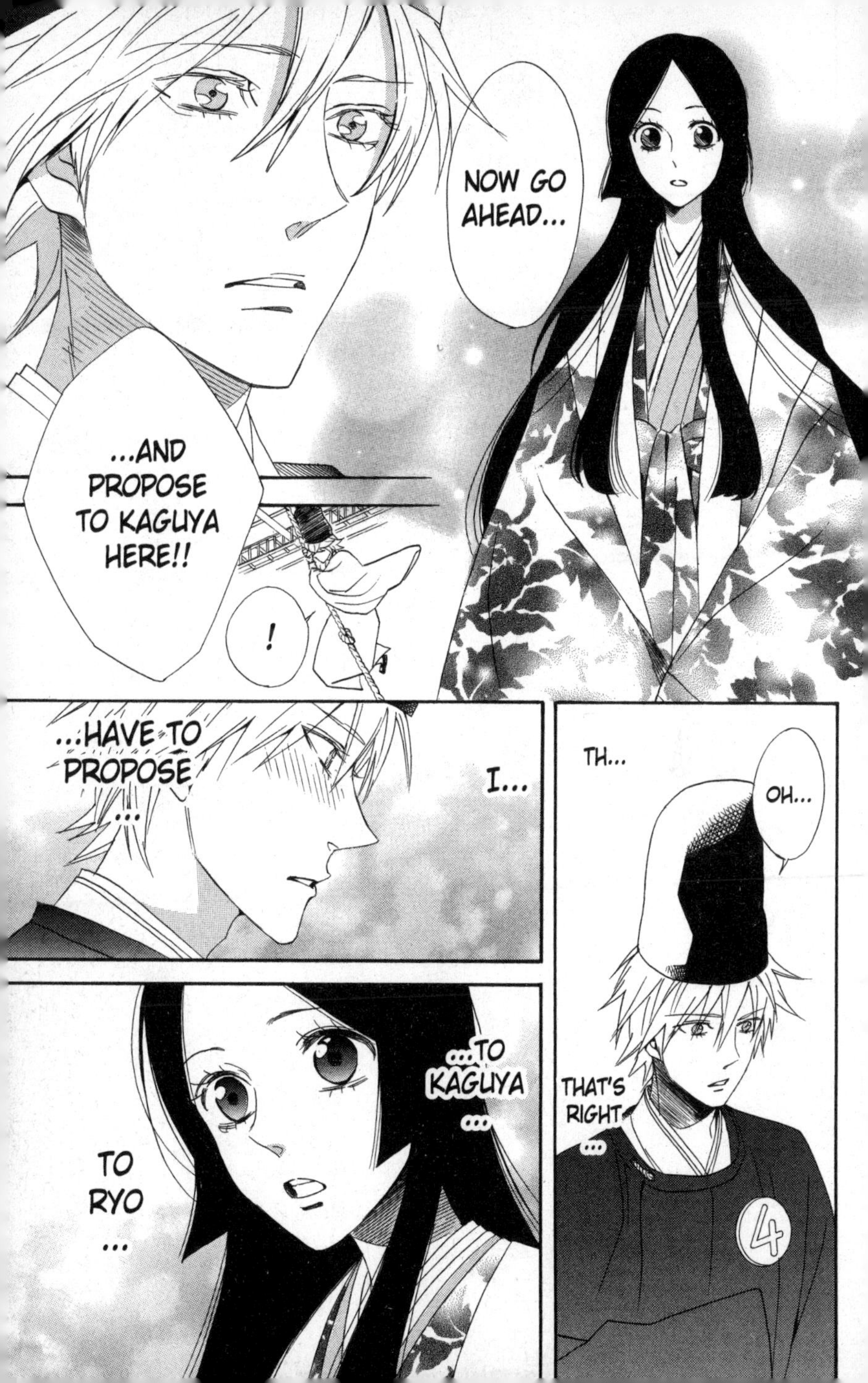
NOW GO AHEAD...
...AND PROPOSE TO KAGUYA HERE!!
!
TH...
OH...
THAT'S RIGHT...
I...
...HAVE TO PROPOSE...
...TO KAGUYA...
TO RYO...

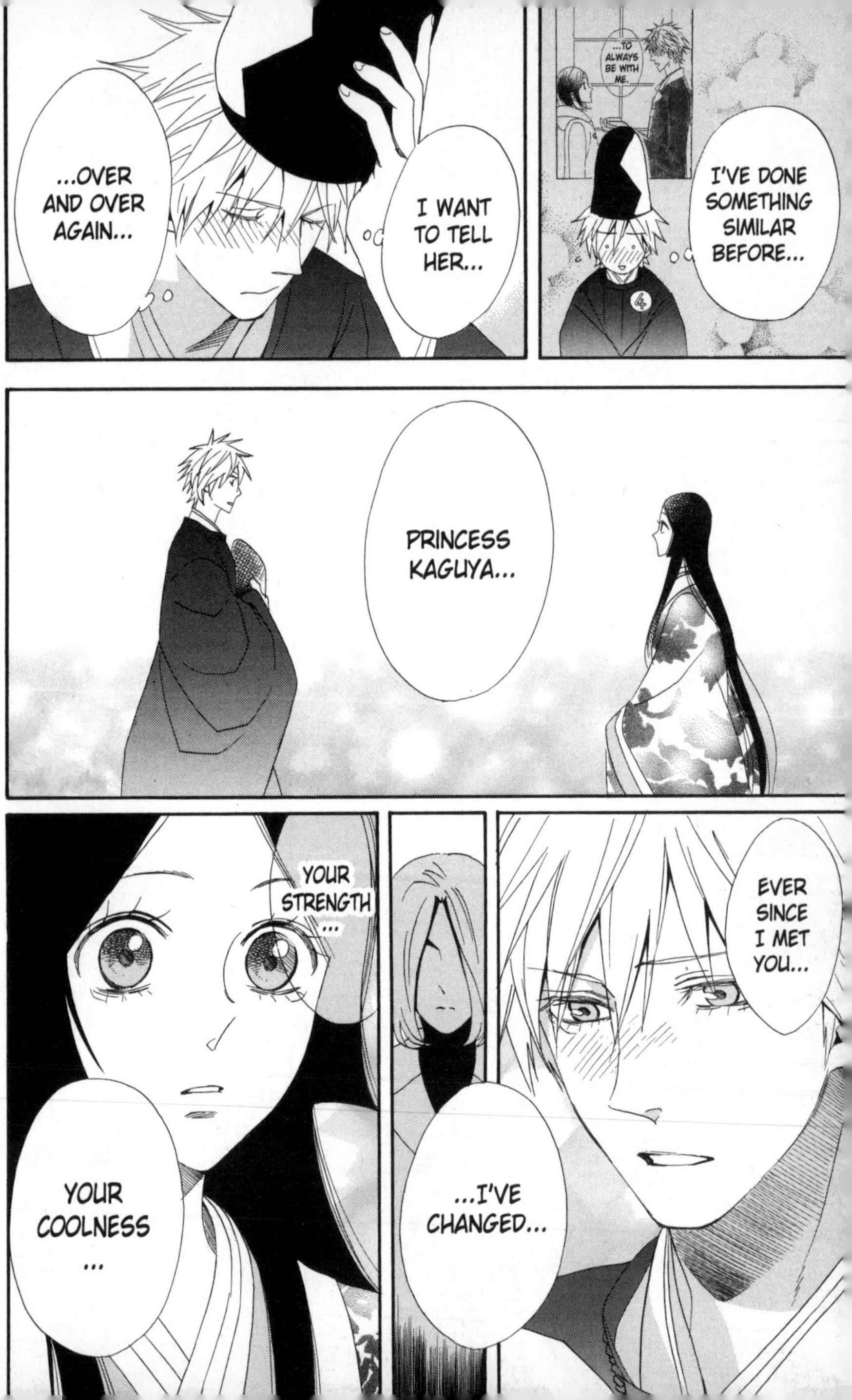

...TO ALWAYS BE WITH ME.
I'VE DONE SOMETHING SIMILAR BEFORE...
I WANT TO TELL HER...
...OVER AND OVER AGAIN...
PRINCESS KAGUYA...
EVER SINCE I MET YOU...
...I'VE CHANGED...
YOUR STRENGTH...
YOUR COOLNESS...

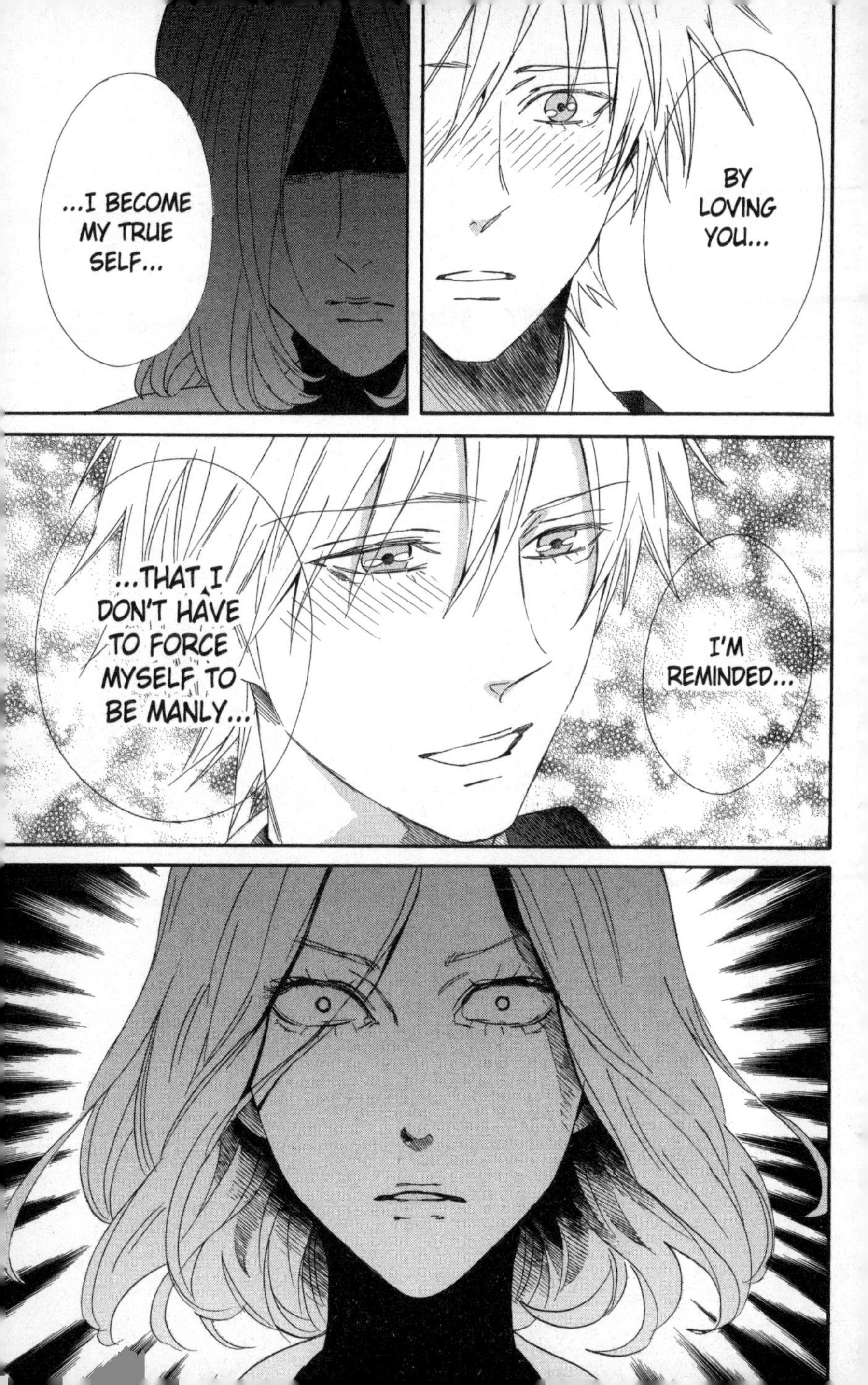
BY LOVING YOU...
...I BECOME MY TRUE SELF...
I'M REMINDED...
...THAT I DON'T HAVE TO FORCE MYSELF TO BE MANLY...

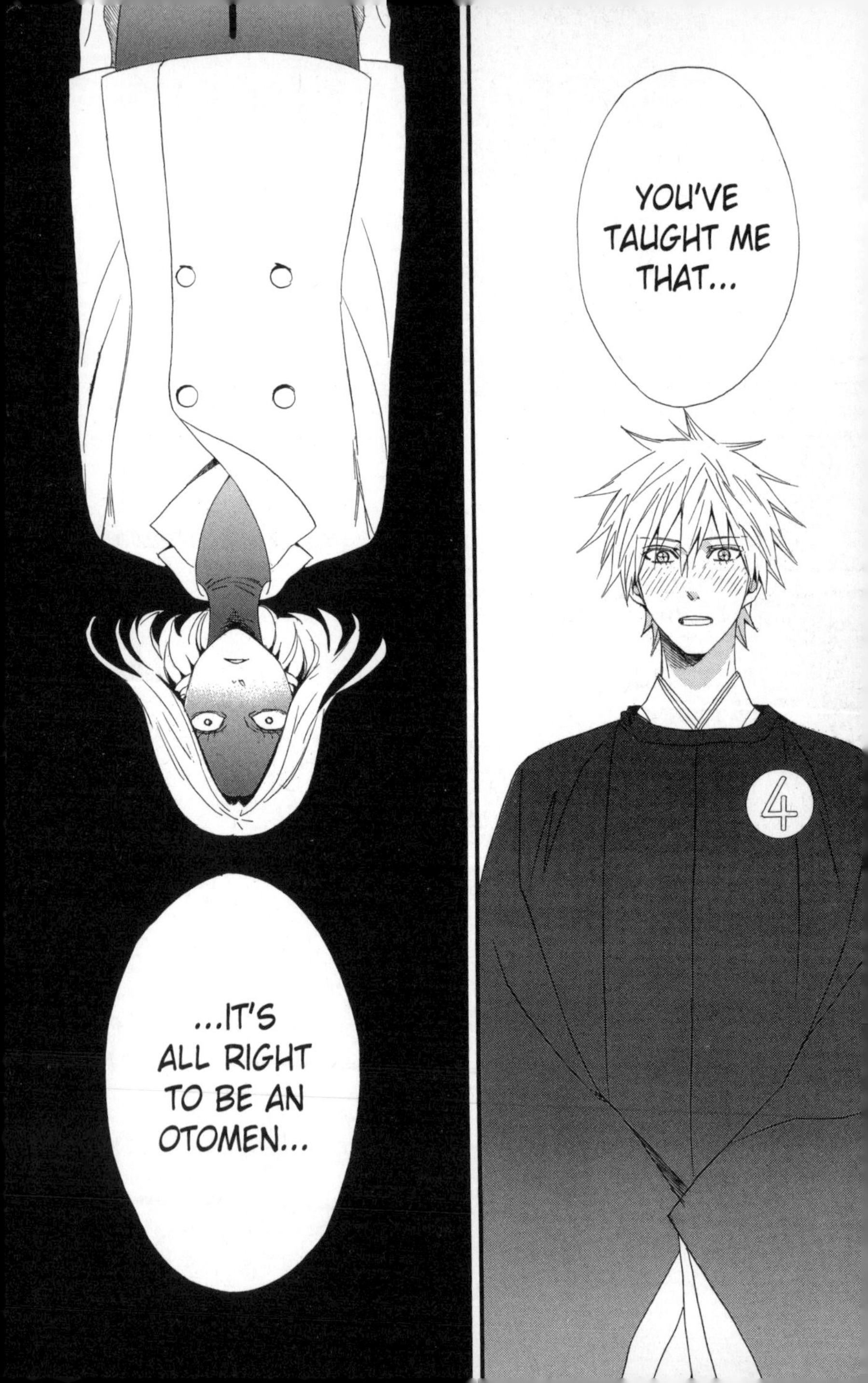
YOU'VE TAUGHT ME THAT...
...IT'S ALL RIGHT TO BE AN OTOMEN...

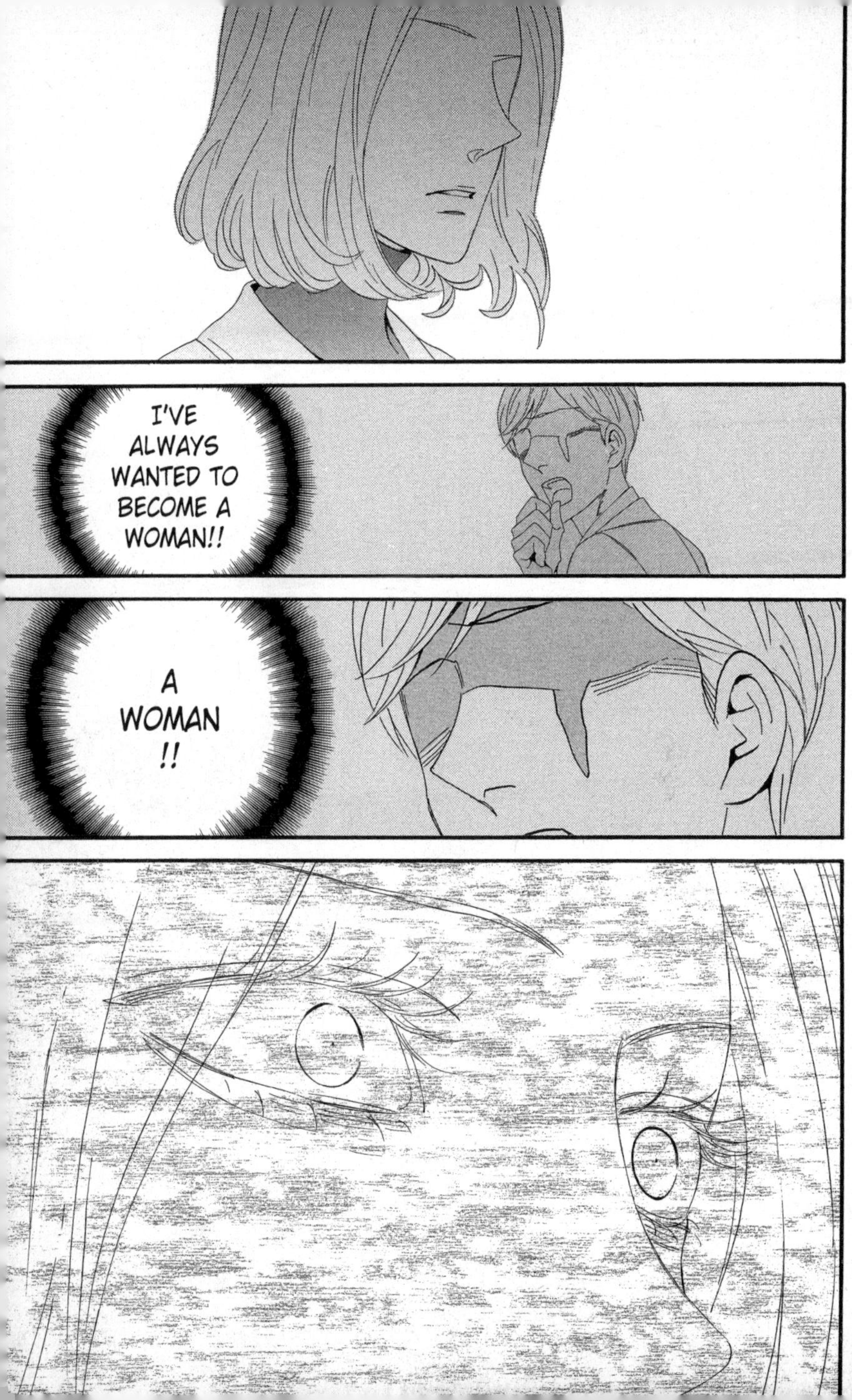
I'VE ALWAYS WANTED TO BECOME A WOMAN!!
A WOMAN !!

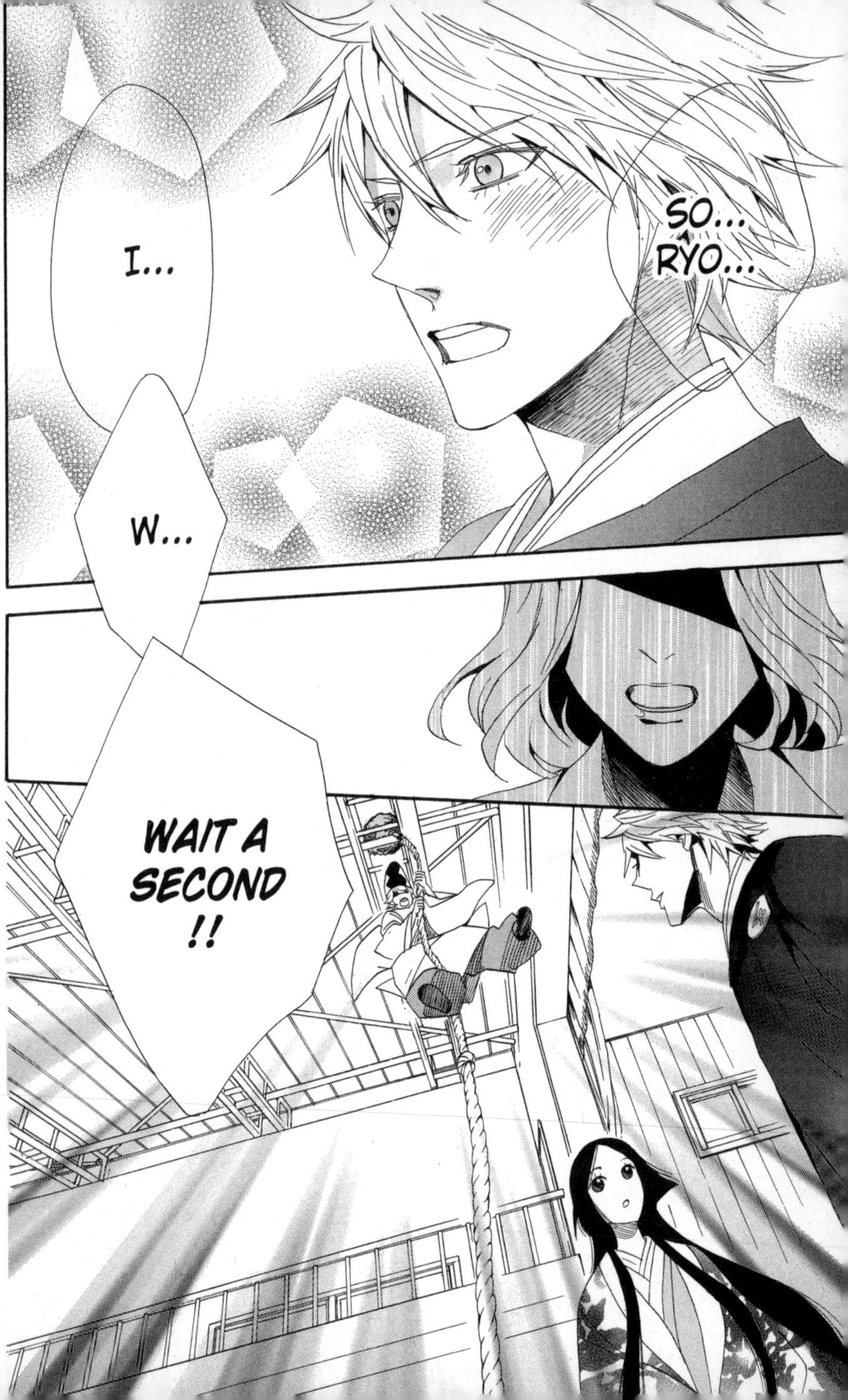
SO... RYO...
I...
W...
WAIT A SECOND !!

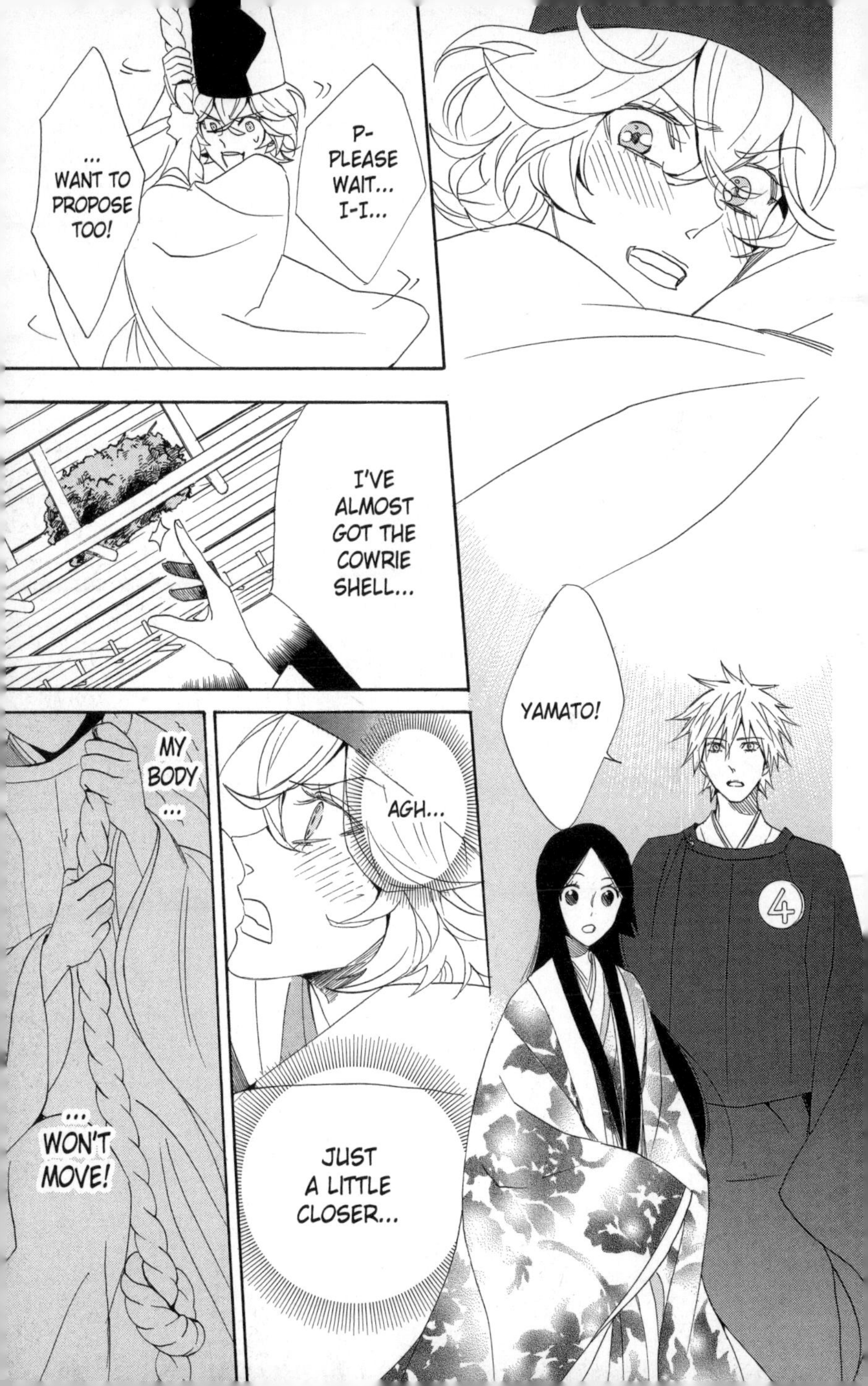
P- PLEASE WAIT... I-I...
... WANT TO PROPOSE TOO!
YAMATO!
I'VE ALMOST GOT THE COWRIE SHELL...
AGH...
JUST A LITTLE CLOSER...
MY BODY ...
... WON'T MOVE!

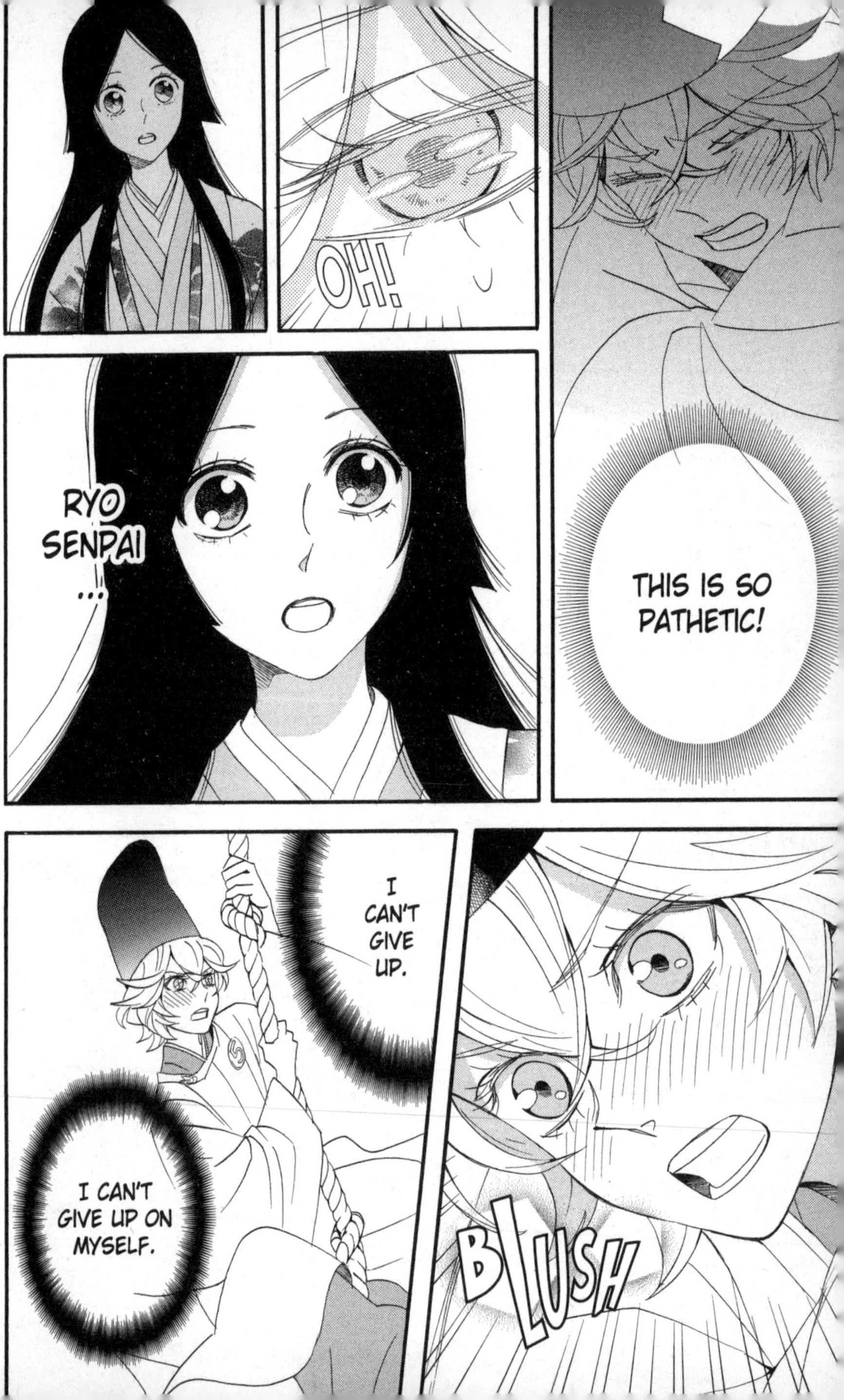
THIS IS SO PATHETIC!
OH!
RYO SENPAI ...
BLUSH
I CAN'T GIVE UP.
I CAN'T GIVE UP ON MYSELF.

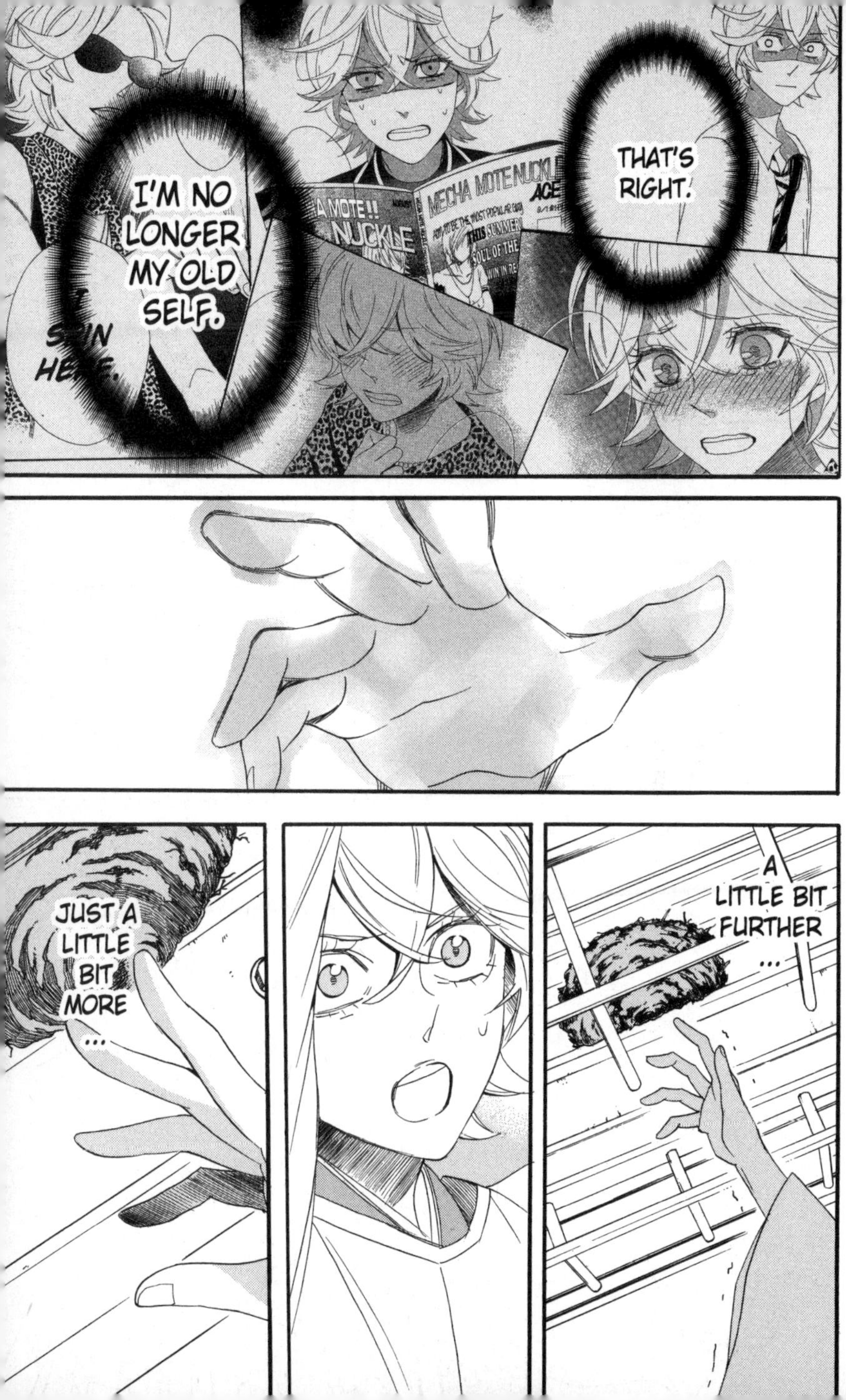
THAT'S RIGHT.
I'M NO LONGER MY OLD SELF.
MECHA MOTE NUCKLE ACE
A LITTLE BIT FURTHER ...
JUST A LITTLE BIT MORE ...

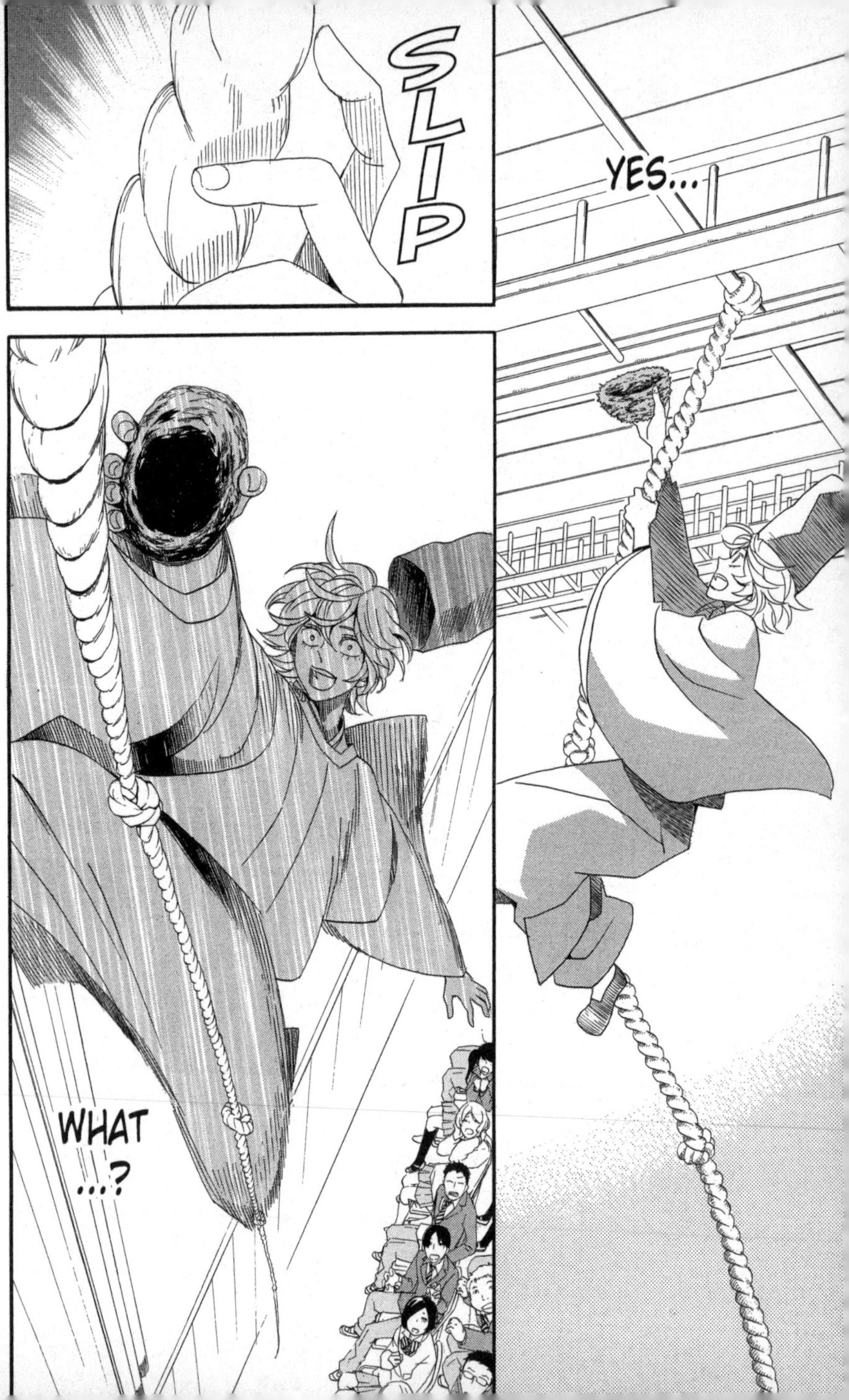
YES...
SLIP
WHAT ...?

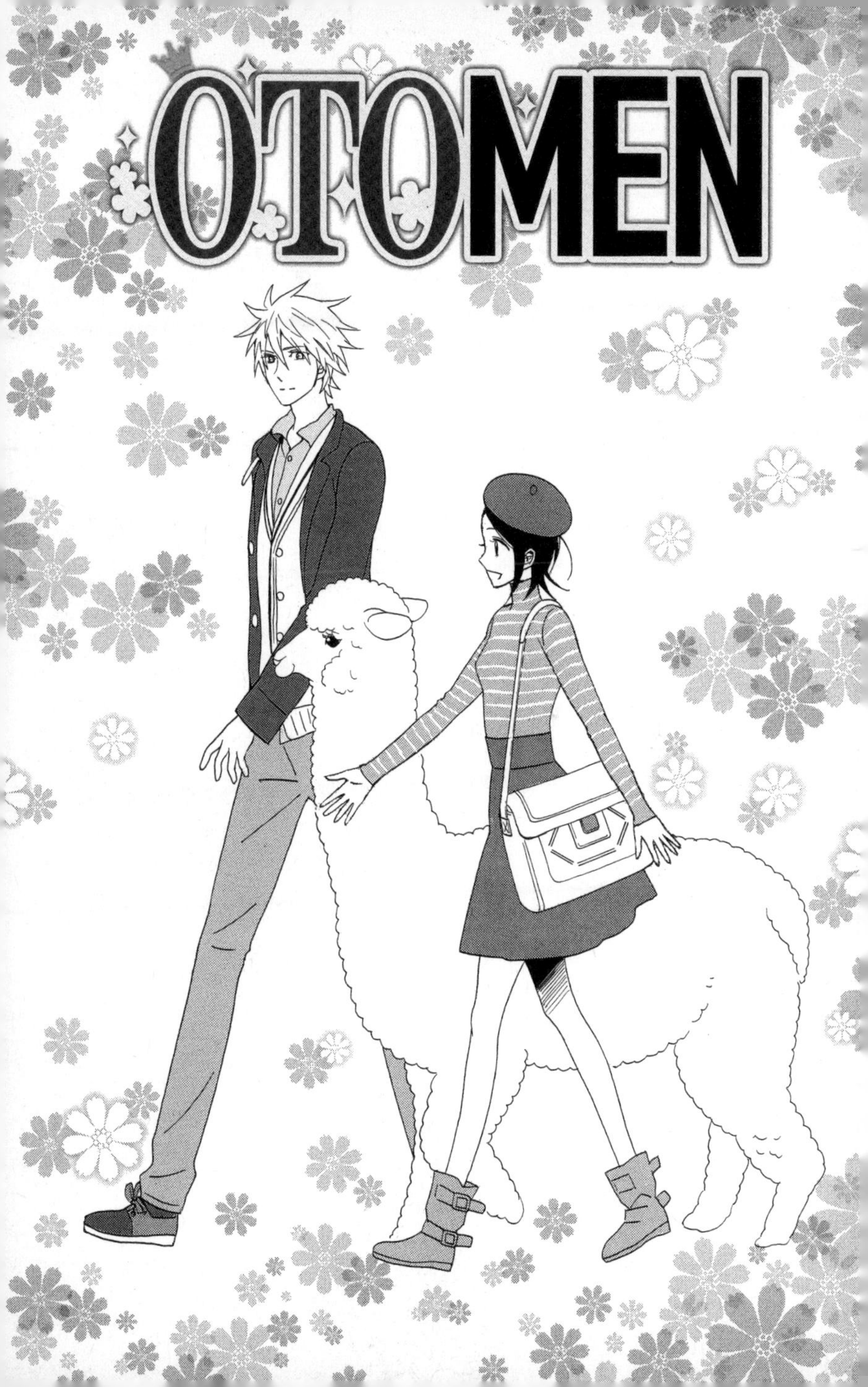
OTOMEN

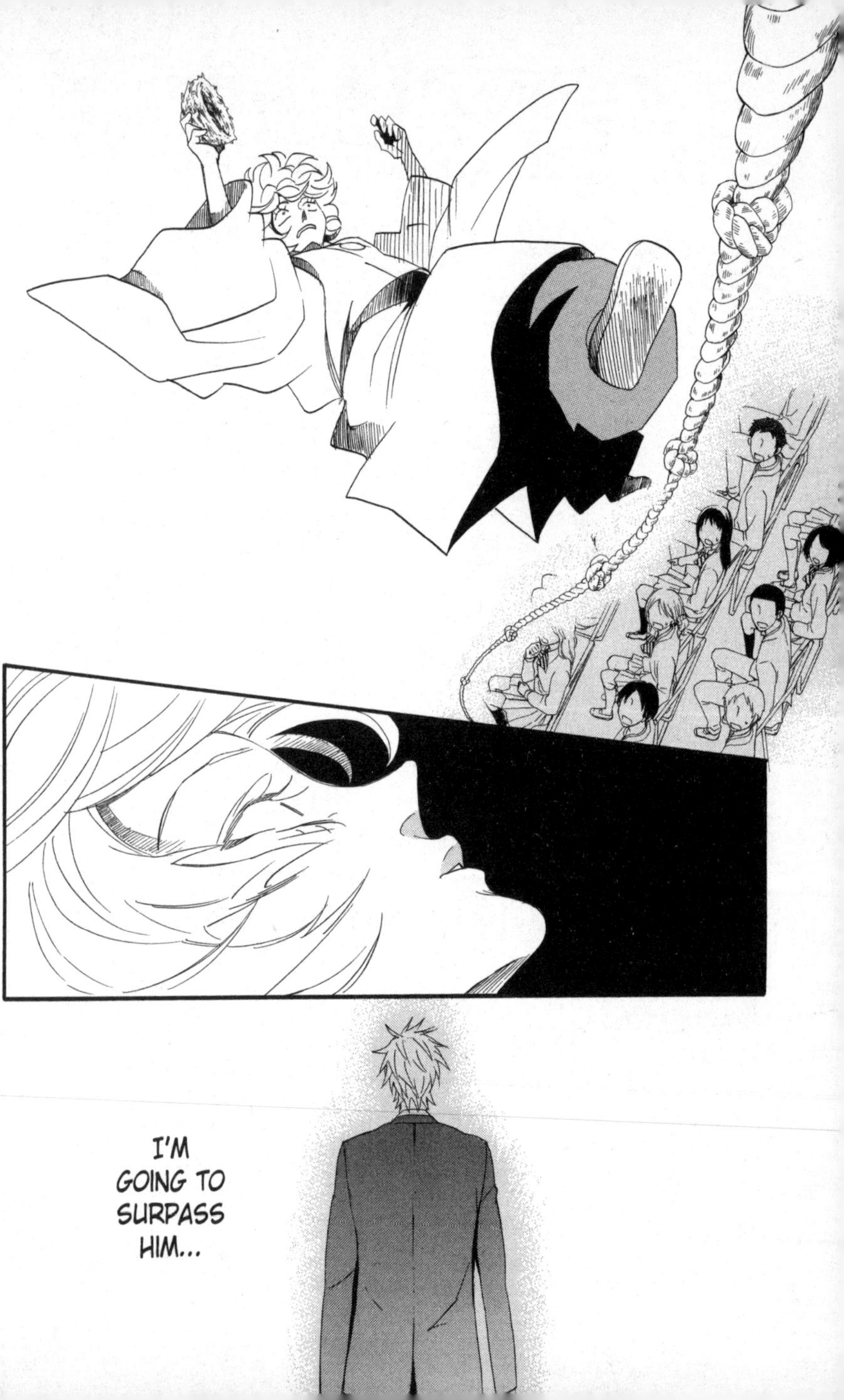
I'M GOING TO SURPASS HIM...

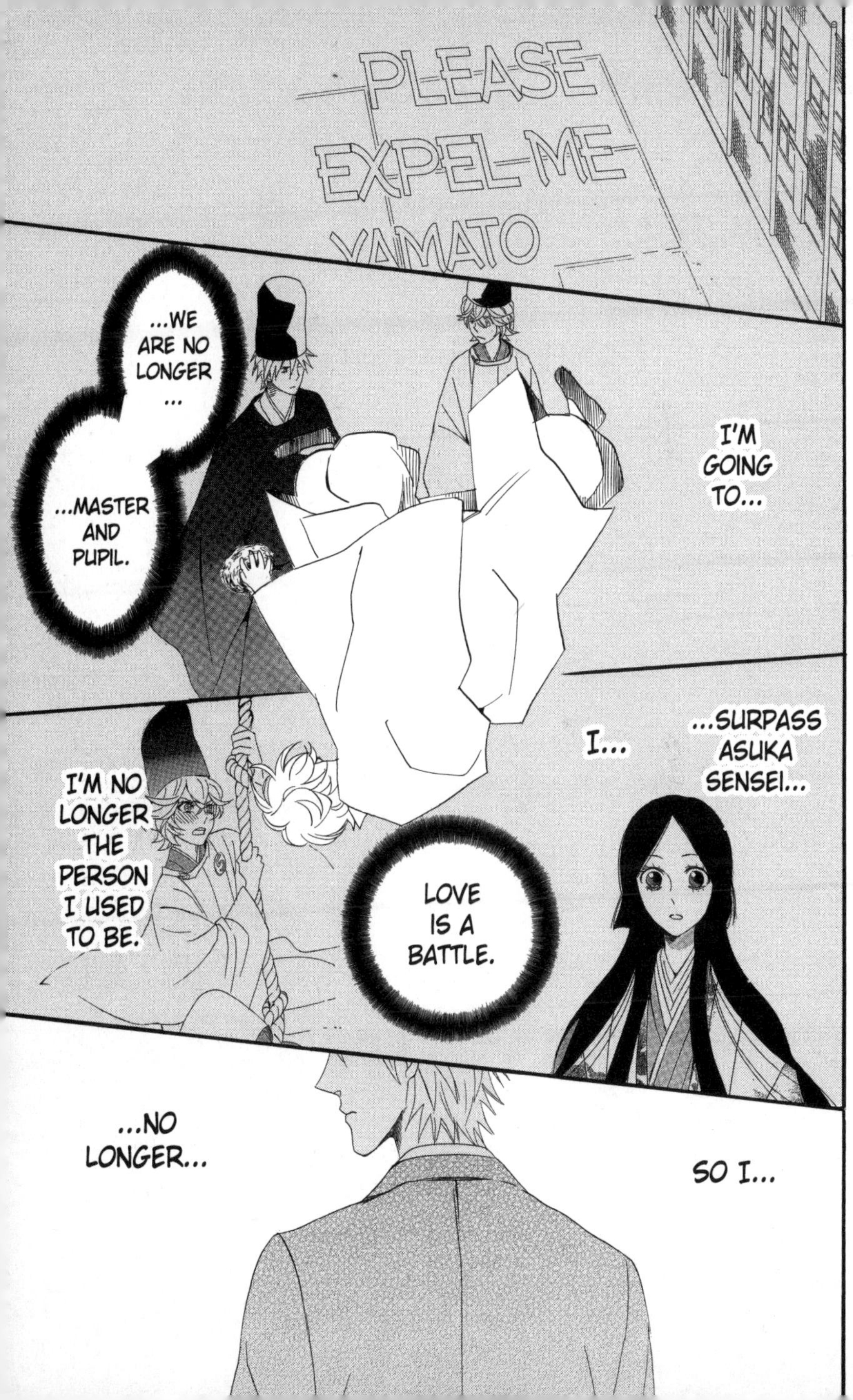
PLEASE EXPEL ME
YAMATO
I'M GOING TO...
...WE ARE NO LONGER...
...MASTER AND PUPIL.
...SURPASS ASUKA SENSEI...
I...
LOVE IS A BATTLE.
I'M NO LONGER THE PERSON I USED TO BE.
SO I...
...NO LONGER...

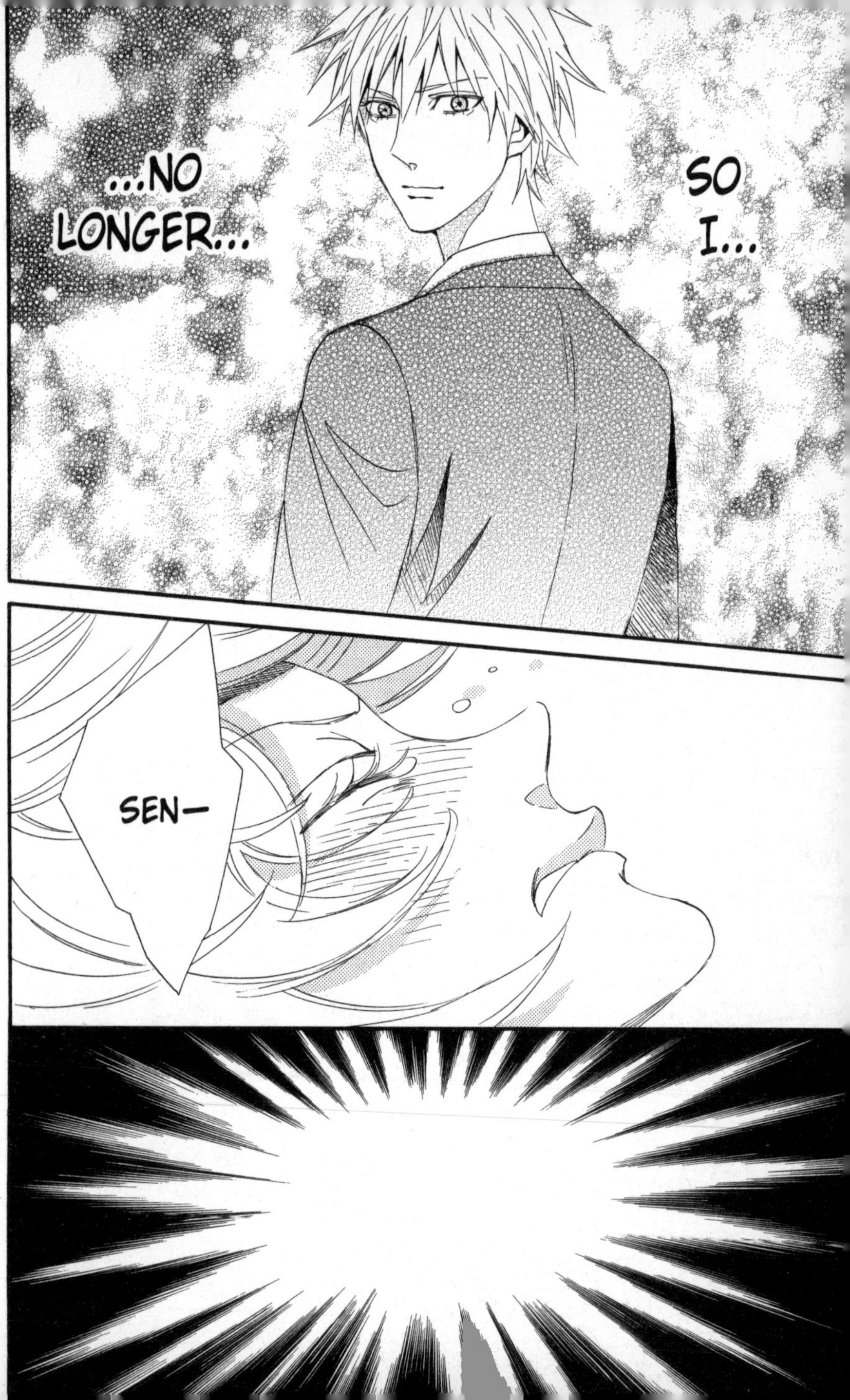
SO I...
...NO LONGER...
SEN—

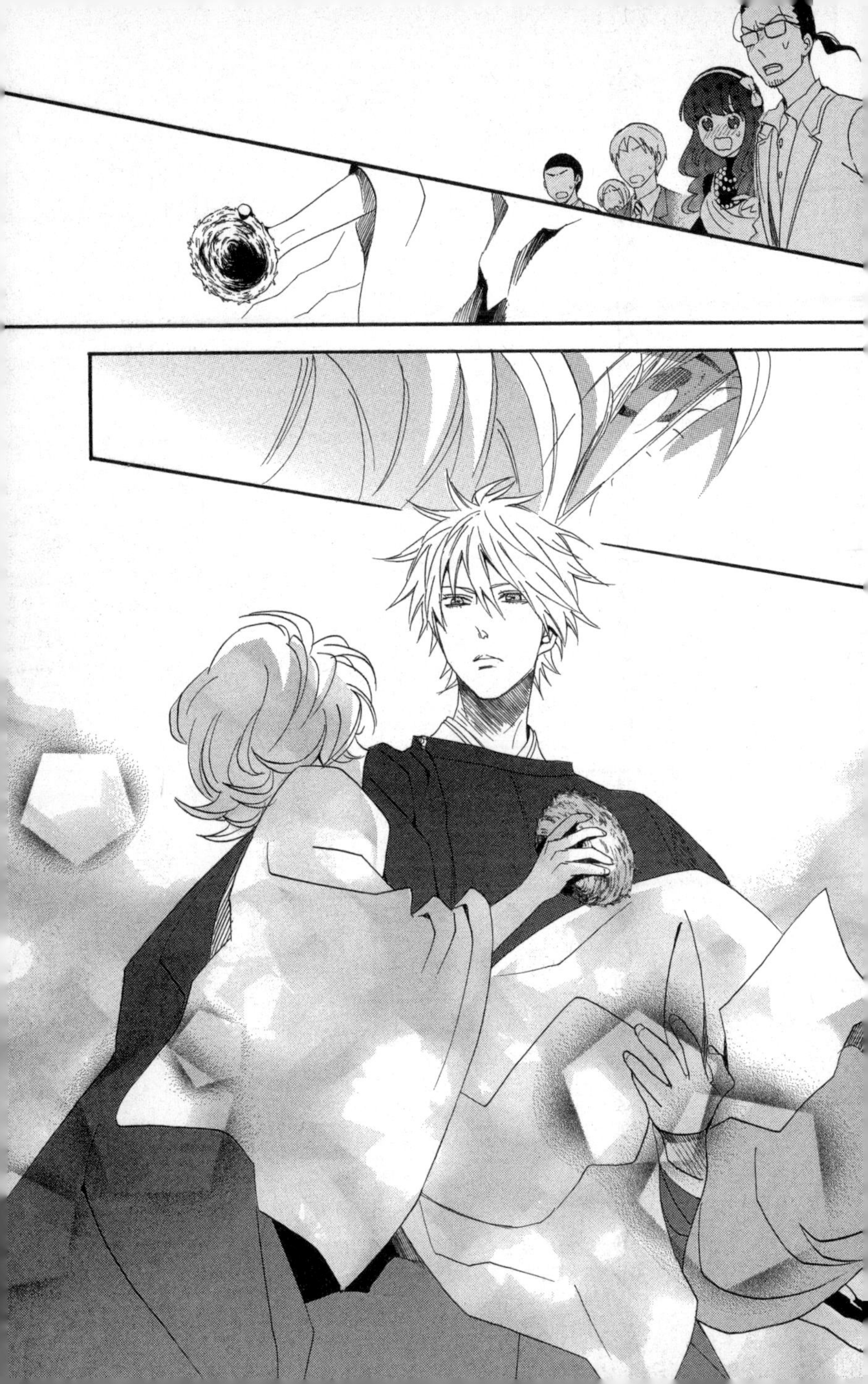

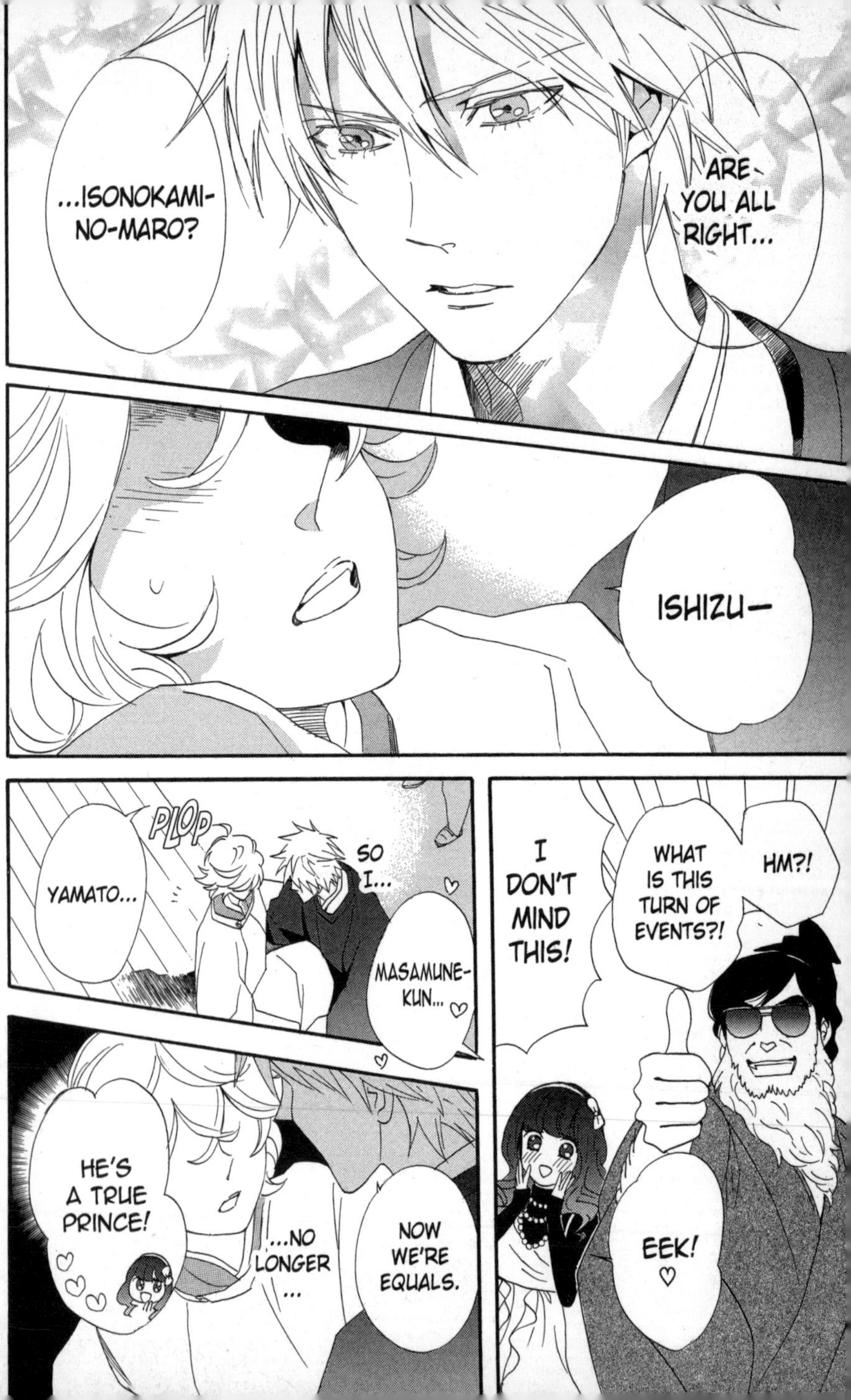
ARE YOU ALL RIGHT...
...ISONOKAMI-NO-MARO?
ISHIZU—
HM?!
WHAT IS THIS TURN OF EVENTS?!
I DON'T MIND THIS!
EEK! ♡
SO I...
MASAMUNE-KUN... ♡
PLOP
YAMATO...
NOW WE'RE EQUALS.
...NO LONGER ...
HE'S A TRUE PRINCE!

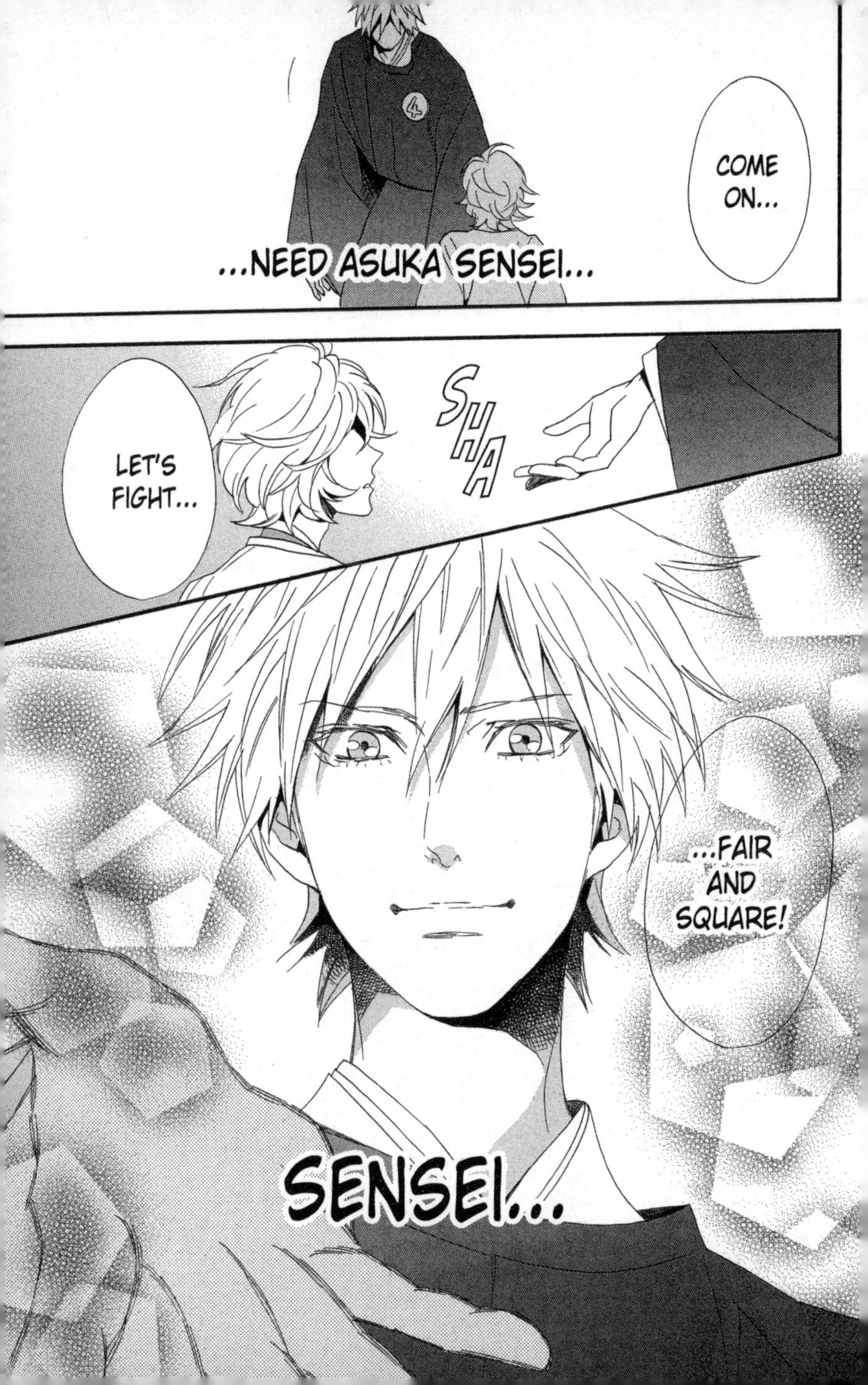
COME ON...
...NEED ASUKA SENSEI...
SHA
LET'S FIGHT...
...FAIR AND SQUARE!
SENSEI...

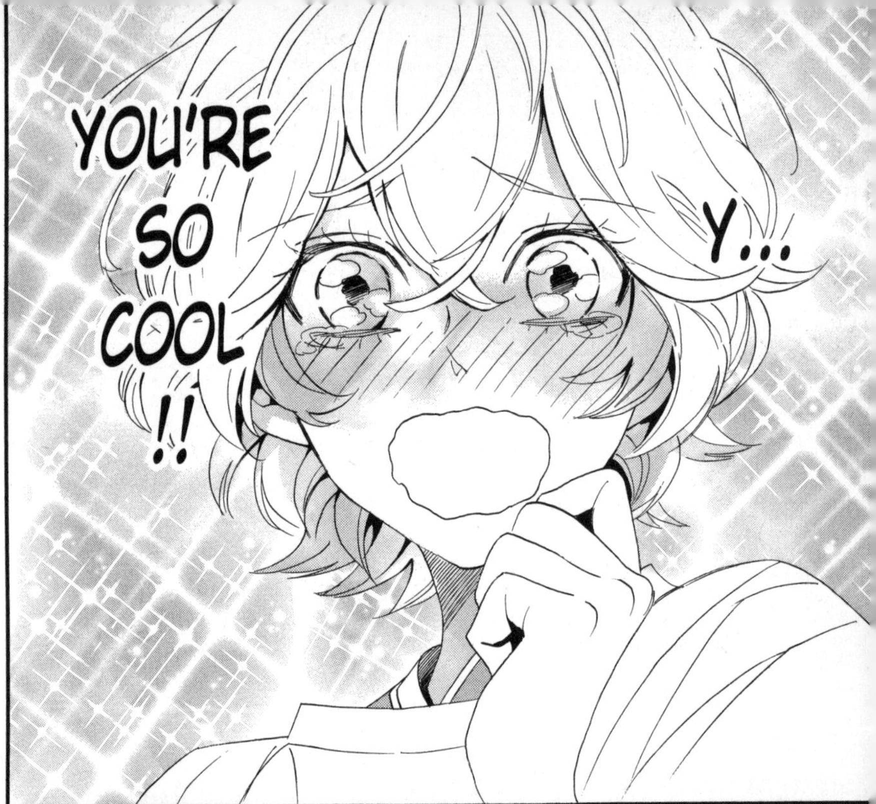
Y...
YOU'RE SO COOL!!

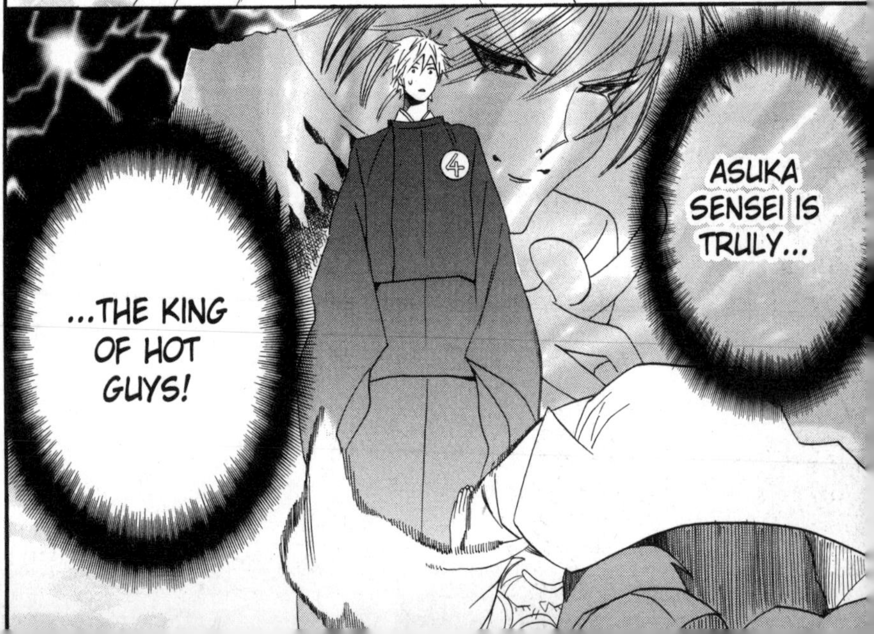
ASUKA SENSEI IS TRULY...
...THE KING OF HOT GUYS!

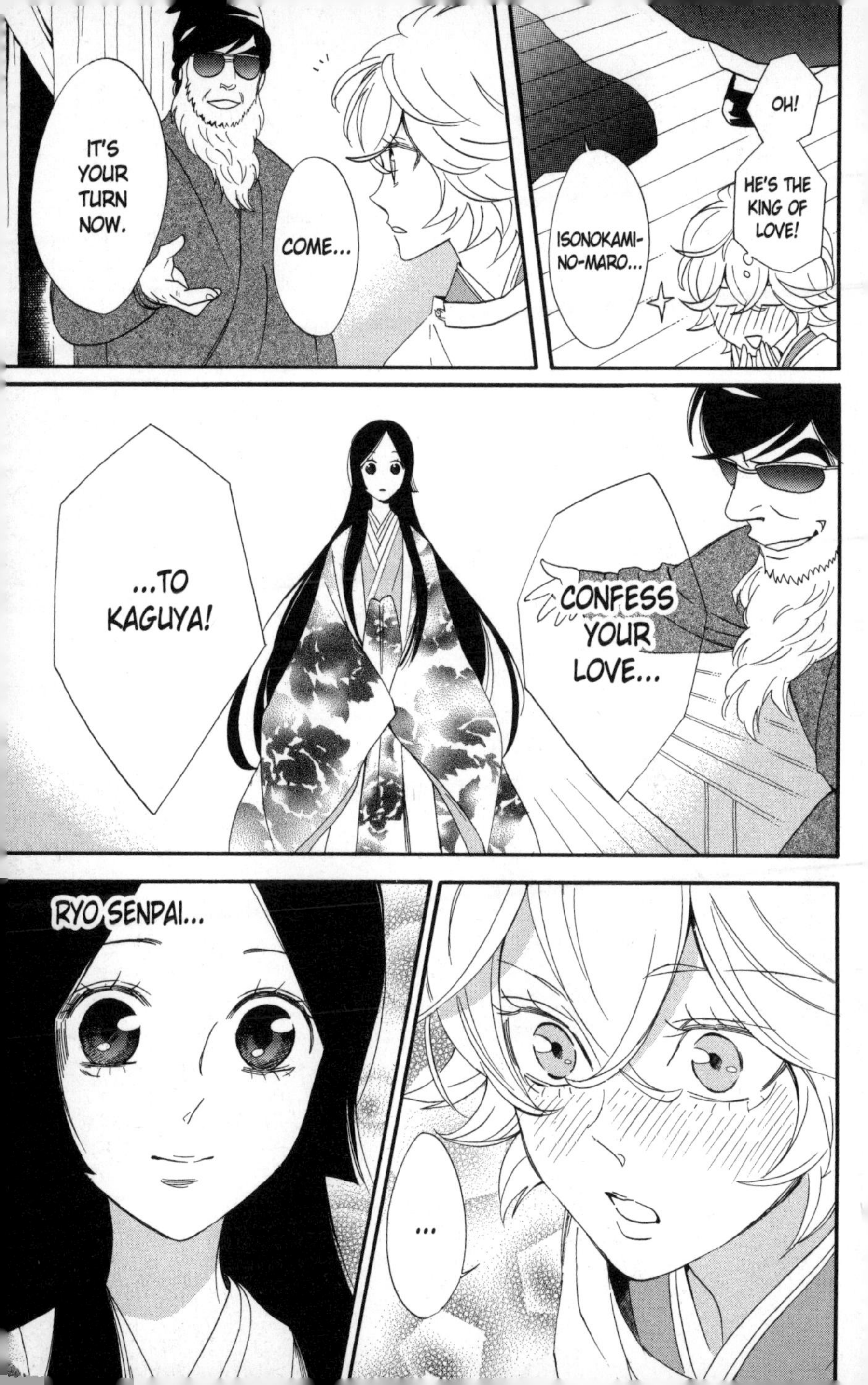
OH!
HE'S THE KING OF LOVE!
ISONOKAMI-NO-MARO...
IT'S YOUR TURN NOW.
COME...
CONFESS YOUR LOVE...
...TO KAGUYA!
...
RYO SENPAI...

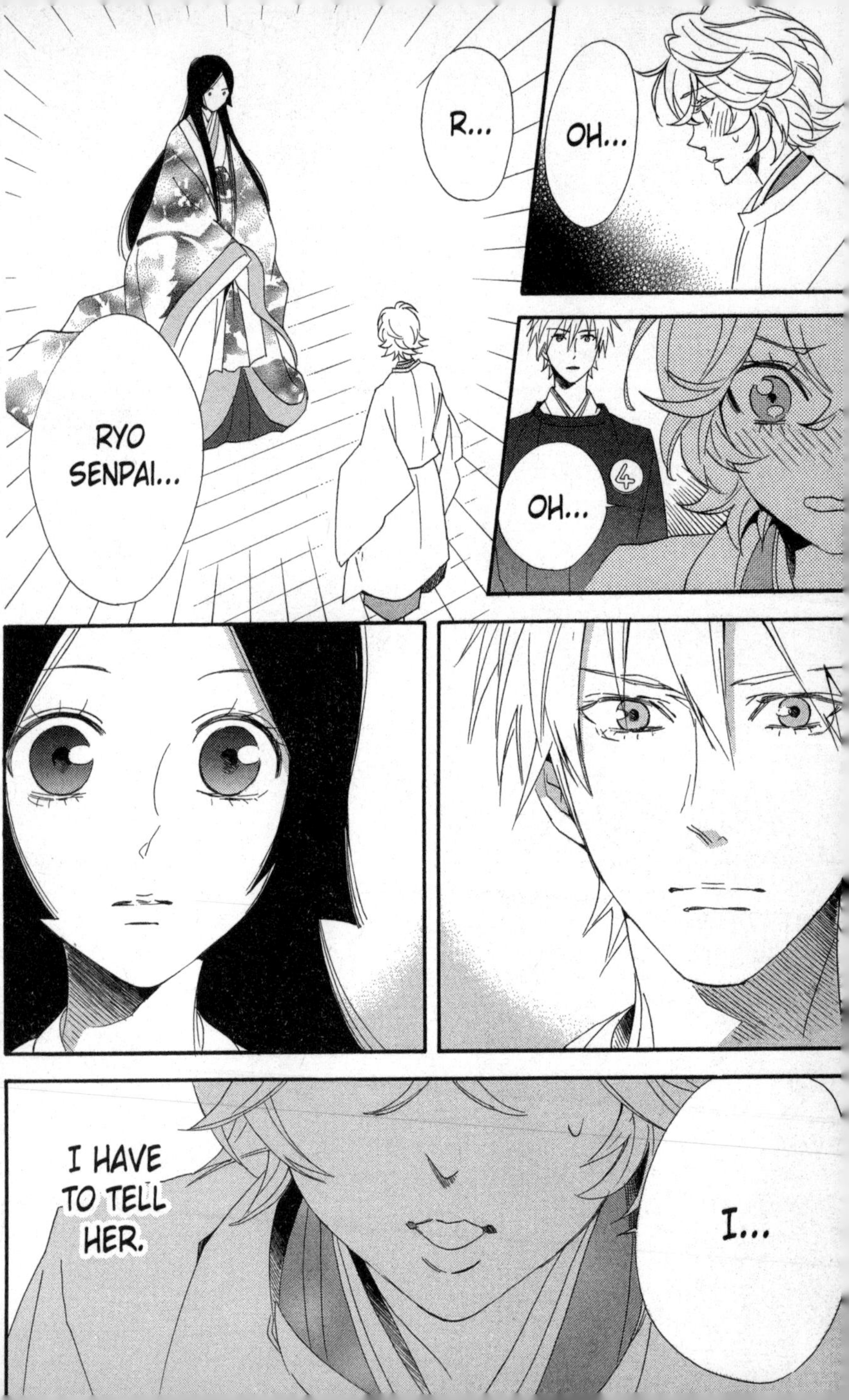
OH...
R...
OH...
RYO SENPAI...
I...
I HAVE TO TELL HER.

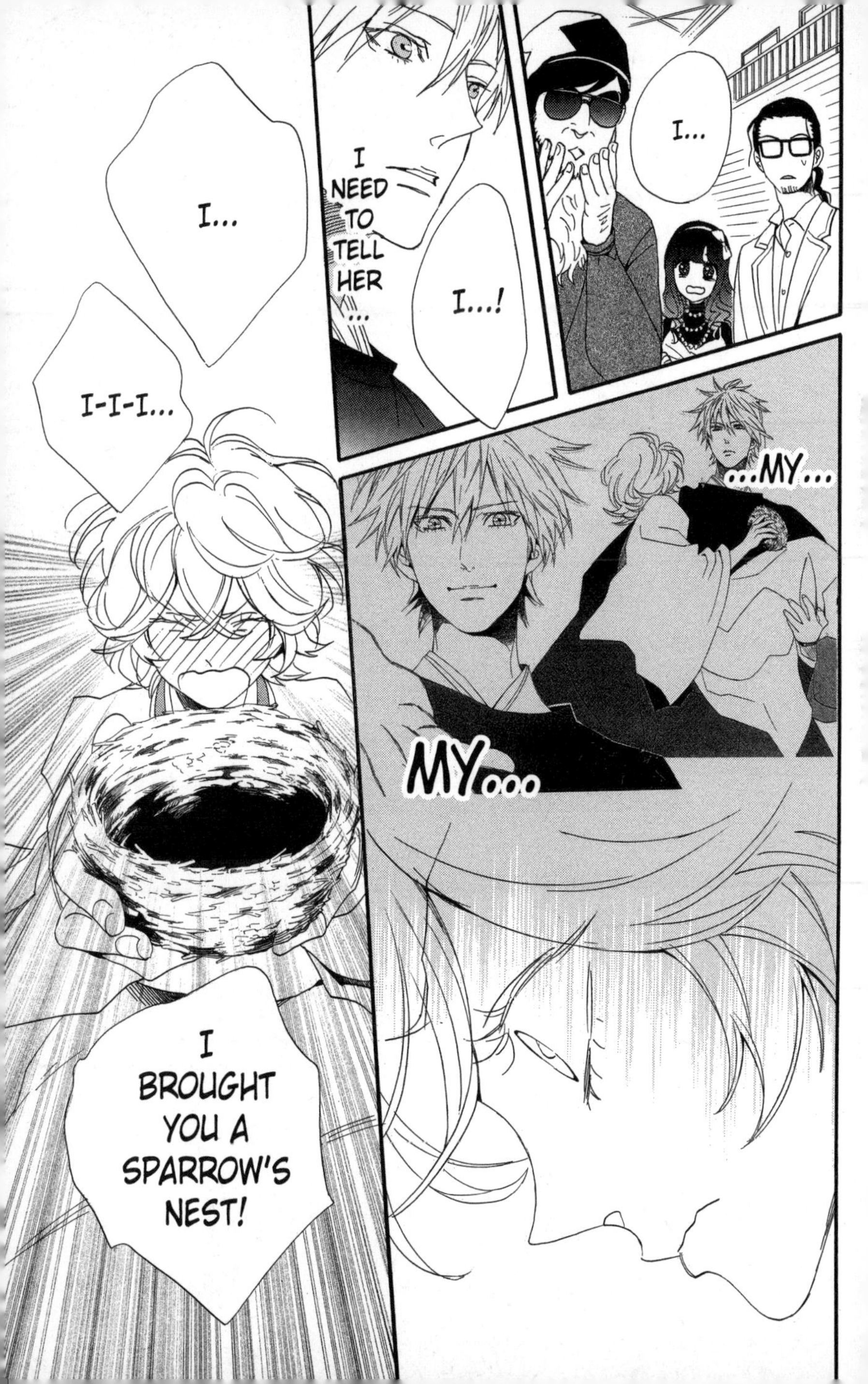
I...
I NEED TO TELL HER...
I...!
...MY...
MY...
I...
I-I-I...
I BROUGHT YOU A SPARROW'S NEST!

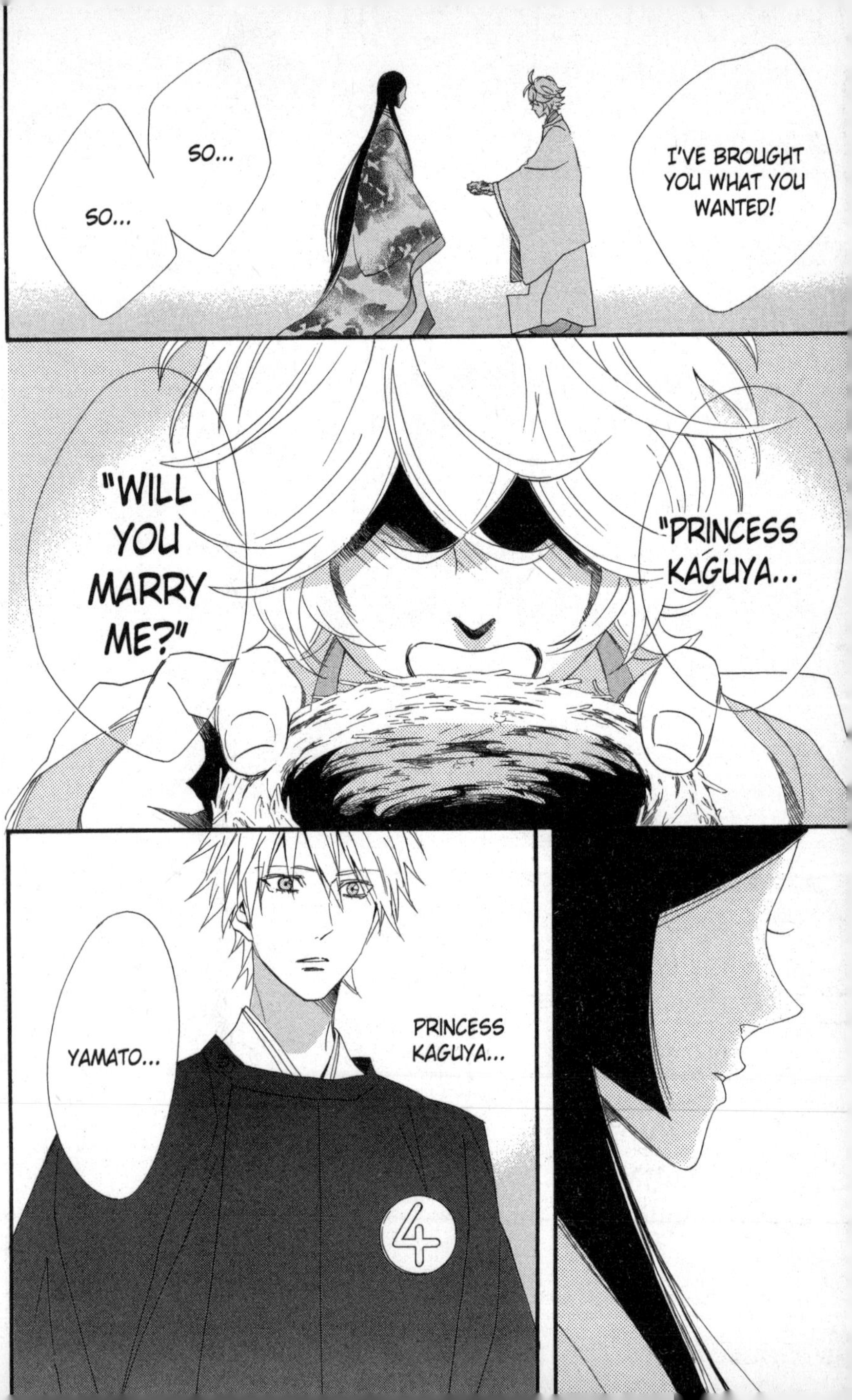
I'VE BROUGHT YOU WHAT YOU WANTED!
SO...
SO...
"PRINCESS KAGUYA...
"WILL YOU MARRY ME?"
PRINCESS KAGUYA...
YAMATO...
4

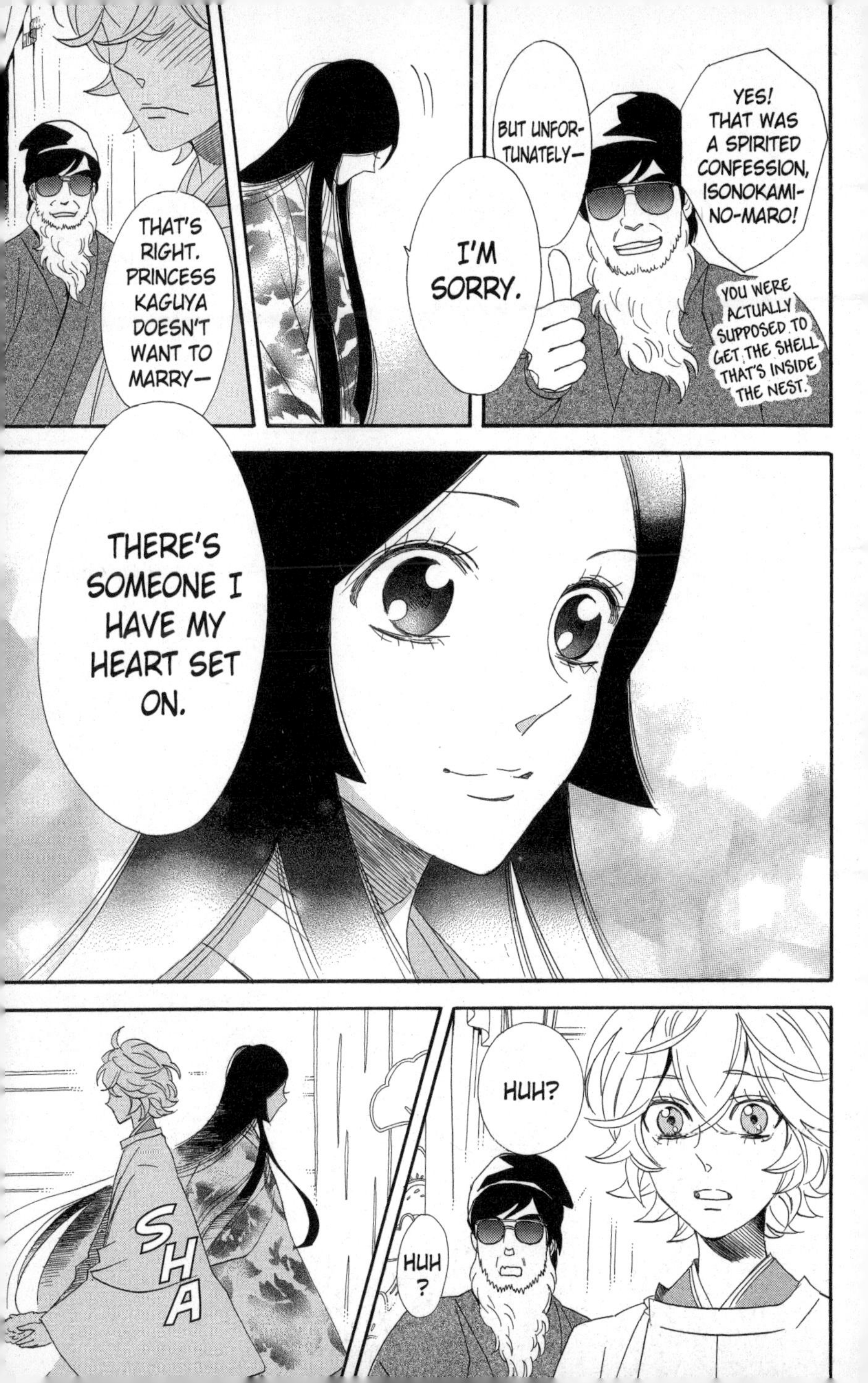
YES! THAT WAS A SPIRITED CONFESSION, ISONOKAMI-NO-MARO!
YOU WERE ACTUALLY SUPPOSED TO GET THE SHELL THAT'S INSIDE THE NEST.
BUT UNFORTUNATELY—
I'M SORRY.
THAT'S RIGHT. PRINCESS KAGUYA DOESN'T WANT TO MARRY—
THERE'S SOMEONE I HAVE MY HEART SET ON.
HUH?
HUH ?
SHA

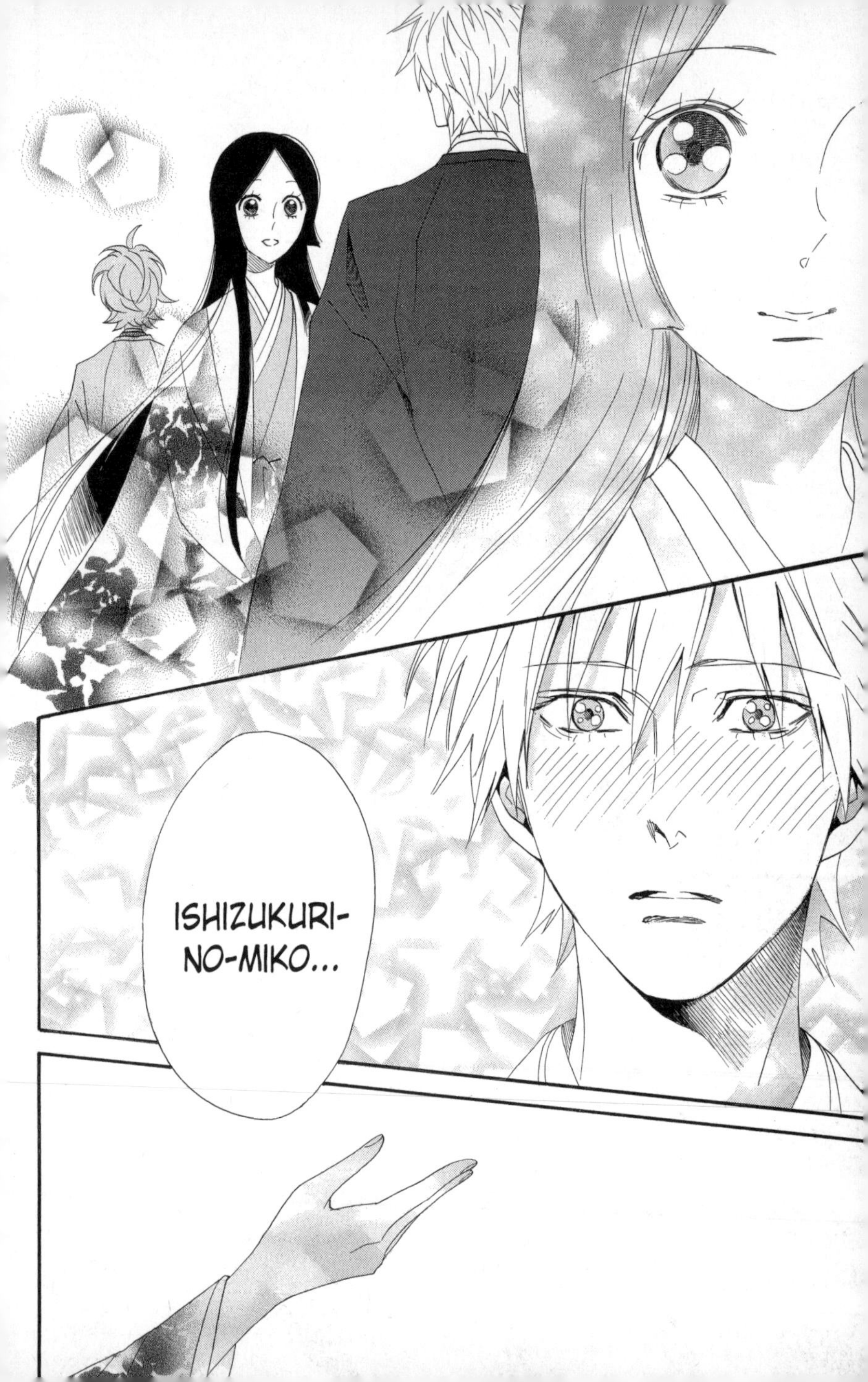
ISHIZUKURI-NO-MIKO...

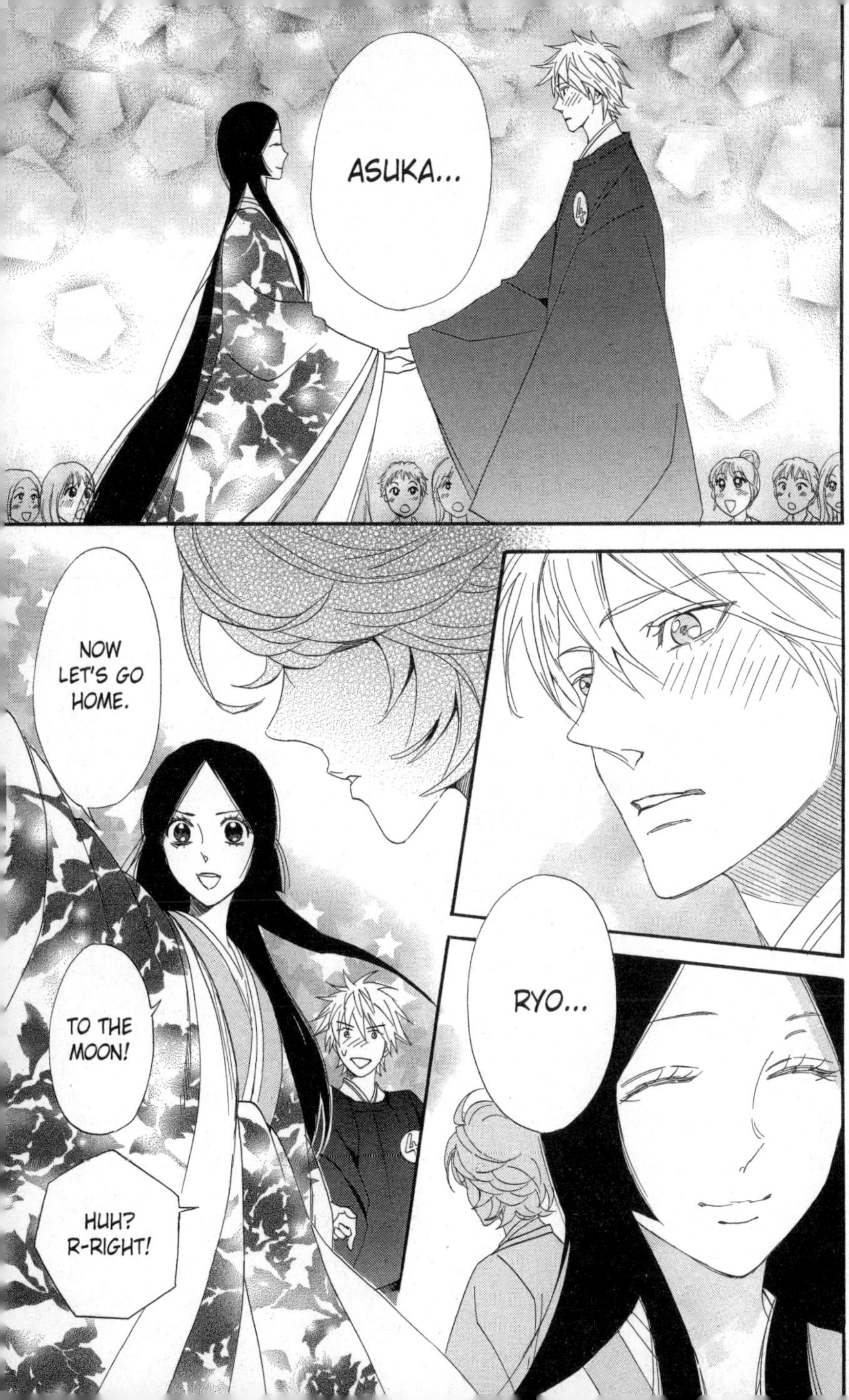
ASUKA...
RYO...
NOW LET'S GO HOME.
TO THE MOON!
HUH? R-RIGHT!

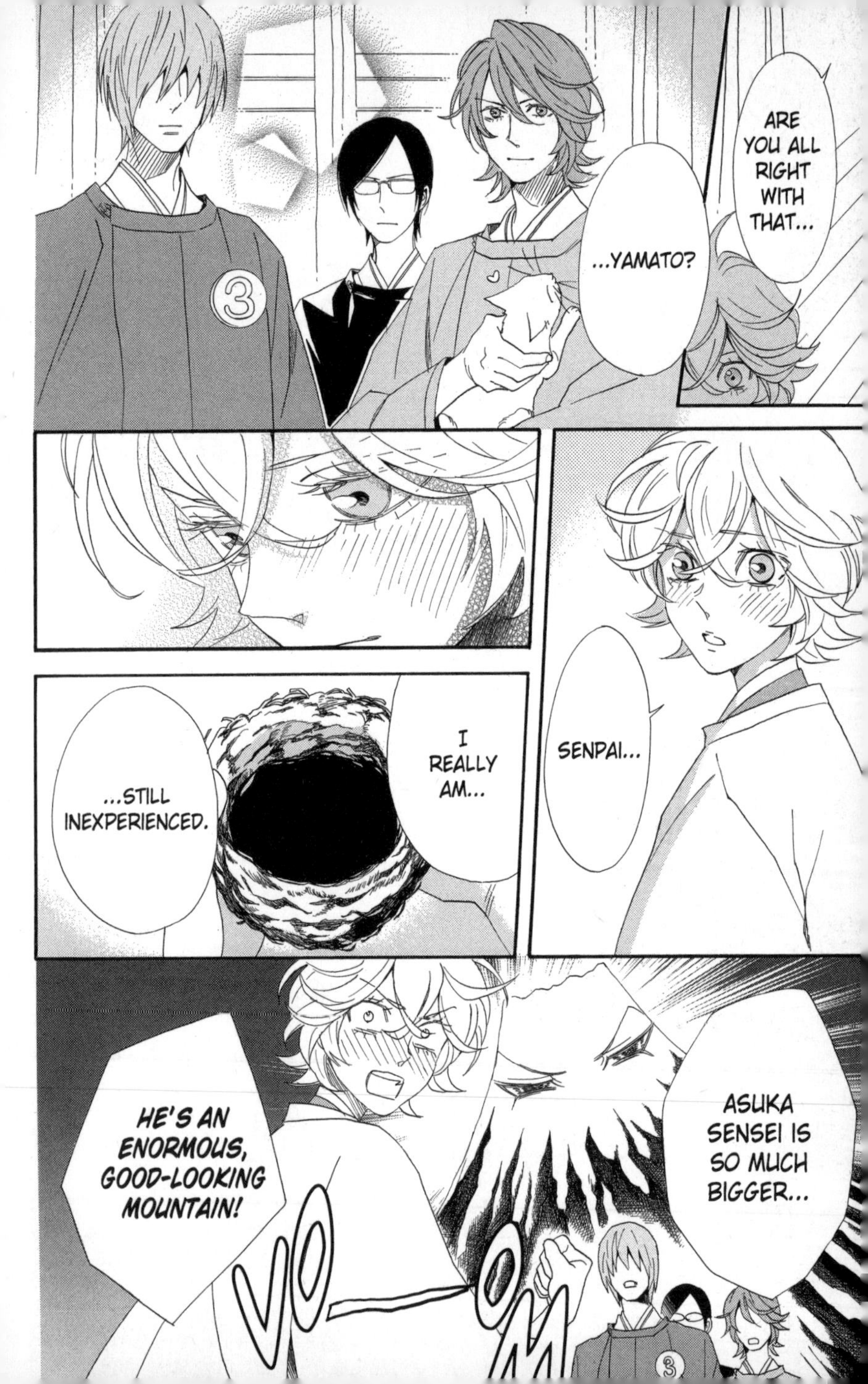
ARE YOU ALL RIGHT WITH THAT...
...YAMATO?
SENPAI...
I REALLY AM...
...STILL INEXPERIENCED.
ASUKA SENSEI IS SO MUCH BIGGER...
HE'S AN ENORMOUS, GOOD-LOOKING MOUNTAIN!
VO—OM

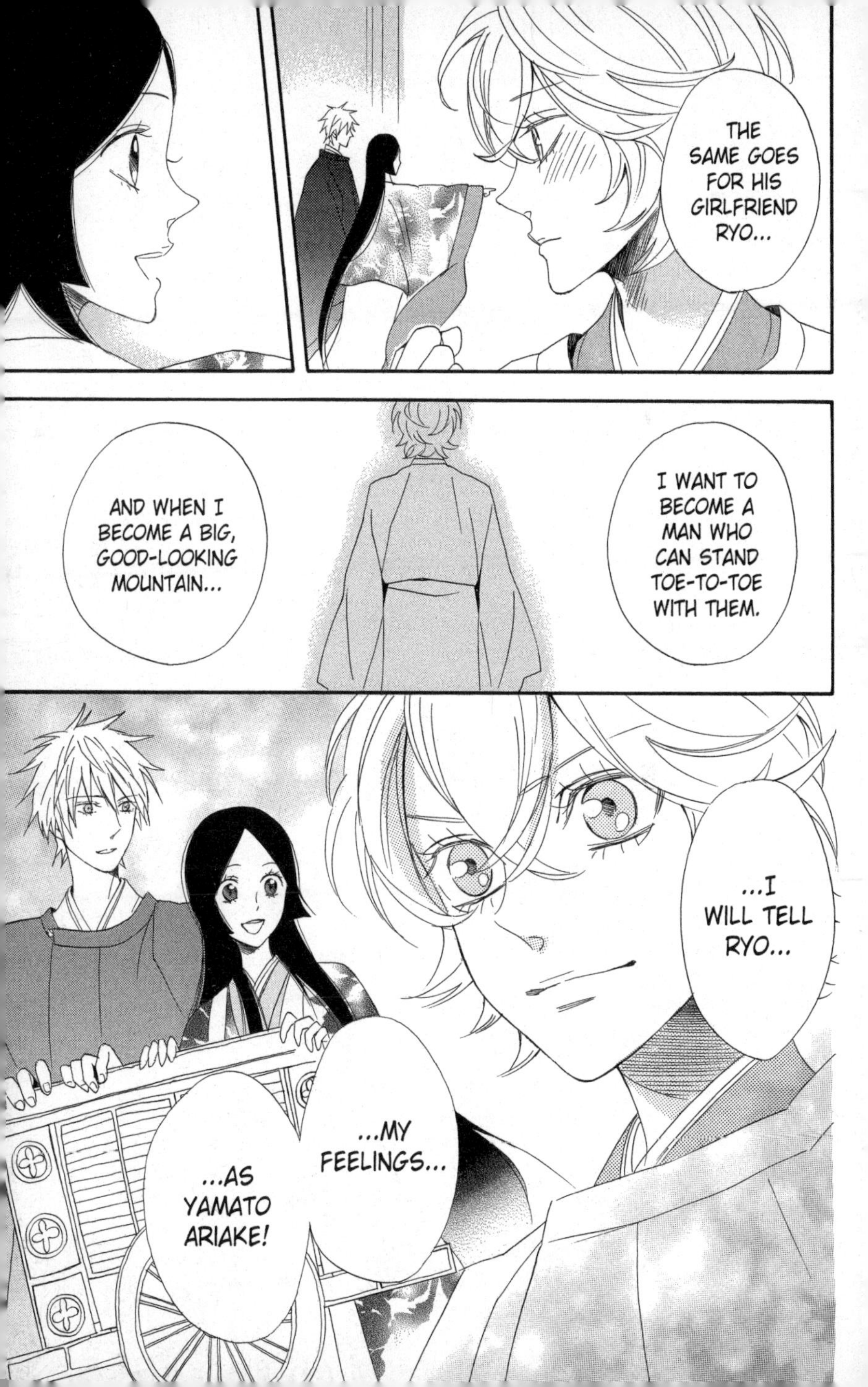
THE SAME GOES FOR HIS GIRLFRIEND RYO...
I WANT TO BECOME A MAN WHO CAN STAND TOE-TO-TOE WITH THEM.
AND WHEN I BECOME A BIG, GOOD-LOOKING MOUNTAIN...
...I WILL TELL RYO...
...MY FEELINGS...
...AS YAMATO ARIAKE!

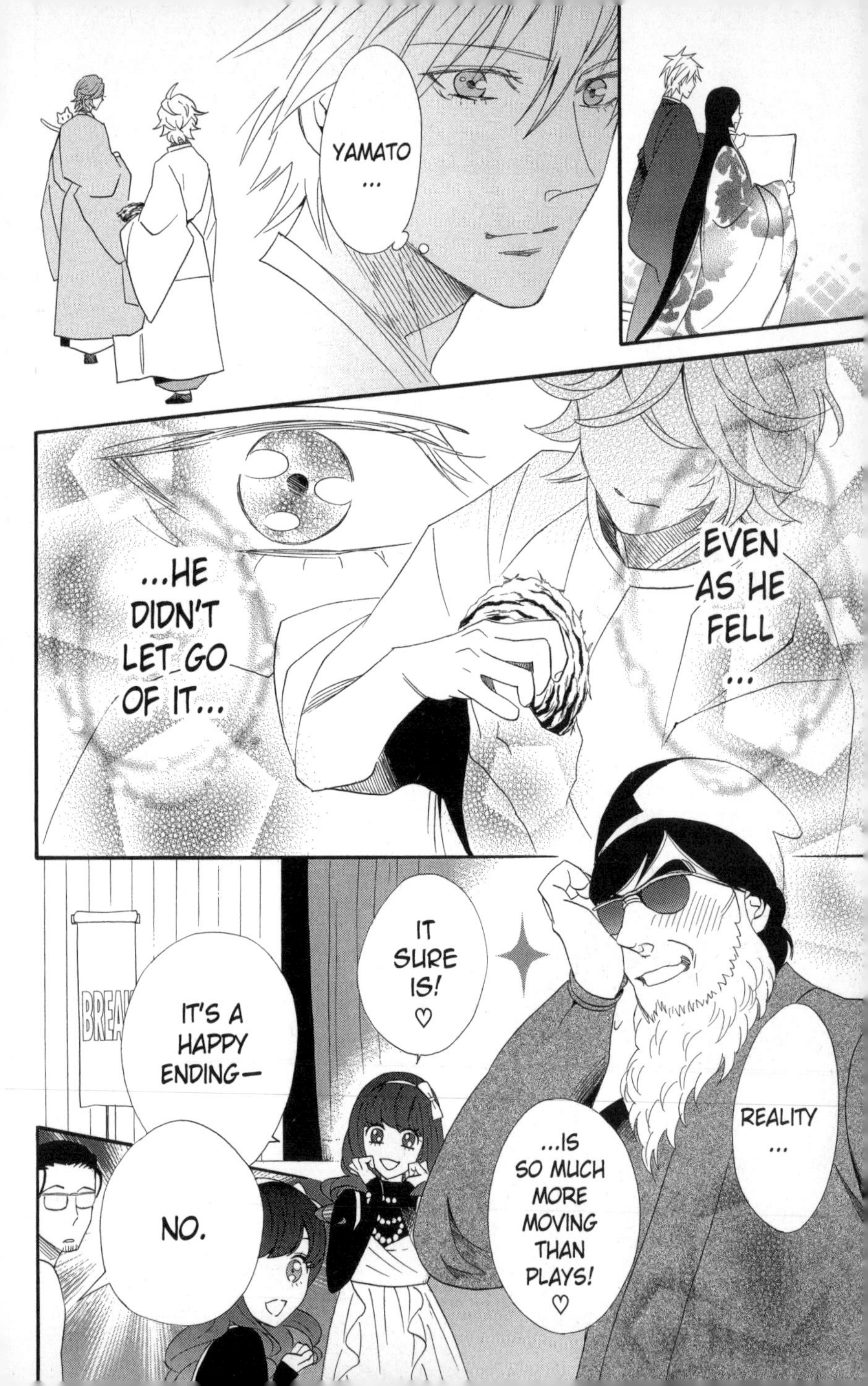
YAMATO ...
EVEN AS HE FELL ...
...HE DIDN'T LET GO OF IT...
REALITY ...
...IS SO MUCH MORE MOVING THAN PLAYS! ♡
IT SURE IS! ♡
IT'S A HAPPY ENDING—
NO.

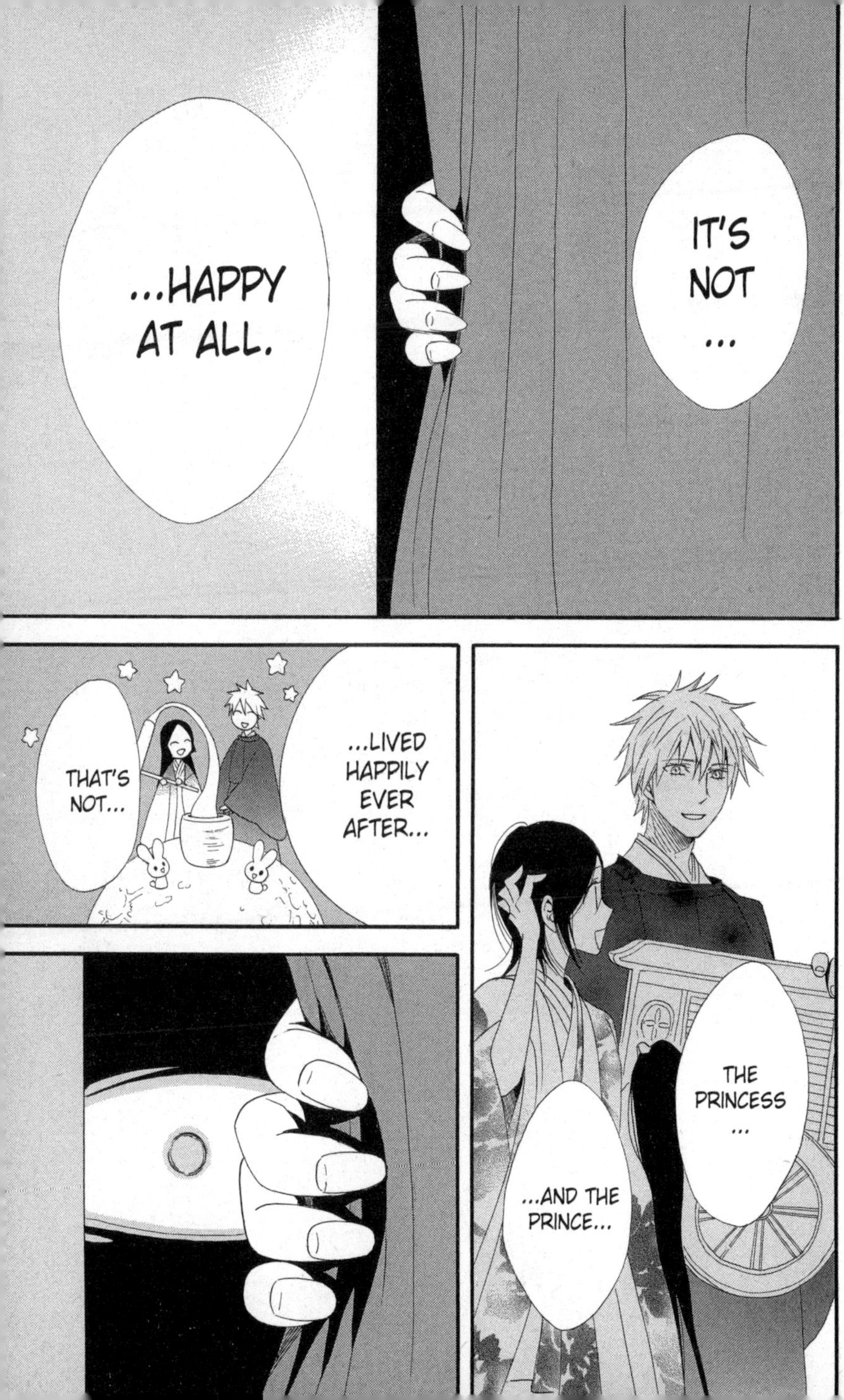
IT'S NOT ...
...HAPPY AT ALL.
THE PRINCESS ...
...AND THE PRINCE...
...LIVED HAPPILY EVER AFTER...
THAT'S NOT...

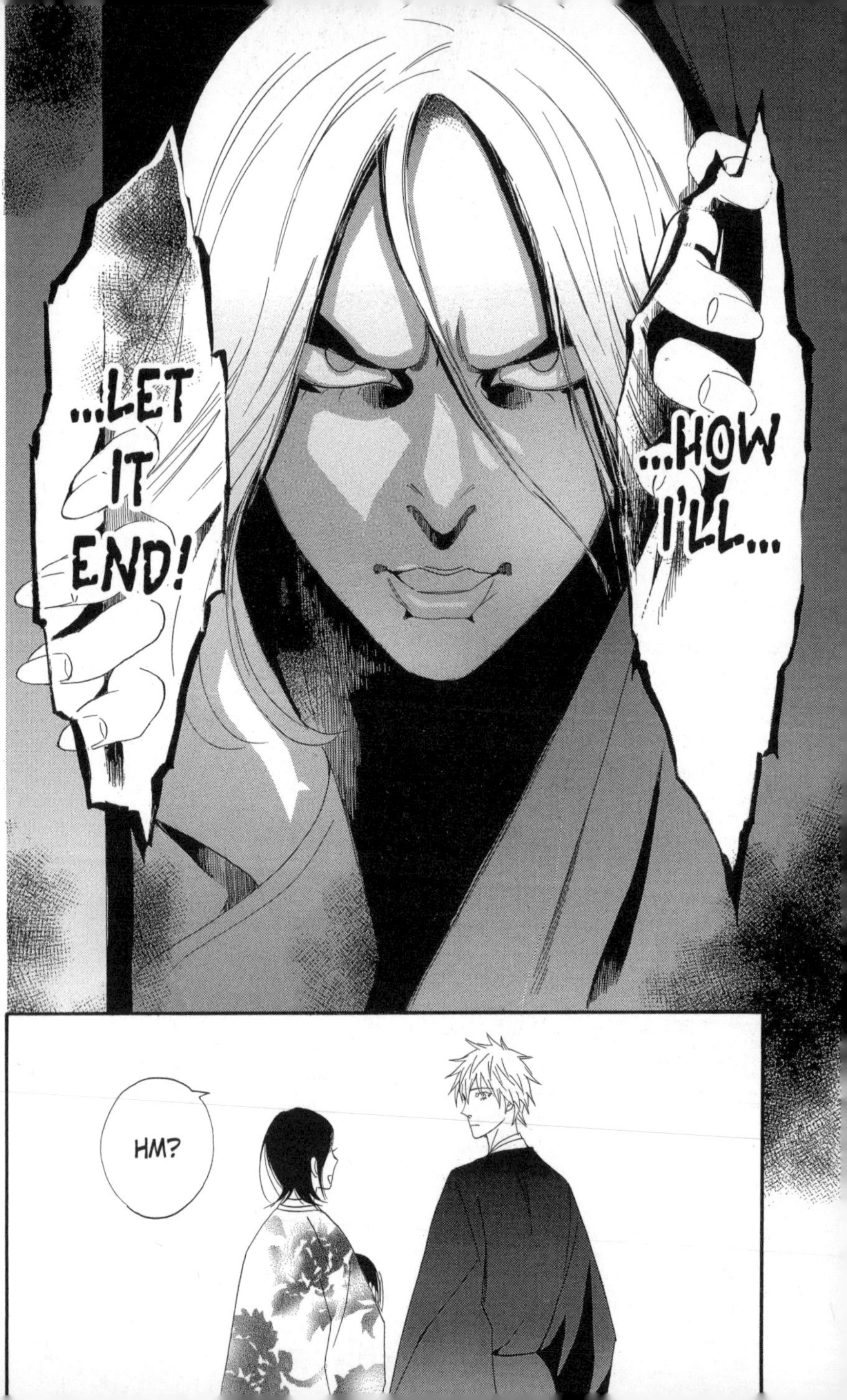
...HOW I'LL...
...LET IT END!
HM?

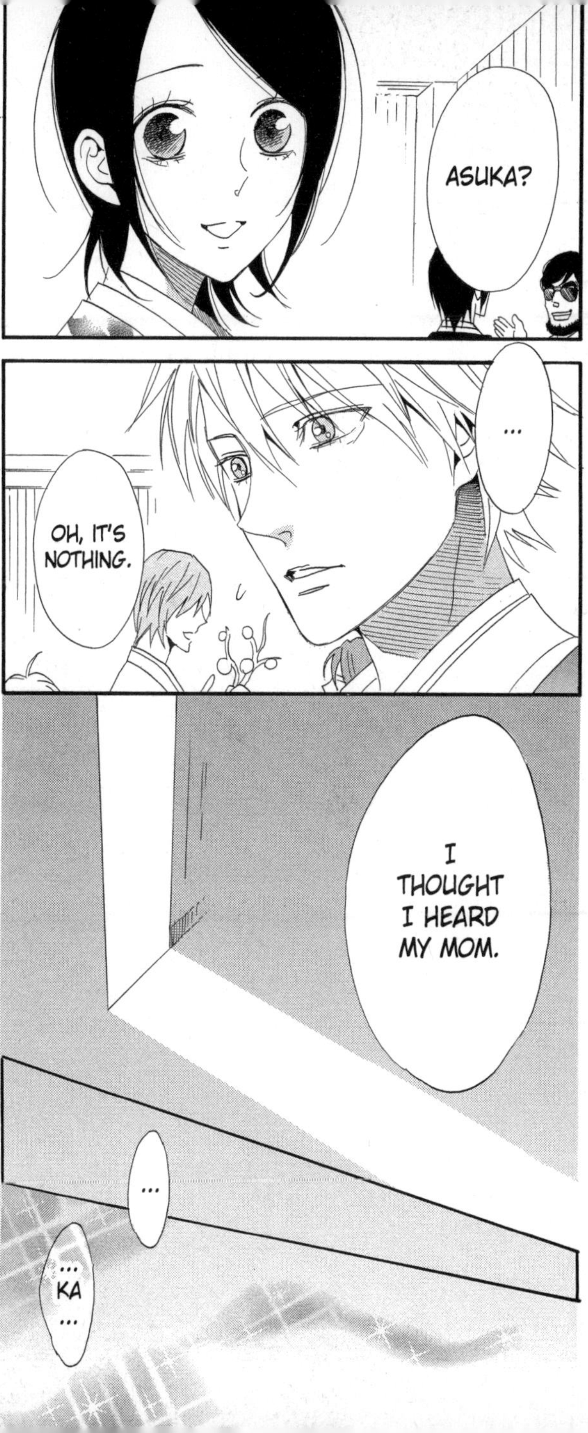
ASUKA?
...
OH, IT'S NOTHING.
I THOUGHT I HEARD MY MOM.
...
...KA...

Looking back, I've been drawing *Otomen* for seven years now. In the extra pages at the end of this volume, I want to introduce you to all of the assistants that have helped me.

Otomen couldn't have been possible without my assistants. They draw major accessories and items. They add the necessary backgrounds and effects to complete each page. *Otomen* is made possible because of the help of my assistants.

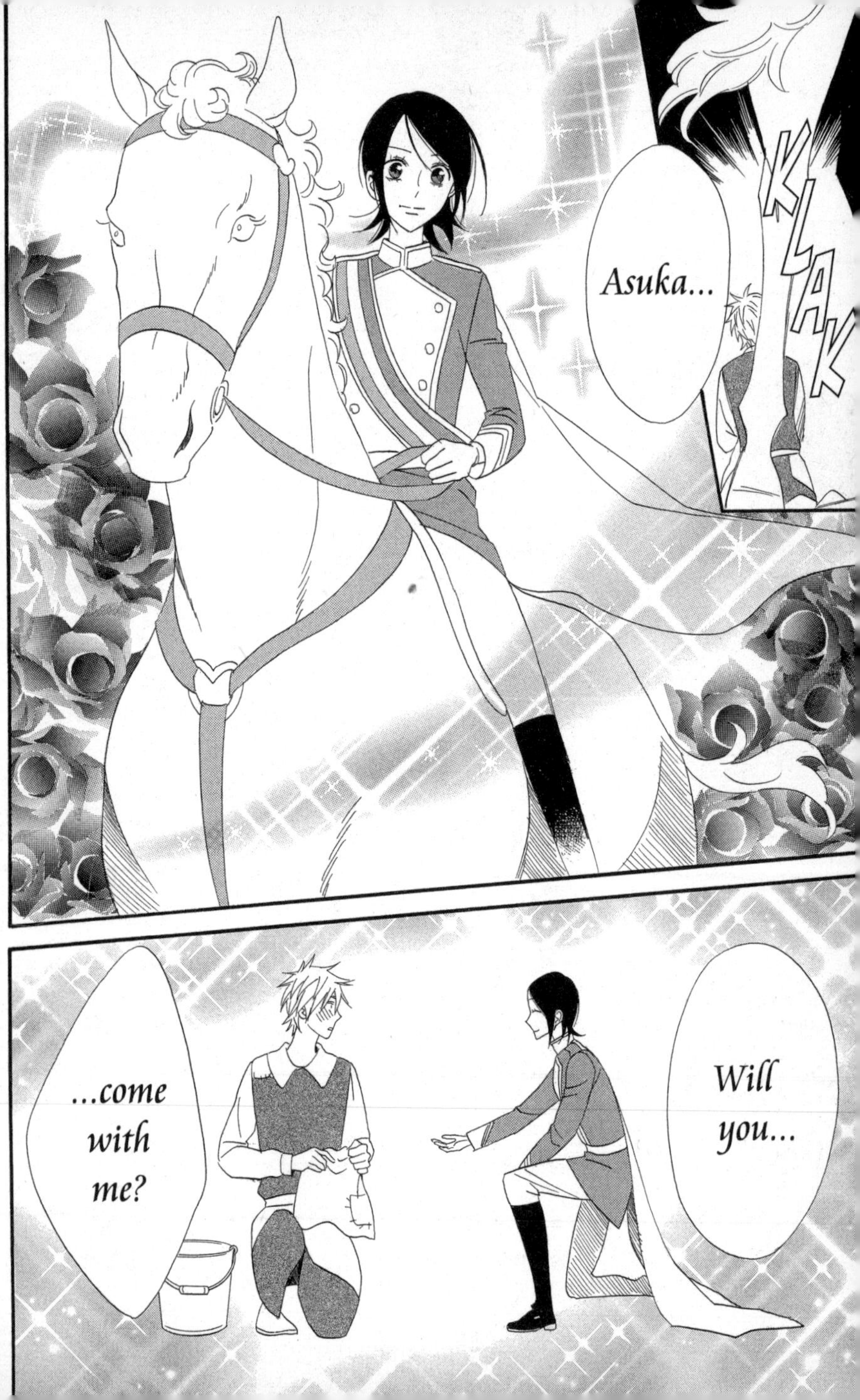
KLAK
Asuka...
Will you...
...come with me?

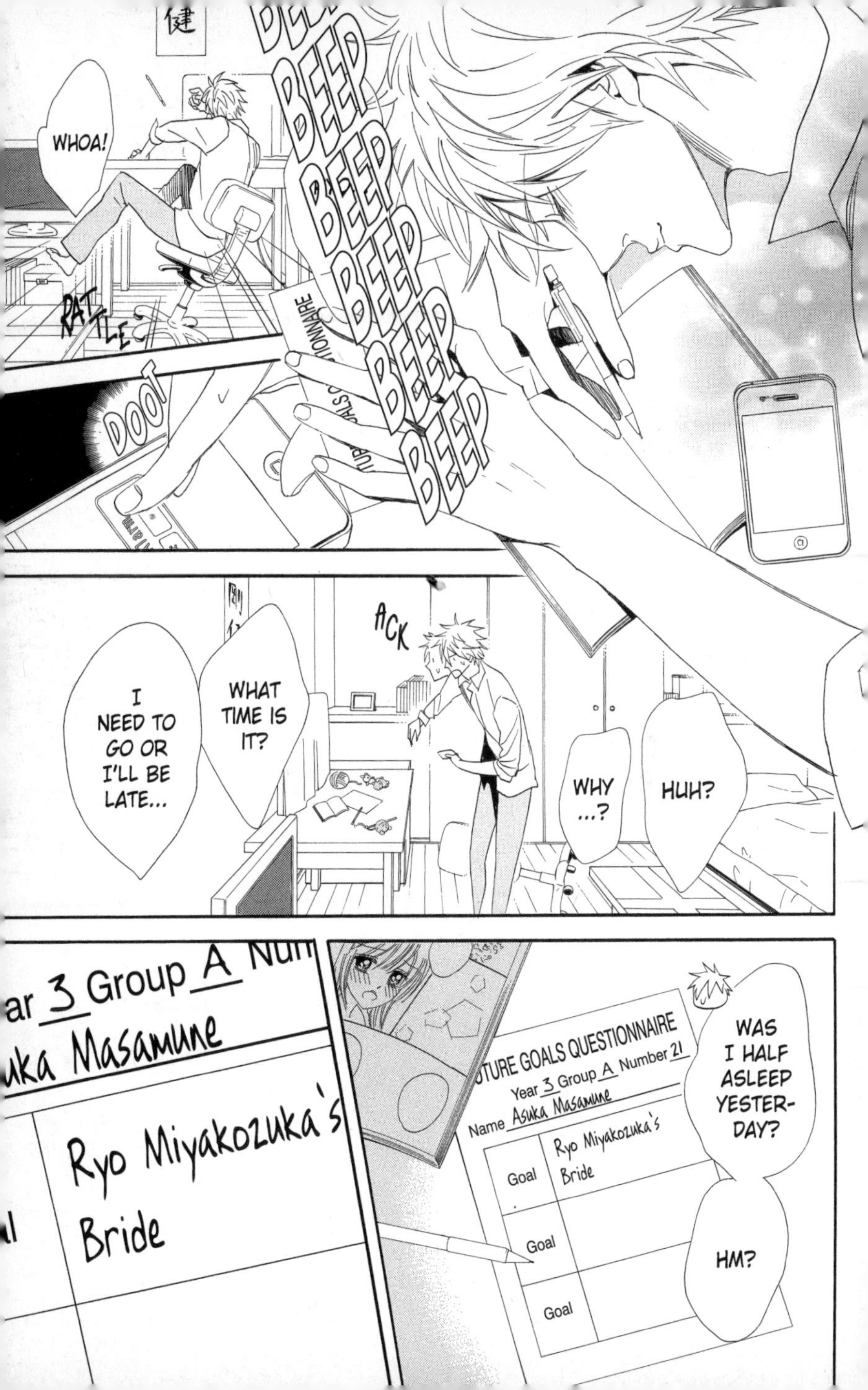
BEEP BEEP BEEP BEEP BEEP BEEP
WHOA!
RATTLE
DOOT
HUH?
WHY ...?
ACK
WHAT TIME IS IT?
I NEED TO GO OR I'LL BE LATE...
WAS I HALF ASLEEP YESTERDAY?
HM?
UTURE GOALS QUESTIONNAIRE
Year 3 Group A Number 21
Name Asuka Masamune
Goal Ryo Miyakozuka's Bride
Goal
Goal
ar 3 Group A Num
uka Masamune
Ryo Miyakozuka's Bride

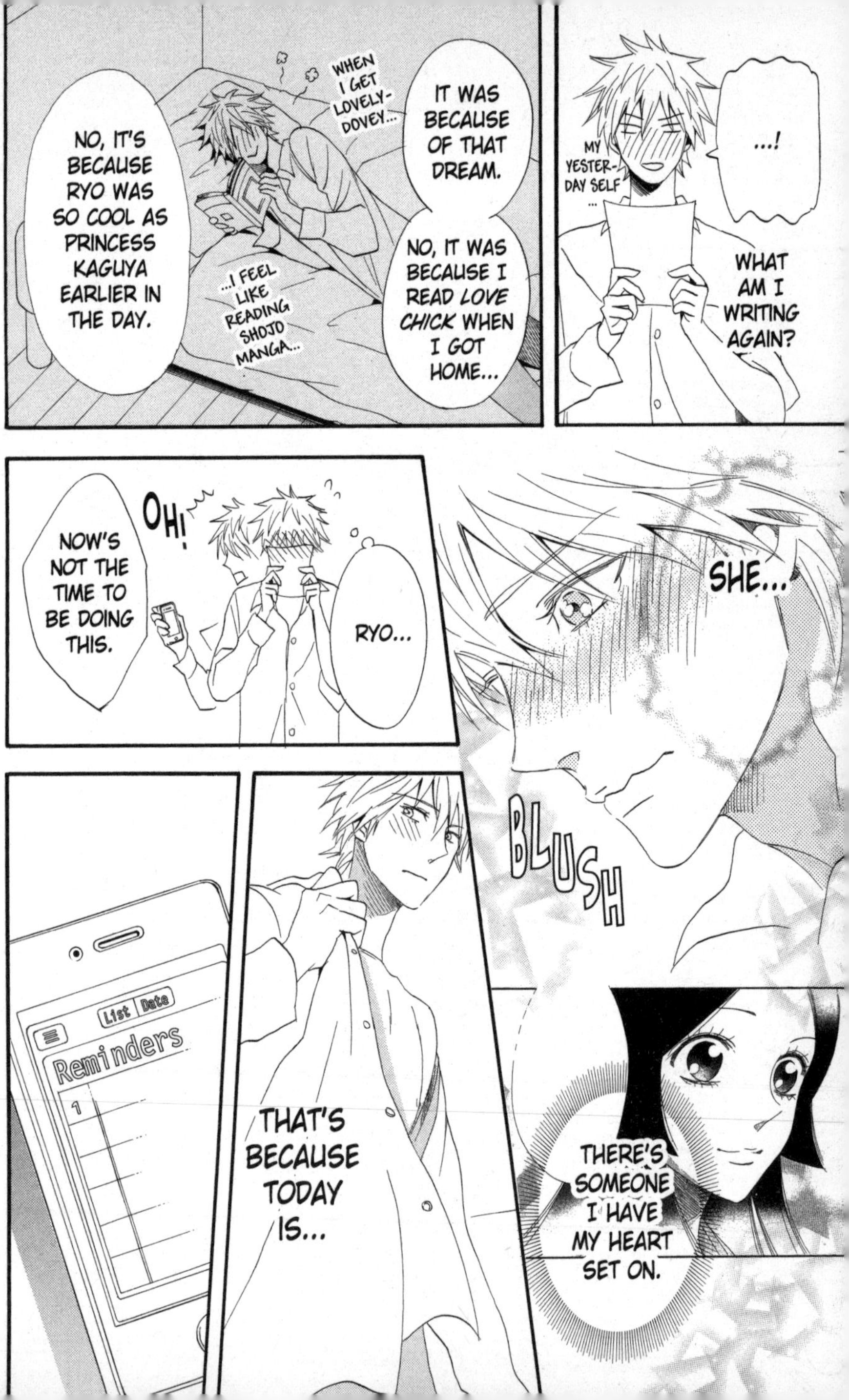
...!
MY YESTER-DAY SELF ...
WHAT AM I WRITING AGAIN?
IT WAS BECAUSE OF THAT DREAM.
WHEN I GET LOVELY-DOVEY...
NO, IT WAS BECAUSE I READ *LOVE CHICK* WHEN I GOT HOME...
...I FEEL LIKE READING SHOJO MANGA...
NO, IT'S BECAUSE RYO WAS SO COOL AS PRINCESS KAGUYA EARLIER IN THE DAY.
SHE...
BLUSH
THERE'S SOMEONE I HAVE MY HEART SET ON.
RYO...
OH!
NOW'S NOT THE TIME TO BE DOING THIS.
THAT'S BECAUSE TODAY IS...
List Date
Reminders
1

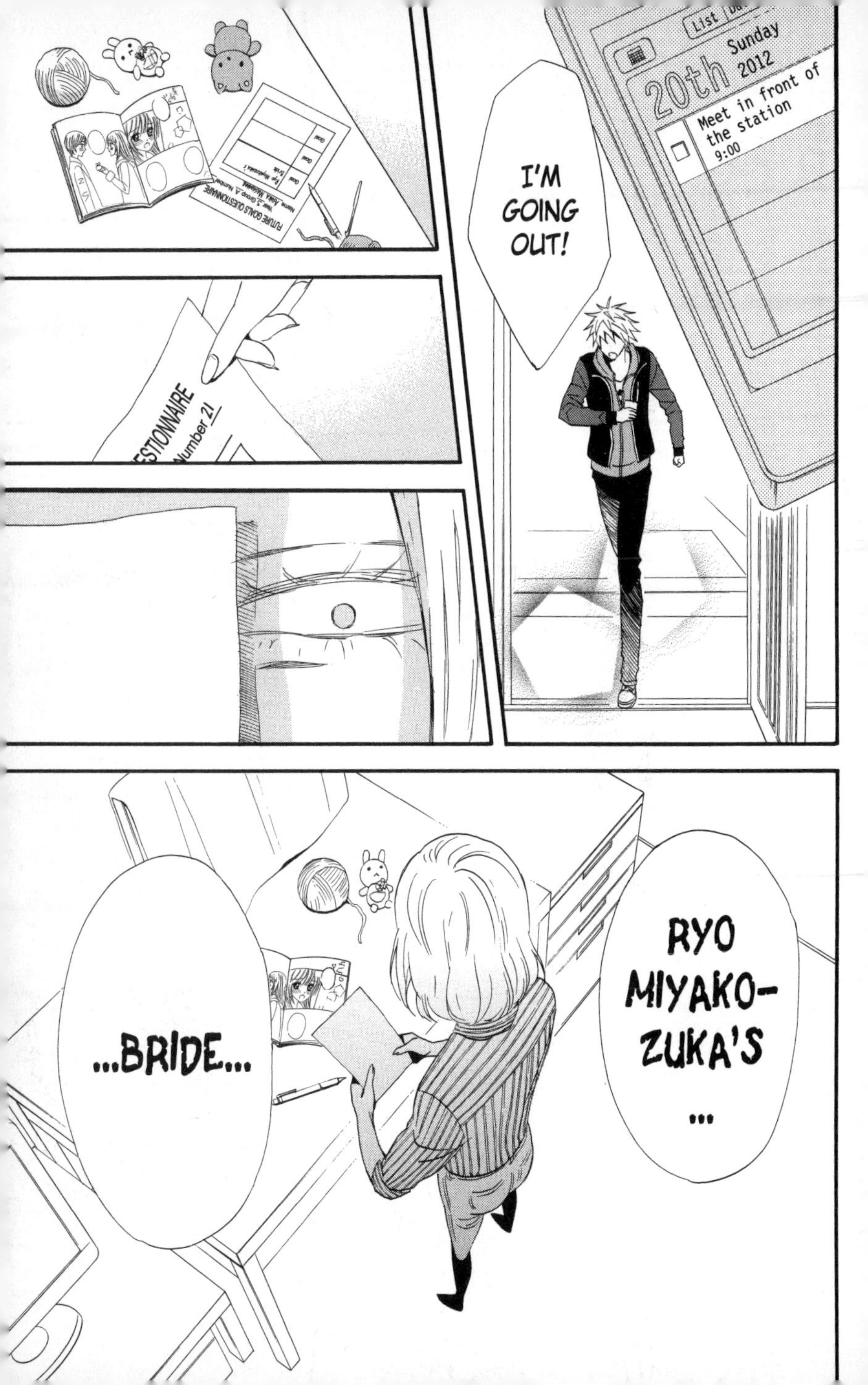
List
20th Sunday 2012
Meet in front of the station 9:00
I'M GOING OUT!
FUTURE GOALS QUESTIONNAIRE
Number 2!
RYO MIYAKO-ZUKA'S ...
...BRIDE...

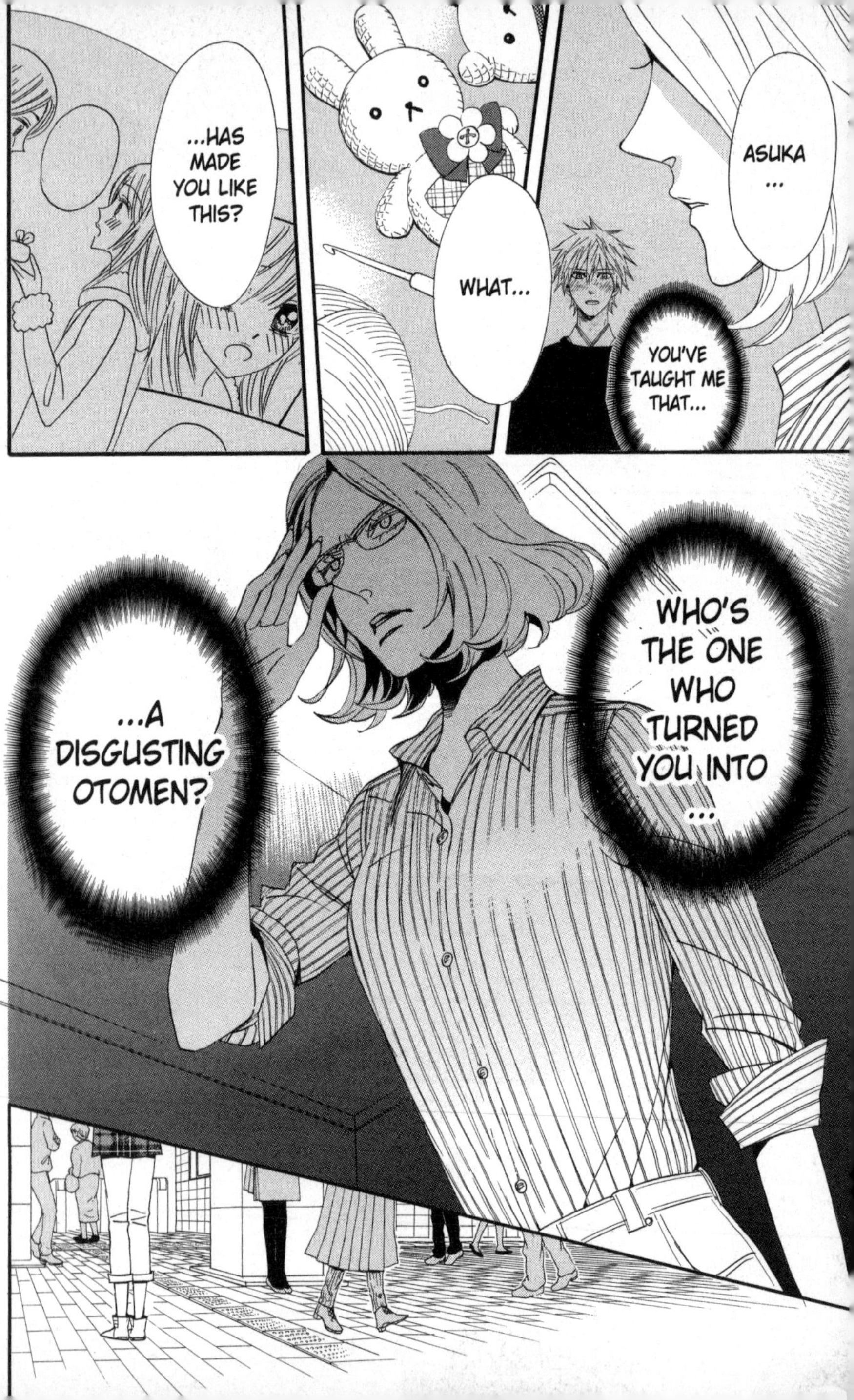
ASUKA ...
YOU'VE TAUGHT ME THAT...
WHAT...
...HAS MADE YOU LIKE THIS?
WHO'S THE ONE WHO TURNED YOU INTO ...
...A DISGUSTING OTOMEN?

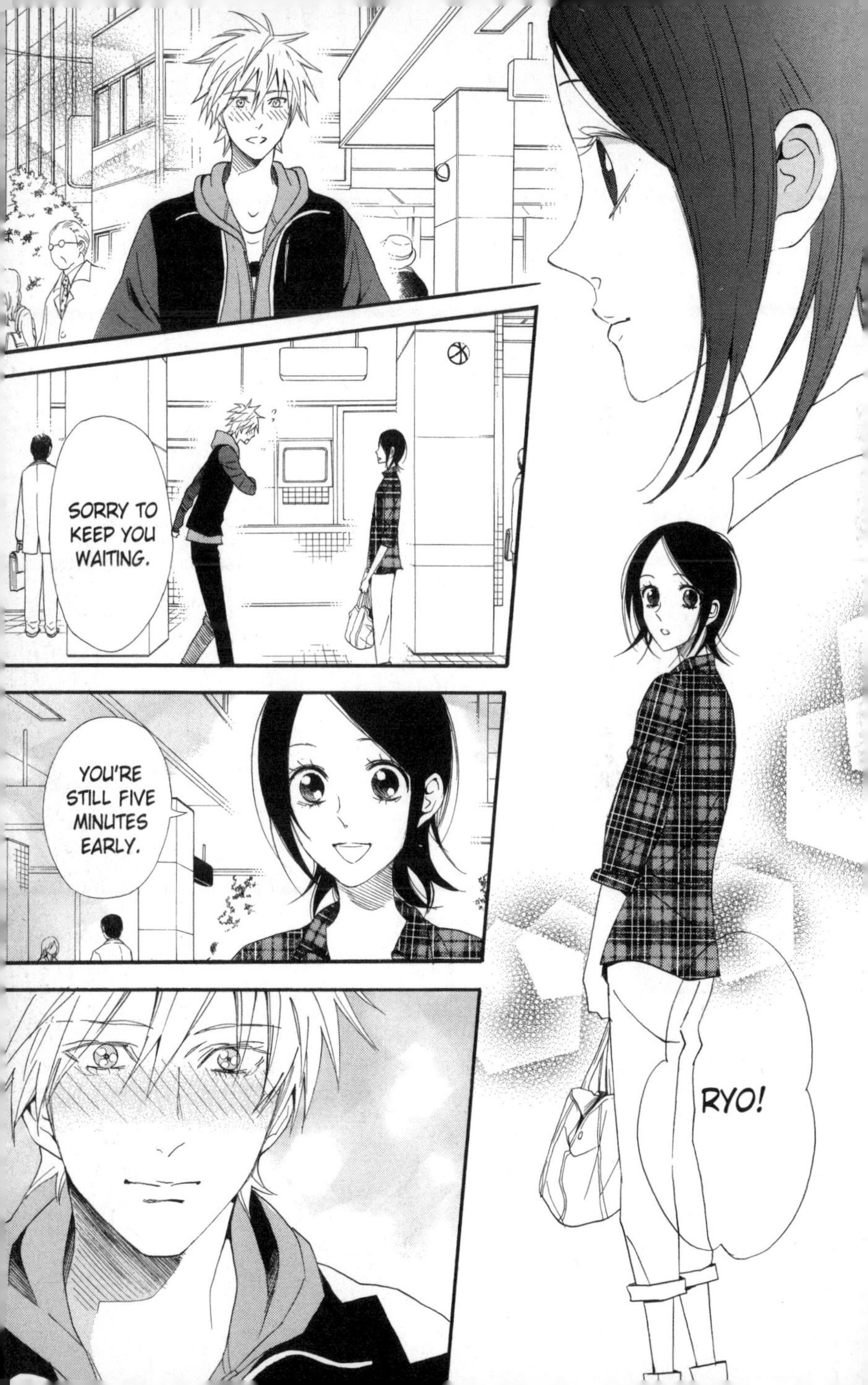
RYO!
SORRY TO KEEP YOU WAITING.
YOU'RE STILL FIVE MINUTES EARLY.

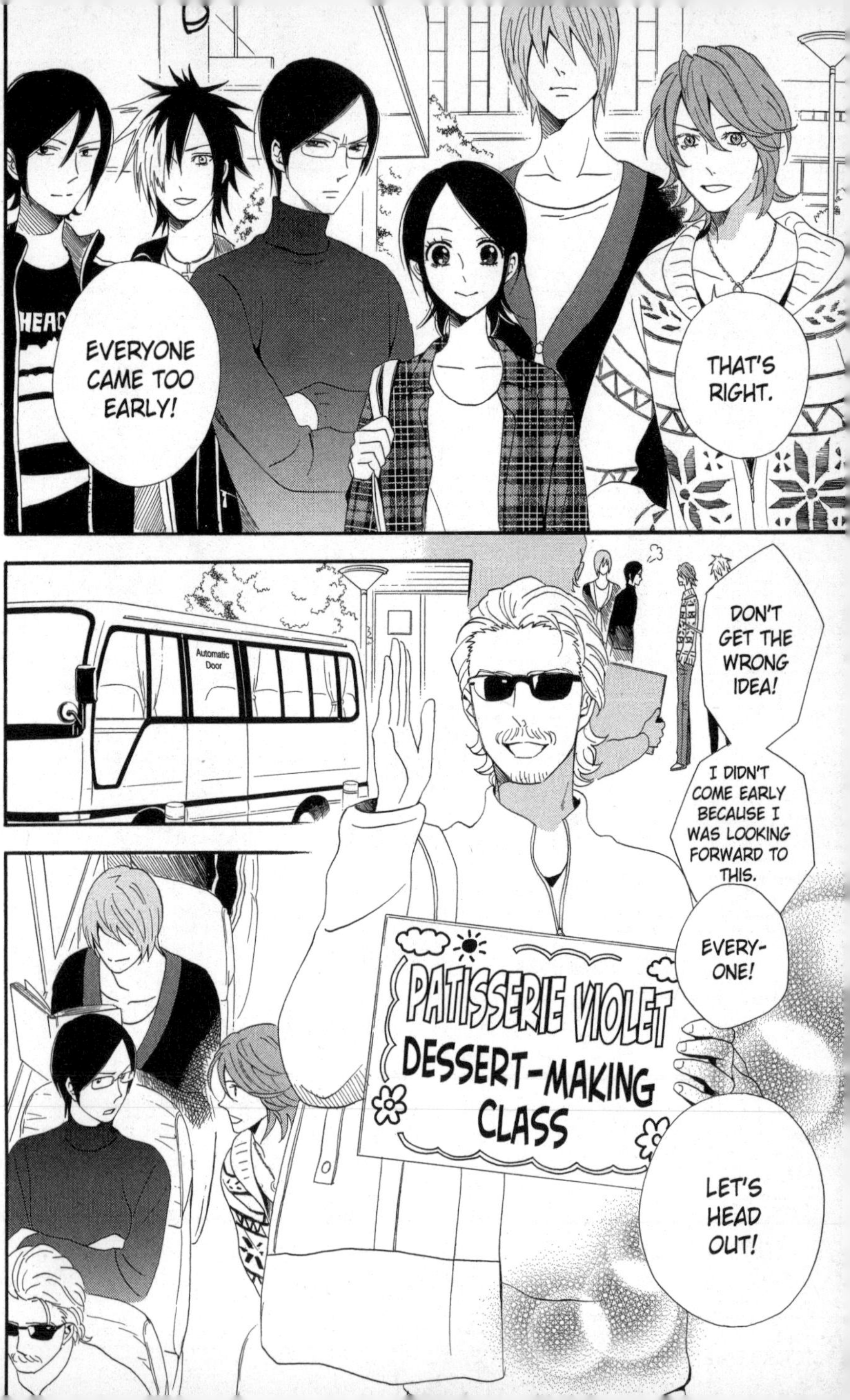
THAT'S RIGHT.
EVERYONE CAME TOO EARLY!
DON'T GET THE WRONG IDEA!
I DIDN'T COME EARLY BECAUSE I WAS LOOKING FORWARD TO THIS.
Automatic Door
EVERY-ONE!
LET'S HEAD OUT!
PATISSERIE VIOLET
DESSERT-MAKING CLASS

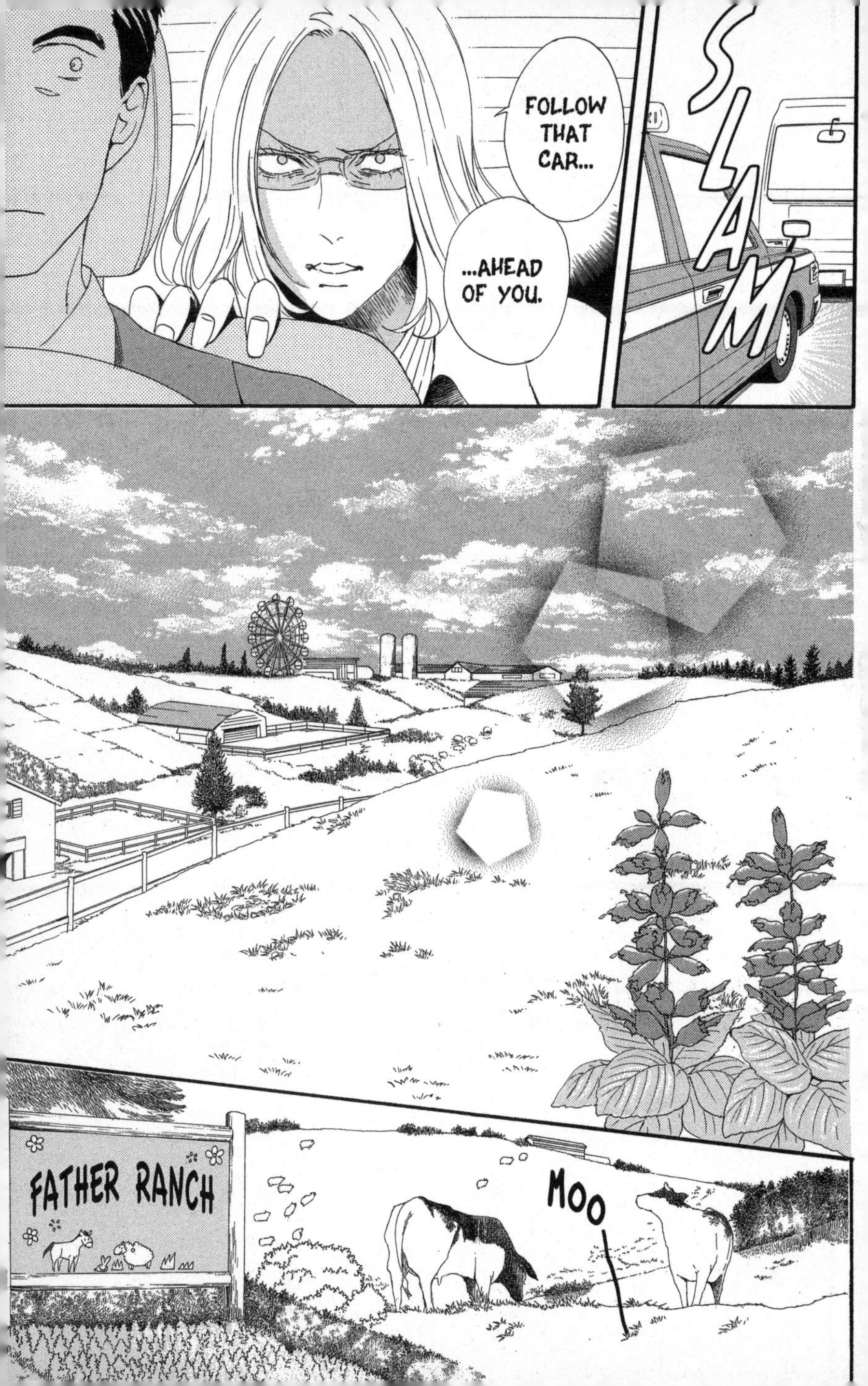
SLAM
FOLLOW THAT CAR...
...AHEAD OF YOU.
MOO
FATHER RANCH

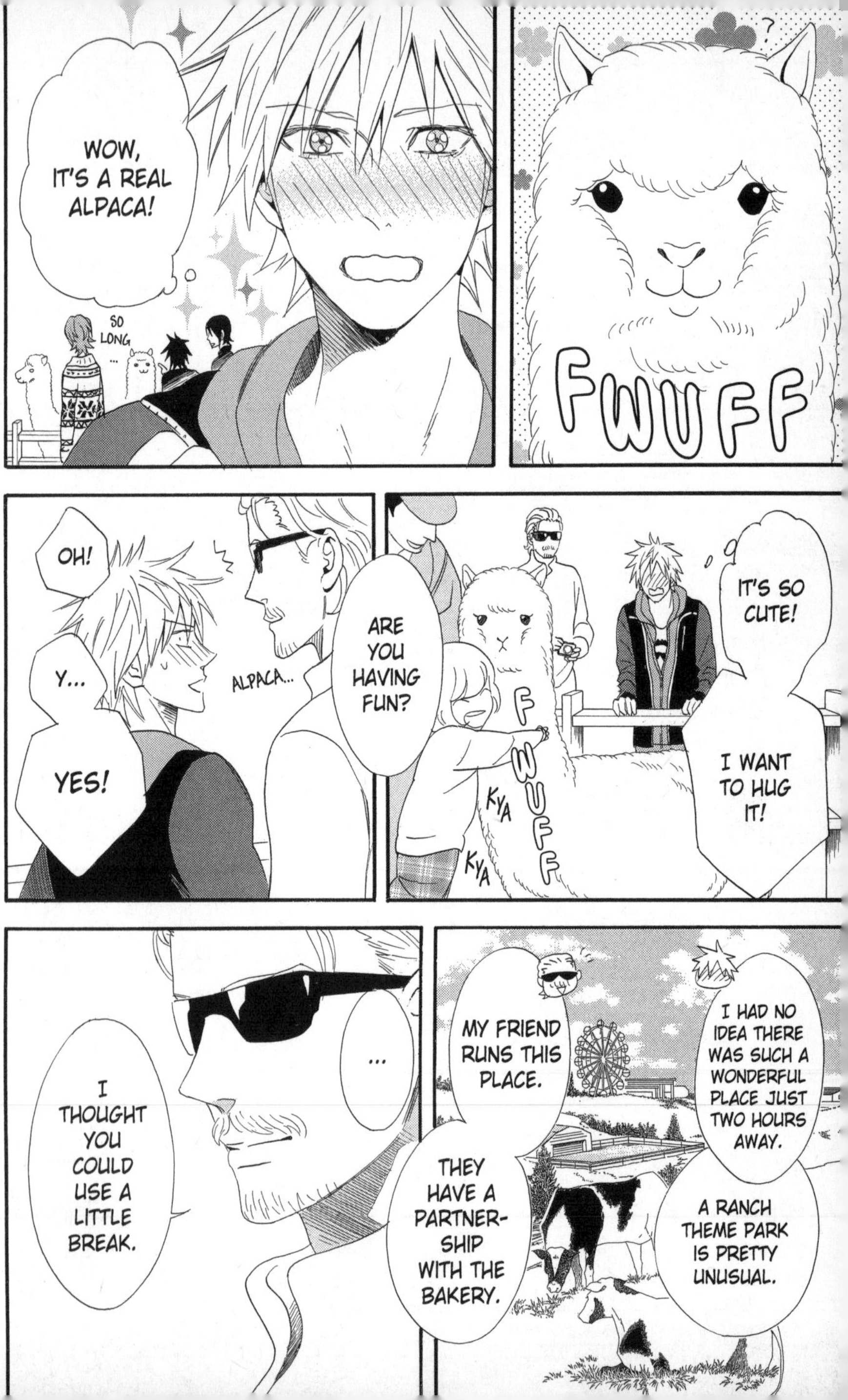
?
FWUFF
WOW, IT'S A REAL ALPACA!
SO LONG ...
IT'S SO CUTE!
I WANT TO HUG IT!
FWUFF
KYA
KYA
ARE YOU HAVING FUN?
OH!
Y...
YES!
ALPACA...
I HAD NO IDEA THERE WAS SUCH A WONDERFUL PLACE JUST TWO HOURS AWAY.
A RANCH THEME PARK IS PRETTY UNUSUAL.
MY FRIEND RUNS THIS PLACE.
THEY HAVE A PARTNER-SHIP WITH THE BAKERY.
...
I THOUGHT YOU COULD USE A LITTLE BREAK.

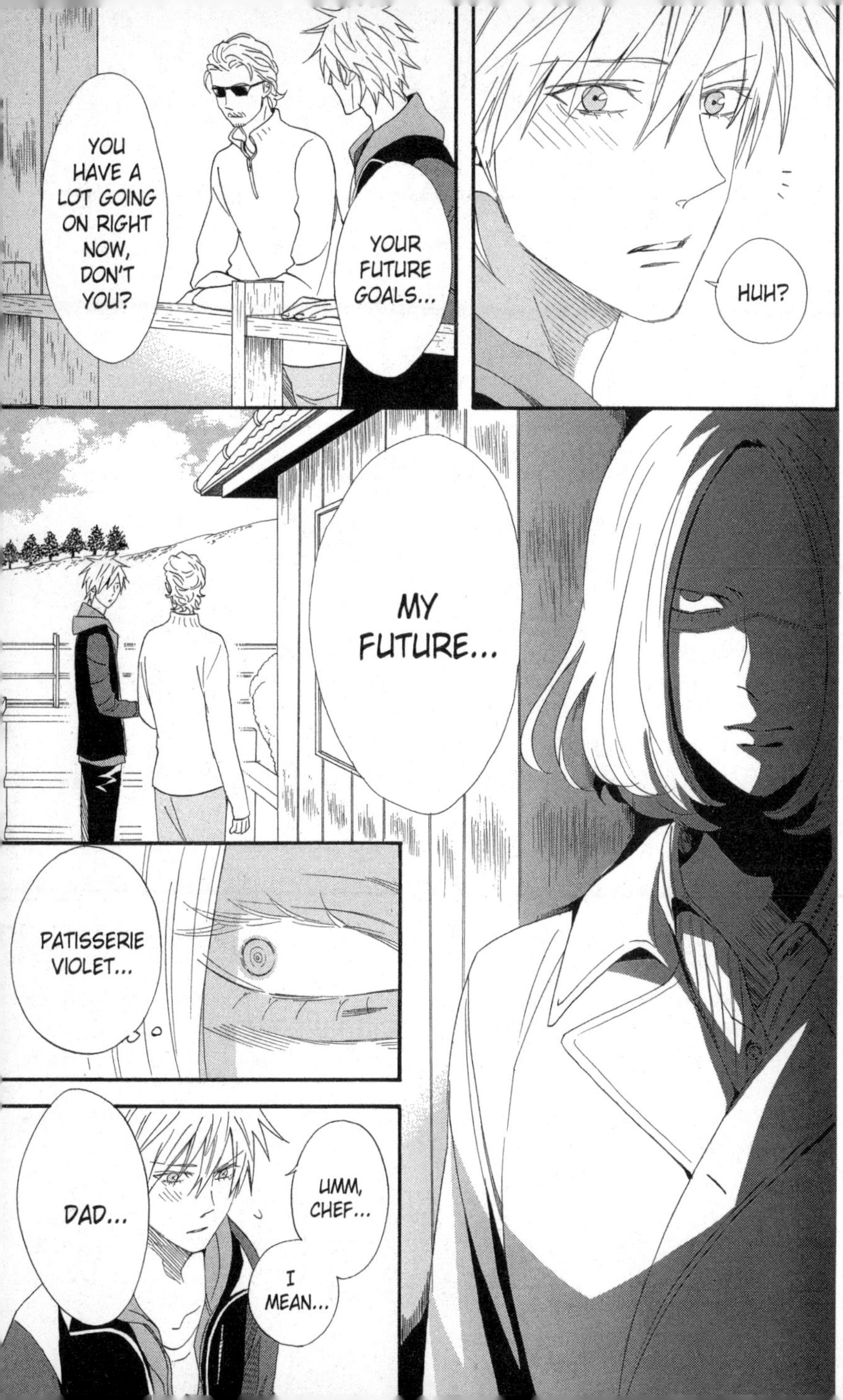
HUH?
YOUR FUTURE GOALS...
YOU HAVE A LOT GOING ON RIGHT NOW, DON'T YOU?
MY FUTURE...
PATISSERIE VIOLET...
UMM, CHEF...
I MEAN...
DAD...

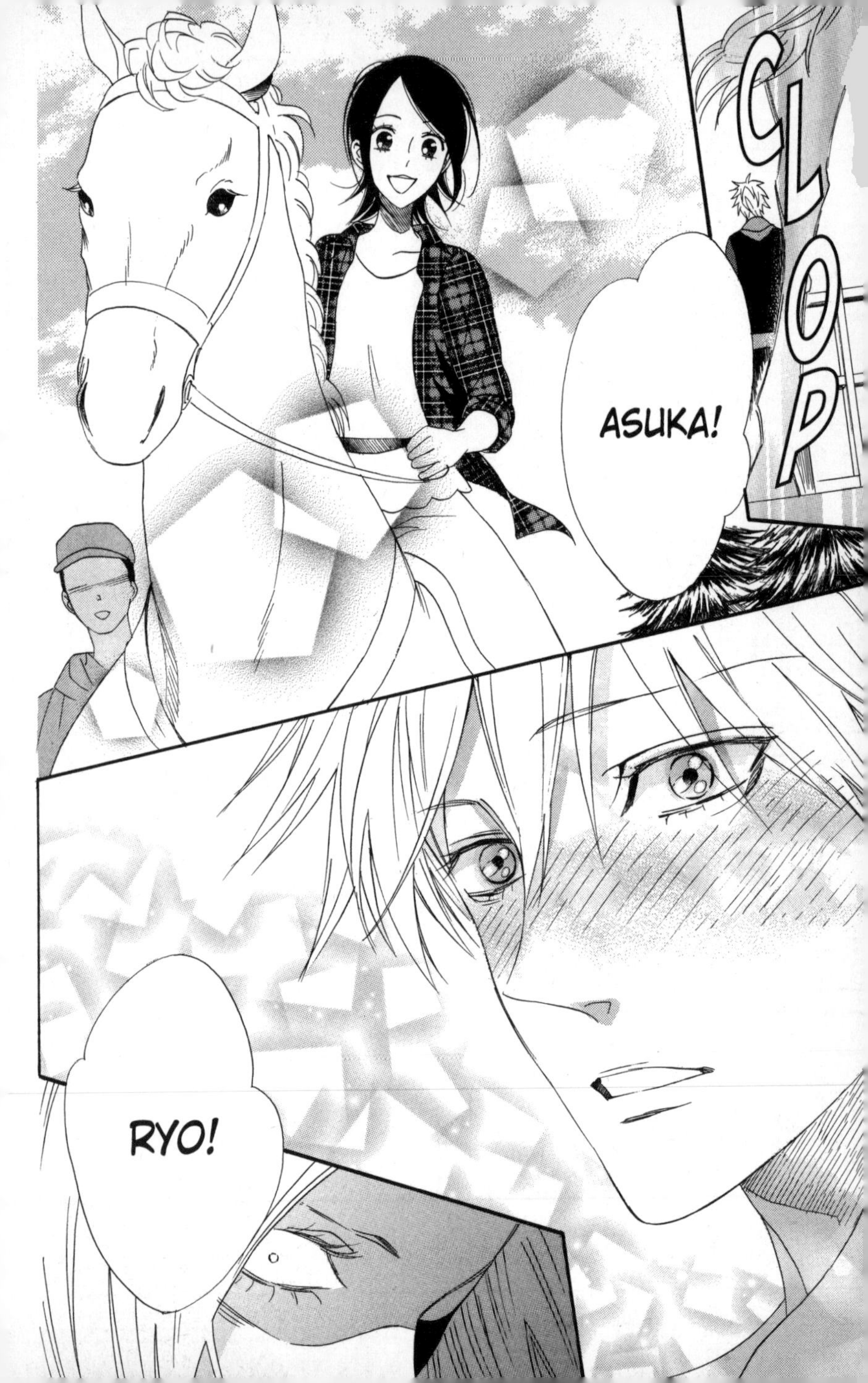
CLOP
ASUKA!
RYO!

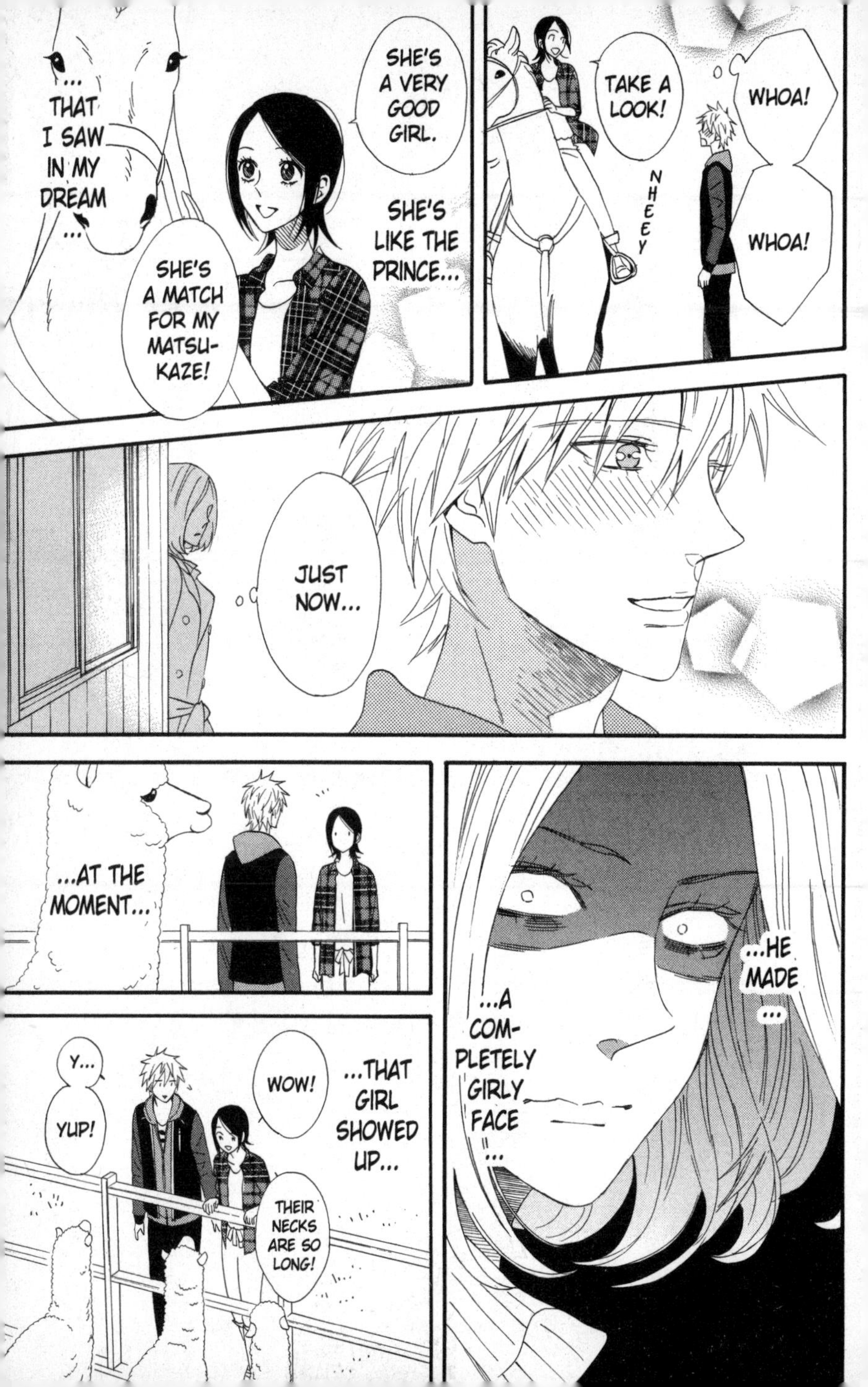
WHOA!
TAKE A LOOK!
NHEEY
WHOA!
SHE'S A VERY GOOD GIRL.
SHE'S LIKE THE PRINCE...
...THAT I SAW IN MY DREAM...
SHE'S A MATCH FOR MY MATSU-KAZE!
JUST NOW...
...HE MADE...
...A COM-PLETELY GIRLY FACE...
...AT THE MOMENT...
...THAT GIRL SHOWED UP...
WOW!
Y...
YUP!
THEIR NECKS ARE SO LONG!

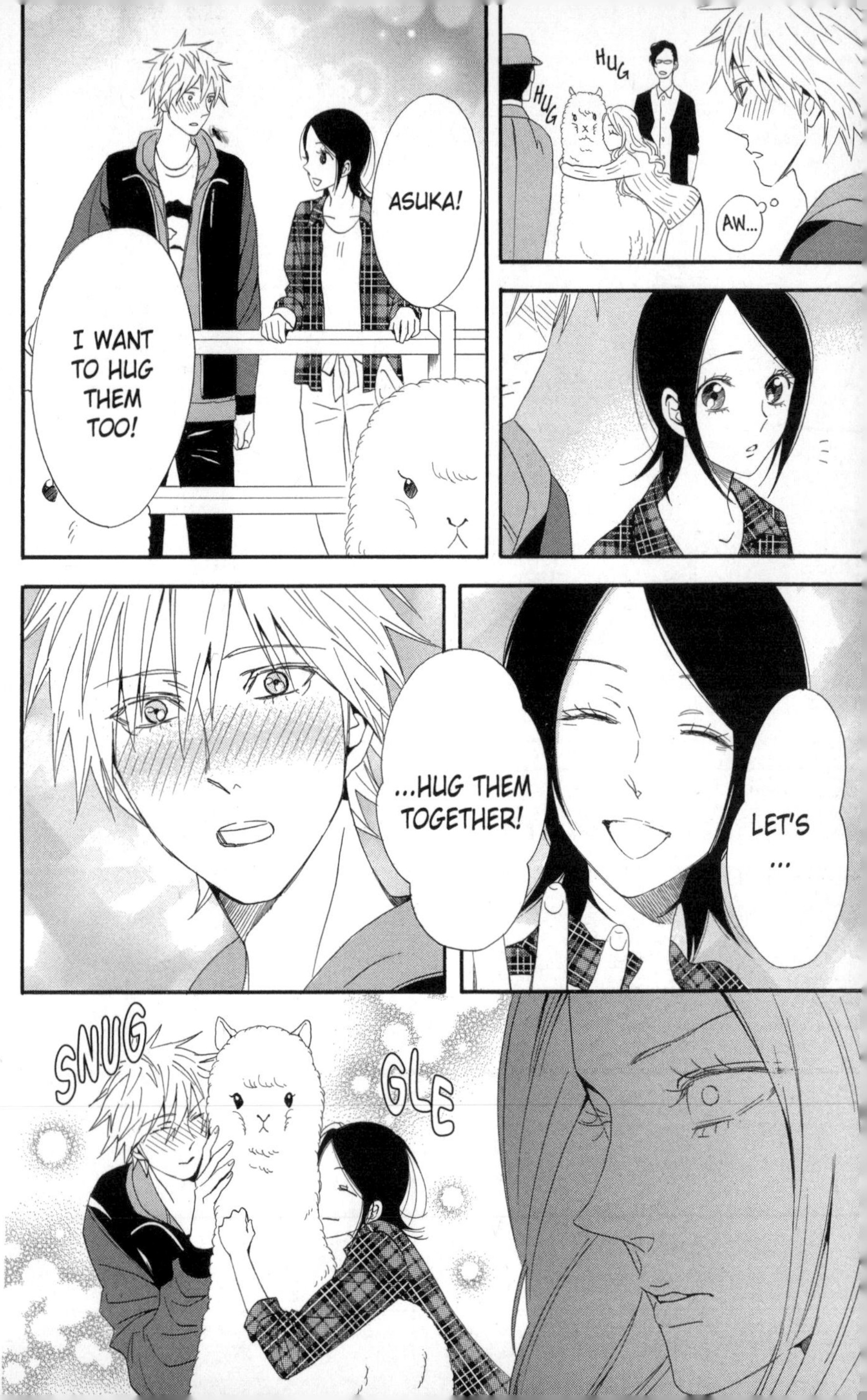
HUG
HUG
AW...
ASUKA!
I WANT TO HUG THEM TOO!
LET'S ...
...HUG THEM TOGETHER!
SNUG
GLE

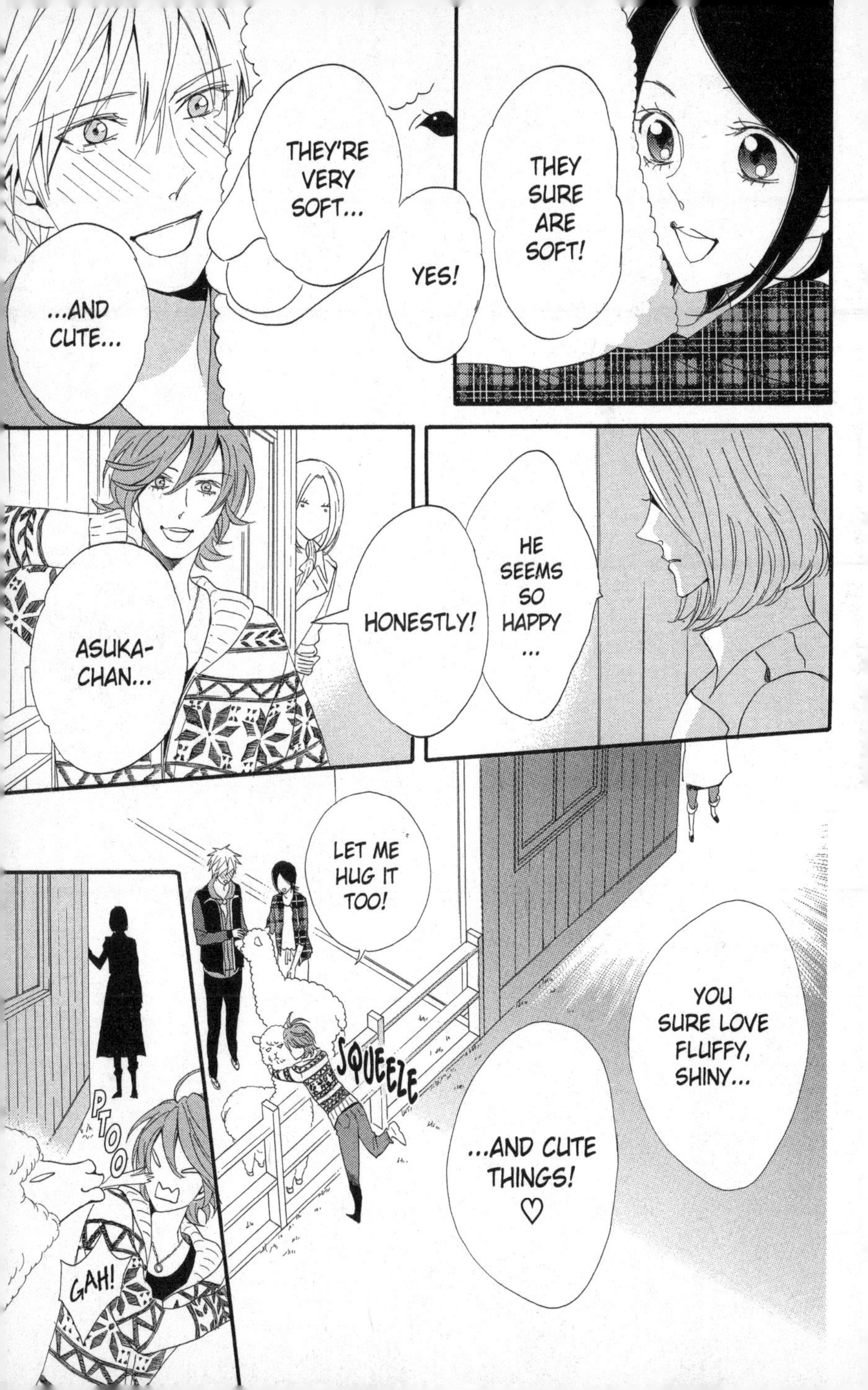
THEY SURE ARE SOFT!
THEY'RE VERY SOFT...
YES!
...AND CUTE...
HE SEEMS SO HAPPY ...
HONESTLY!
ASUKA-CHAN...
YOU SURE LOVE FLUFFY, SHINY...
...AND CUTE THINGS! ♡
LET ME HUG IT TOO!
SQUEEZE
PTOO
GAH!

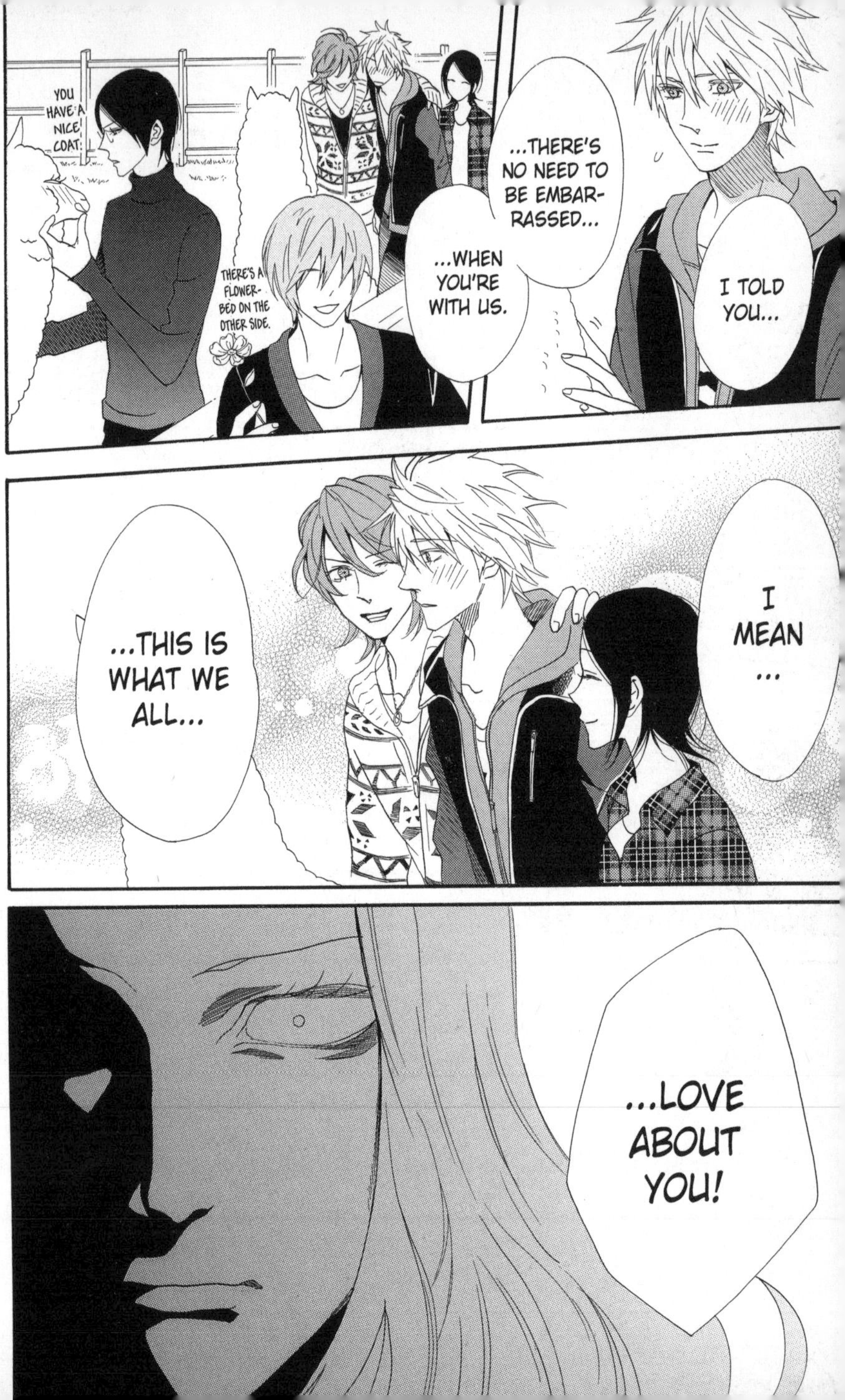
I TOLD YOU...
...THERE'S NO NEED TO BE EMBARRASSED...
...WHEN YOU'RE WITH US.
YOU HAVE A NICE COAT.
THERE'S A FLOWERBED ON THE OTHER SIDE.
I MEAN...
...THIS IS WHAT WE ALL...
...LOVE ABOUT YOU!

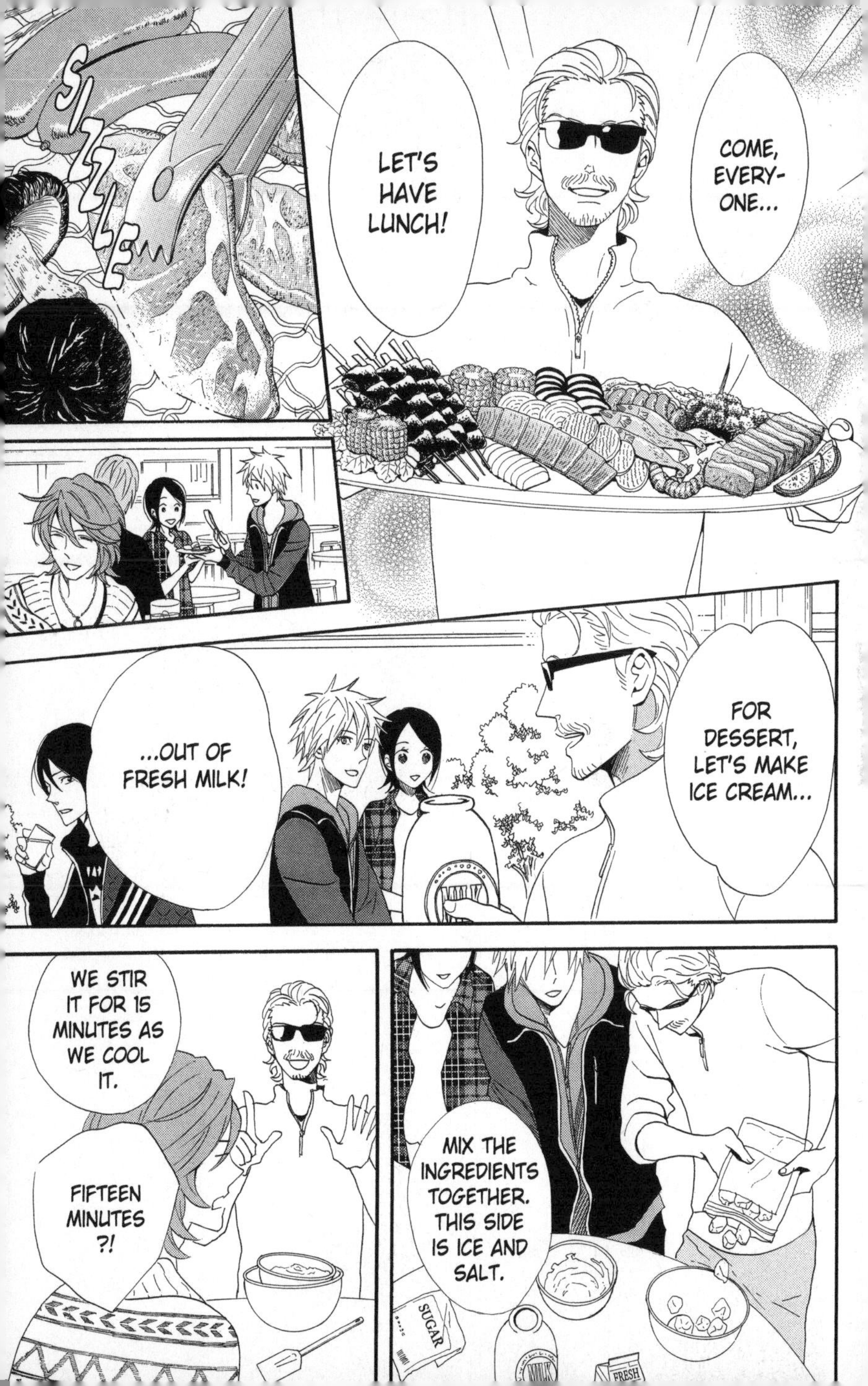
COME, EVERY-ONE...
LET'S HAVE LUNCH!
SIZZLE
FOR DESSERT, LET'S MAKE ICE CREAM...
...OUT OF FRESH MILK!
MIX THE INGREDIENTS TOGETHER. THIS SIDE IS ICE AND SALT.
SUGAR
FRESH
WE STIR IT FOR 15 MINUTES AS WE COOL IT.
FIFTEEN MINUTES ?!

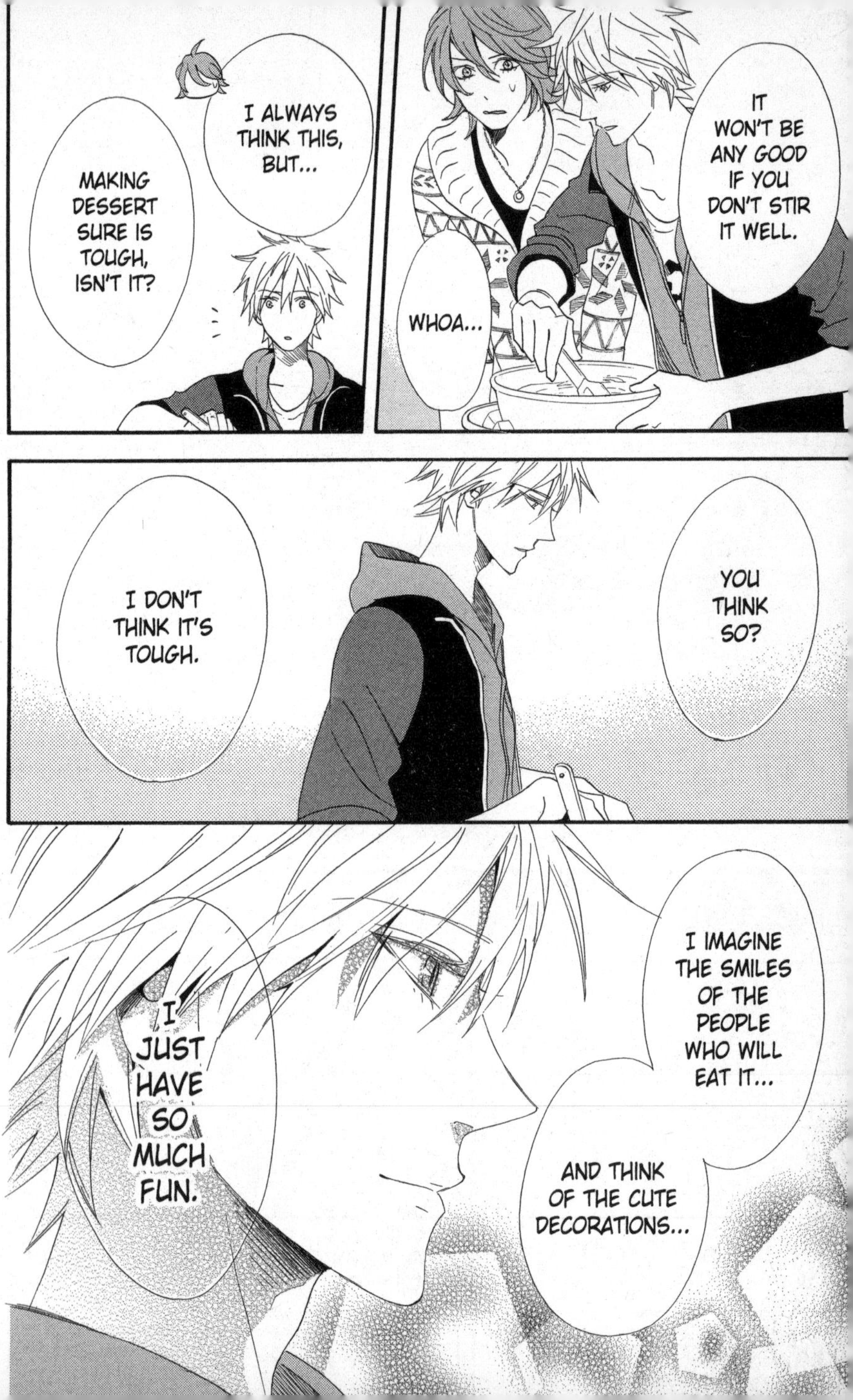
IT WON'T BE ANY GOOD IF YOU DON'T STIR IT WELL.
WHOA...
I ALWAYS THINK THIS, BUT...
MAKING DESSERT SURE IS TOUGH, ISN'T IT?
YOU THINK SO?
I DON'T THINK IT'S TOUGH.
I IMAGINE THE SMILES OF THE PEOPLE WHO WILL EAT IT...
AND THINK OF THE CUTE DECORATIONS...
I JUST HAVE SO MUCH FUN.

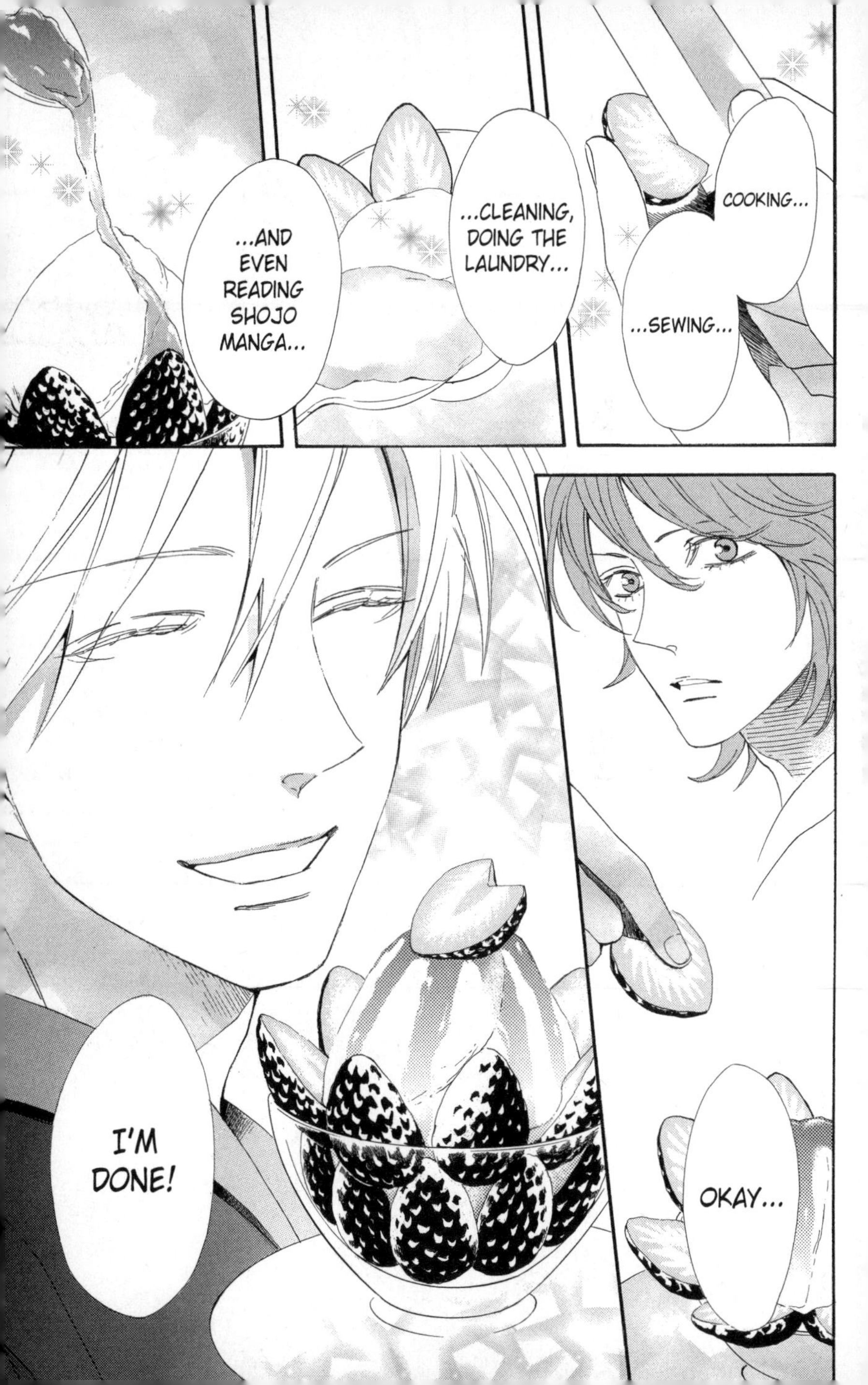

COOKING...
...SEWING...
...CLEANING, DOING THE LAUNDRY...
...AND EVEN READING SHOJO MANGA...
OKAY...
I'M DONE!

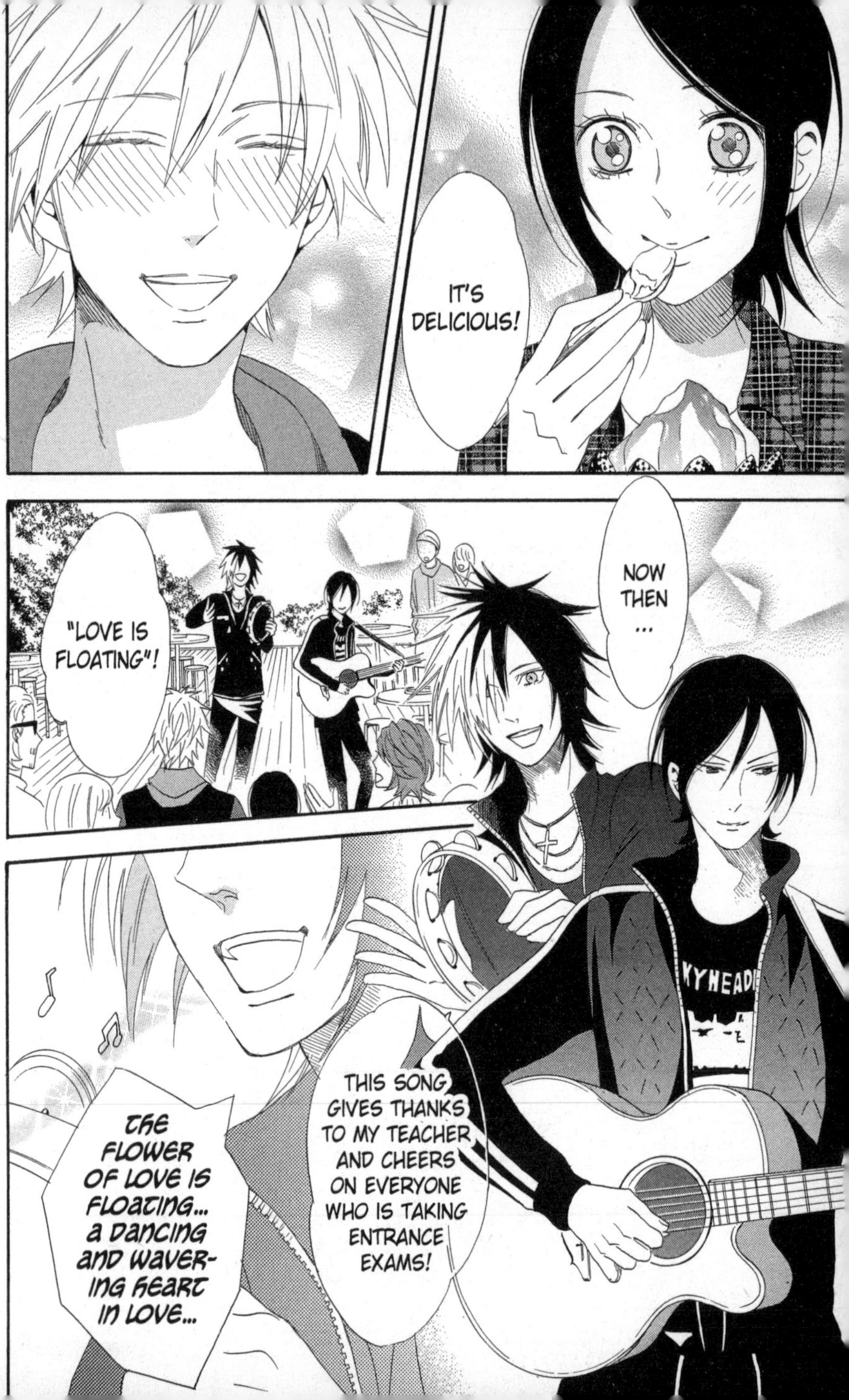
IT'S DELICIOUS!
NOW THEN ...
"LOVE IS FLOATING"!
THIS SONG GIVES THANKS TO MY TEACHER AND CHEERS ON EVERYONE WHO IS TAKING ENTRANCE EXAMS!
THE FLOWER OF LOVE IS FLOATING... A DANCING AND WAVER-ING HEART IN LOVE...

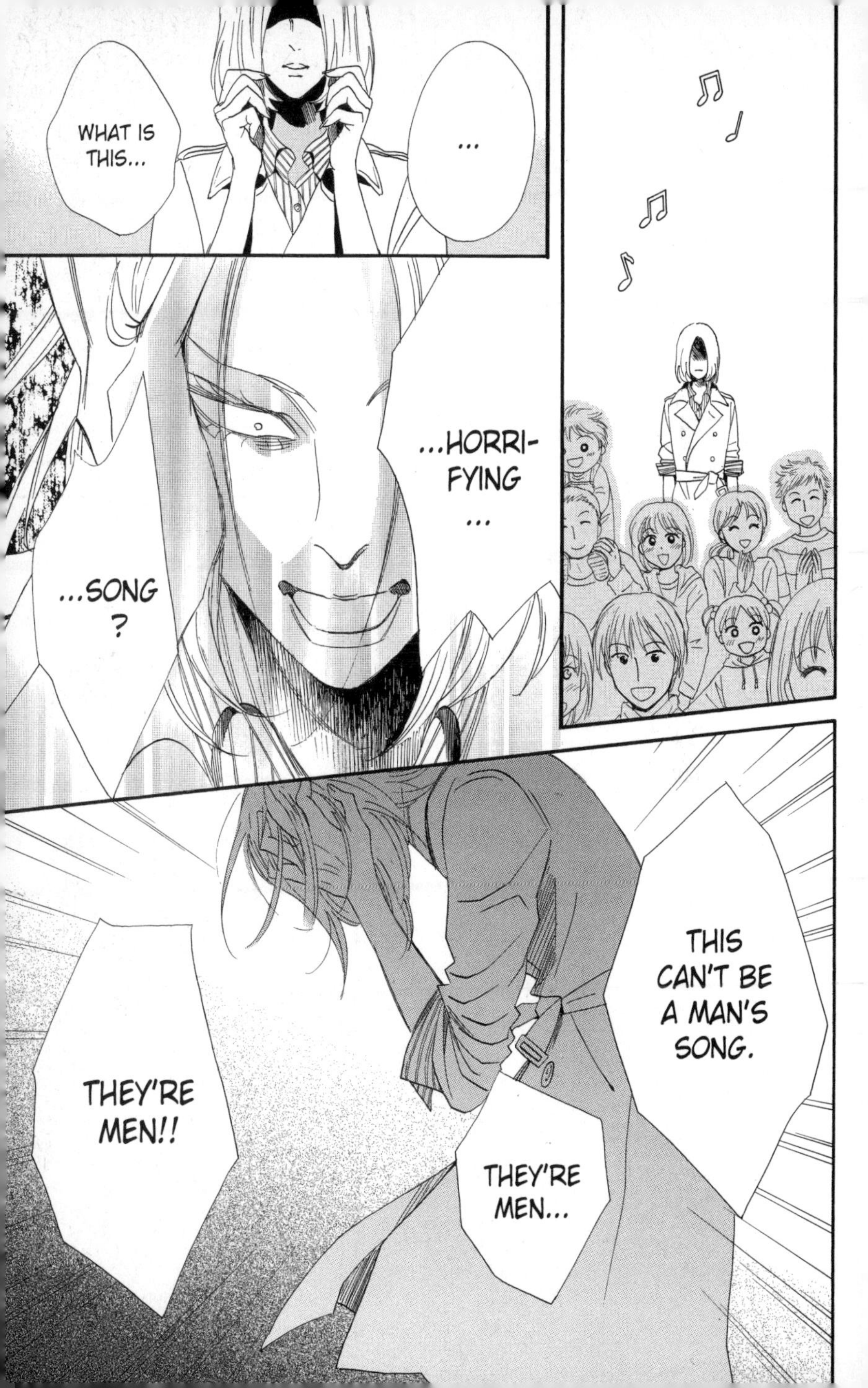
...
WHAT IS THIS...
...HORRI-FYING...
...SONG?
THIS CAN'T BE A MAN'S SONG.
THEY'RE MEN...
THEY'RE MEN!!

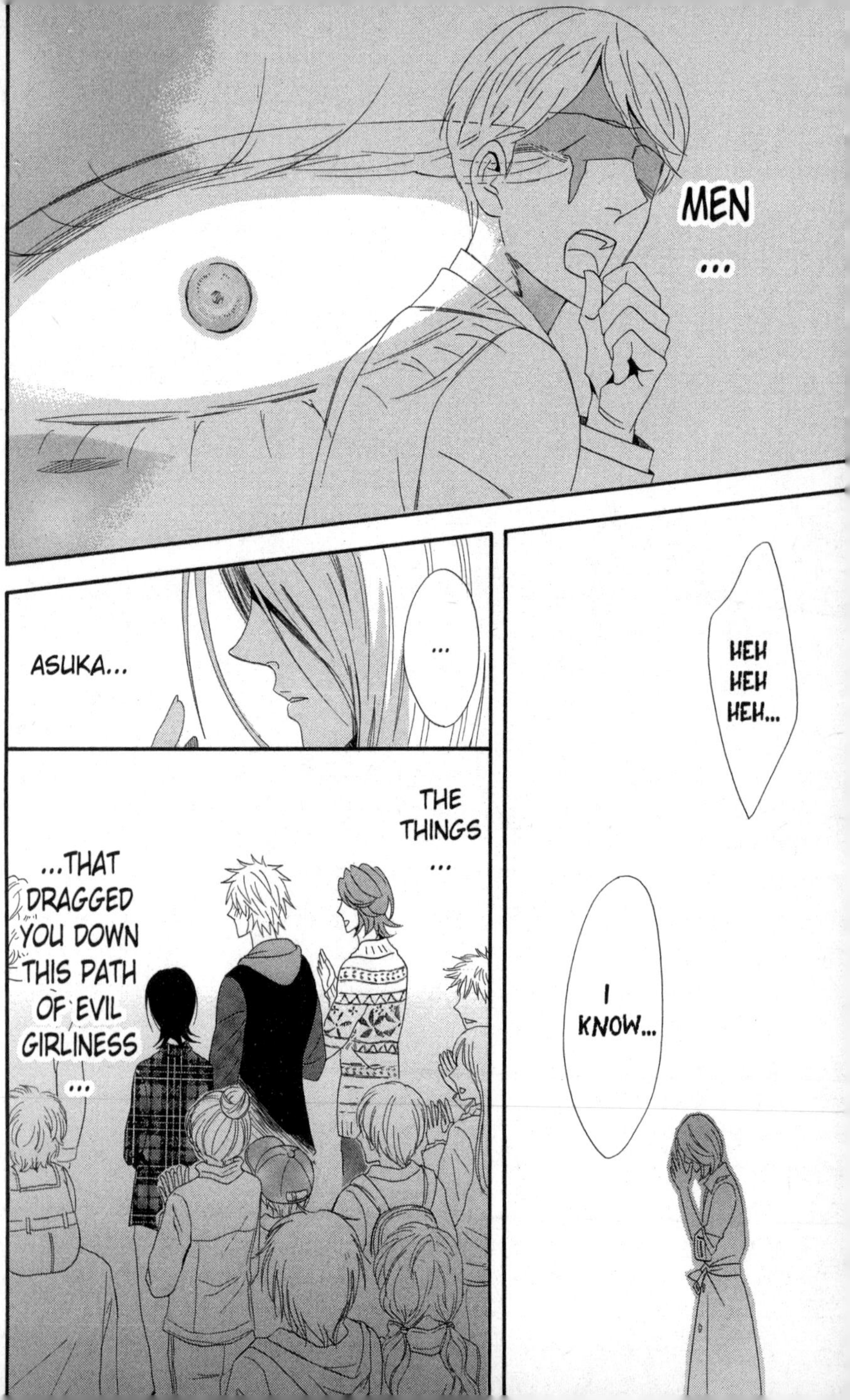
MEN...
HEH HEH HEH...
I KNOW...
...
ASUKA...
THE THINGS...
...THAT DRAGGED YOU DOWN THIS PATH OF EVIL GIRLINESS...

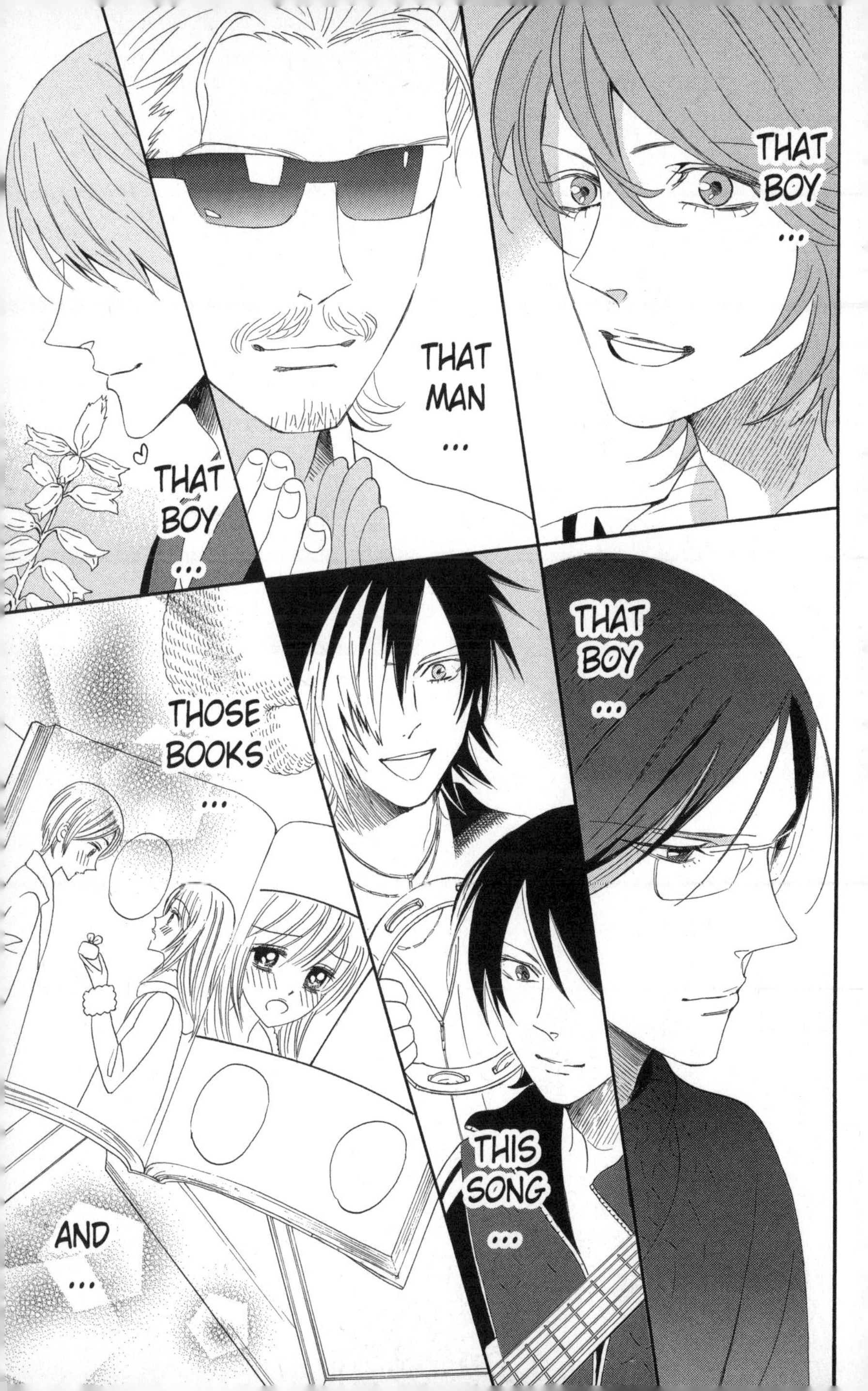
THAT BOY ...
THAT MAN ...
THAT BOY ...
THAT BOY ...
THIS SONG ...
THOSE BOOKS ...
AND ...

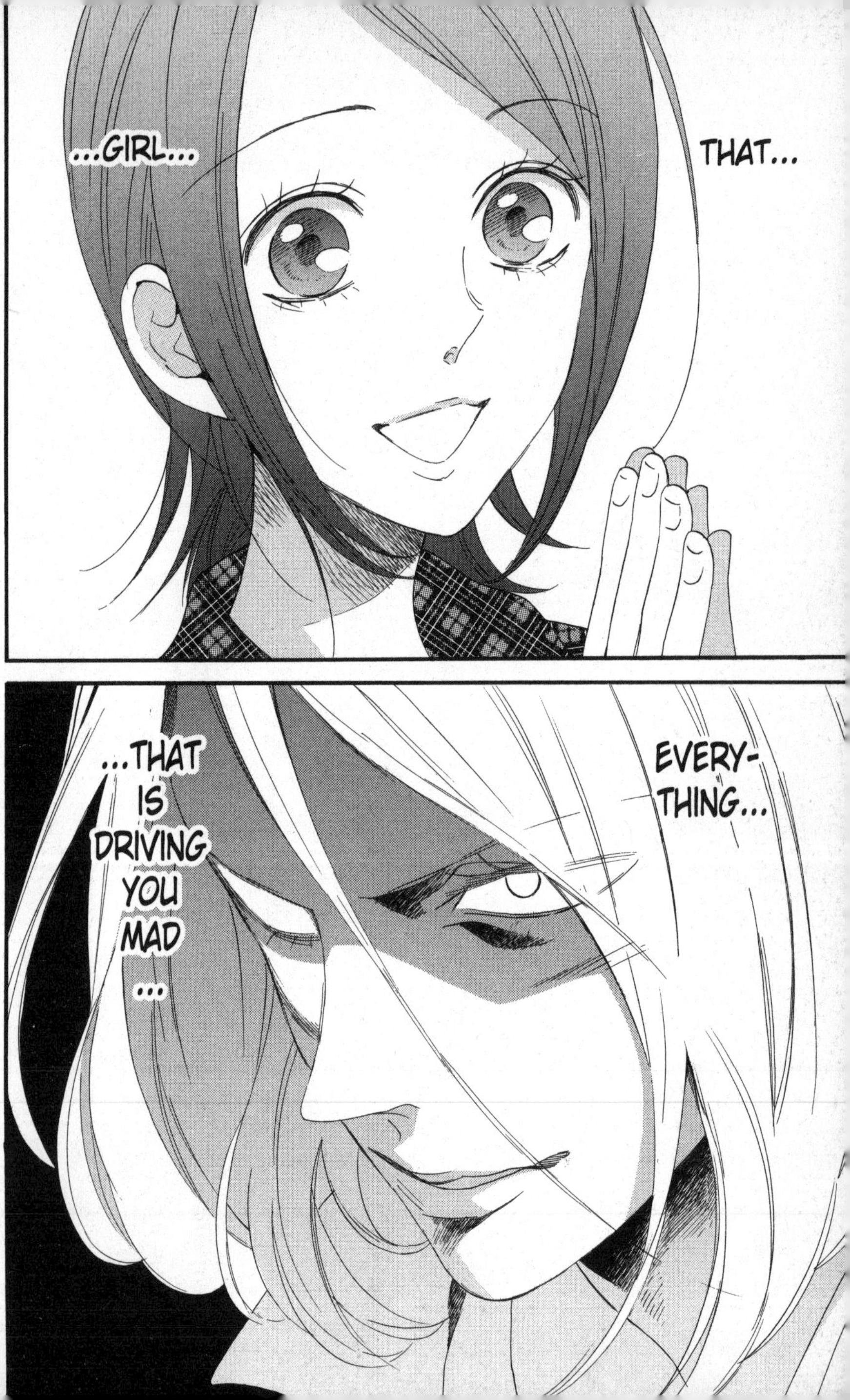
THAT...
...GIRL...
EVERY-THING...
...THAT IS DRIVING YOU MAD ...

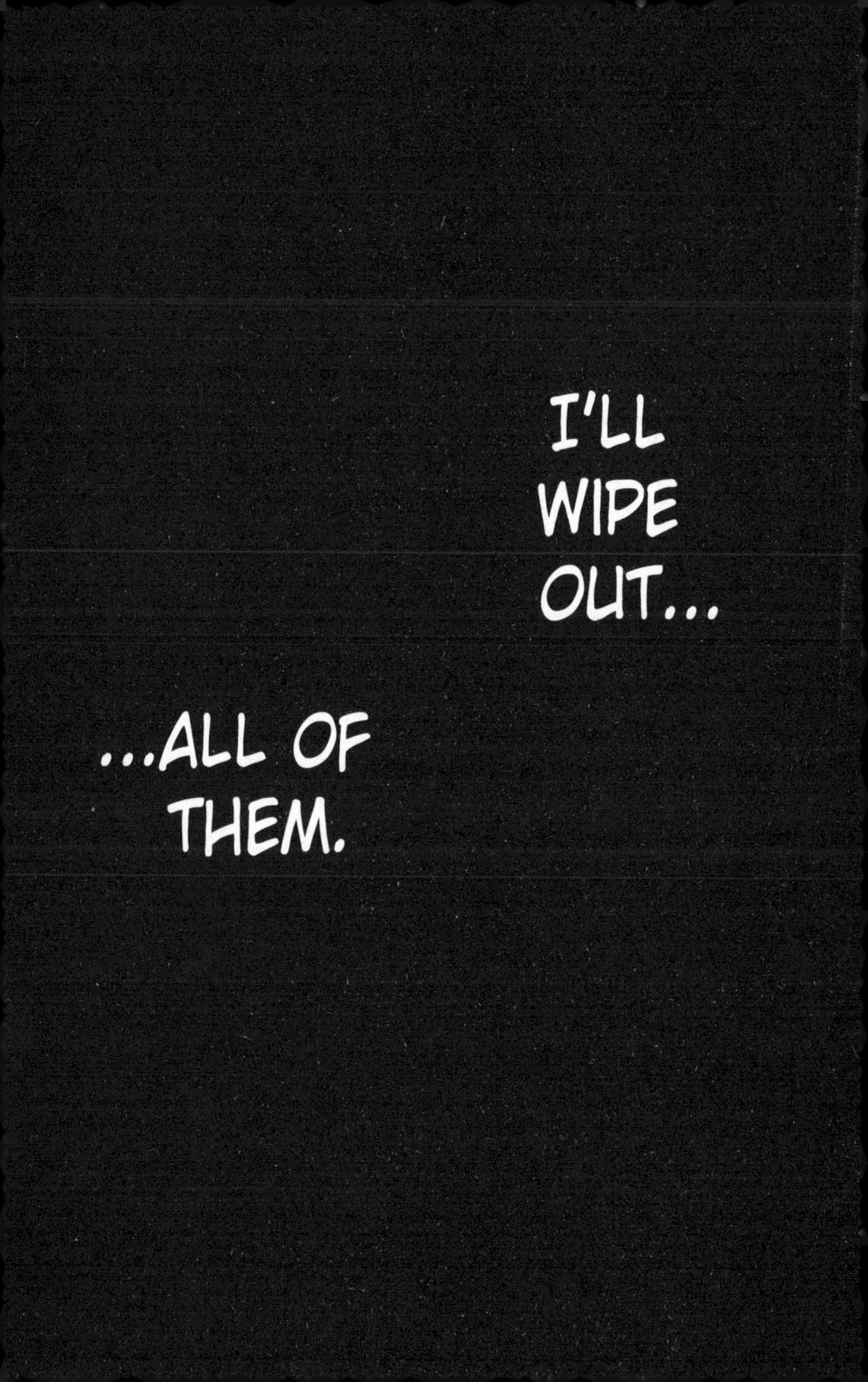
I'LL WIPE OUT...
...ALL OF THEM.

OTOMEN

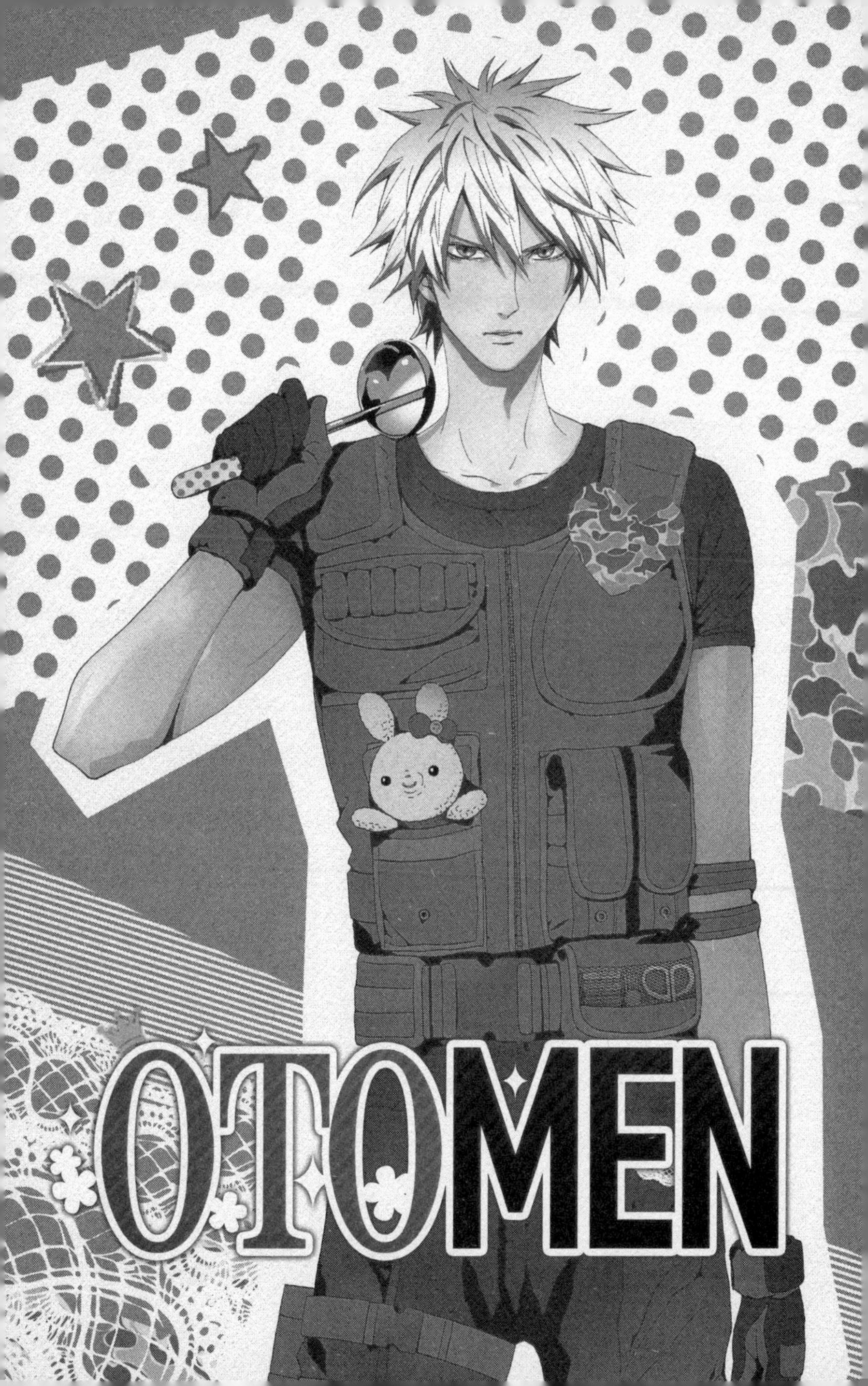
OTOMEN

OTOMEN

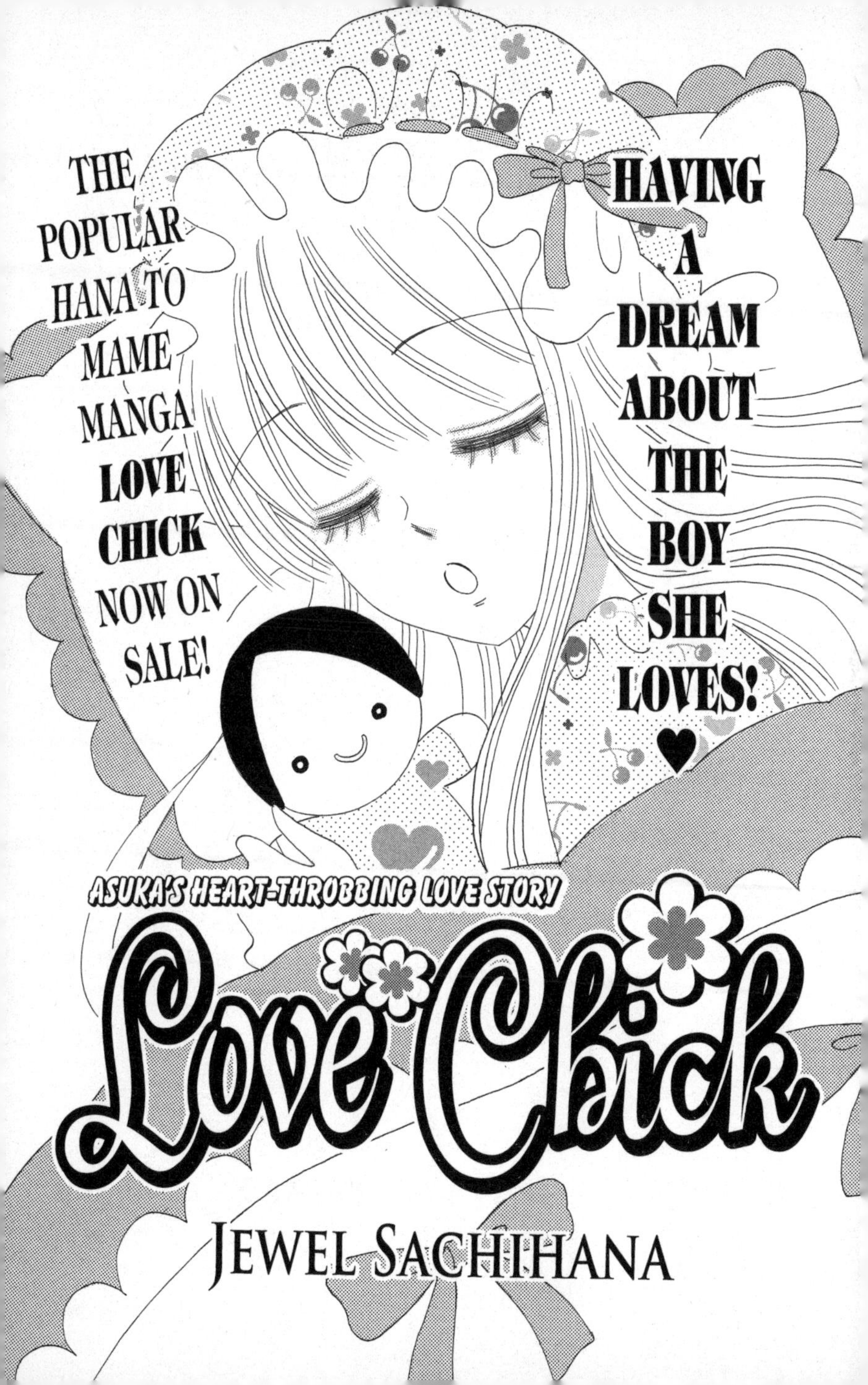
THE POPULAR HANA TO MAME MANGA LOVE CHICK NOW ON SALE!
HAVING A DREAM ABOUT THE BOY SHE LOVES! ♥
ASUKA'S HEART-THROBBING LOVE STORY
Love Chick
JEWEL SACHIHANA

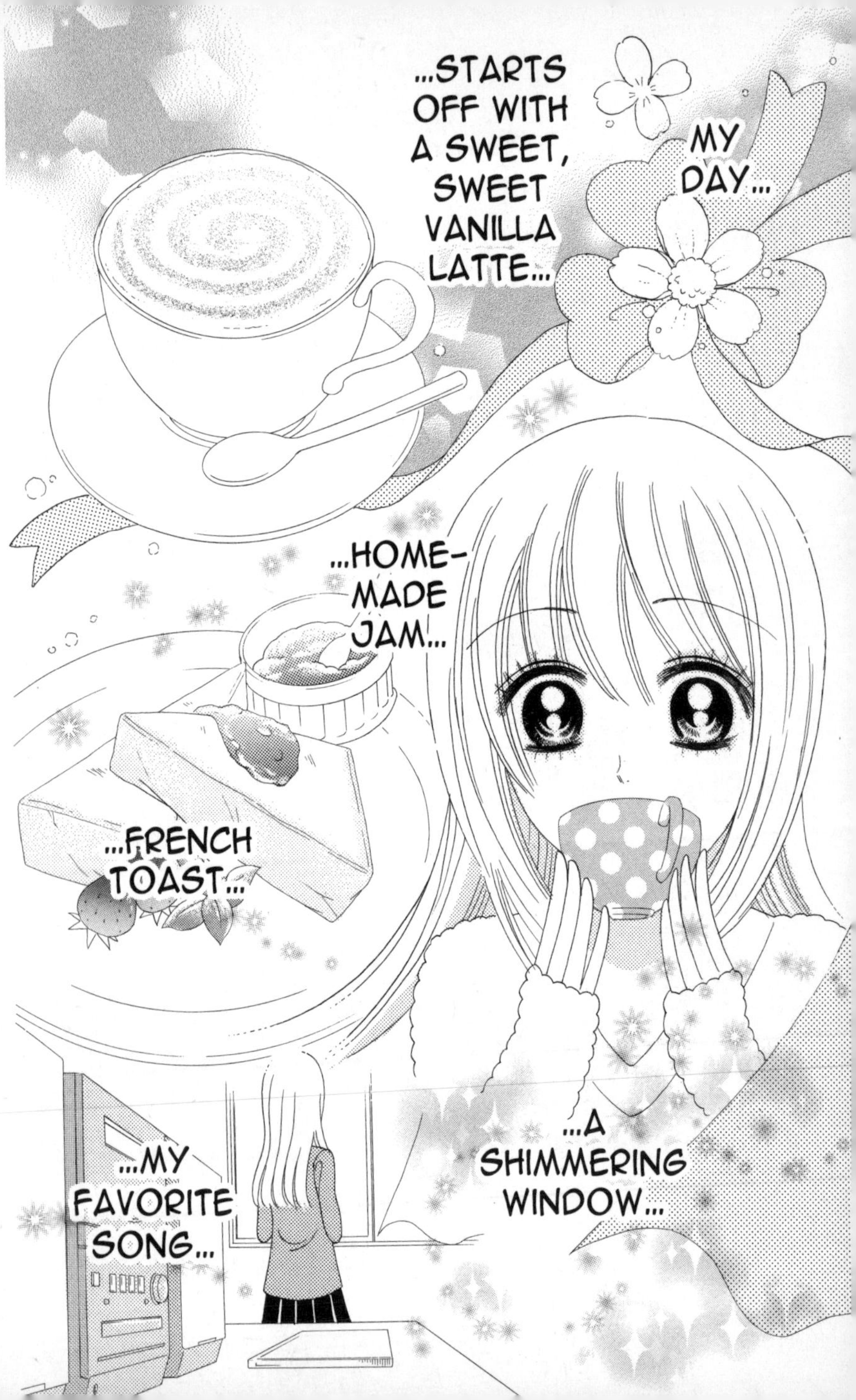
MY DAY...
...STARTS OFF WITH A SWEET, SWEET VANILLA LATTE...
...HOME-MADE JAM...
...FRENCH TOAST...
...A SHIMMERING WINDOW...
...MY FAVORITE SONG...

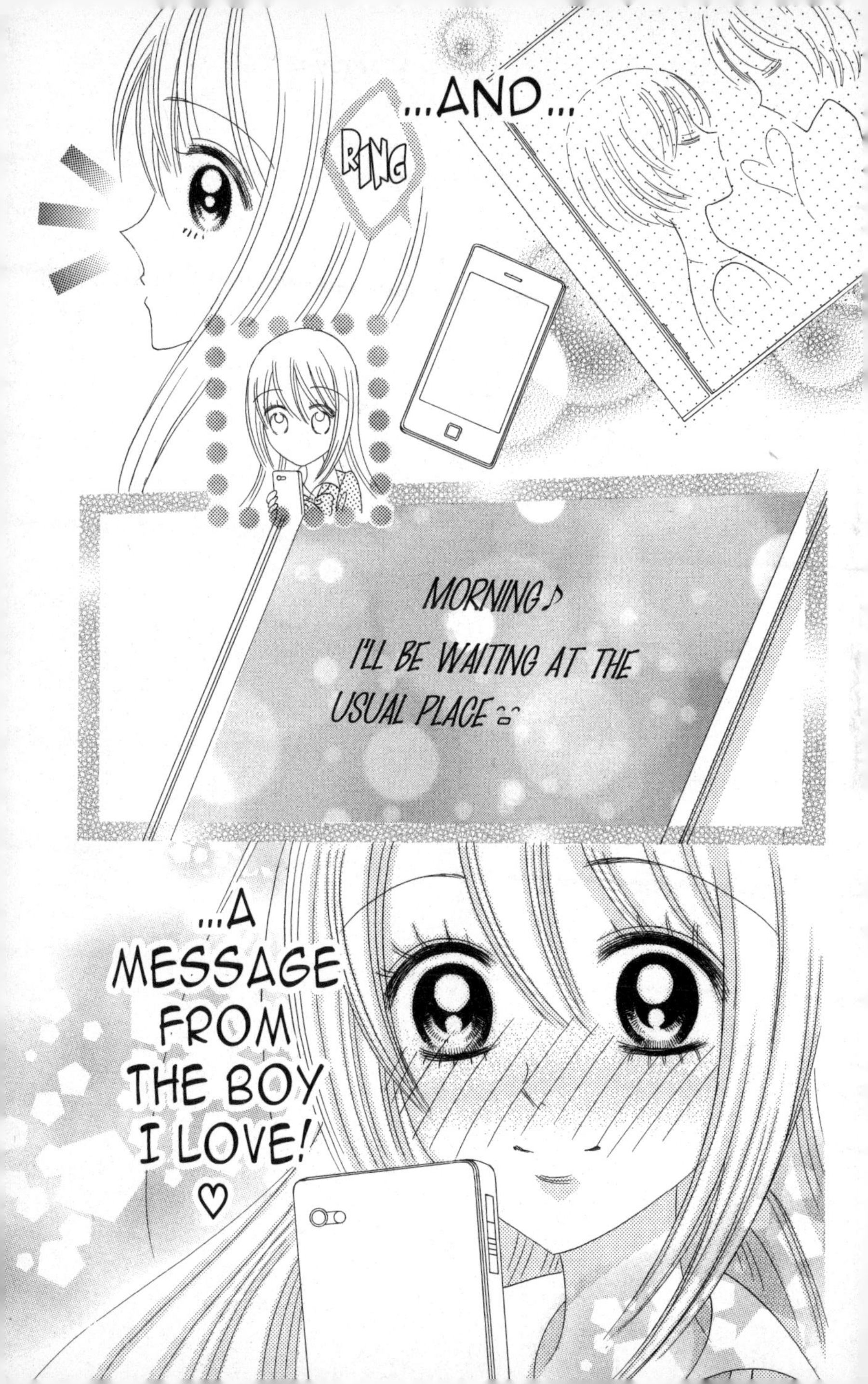
...AND...
RING
MORNING♪
I'LL BE WAITING AT THE USUAL PLACE
...A MESSAGE FROM THE BOY I LOVE! ♡

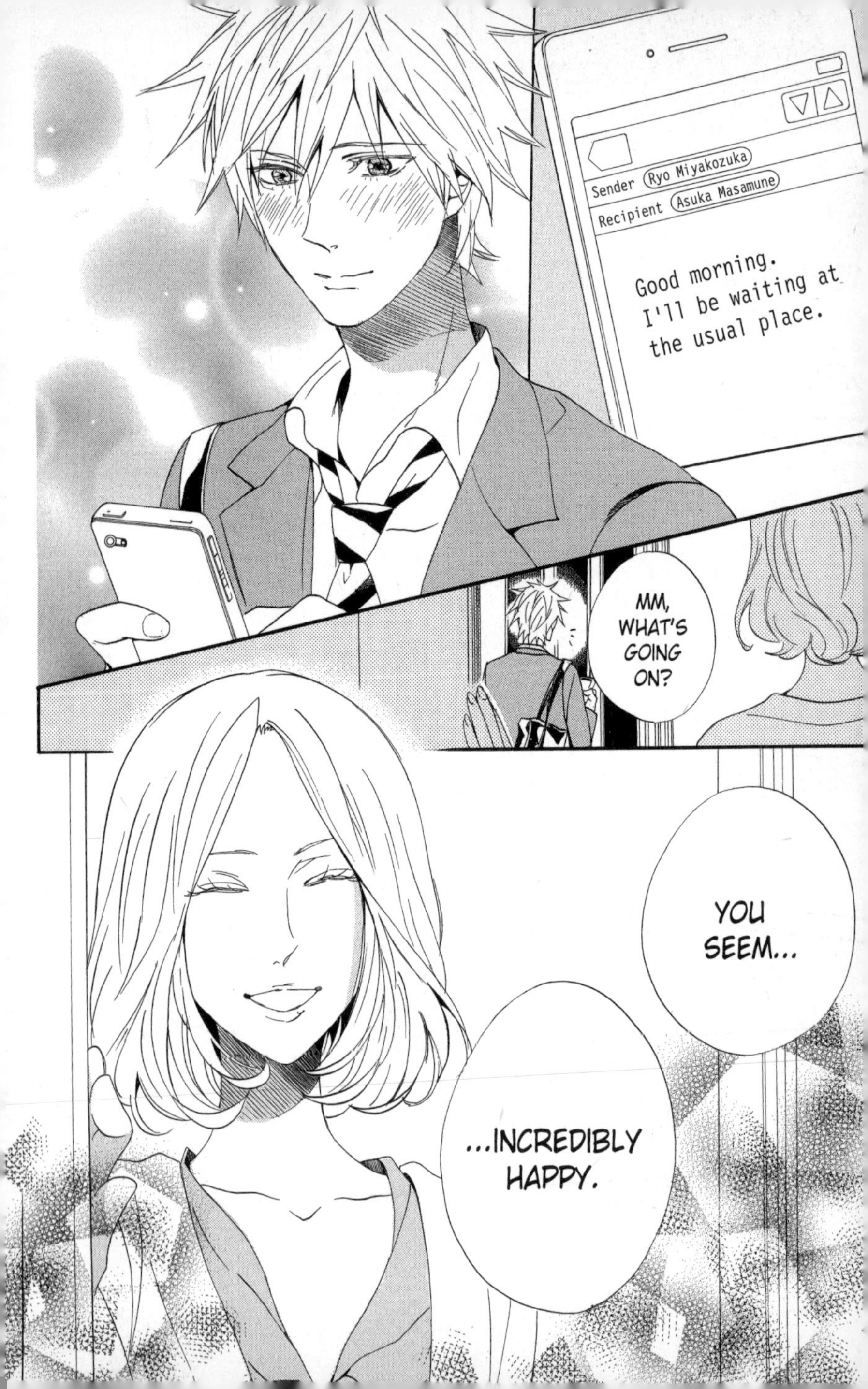
Sender Ryo Miyakozuka
Recipient Asuka Masamune
Good morning. I'll be waiting at the usual place.
MM, WHAT'S GOING ON?
YOU SEEM...
...INCREDIBLY HAPPY.

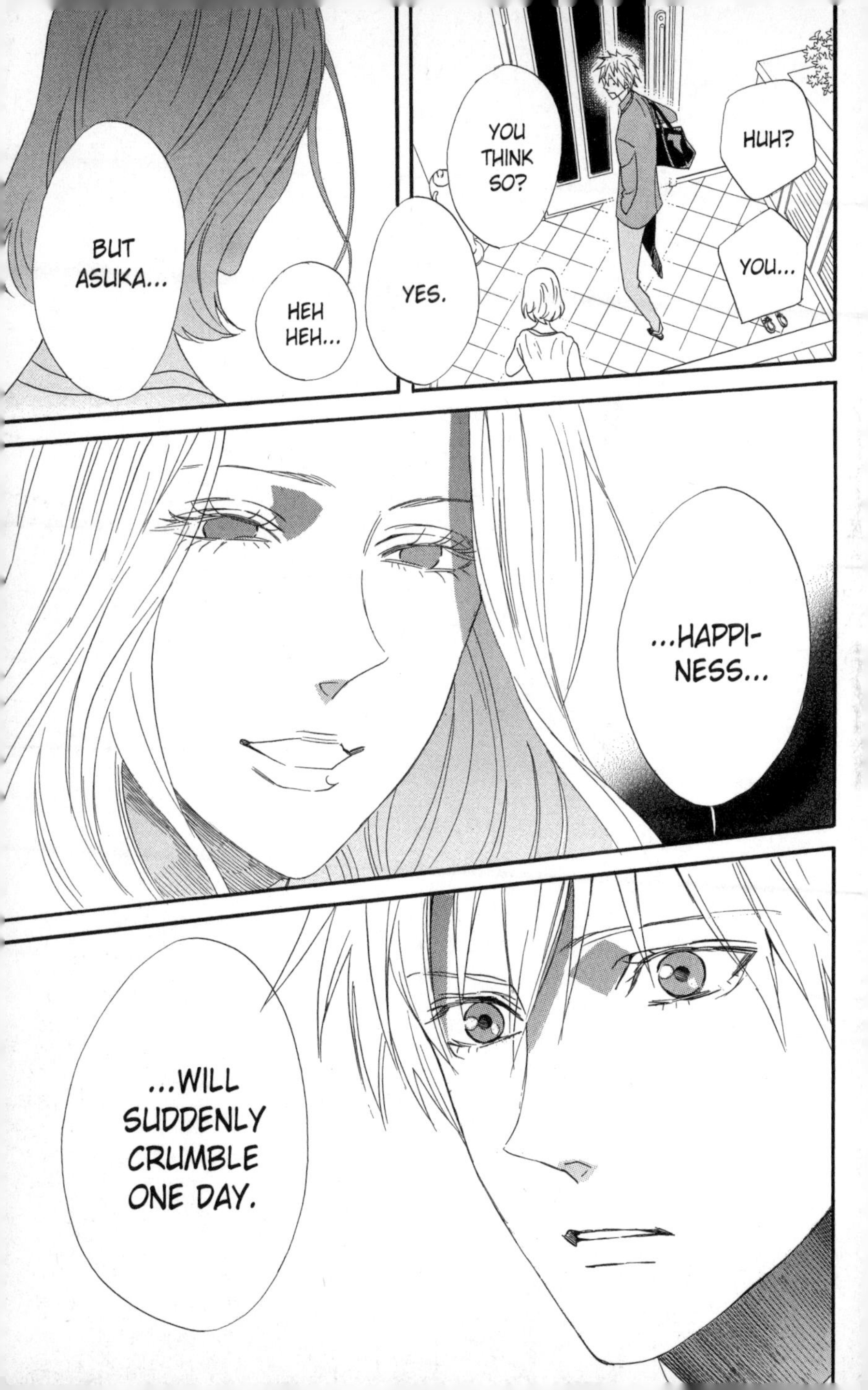
HUH?
YOU...
YOU THINK SO?
YES.
HEH HEH...
BUT ASUKA...
...HAPPINESS...
...WILL SUDDENLY CRUMBLE ONE DAY.

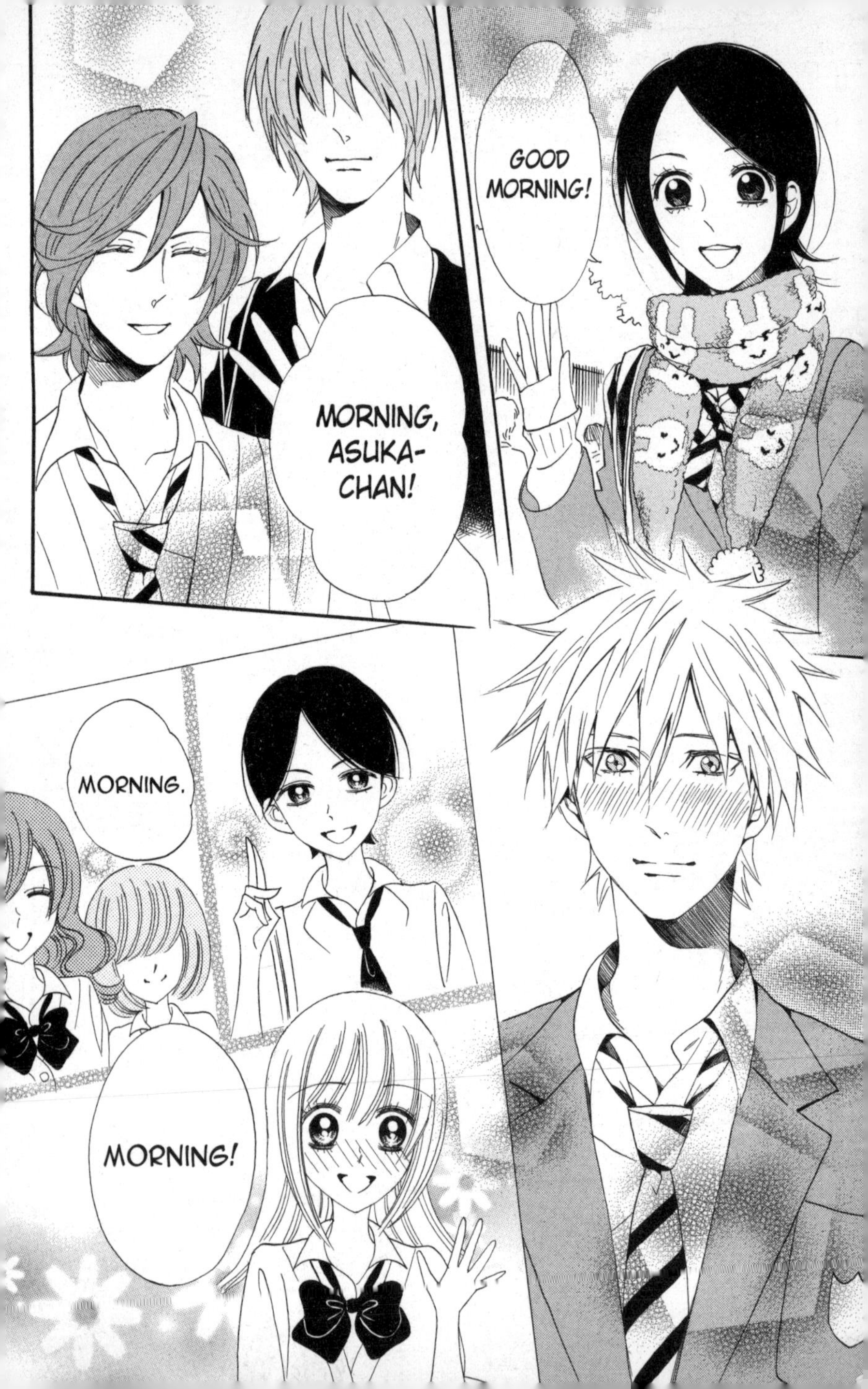
GOOD MORNING!
MORNING, ASUKA-CHAN!
MORNING.
MORNING!

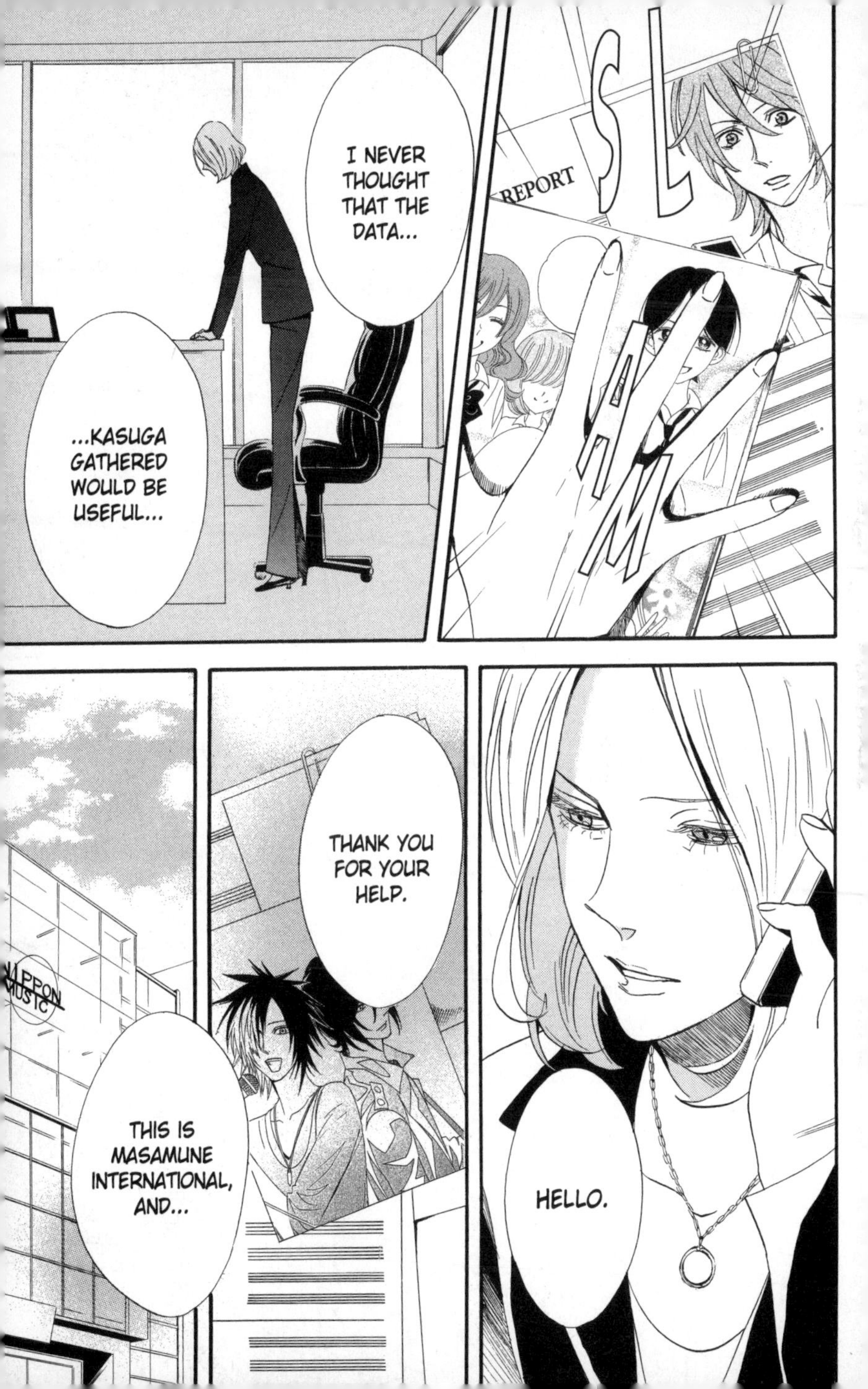
REPORT
I NEVER THOUGHT THAT THE DATA...
...KASUGA GATHERED WOULD BE USEFUL...
HELLO.
THANK YOU FOR YOUR HELP.
THIS IS MASAMUNE INTERNATIONAL, AND...

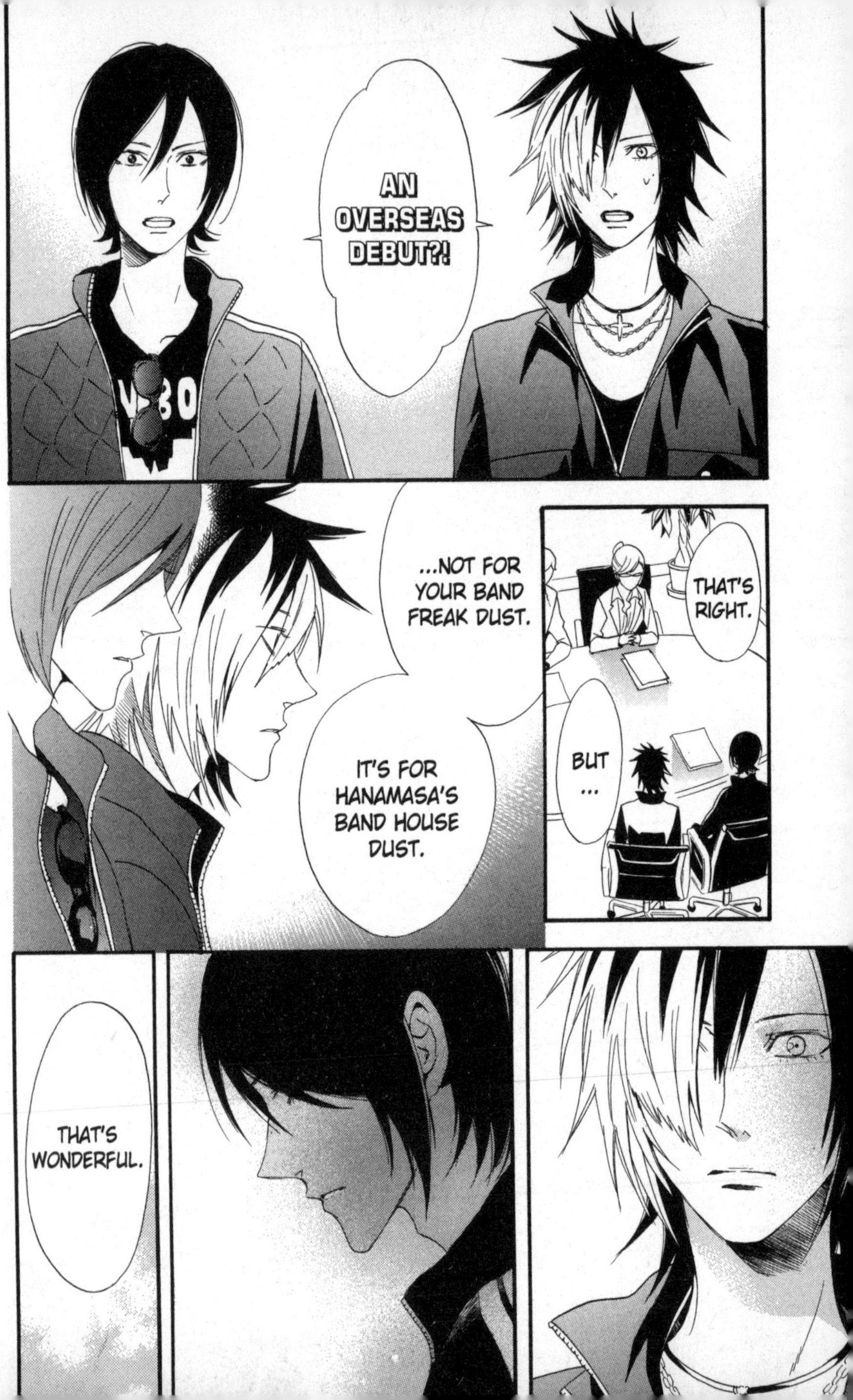
AN OVERSEAS DEBUT?!
THAT'S RIGHT.
BUT ...
...NOT FOR YOUR BAND FREAK DUST.
IT'S FOR HANAMASA'S BAND HOUSE DUST.
THAT'S WONDERFUL.

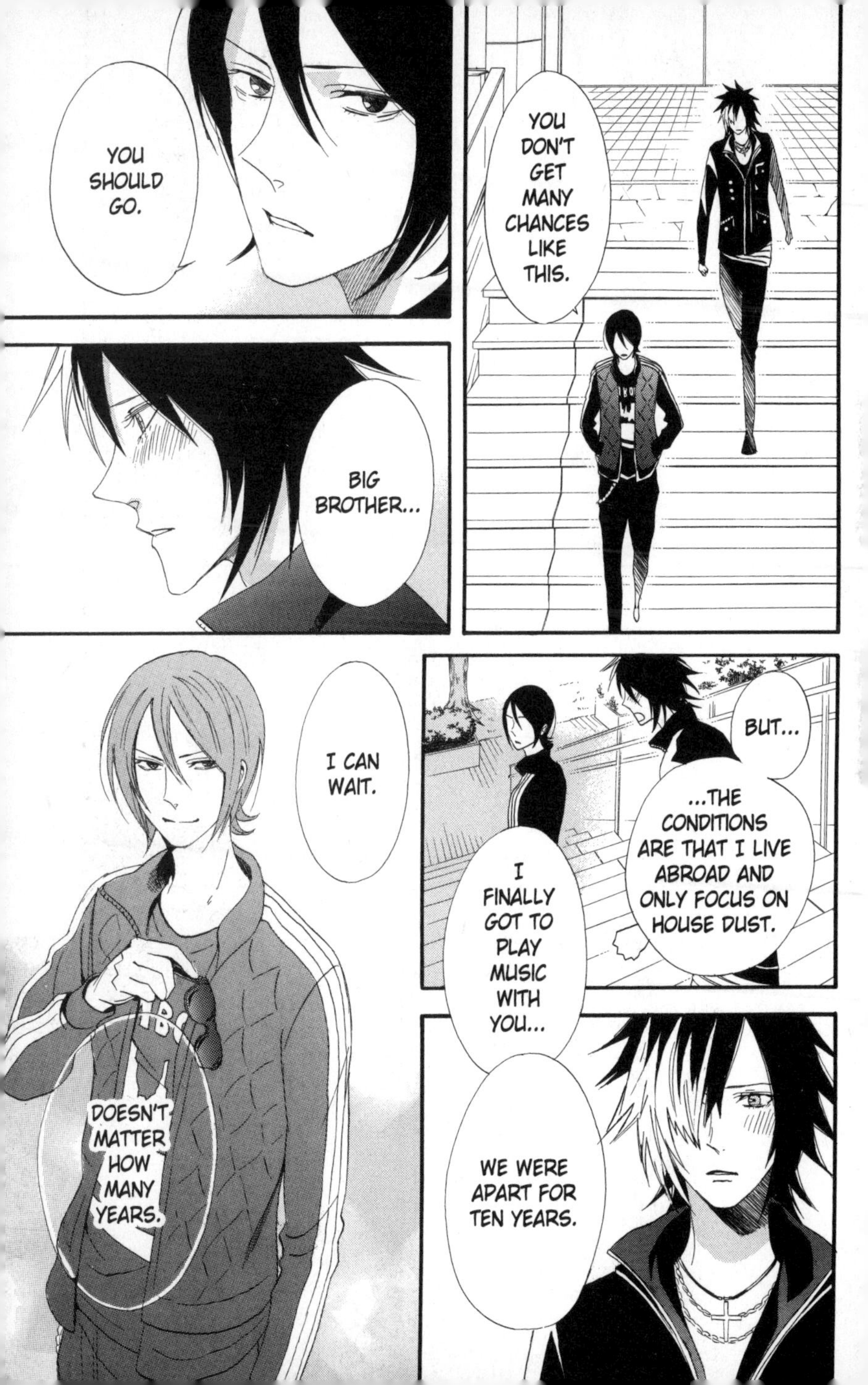
YOU DON'T GET MANY CHANCES LIKE THIS.
YOU SHOULD GO.
BIG BROTHER...
BUT...
...THE CONDITIONS ARE THAT I LIVE ABROAD AND ONLY FOCUS ON HOUSE DUST.
I FINALLY GOT TO PLAY MUSIC WITH YOU...
WE WERE APART FOR TEN YEARS.
I CAN WAIT.
DOESN'T MATTER HOW MANY YEARS.

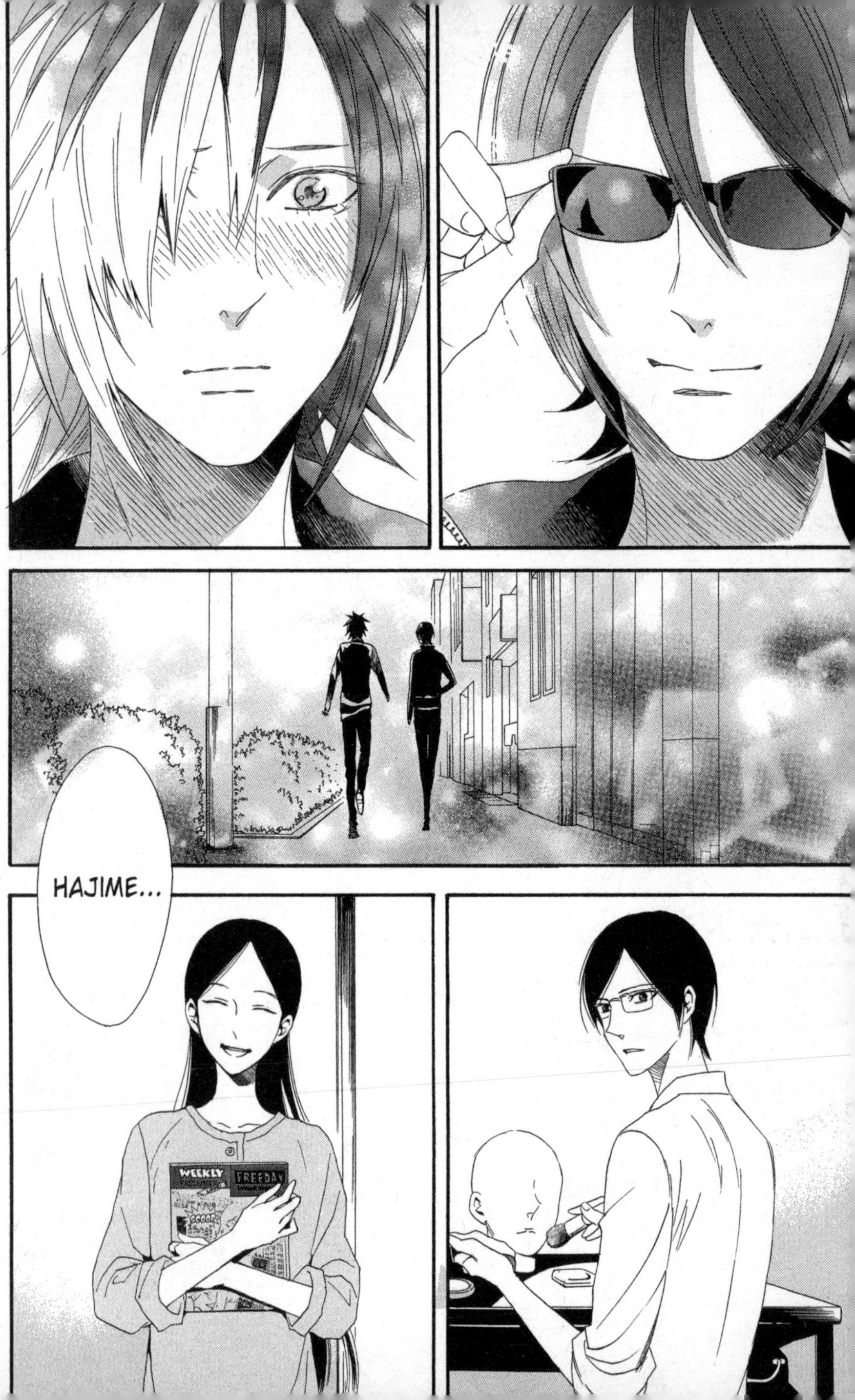
HAJIME...
WEEKLY
FREEDAY

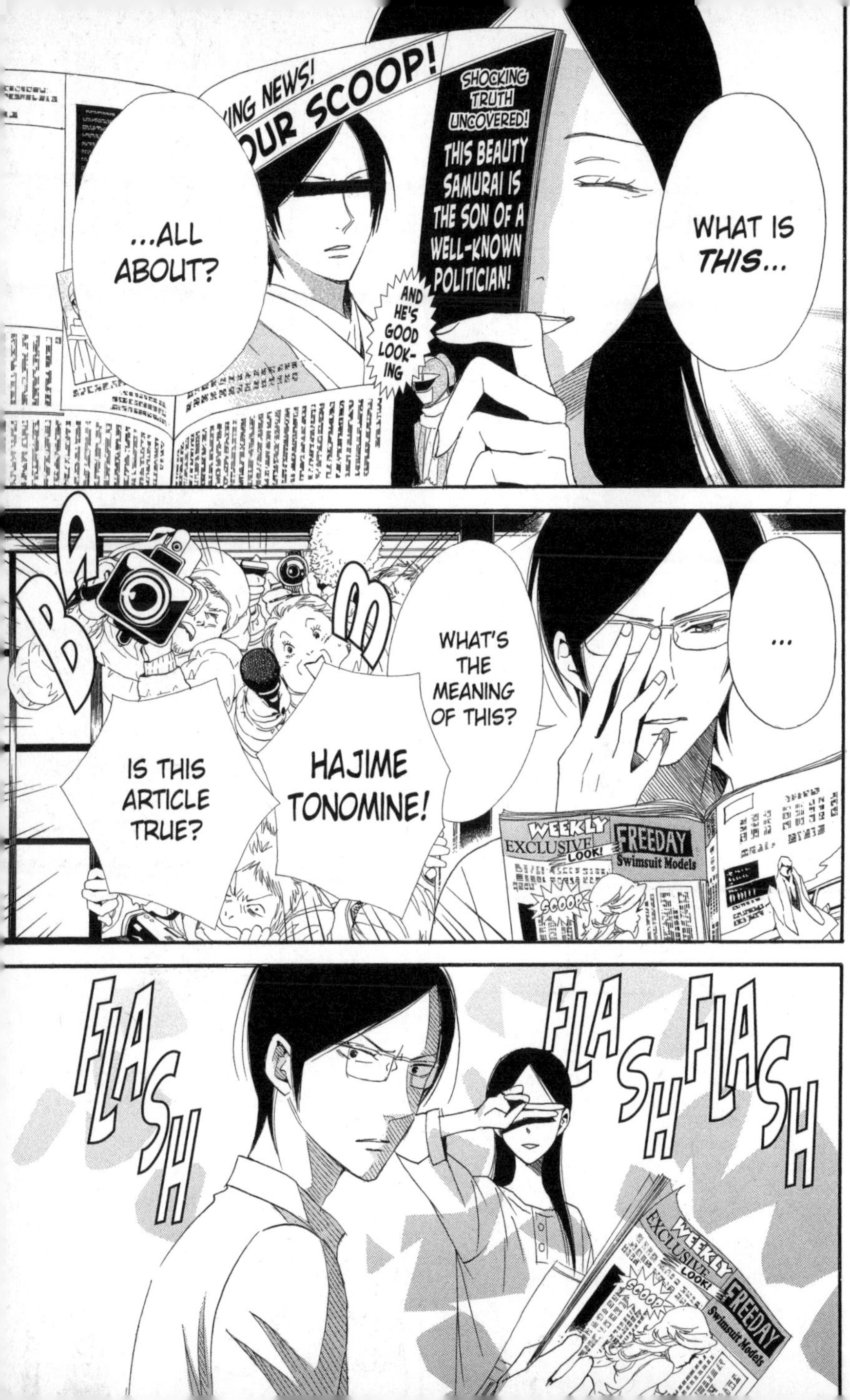
WHAT IS THIS...
...ALL ABOUT?
OUR SCOOP!
SHOCKING TRUTH UNCOVERED! THIS BEAUTY SAMURAI IS THE SON OF A WELL-KNOWN POLITICIAN!
AND HE'S GOOD LOOK-ING
...
WHAT'S THE MEANING OF THIS?
HAJIME TONOMINE!
IS THIS ARTICLE TRUE?
WEEKLY EXCLUSIVE LOOK! FREEDAY Swimsuit Models
SCOOP
FLASH
FLASH
FLASH

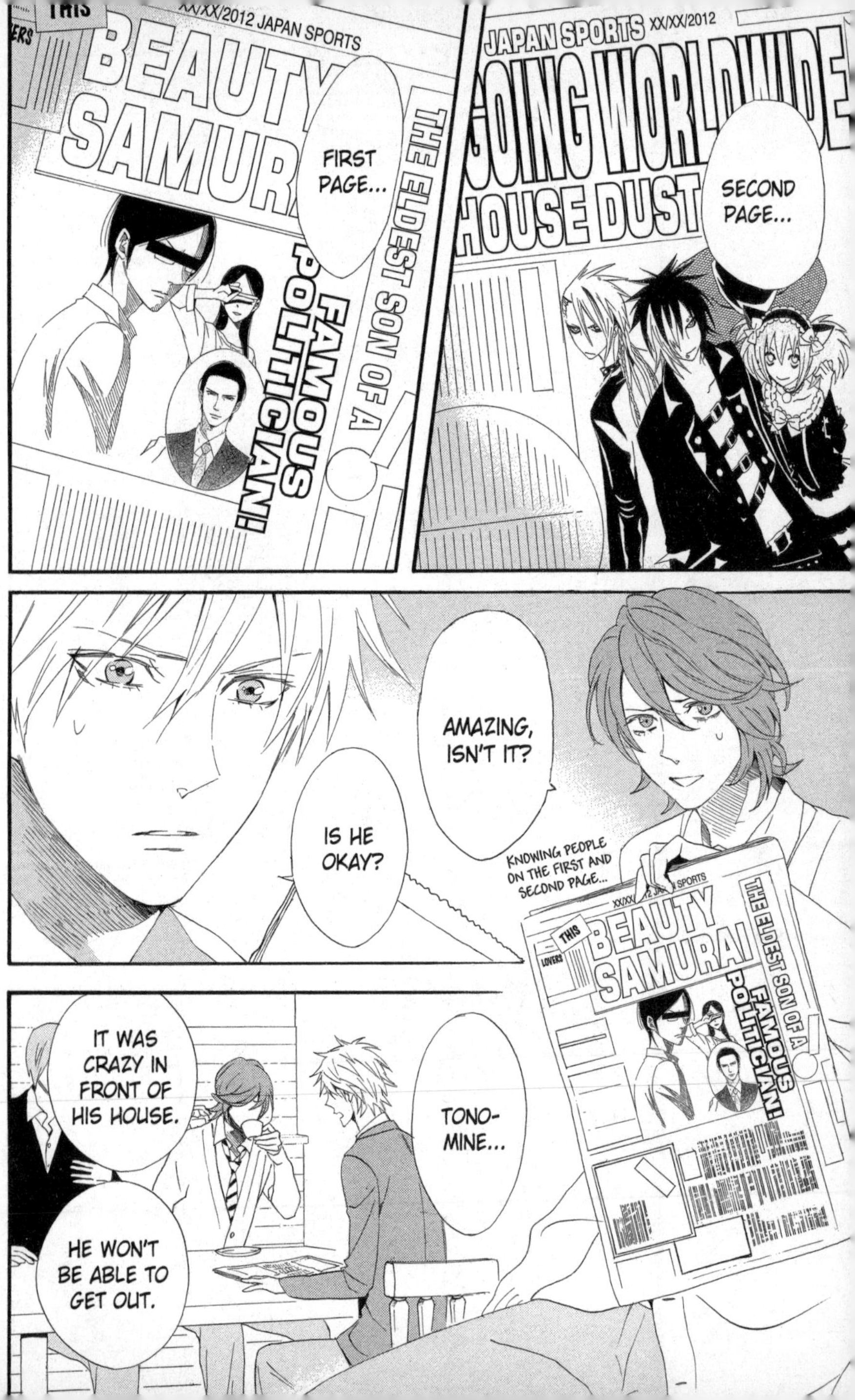
JAPAN SPORTS XX/XX/2012
GOING WORLDWIDE
HOUSE DUST
SECOND PAGE...
XX/XX/2012 JAPAN SPORTS
THE ELDEST SON OF A FAMOUS POLITICIAN!
FIRST PAGE...
AMAZING, ISN'T IT?
KNOWING PEOPLE ON THE FIRST AND SECOND PAGE...
XX/XX/2012 JAPAN SPORTS
THIS
LOVERS
BEAUTY SAMURAI
THE ELDEST SON OF A FAMOUS POLITICIAN!
IS HE OKAY?
TONO-MINE...
IT WAS CRAZY IN FRONT OF HIS HOUSE.
HE WON'T BE ABLE TO GET OUT.

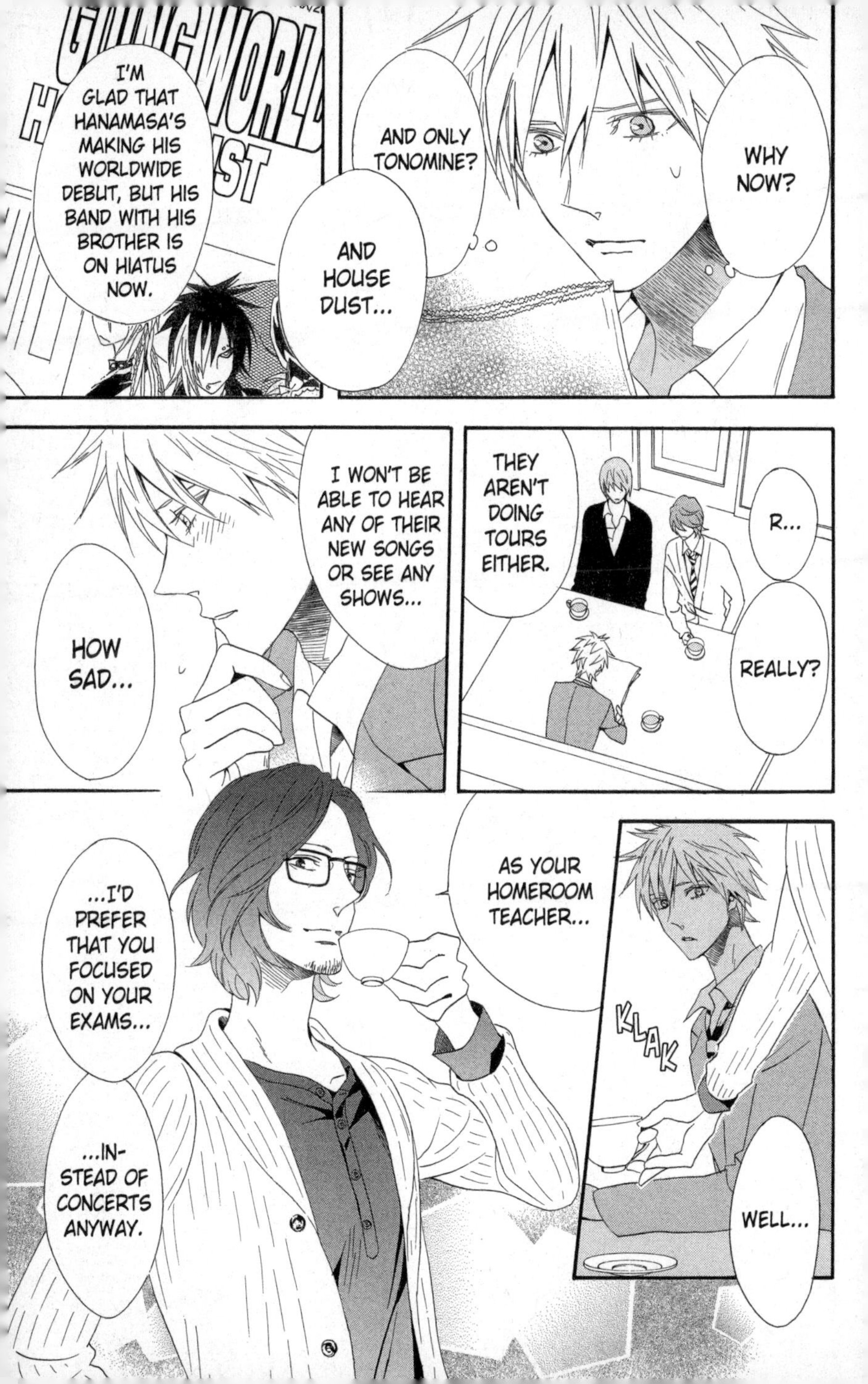
WHY NOW?
AND ONLY TONOMINE?
AND HOUSE DUST...
I'M GLAD THAT HANAMASA'S MAKING HIS WORLDWIDE DEBUT, BUT HIS BAND WITH HIS BROTHER IS ON HIATUS NOW.
R...
REALLY?
THEY AREN'T DOING TOURS EITHER.
I WON'T BE ABLE TO HEAR ANY OF THEIR NEW SONGS OR SEE ANY SHOWS...
HOW SAD...
KLAK
WELL...
AS YOUR HOMEROOM TEACHER...
...I'D PREFER THAT YOU FOCUSED ON YOUR EXAMS...
...IN-STEAD OF CONCERTS ANYWAY.

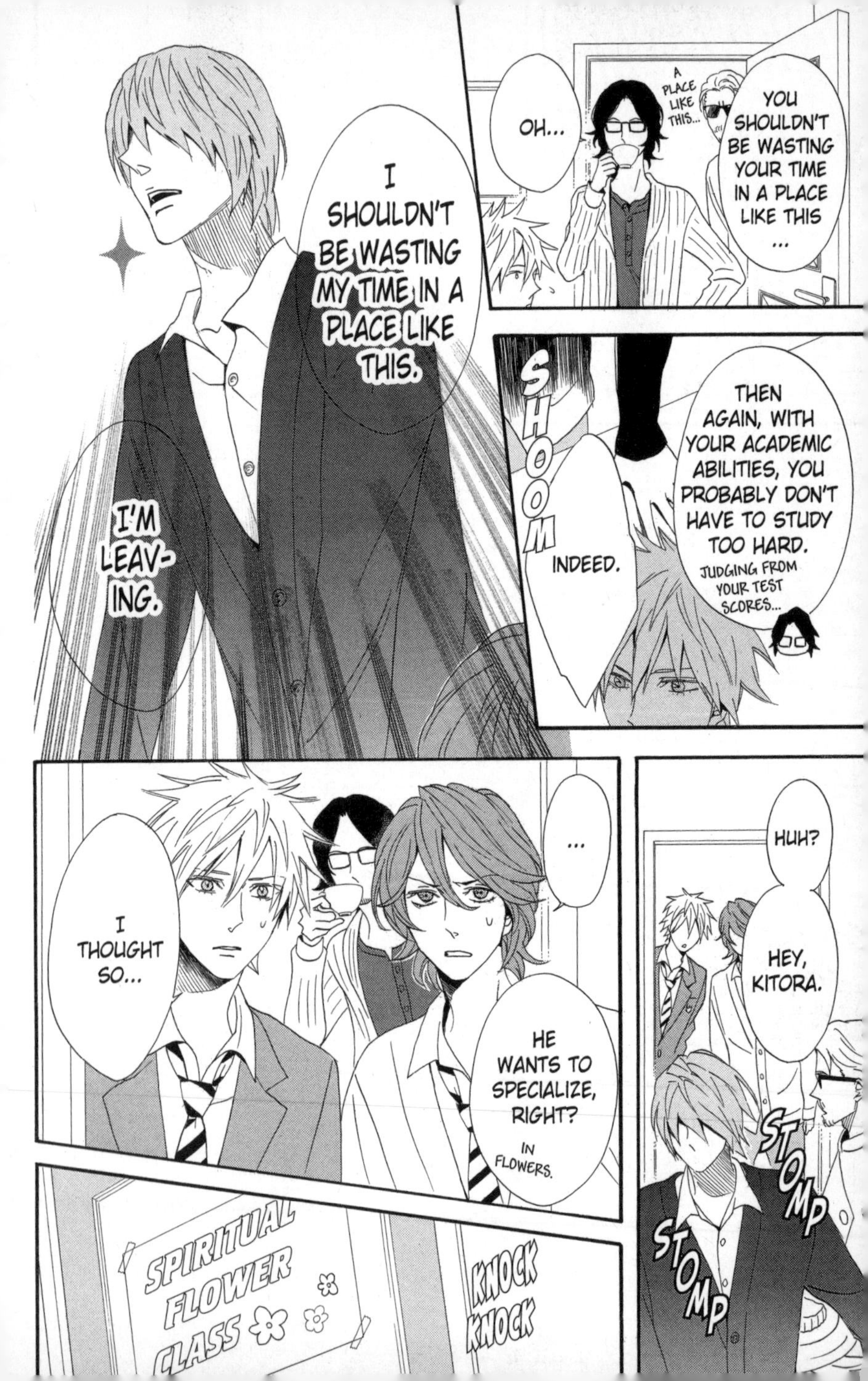
YOU SHOULDN'T BE WASTING YOUR TIME IN A PLACE LIKE THIS ...
A PLACE LIKE THIS...
OH...
THEN AGAIN, WITH YOUR ACADEMIC ABILITIES, YOU PROBABLY DON'T HAVE TO STUDY TOO HARD.
JUDGING FROM YOUR TEST SCORES...
SHOOM
INDEED.
I SHOULDN'T BE WASTING MY TIME IN A PLACE LIKE THIS.
I'M LEAV-ING.
HUH?
HEY, KITORA.
STOMP
STOMP
...
HE WANTS TO SPECIALIZE, RIGHT?
IN FLOWERS.
I THOUGHT SO...
KNOCK KNOCK
SPIRITUAL FLOWER CLASS

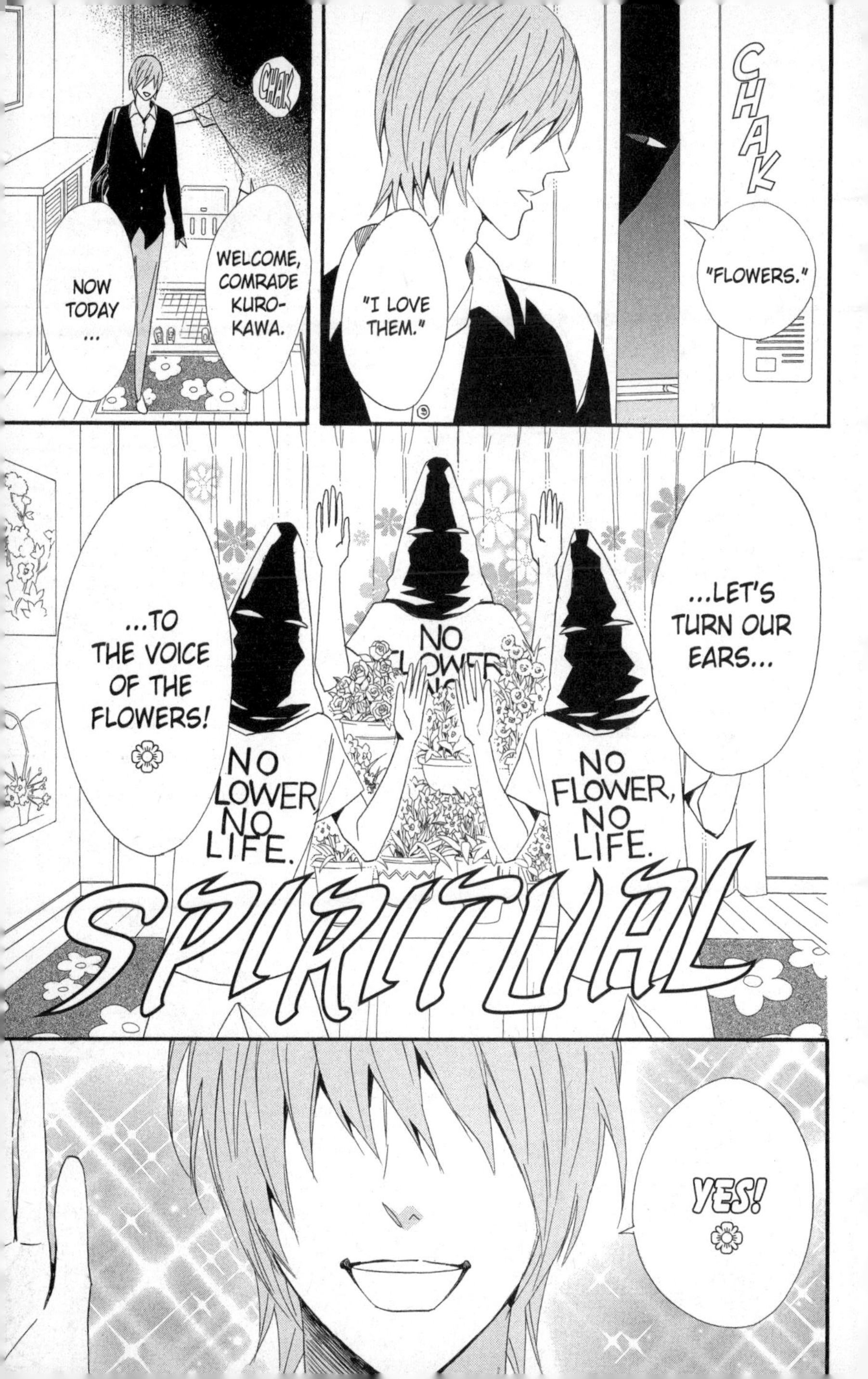
CHAK
"FLOWERS."
"I LOVE THEM."
CHAK
WELCOME, COMRADE KURO-KAWA.
NOW TODAY ...
...LET'S TURN OUR EARS...
NO FLOWER, NO LIFE.
...TO THE VOICE OF THE FLOWERS!
NO LOWER NO LIFE.
SPIRITUAL
YES!

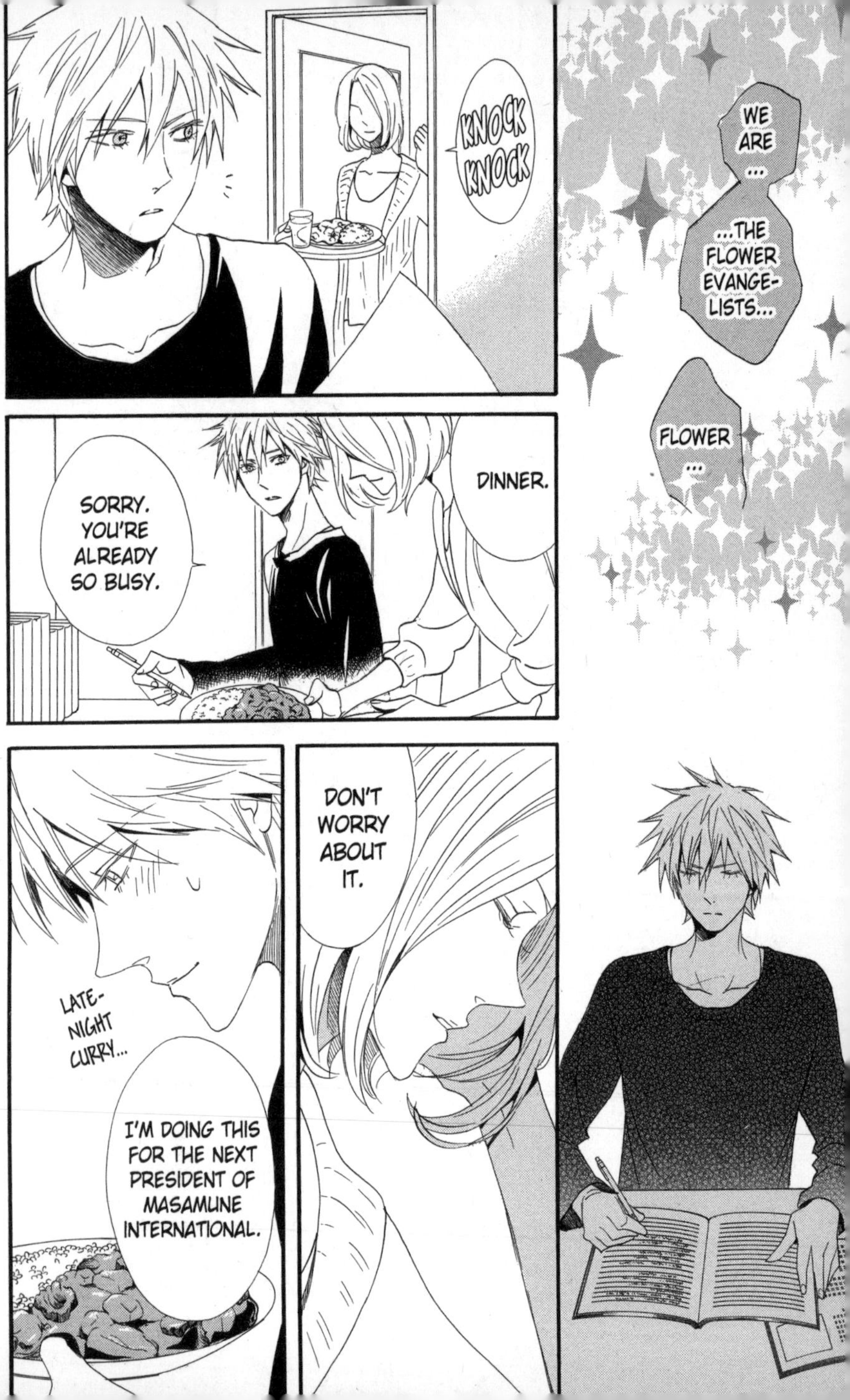
WE ARE ...
...THE FLOWER EVANGE-LISTS...
FLOWER ...
KNOCK KNOCK
DINNER.
SORRY. YOU'RE ALREADY SO BUSY.
DON'T WORRY ABOUT IT.
LATE-NIGHT CURRY...
I'M DOING THIS FOR THE NEXT PRESIDENT OF MASAMUNE INTERNATIONAL.

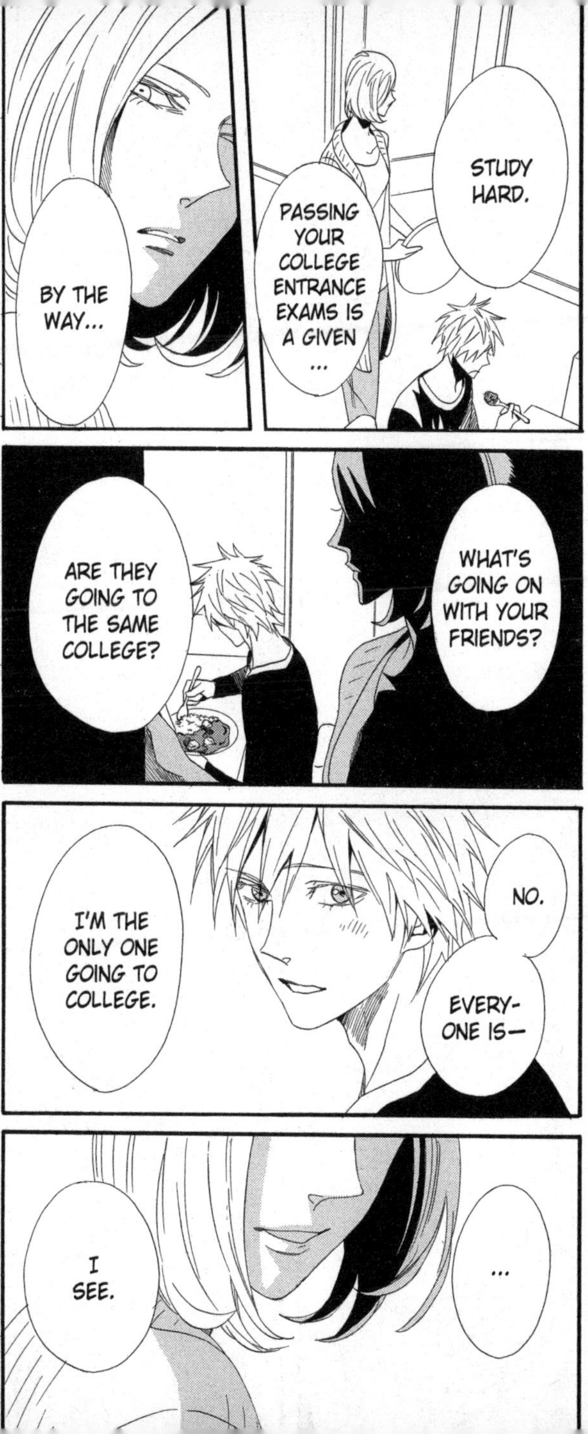
STUDY HARD.
PASSING YOUR COLLEGE ENTRANCE EXAMS IS A GIVEN...
BY THE WAY...
WHAT'S GOING ON WITH YOUR FRIENDS?
ARE THEY GOING TO THE SAME COLLEGE?
NO.
EVERY-ONE IS—
I'M THE ONLY ONE GOING TO COLLEGE.
...
I SEE.

Production Assistance:

Shimada-san
Kuwana-san
Kaneko-san
Sakurai-san
Nakazawa-san
Tanaka-san
Kawashima-san
Sayaka-san
Yone-yan

Special Thanks:

Abe-san
All My Readers
My Family

I hope you keep reading this story about Asuka, Ryo, and their friends until the end.

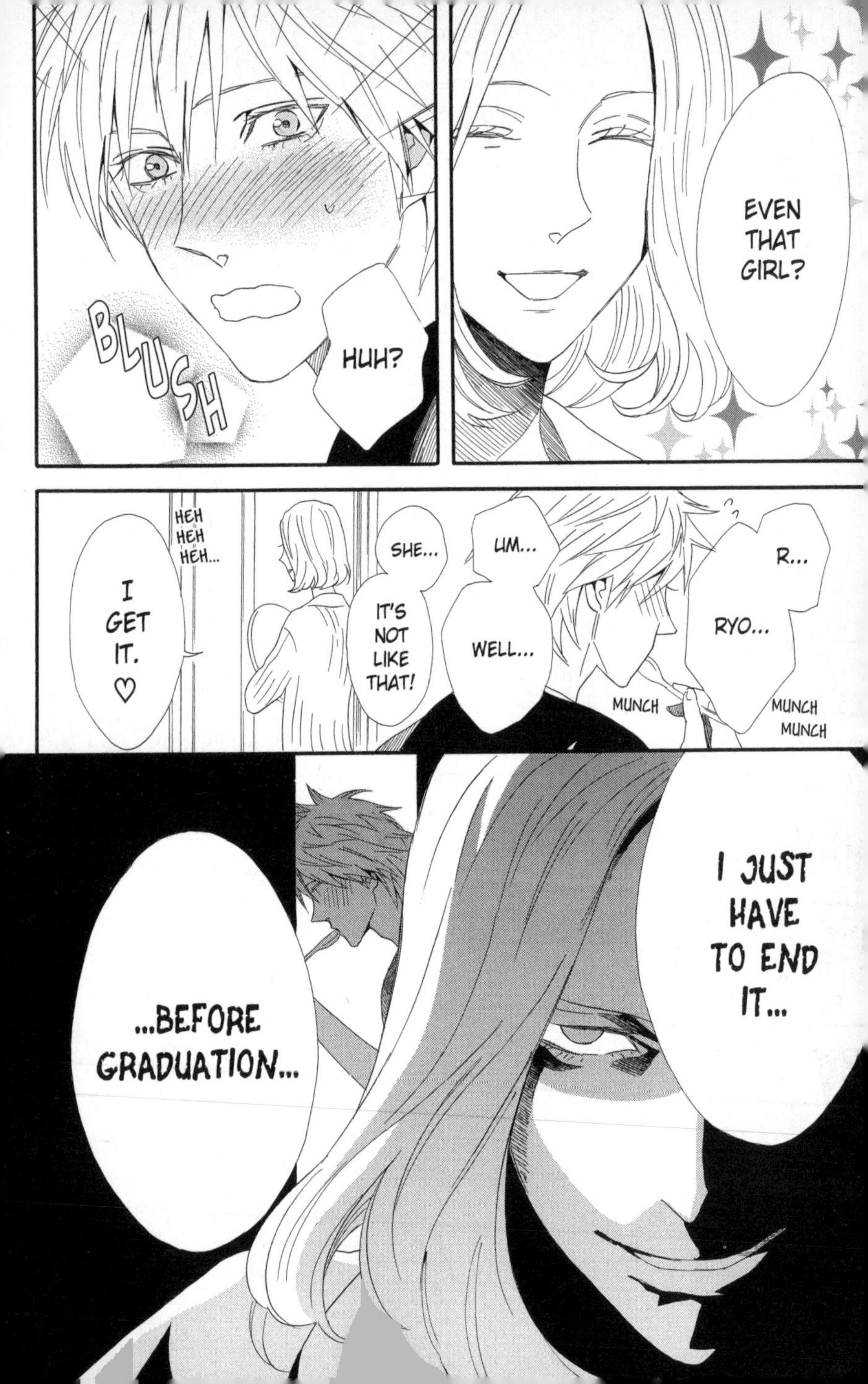
EVEN THAT GIRL?
HUH?
BLUSH
R...
RYO...
MUNCH MUNCH
MUNCH
UM...
WELL...
SHE...
IT'S NOT LIKE THAT!
I GET IT. ♡
HEH HEH HEH...
I JUST HAVE TO END IT...
...BEFORE GRADUATION...

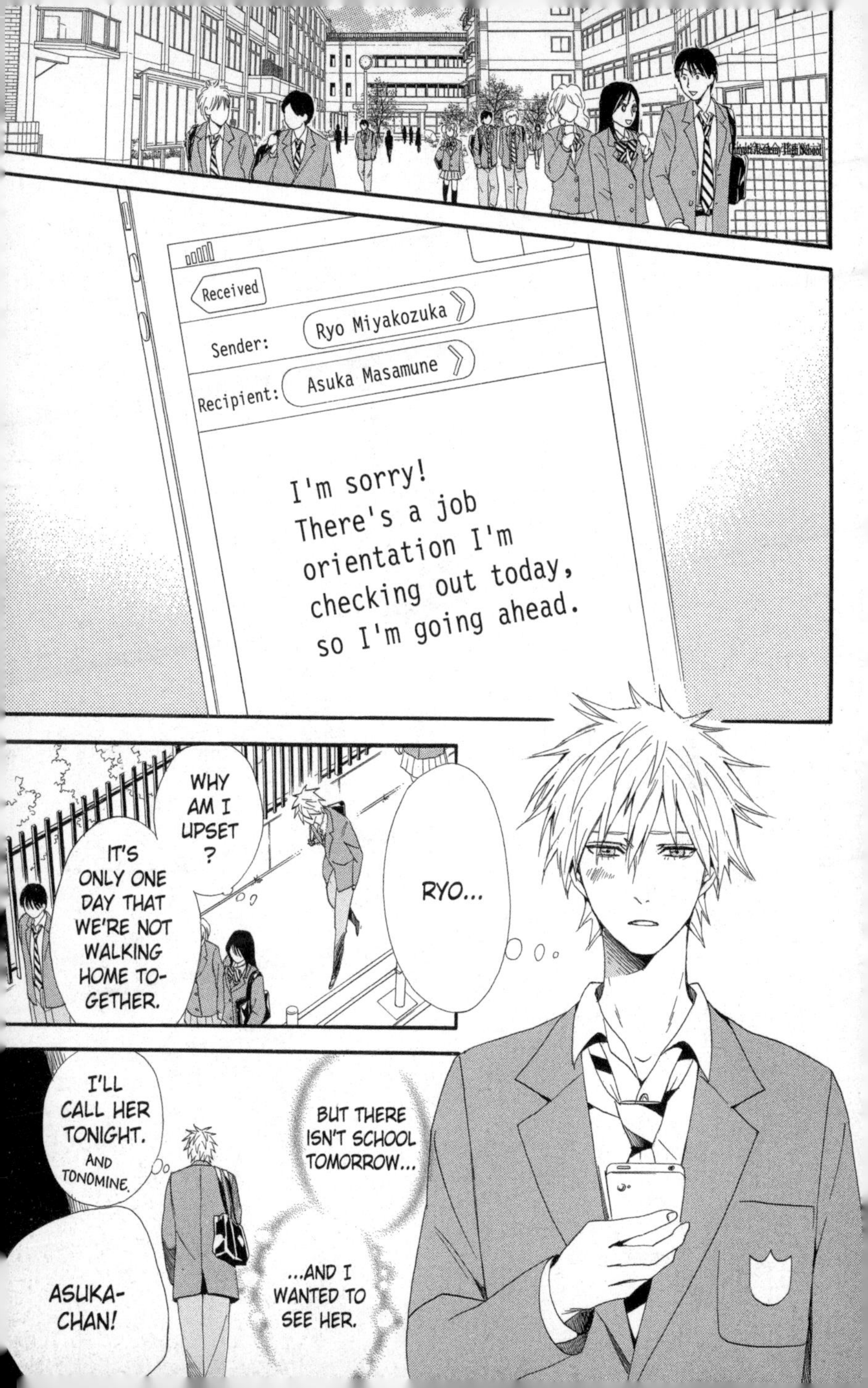
Received
Sender: Ryo Miyakozuka
Recipient: Asuka Masamune
I'm sorry! There's a job orientation I'm checking out today, so I'm going ahead.
RYO...
WHY AM I UPSET?
IT'S ONLY ONE DAY THAT WE'RE NOT WALKING HOME TOGETHER.
BUT THERE ISN'T SCHOOL TOMORROW...
...AND I WANTED TO SEE HER.
I'LL CALL HER TONIGHT. AND TONOMINE.
ASUKA-CHAN!

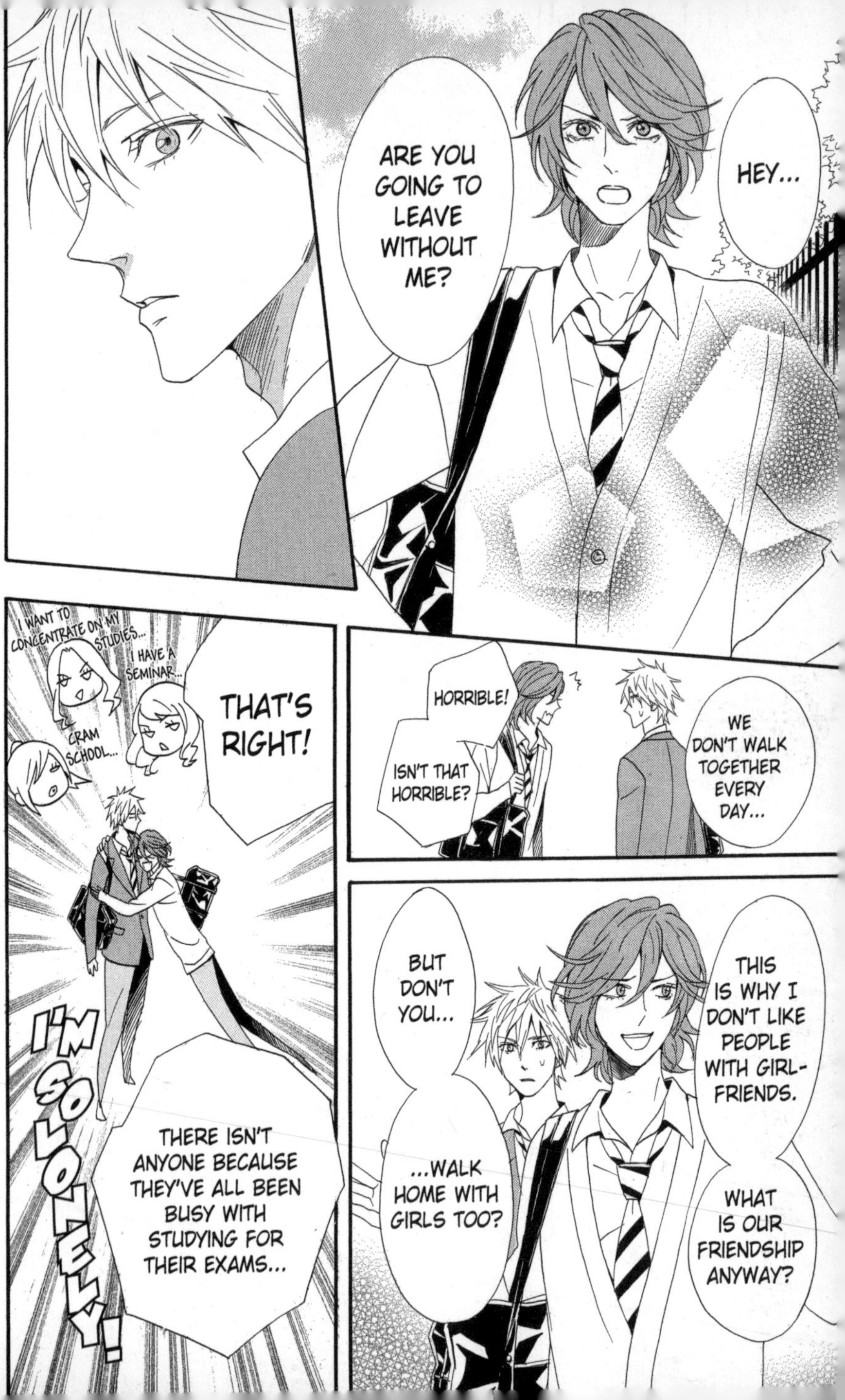
HEY...
ARE YOU GOING TO LEAVE WITHOUT ME?
HORRIBLE!
ISN'T THAT HORRIBLE?
WE DON'T WALK TOGETHER EVERY DAY...
THIS IS WHY I DON'T LIKE PEOPLE WITH GIRL-FRIENDS.
WHAT IS OUR FRIENDSHIP ANYWAY?
BUT DON'T YOU...
...WALK HOME WITH GIRLS TOO?
THAT'S RIGHT!
I WANT TO CONCENTRATE ON MY STUDIES...
I HAVE A SEMINAR...
CRAM SCHOOL...
THERE ISN'T ANYONE BECAUSE THEY'VE ALL BEEN BUSY WITH STUDYING FOR THEIR EXAMS...
I'M SO LONELY!

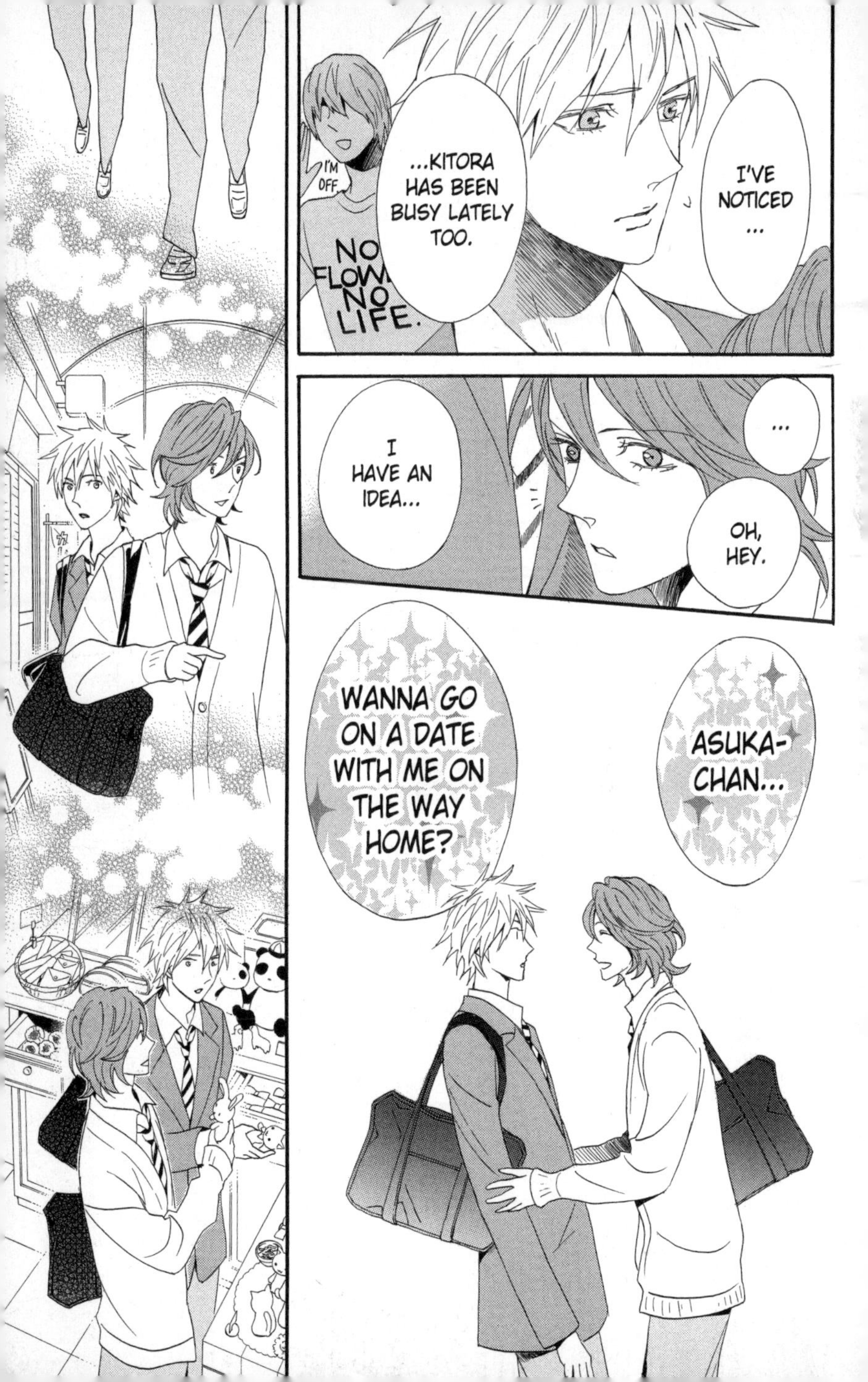
I'VE NOTICED ...
...KITORA HAS BEEN BUSY LATELY TOO.
I'M OFF.
NO FLOW NO LIFE.
...
OH, HEY.
I HAVE AN IDEA...
ASUKA-CHAN...
WANNA GO ON A DATE WITH ME ON THE WAY HOME?

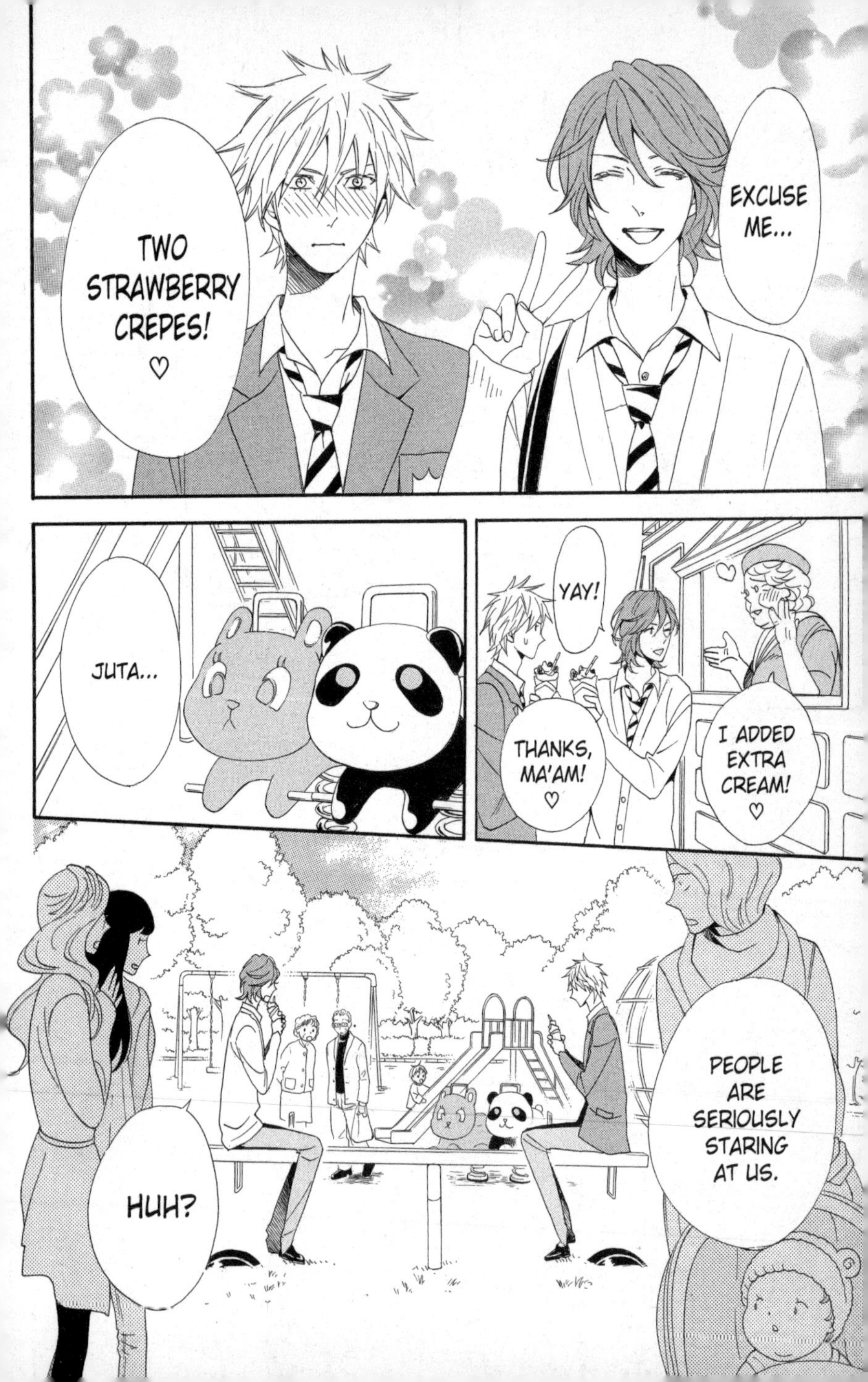
EXCUSE ME...
TWO STRAWBERRY CREPES! ♡
YAY!
I ADDED EXTRA CREAM! ♡
THANKS, MA'AM! ♡
JUTA...
PEOPLE ARE SERIOUSLY STARING AT US.
HUH?

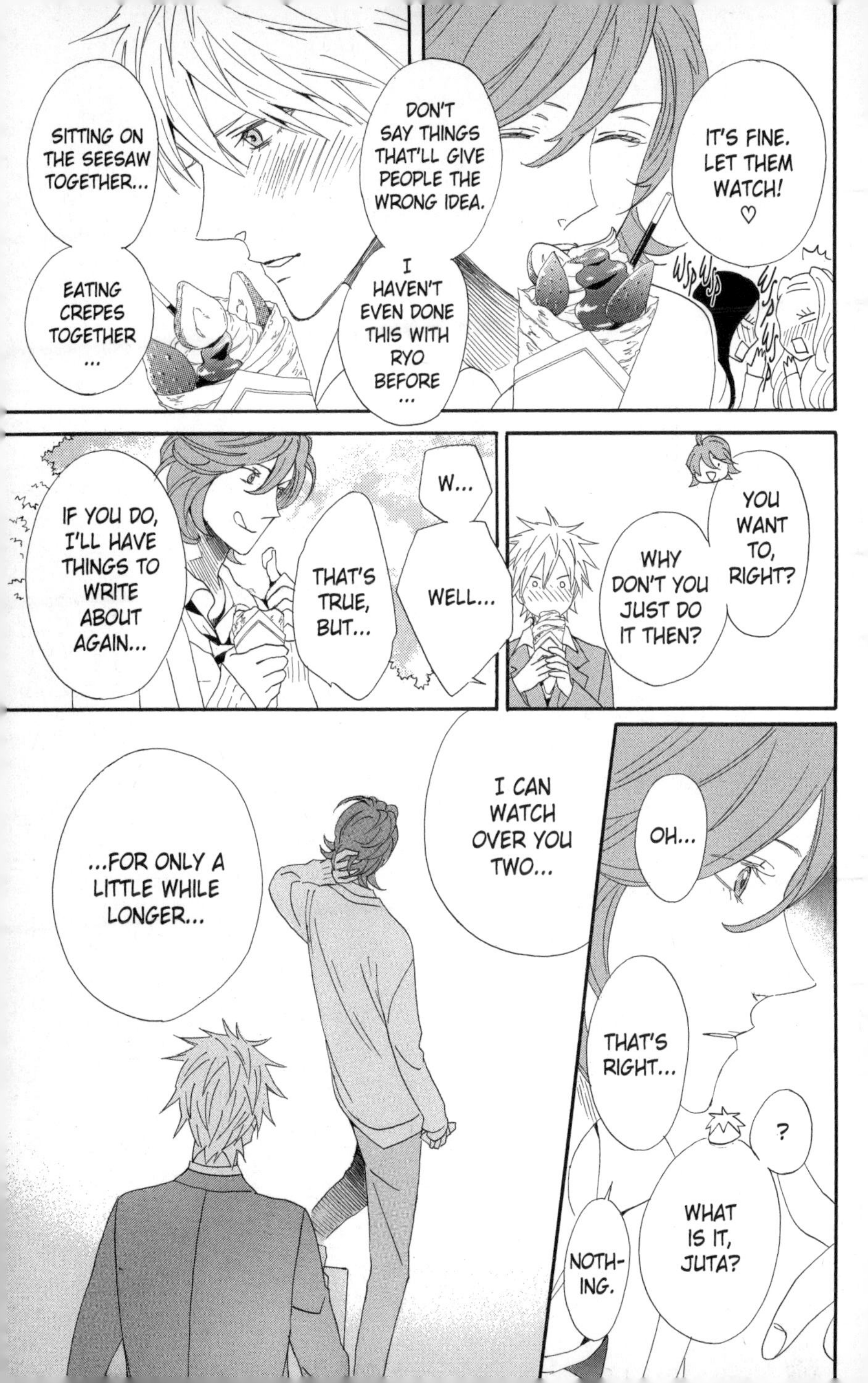
DON'T SAY THINGS THAT'LL GIVE PEOPLE THE WRONG IDEA.
I HAVEN'T EVEN DONE THIS WITH RYO BEFORE...
IT'S FINE. LET THEM WATCH! ♡
WSP WSP
WSP WSP WSP
SITTING ON THE SEESAW TOGETHER...
EATING CREPES TOGETHER...
YOU WANT TO, RIGHT?
WHY DON'T YOU JUST DO IT THEN?
W...
WELL...
THAT'S TRUE, BUT...
IF YOU DO, I'LL HAVE THINGS TO WRITE ABOUT AGAIN...
OH...
THAT'S RIGHT...
?
WHAT IS IT, JUTA?
NOTH-ING.
I CAN WATCH OVER YOU TWO...
...FOR ONLY A LITTLE WHILE LONGER...

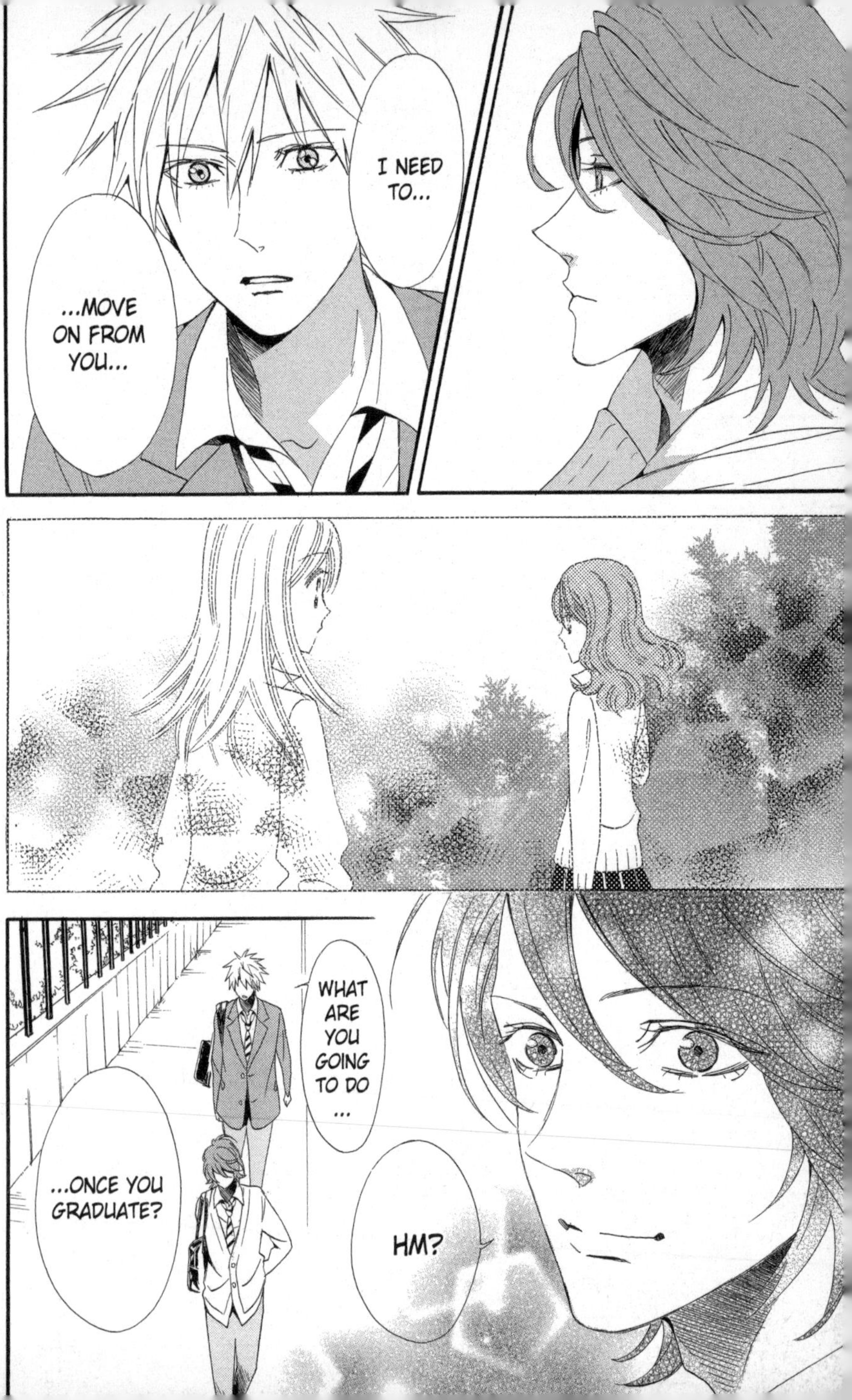
I NEED TO...
...MOVE ON FROM YOU...
HM?
WHAT ARE YOU GOING TO DO ...
...ONCE YOU GRADUATE?

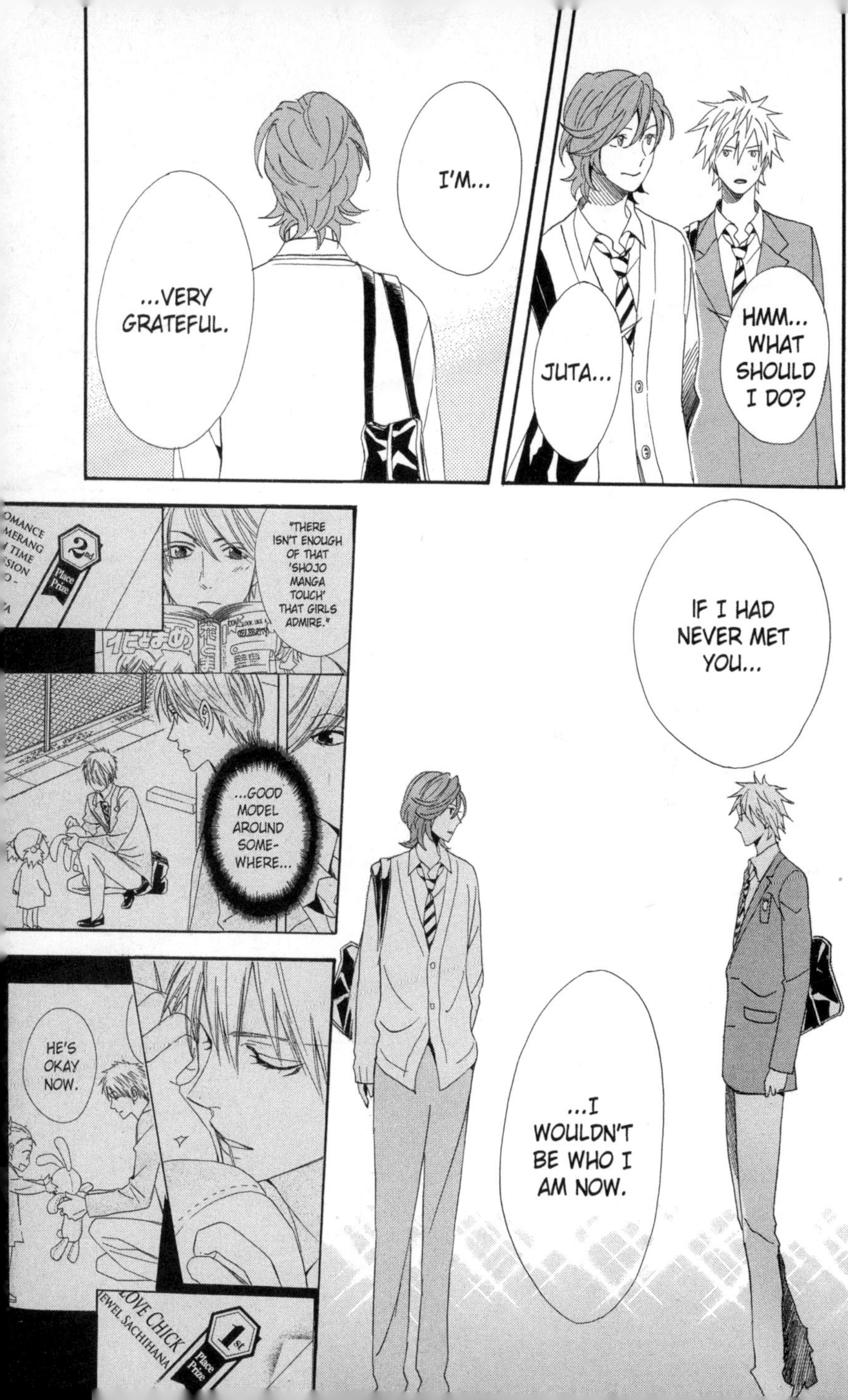
HMM... WHAT SHOULD I DO?
JUTA...
I'M...
...VERY GRATEFUL.
IF I HAD NEVER MET YOU...
...I WOULDN'T BE WHO I AM NOW.
2nd Place Prize
"THERE ISN'T ENOUGH OF THAT 'SHOJO MANGA TOUCH' THAT GIRLS ADMIRE."
...GOOD MODEL AROUND SOME-WHERE...
HE'S OKAY NOW.
LOVE CHICK
JEWEL SACHIHANA
1st Place Prize

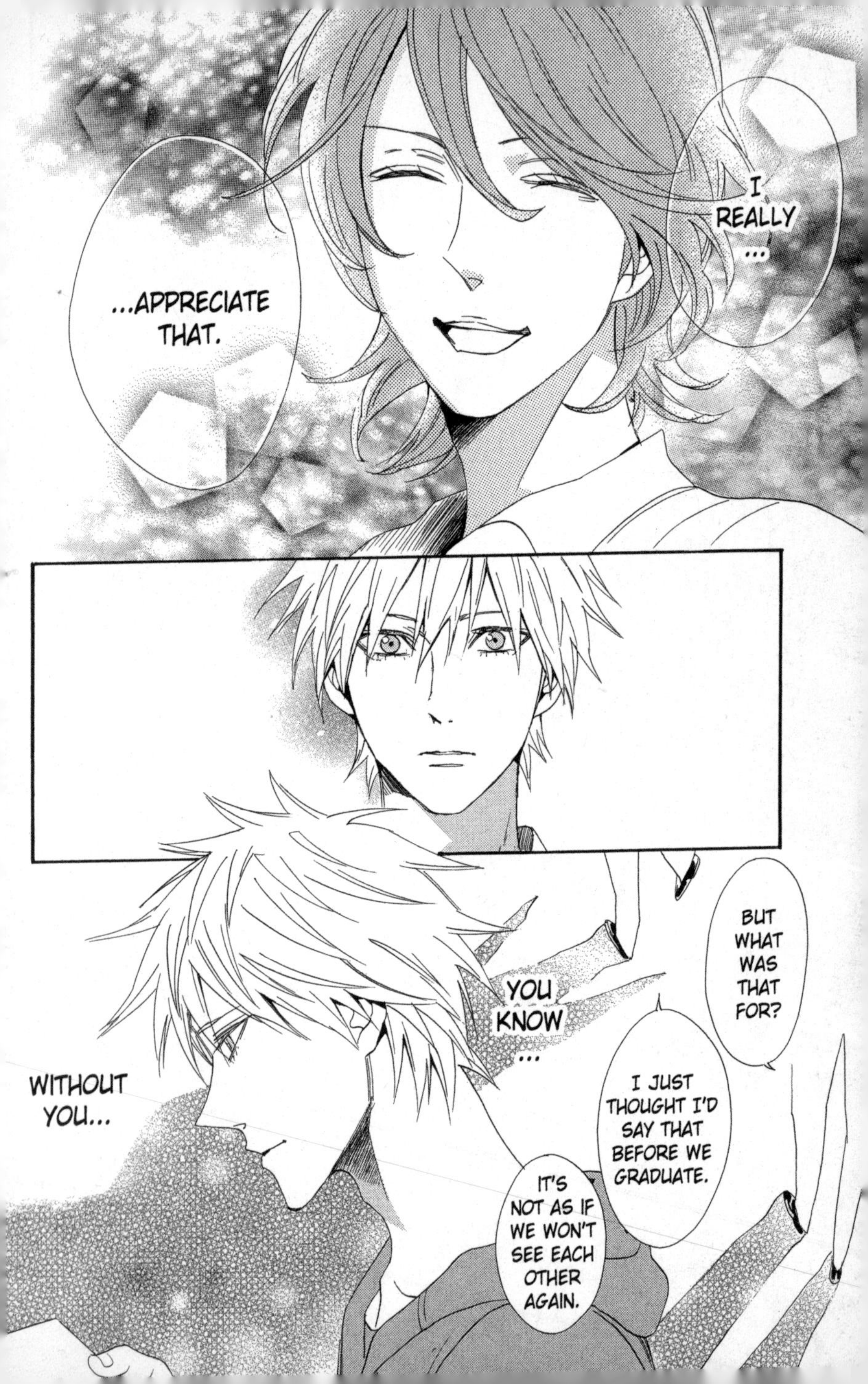
I REALLY...
...APPRECIATE THAT.
BUT WHAT WAS THAT FOR?
I JUST THOUGHT I'D SAY THAT BEFORE WE GRADUATE.
YOU KNOW...
IT'S NOT AS IF WE WON'T SEE EACH OTHER AGAIN.
WITHOUT YOU...

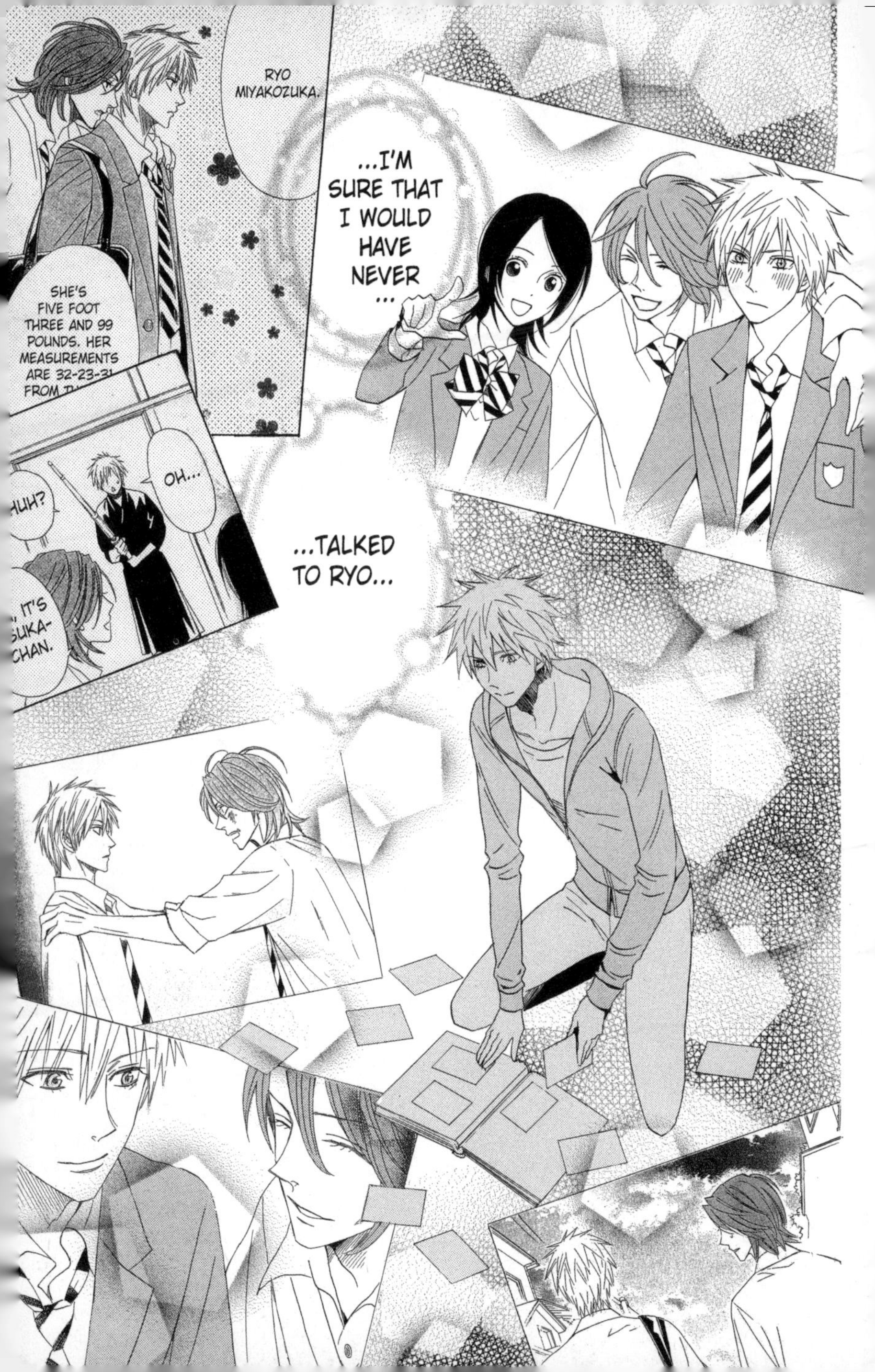
...I'M SURE THAT I WOULD HAVE NEVER ...
RYO MIYAKOZUKA.
SHE'S FIVE FOOT THREE AND 99 POUNDS. HER MEASUREMENTS ARE 32-23-31 FROM
OH...
HUH?
IT'S SUKA-CHAN.
...TALKED TO RYO...

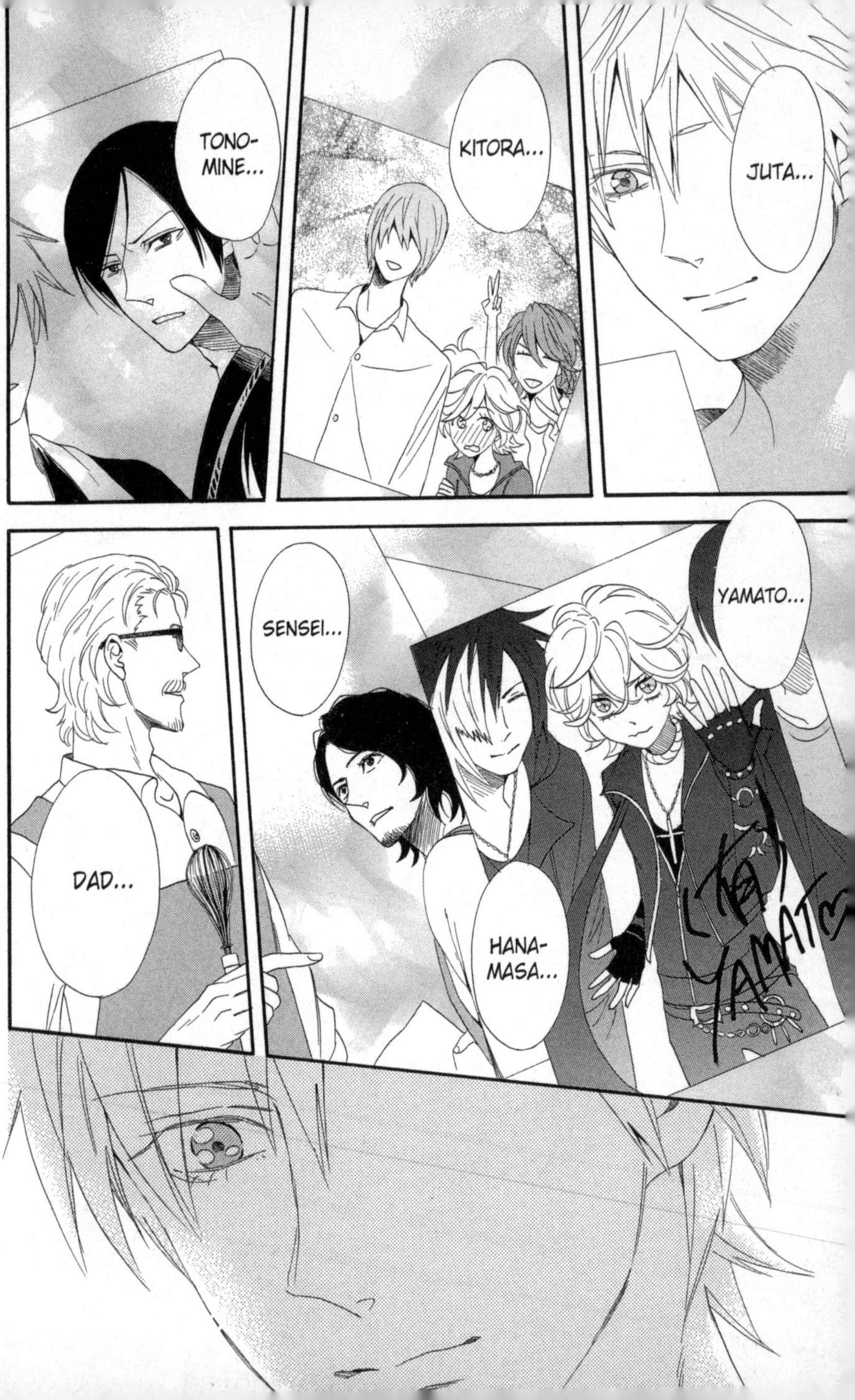
JUTA...
KITORA...
TONO-
MINE...
YAMATO...
SENSEI...
HANA-
MASA...
YAMATO
DAD...

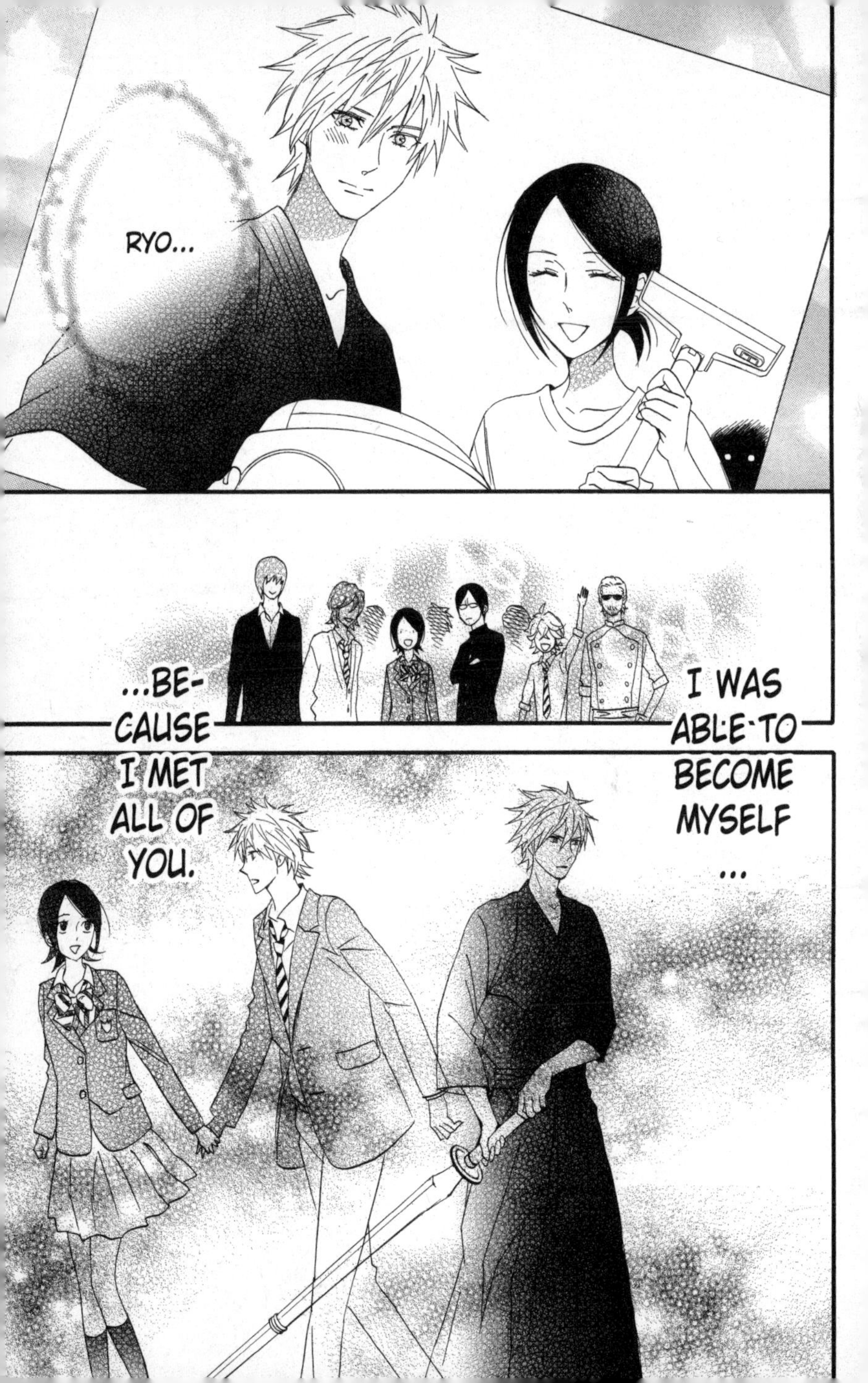
RYO...
I WAS ABLE TO BECOME MYSELF ...
...BE-CAUSE I MET ALL OF YOU.

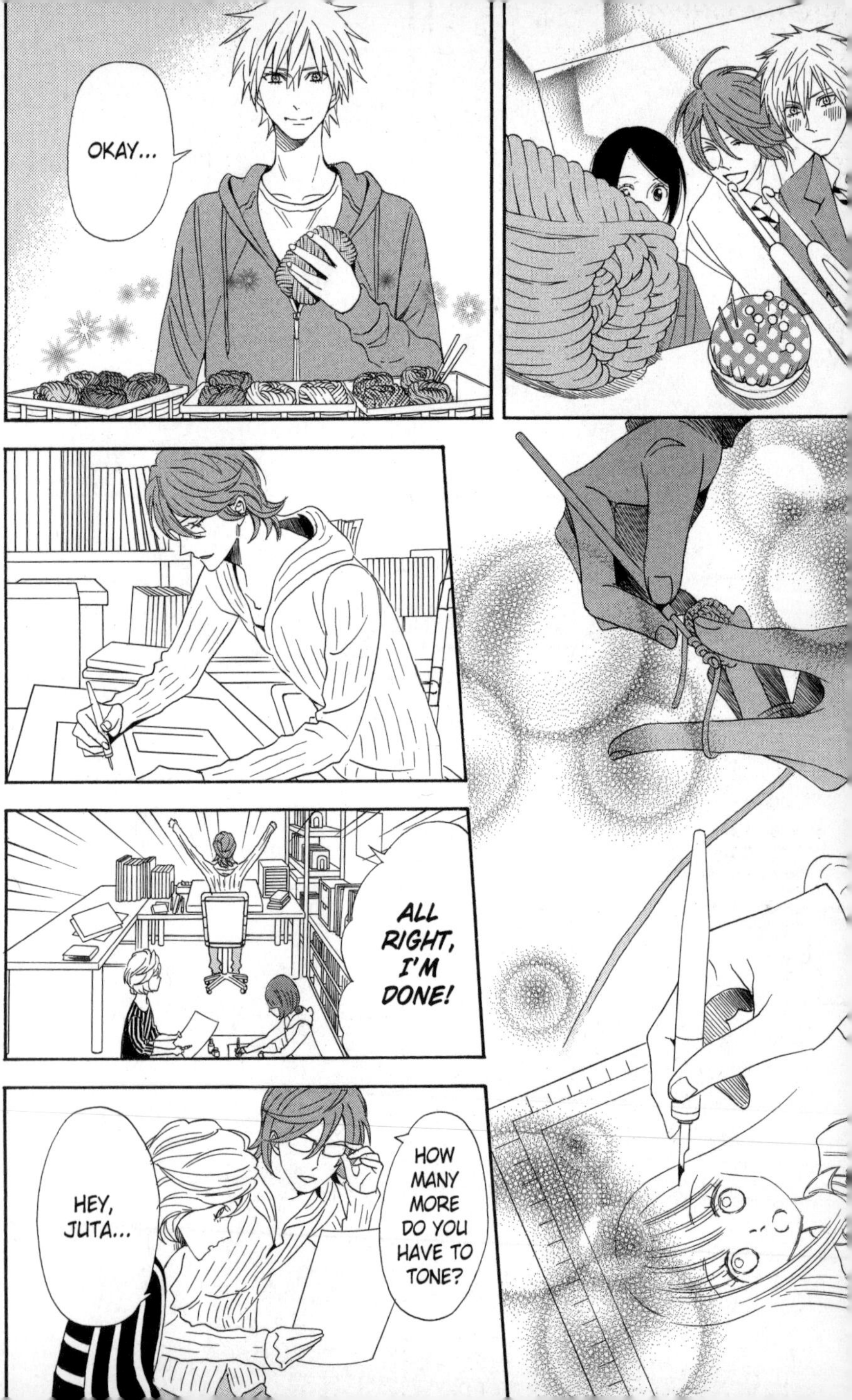
OKAY...
ALL RIGHT, I'M DONE!
HOW MANY MORE DO YOU HAVE TO TONE?
HEY, JUTA...

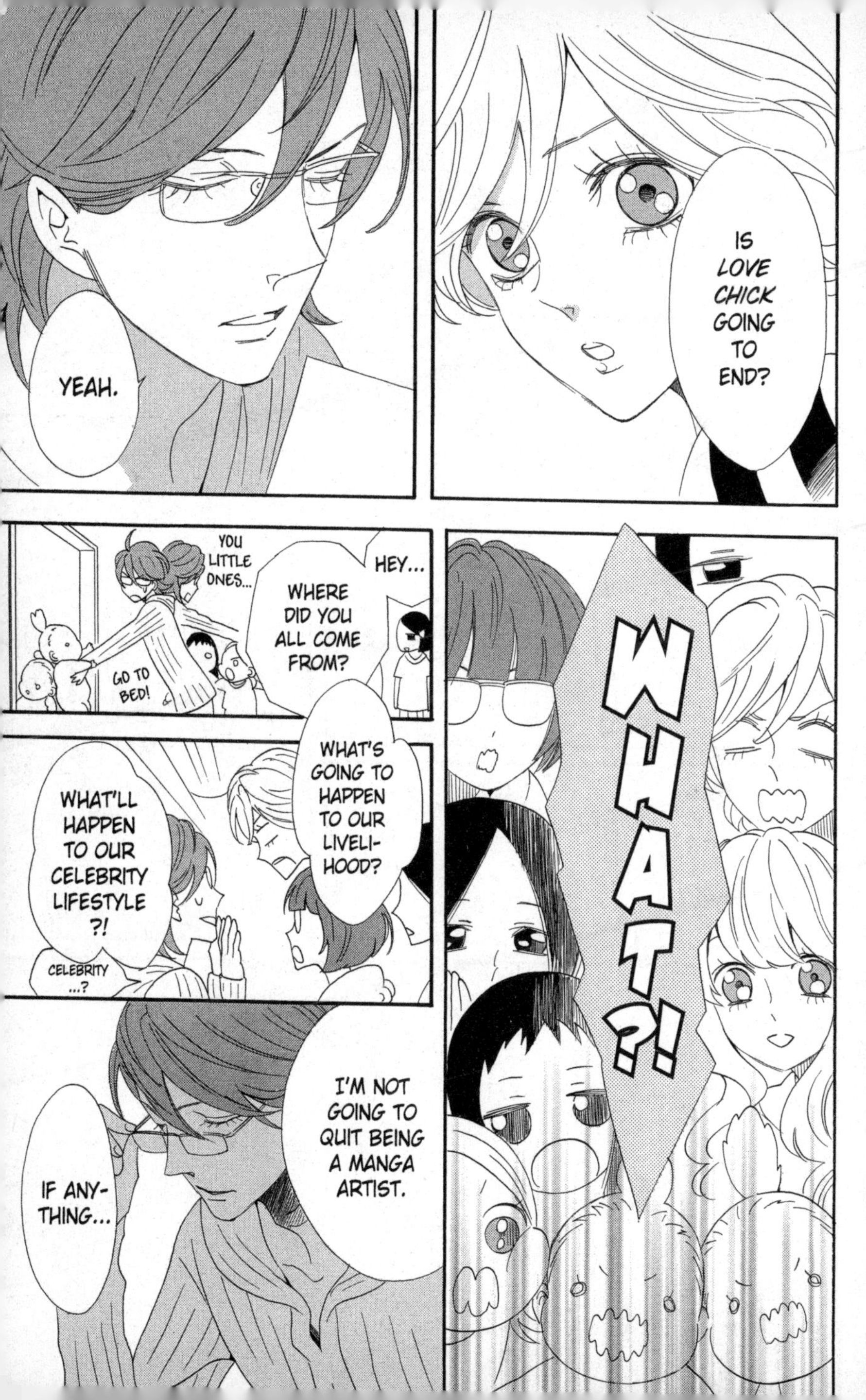
IS LOVE CHICK GOING TO END?
YEAH.
WHAT?!
HEY...
WHERE DID YOU ALL COME FROM?
YOU LITTLE ONES...
GO TO BED!
WHAT'S GOING TO HAPPEN TO OUR LIVELI-HOOD?
WHAT'LL HAPPEN TO OUR CELEBRITY LIFESTYLE ?!
CELEBRITY ...?
I'M NOT GOING TO QUIT BEING A MANGA ARTIST.
IF ANY-THING...

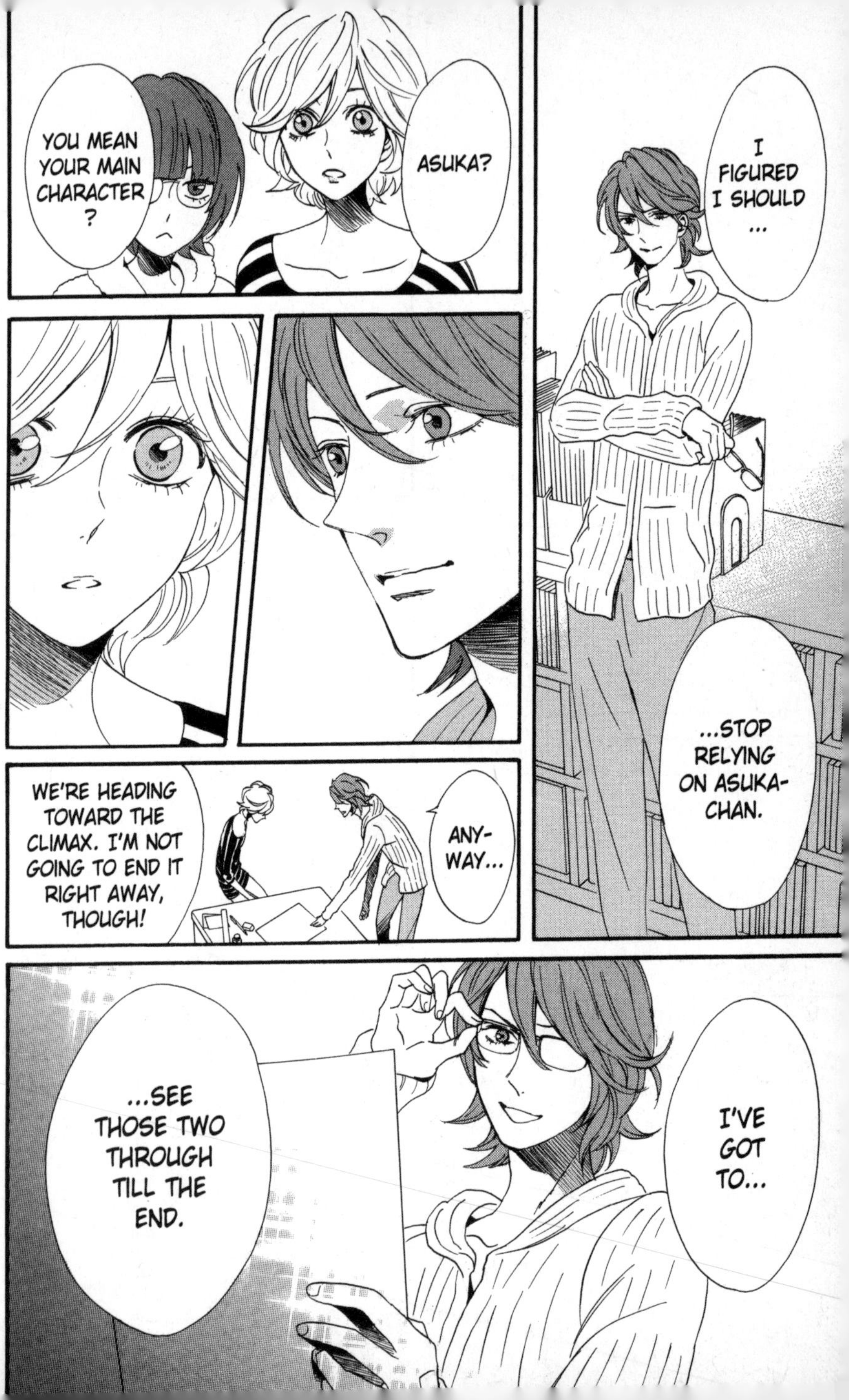
I FIGURED I SHOULD...
...STOP RELYING ON ASUKA-CHAN.
ASUKA?
YOU MEAN YOUR MAIN CHARACTER?
ANYWAY...
WE'RE HEADING TOWARD THE CLIMAX. I'M NOT GOING TO END IT RIGHT AWAY, THOUGH!
I'VE GOT TO...
...SEE THOSE TWO THROUGH TILL THE END.

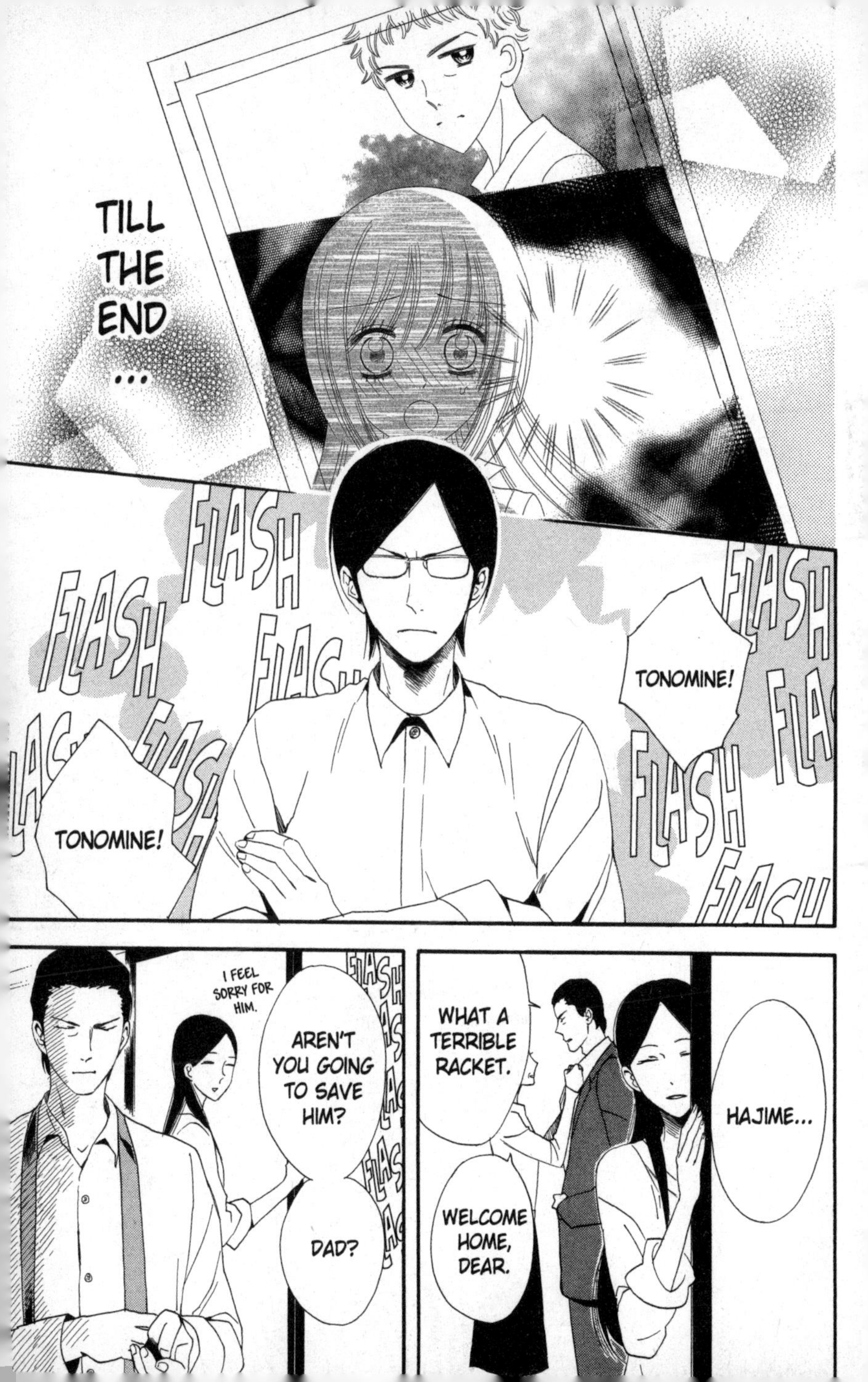
TILL THE END...
FLASH
FLASH
FLASH
FLASH
TONOMINE!
TONOMINE!
HAJIME...
WHAT A TERRIBLE RACKET.
WELCOME HOME, DEAR.
I FEEL SORRY FOR HIM.
AREN'T YOU GOING TO SAVE HIM?
DAD?

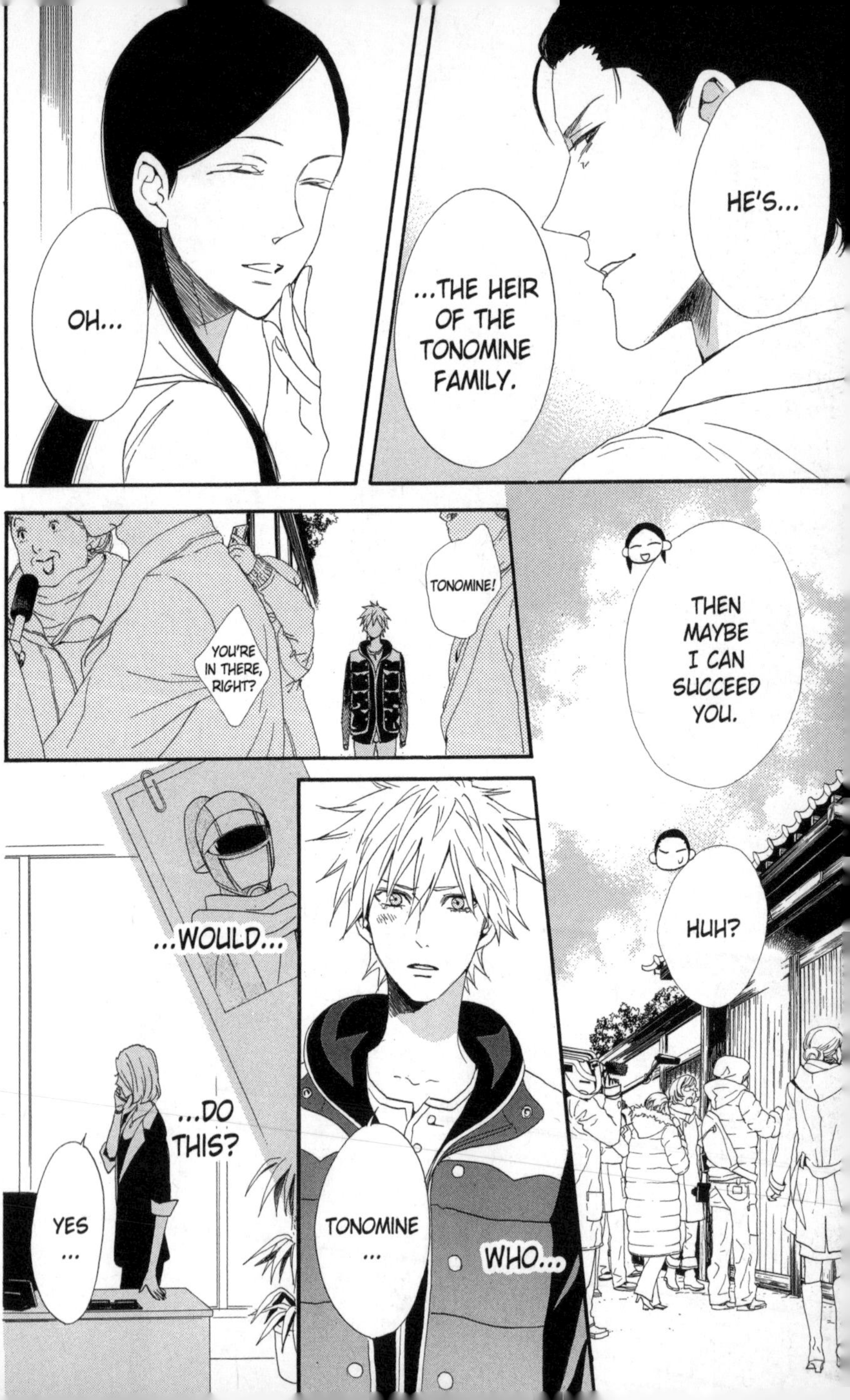
HE'S...
...THE HEIR OF THE TONOMINE FAMILY.
OH...
THEN MAYBE I CAN SUCCEED YOU.
HUH?
TONOMINE!
YOU'RE IN THERE, RIGHT?
TONOMINE ...
WHO...
...WOULD...
...DO THIS?
YES ...

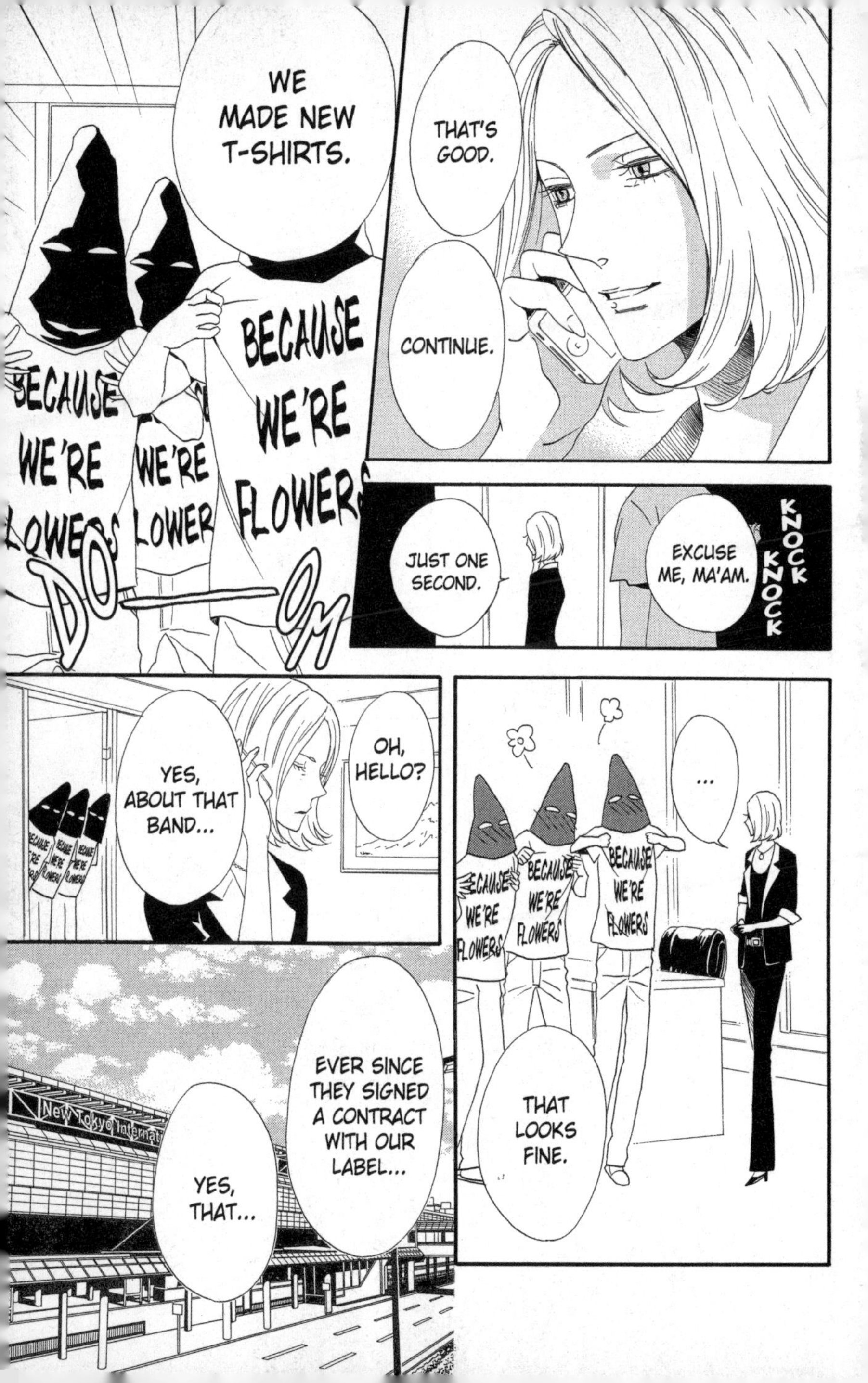
THAT'S GOOD.
CONTINUE.
KNOCK KNOCK
EXCUSE ME, MA'AM.
JUST ONE SECOND.
WE MADE NEW T-SHIRTS.
BECAUSE WE'RE FLOWERS
DO—OM
...
THAT LOOKS FINE.
OH, HELLO?
YES, ABOUT THAT BAND...
BECAUSE WE'RE FLOWERS
EVER SINCE THEY SIGNED A CONTRACT WITH OUR LABEL...
YES, THAT...
New Tokyo Internat

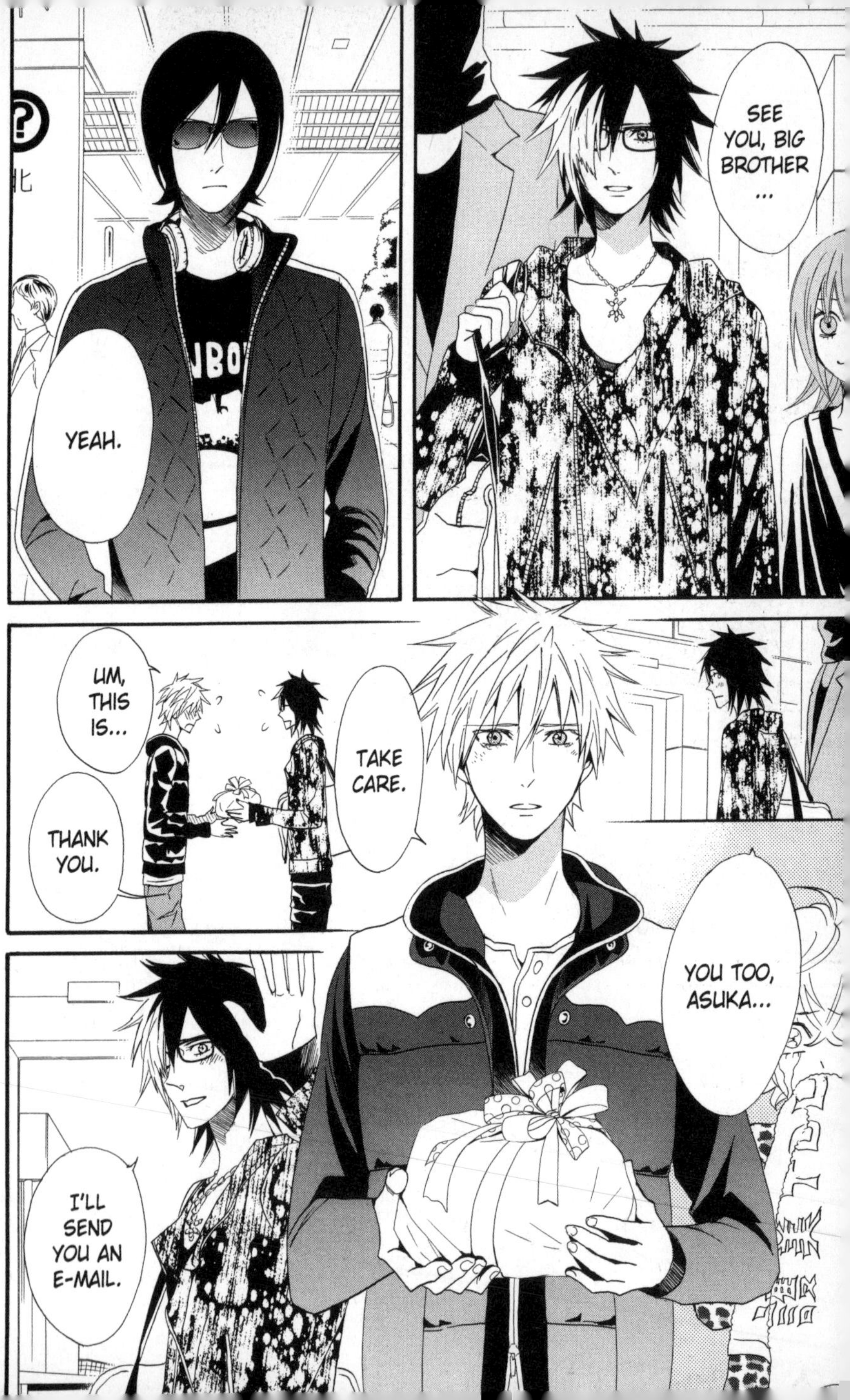

SEE YOU, BIG BROTHER ...
YEAH.
UM, THIS IS...
THANK YOU.
TAKE CARE.
YOU TOO, ASUKA...
I'LL SEND YOU AN E-MAIL.

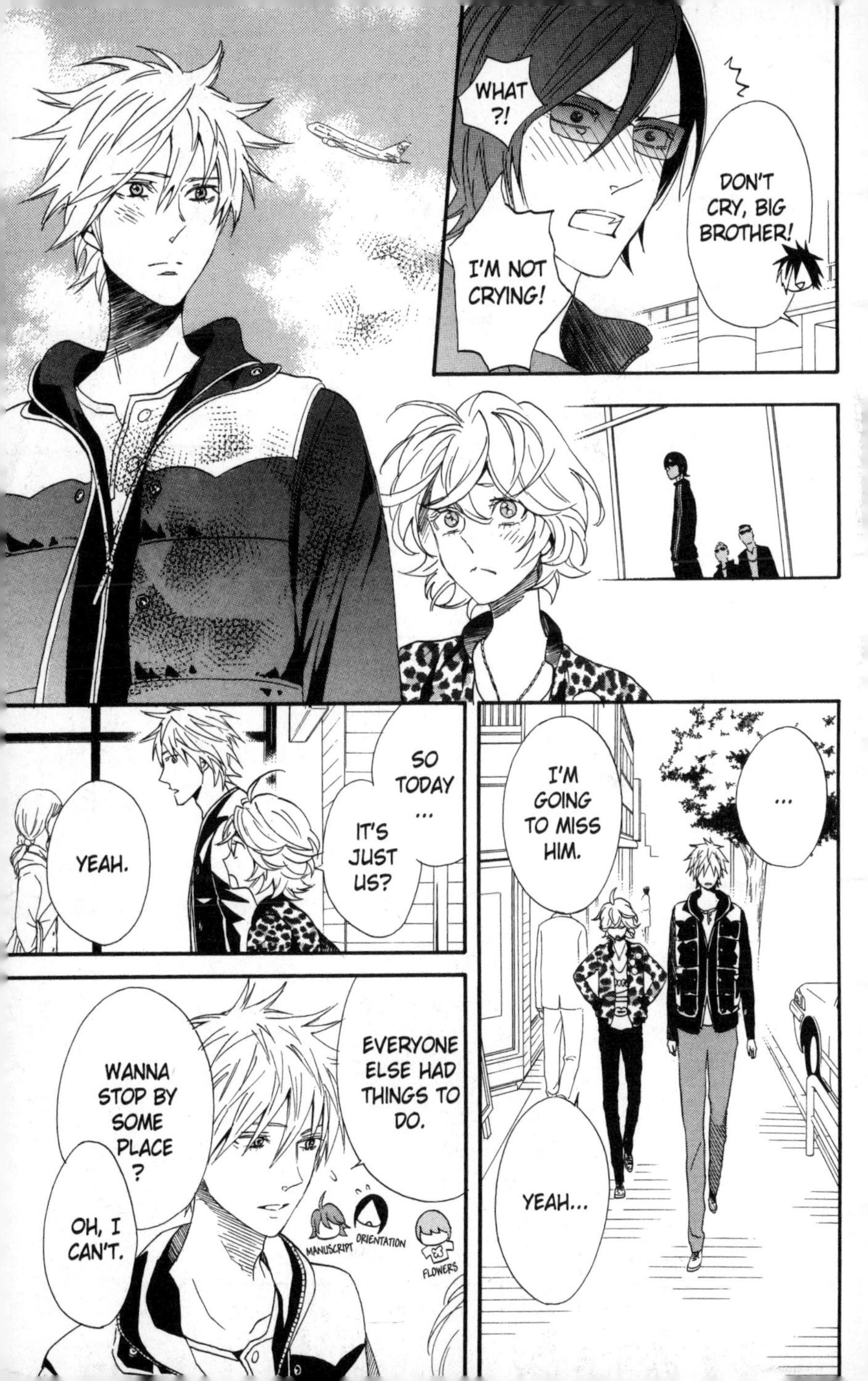
DON'T CRY, BIG BROTHER!
WHAT ?!
I'M NOT CRYING!
...
I'M GOING TO MISS HIM.
YEAH...
SO TODAY ...
IT'S JUST US?
YEAH.
EVERYONE ELSE HAD THINGS TO DO.
WANNA STOP BY SOME PLACE ?
OH, I CAN'T.
ORIENTATION
MANUSCRIPT
FLOWERS

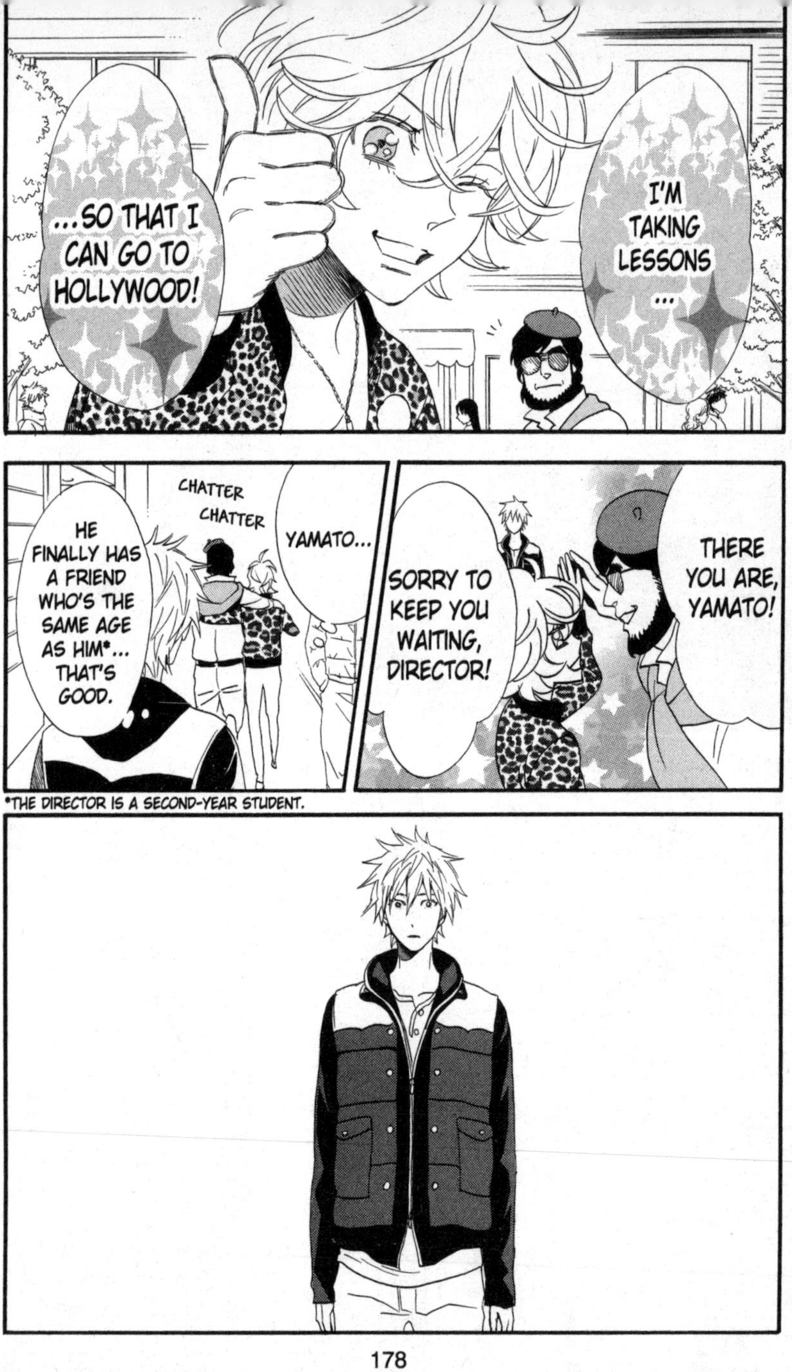
I'M TAKING LESSONS ...
...SO THAT I CAN GO TO HOLLYWOOD!
THERE YOU ARE, YAMATO!
SORRY TO KEEP YOU WAITING, DIRECTOR!
YAMATO...
CHATTER CHATTER
HE FINALLY HAS A FRIEND WHO'S THE SAME AGE AS HIM*... THAT'S GOOD.

*THE DIRECTOR IS A SECOND-YEAR STUDENT.

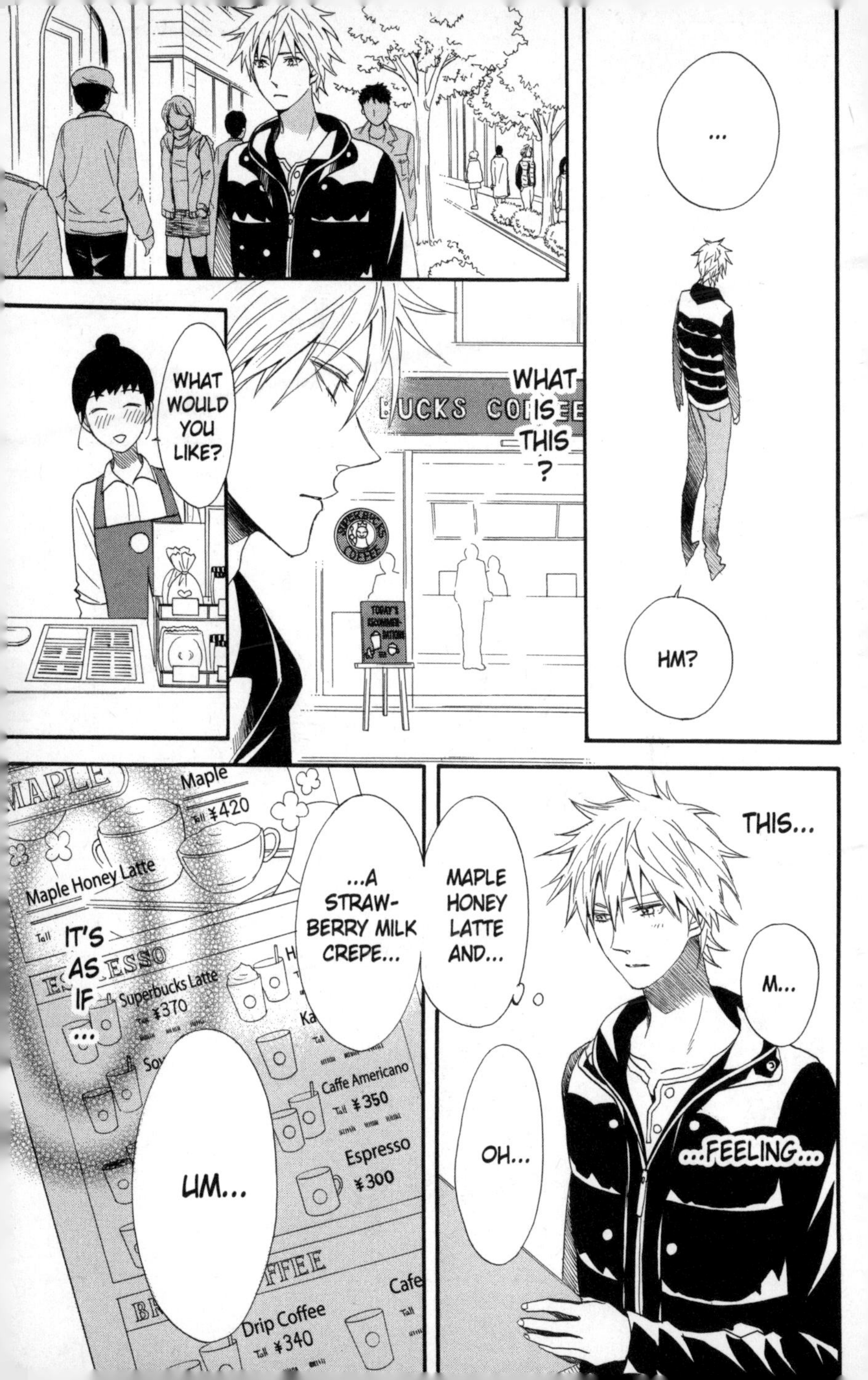
...
HM?
WHAT IS THIS?
WHAT WOULD YOU LIKE?
THIS...
M...
...FEELING...
OH...
MAPLE HONEY LATTE AND...
...A STRAWBERRY MILK CREPE...
IT'S AS IF ...
UM...
Maple
Tall ¥420
Maple Honey Latte
Superbucks Latte
Tall ¥370
Caffe Americano
Tall ¥350
Espresso
¥300
Drip Coffee
Tall ¥340

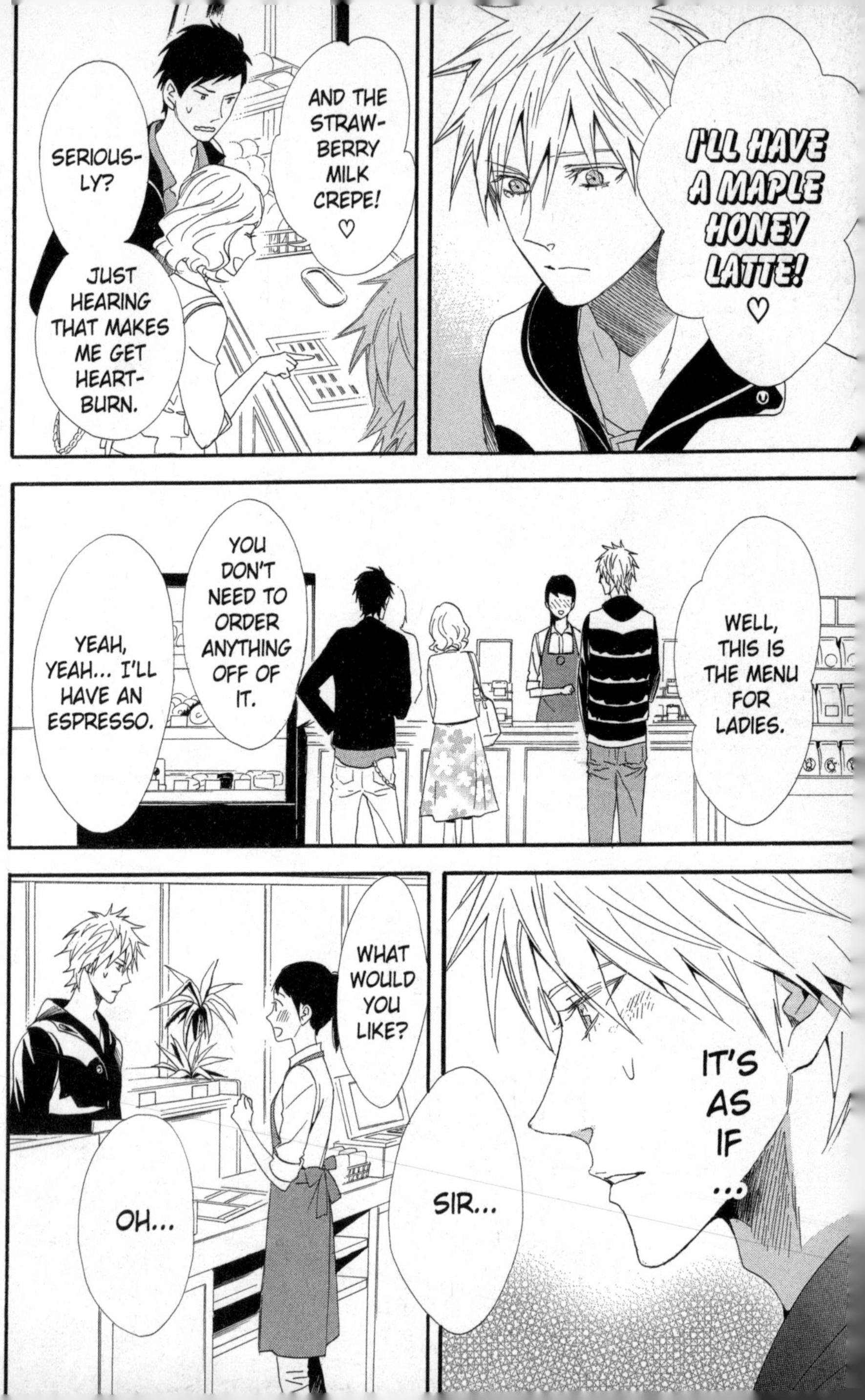
I'LL HAVE A MAPLE HONEY LATTE! ♡
AND THE STRAWBERRY MILK CREPE! ♡
SERIOUSLY?
JUST HEARING THAT MAKES ME GET HEARTBURN.
WELL, THIS IS THE MENU FOR LADIES.
YOU DON'T NEED TO ORDER ANYTHING OFF OF IT.
YEAH, YEAH... I'LL HAVE AN ESPRESSO.
IT'S AS IF ...
SIR...
WHAT WOULD YOU LIKE?
OH...

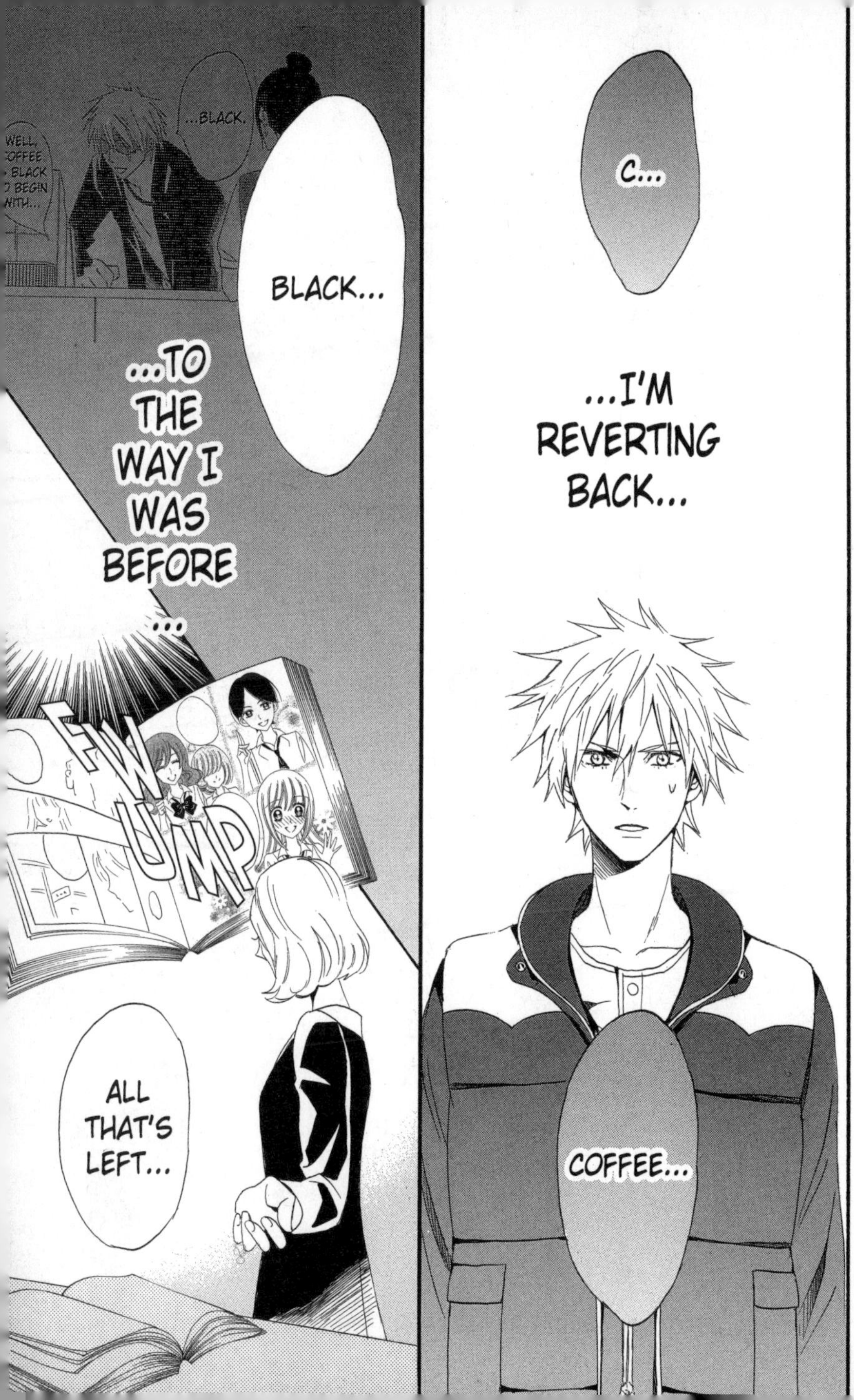
C...
...I'M REVERTING BACK...
COFFEE...
BLACK...
...BLACK.
WELL,
...TO THE WAY I WAS BEFORE...
FWUMP
ALL THAT'S LEFT...

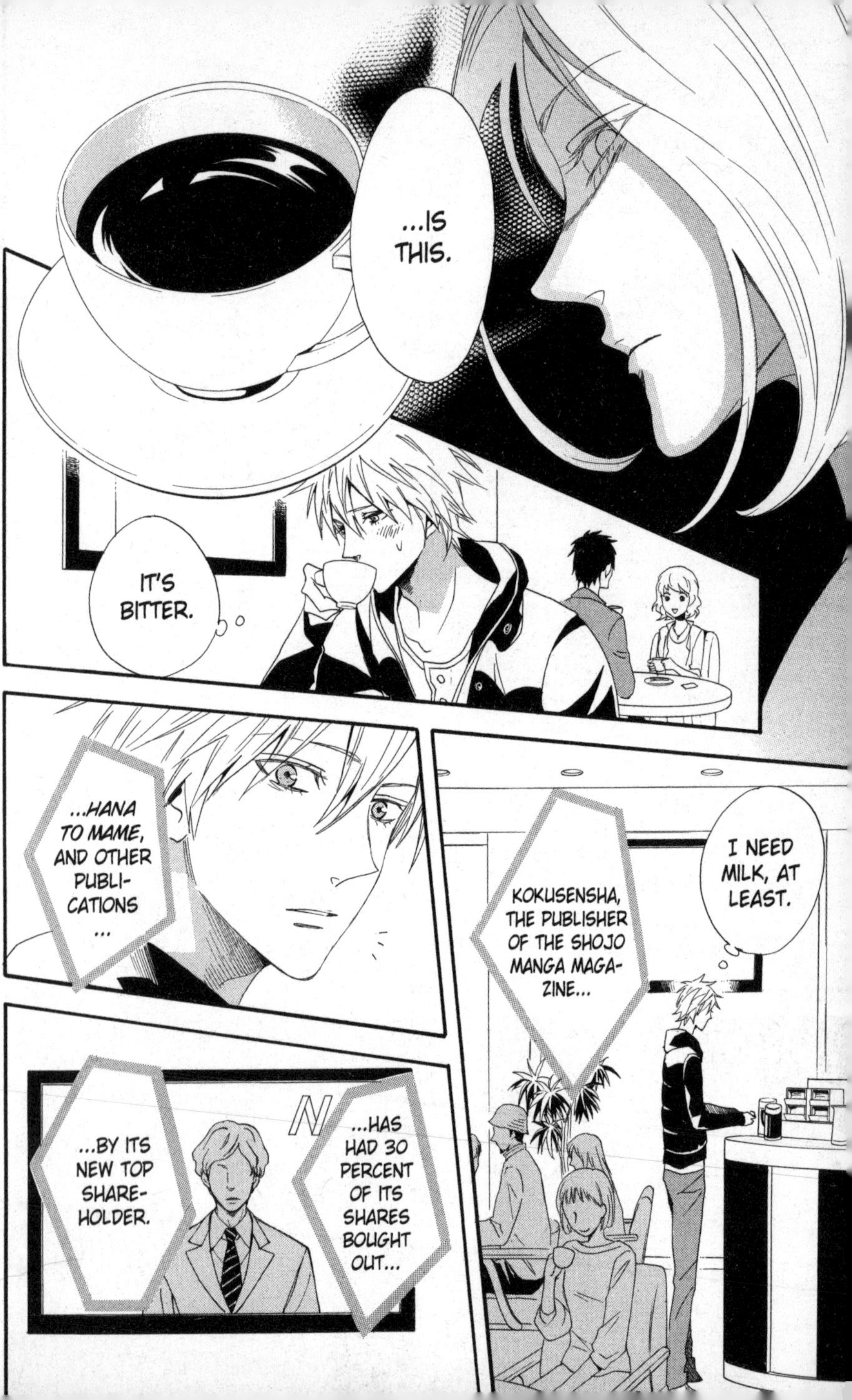
...IS THIS.
IT'S BITTER.
I NEED MILK, AT LEAST.
KOKUSENSHA, THE PUBLISHER OF THE SHOJO MANGA MAGAZINE...
...HANA TO MAME, AND OTHER PUBLICATIONS...
...HAS HAD 30 PERCENT OF ITS SHARES BOUGHT OUT...
...BY ITS NEW TOP SHAREHOLDER.
N

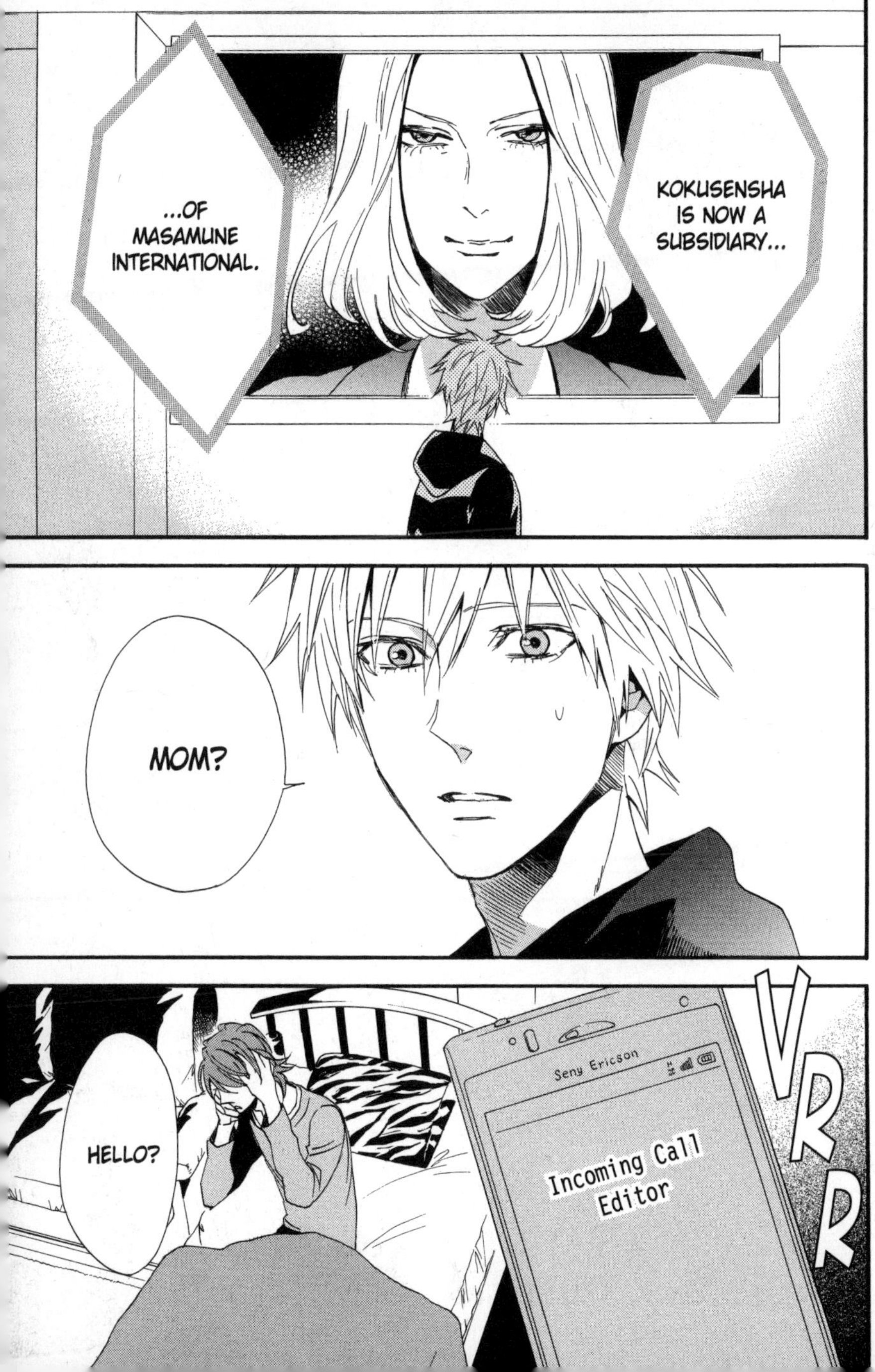
KOKUSENSHA IS NOW A SUBSIDIARY...
...OF MASAMUNE INTERNATIONAL.
MOM?
VRR
Seny Ericson
Incoming Call
Editor
HELLO?

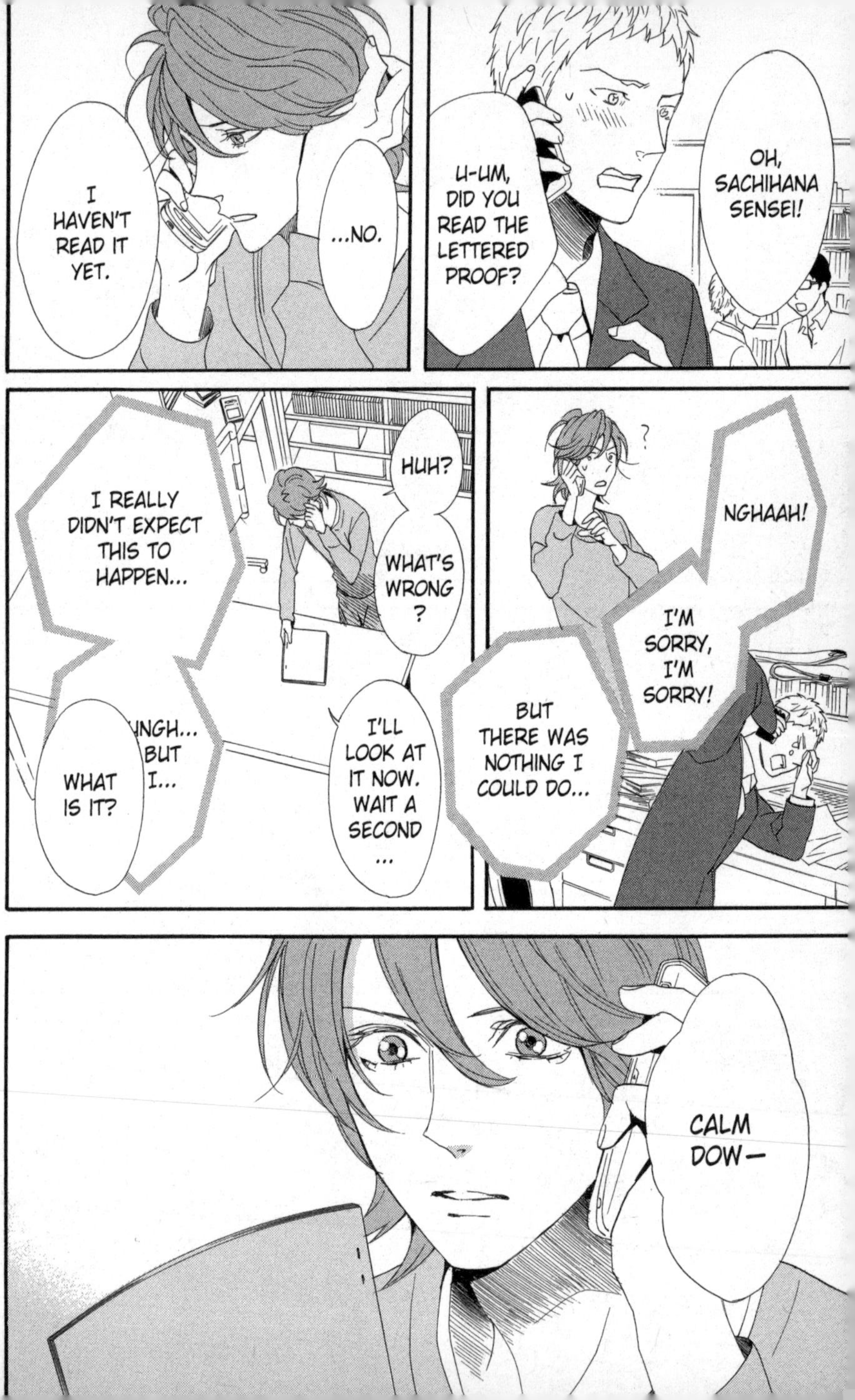
OH, SACHIHANA SENSEI!
U-UM, DID YOU READ THE LETTERED PROOF?
...NO.
I HAVEN'T READ IT YET.
NGHAAH!
I'M SORRY, I'M SORRY!
BUT THERE WAS NOTHING I COULD DO...
HUH?
WHAT'S WRONG?
I'LL LOOK AT IT NOW. WAIT A SECOND...
I REALLY DIDN'T EXPECT THIS TO HAPPEN...
NGH... BUT I...
WHAT IS IT?
CALM DOW—

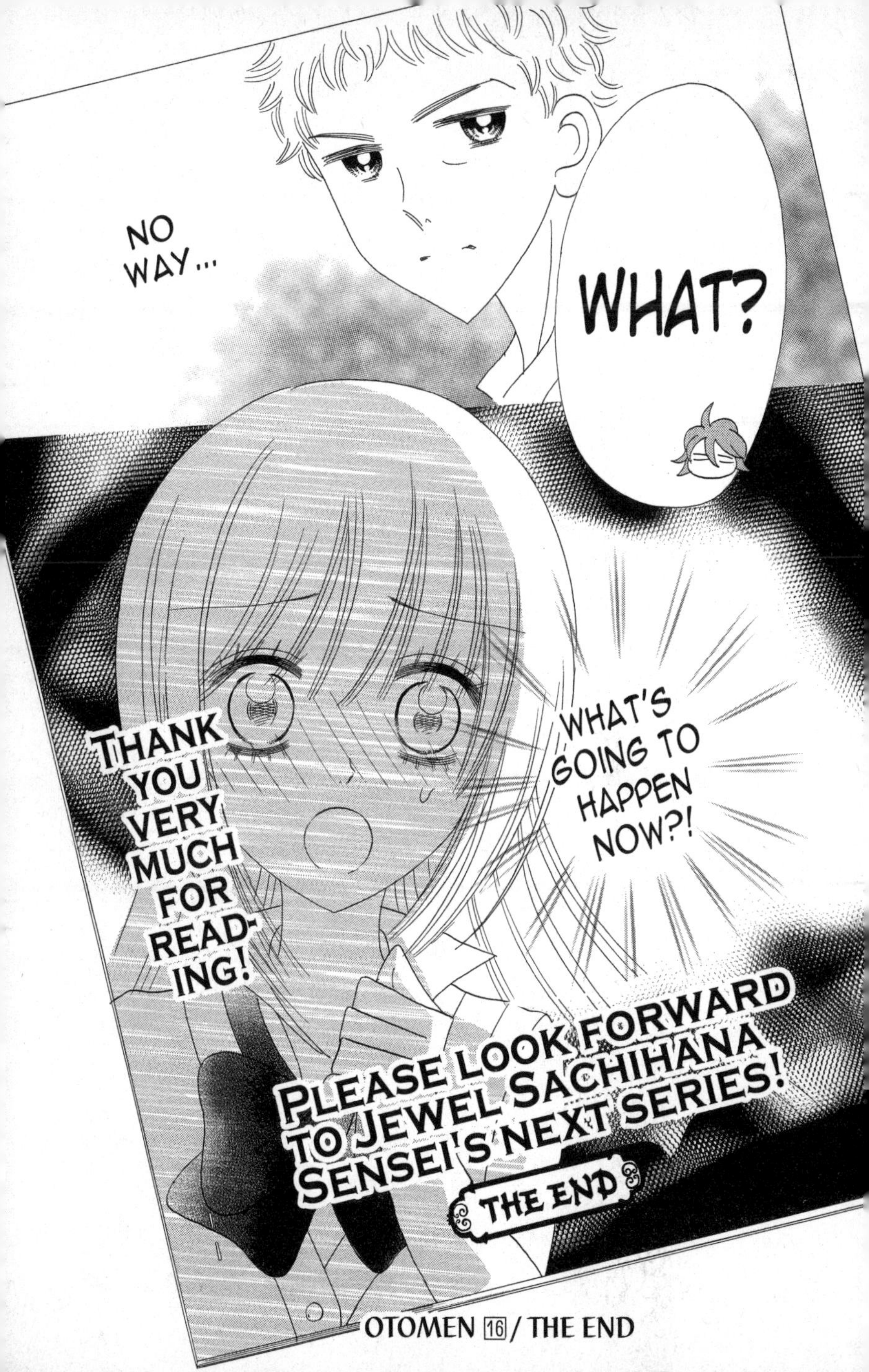
WHAT?
NO WAY...
WHAT'S GOING TO HAPPEN NOW?!
THANK YOU VERY MUCH FOR READ-ING!
PLEASE LOOK FORWARD TO JEWEL SACHIHANA SENSEI'S NEXT SERIES!
THE END

OTOMEN

COMMEMORATING THE UPCOMING **FINAL CHAPTER**

INTRODUCING THE ASSISTANTS WHO WORKED ON OTOMEN

THESE ARE THE ASSISTANTS WHO WORKED ON OTOMEN ALMOST ENTIRELY FROM BEGINNING TO END. THERE ARE EIGHT (PLUS TWO).

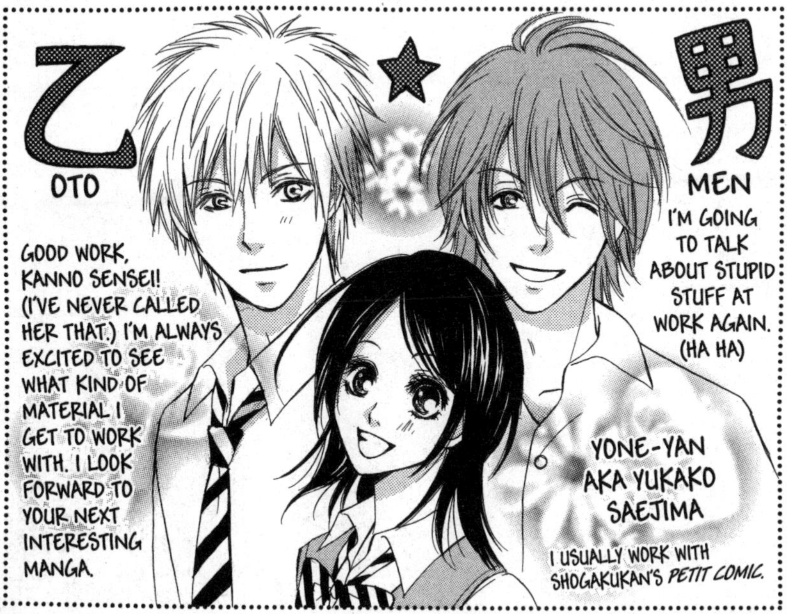

乙★男
OTO
MEN
I'M GOING TO TALK ABOUT STUPID STUFF AT WORK AGAIN. (HA HA)
YONE-YAN AKA YUKAKO SAEJIMA
I USUALLY WORK WITH SHOGAKUKAN'S *PETIT COMIC*.
GOOD WORK, KANNO SENSEI! (I'VE NEVER CALLED HER THAT.) I'M ALWAYS EXCITED TO SEE WHAT KIND OF MATERIAL I GET TO WORK WITH. I LOOK FORWARD TO YOUR NEXT INTERESTING MANGA.

KANNO SENSEI, THANK YOU VERY MUCH FOR THESE OTOMEN WHO ARE ALWAYS SO CUTE AND COOL!

I, NAKADA, ALWAYS LOOK FORWARD TO WORKING WITH YOU EVERY MONTH.

AT WORK, YOU ALWAYS WANT ME TO DO THINGS I'VE NEVER DRAWN BEFORE, SO I'VE OFTEN FELT CONFUSED...

ALSO, THE FOOD YOU DRAW LOOKS GOOD AND MAKES ME HUNGRY...

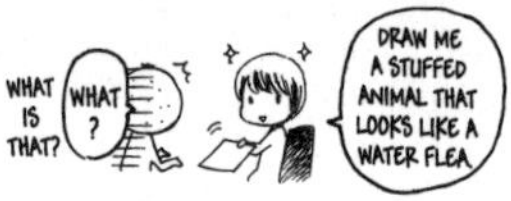
DRAW ME A STUFFED ANIMAL THAT LOOKS LIKE A WATER FLEA
WHAT ?
WHAT IS THAT?

THE ENDING IS COMING SOON! PLEASE HANG IN THERE UNTIL THE END!

ALSO, MY FAVORITE OTOMEN IS TONOMINE! ∞

MAYU NAKATA

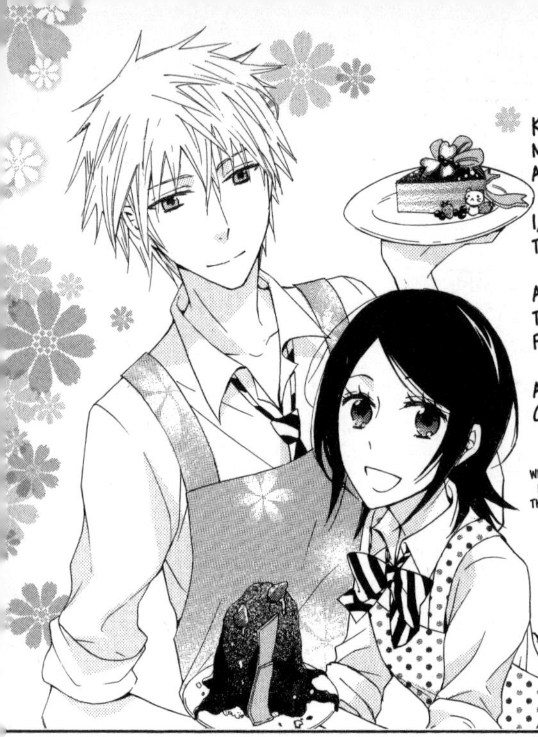

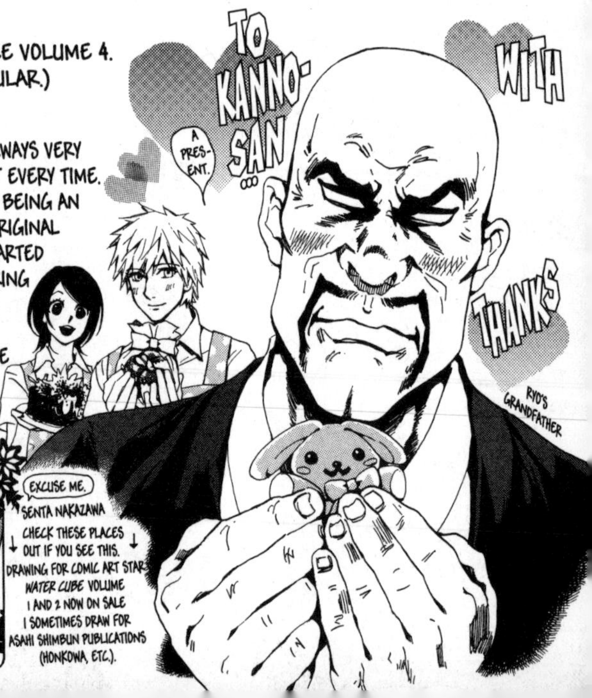
TO KANNO-SAN
WITH THANKS
A PRESENT.
RYO'S GRANDFATHER

I'VE BEEN AN ASSISTANT SINCE VOLUME 4. (CURRENTLY AN IRREGULAR.)

I'M SENTA NAKAZAWA.
THE MANUSCRIPT FOR *OTOMEN* IS ALWAYS VERY PLAYFUL. I HAVE FUN WORKING ON IT EVERY TIME. ONE OF THE SPECIAL PRIVILEGES OF BEING AN ASSISTANT IS THAT I CAN SEE THE ORIGINAL ROUGH DRAFT. BUT WHEN I FIRST STARTED WORKING, I WAS OFTEN ABSENT DURING THE DRAFTING. SO EVEN FIVE YEARS LATER, I SECRETLY MARVEL AT HOW BEAUTIFUL THE LINES ARE WHEN THE ORIGINAL DRAFT IS INKED.

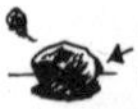

KANNO-SAN'S ERASER IS ALWAYS BLACK IN REACTION TO THIS BEAUTY.

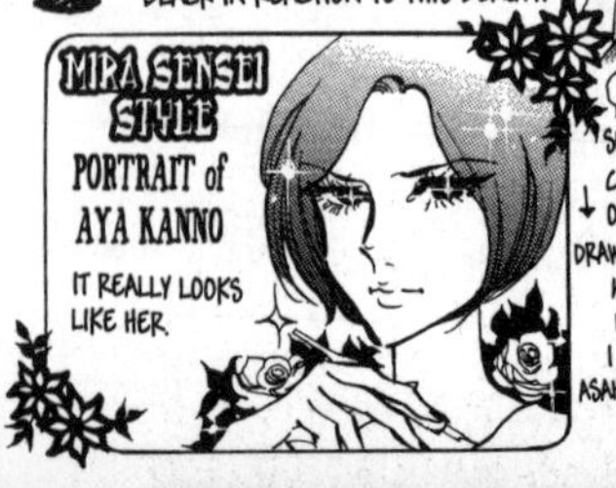
MIRA SENSEI STYLE
PORTRAIT of AYA KANNO
IT REALLY LOOKS LIKE HER.

EXCUSE ME.

SENTA NAKAZAWA

CHECK THESE PLACES OUT IF YOU SEE THIS.
DRAWING FOR COMIC ART STAR
WATER CUBE VOLUME 1 AND 2 NOW ON SALE
I SOMETIMES DRAW FOR ASAHI SHIMBUN PUBLICATIONS (HONKOWA, ETC.).

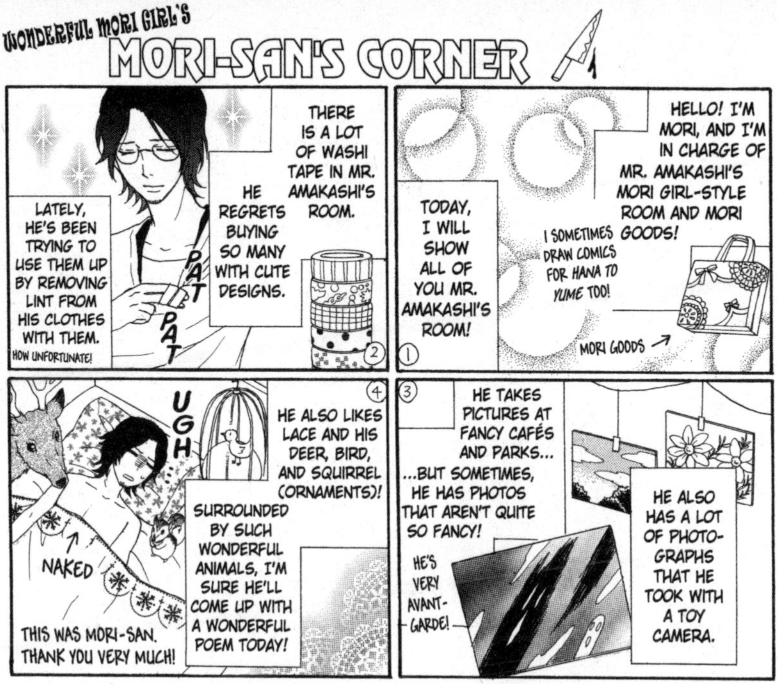
WONDERFUL MORI GIRL'S
MORI-SAN'S CORNER
HELLO! I'M MORI, AND I'M IN CHARGE OF MR. AMAKASHI'S MORI GIRL-STYLE ROOM AND MORI GOODS!
I SOMETIMES DRAW COMICS FOR HANA TO YUME TOO!
TODAY, I WILL SHOW ALL OF YOU MR. AMAKASHI'S ROOM!
MORI GOODS →
1
THERE IS A LOT OF WASHI TAPE IN MR. AMAKASHI'S ROOM.
HE REGRETS BUYING SO MANY WITH CUTE DESIGNS.
PAT PAT
LATELY, HE'S BEEN TRYING TO USE THEM UP BY REMOVING LINT FROM HIS CLOTHES WITH THEM.
HOW UNFORTUNATE!
2
3
HE TAKES PICTURES AT FANCY CAFÉS AND PARKS...
...BUT SOMETIMES, HE HAS PHOTOS THAT AREN'T QUITE SO FANCY!
HE ALSO HAS A LOT OF PHOTOGRAPHS THAT HE TOOK WITH A TOY CAMERA.
HE'S VERY AVANT-GARDE!
4
HE ALSO LIKES LACE AND HIS DEER, BIRD, AND SQUIRREL (ORNAMENTS)!
UGH
SURROUNDED BY SUCH WONDERFUL ANIMALS, I'M SURE HE'LL COME UP WITH A WONDERFUL POEM TODAY!
NAKED
THIS WAS MORI-SAN. THANK YOU VERY MUCH!

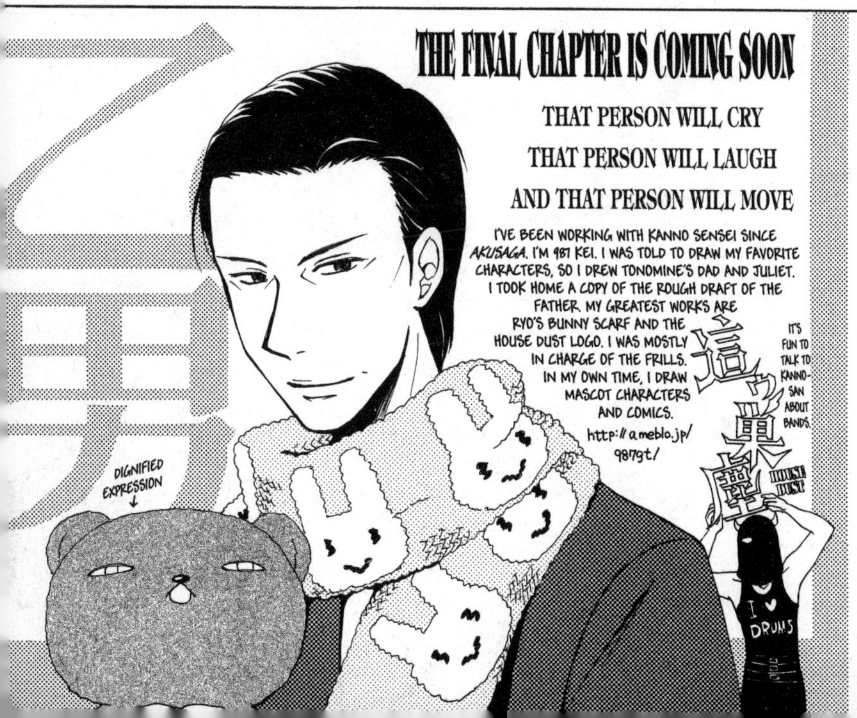
THE FINAL CHAPTER IS COMING SOON
THAT PERSON WILL CRY
THAT PERSON WILL LAUGH
AND THAT PERSON WILL MOVE
I'VE BEEN WORKING WITH KANNO SENSEI SINCE *AKUSAGA*. I'M 987 KEI. I WAS TOLD TO DRAW MY FAVORITE CHARACTERS, SO I DREW TONOMINE'S DAD AND JULIET. I TOOK HOME A COPY OF THE ROUGH DRAFT OF THE FATHER. MY GREATEST WORKS ARE RYO'S BUNNY SCARF AND THE HOUSE DUST LOGO. I WAS MOSTLY IN CHARGE OF THE FRILLS. IN MY OWN TIME, I DRAW MASCOT CHARACTERS AND COMICS.
http://ameblo.jp/9879t/
IT'S FUN TO TALK TO KANNO-SAN ABOUT BANDS.
HOUSE DUST
DIGNIFIED EXPRESSION ↓
I ♥ DRUMS

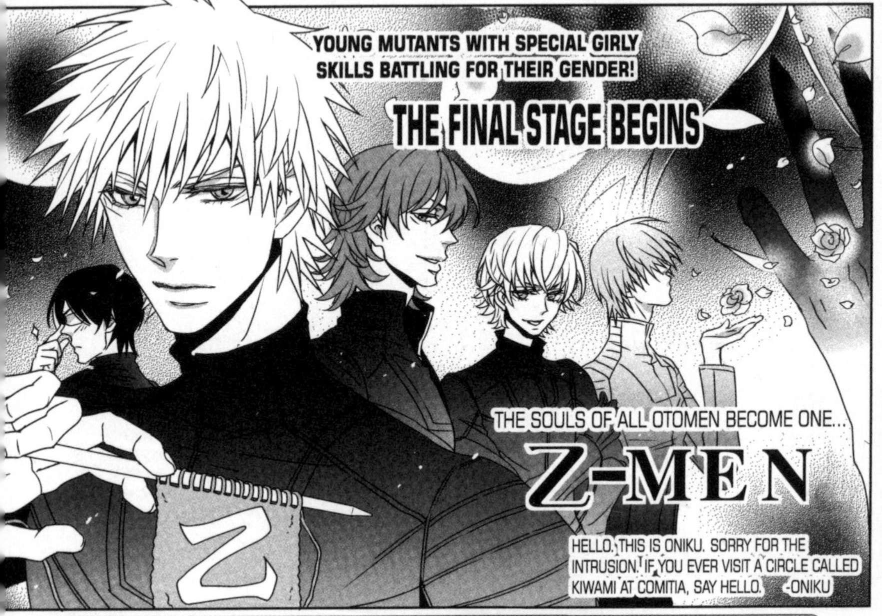
YOUNG MUTANTS WITH SPECIAL GIRLY SKILLS BATTLING FOR THEIR GENDER!
THE FINAL STAGE BEGINS
THE SOULS OF ALL OTOMEN BECOME ONE...
Z-MEN
HELLO. THIS IS ONIKU. SORRY FOR THE INTRUSION. IF YOU EVER VISIT A CIRCLE CALLED KIWAMI AT COMITIA, SAY HELLO. -ONIKU
Z

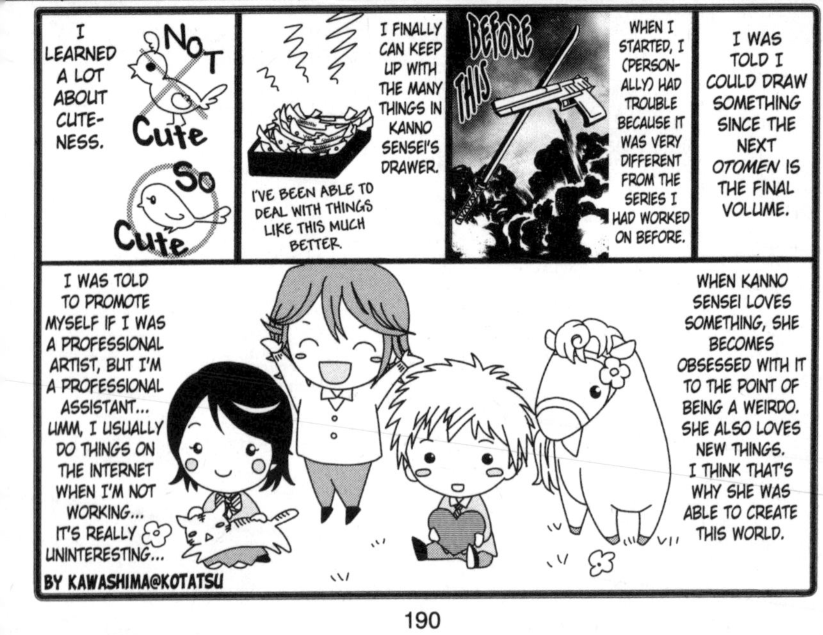
I WAS TOLD I COULD DRAW SOMETHING SINCE THE NEXT *OTOMEN* IS THE FINAL VOLUME.
WHEN I STARTED, I (PERSONALLY) HAD TROUBLE BECAUSE IT WAS VERY DIFFERENT FROM THE SERIES I HAD WORKED ON BEFORE.
BEFORE THIS
I FINALLY CAN KEEP UP WITH THE MANY THINGS IN KANNO SENSEI'S DRAWER.
I'VE BEEN ABLE TO DEAL WITH THINGS LIKE THIS MUCH BETTER.
I LEARNED A LOT ABOUT CUTENESS.
NOT Cute
So Cute
WHEN KANNO SENSEI LOVES SOMETHING, SHE BECOMES OBSESSED WITH IT TO THE POINT OF BEING A WEIRDO. SHE ALSO LOVES NEW THINGS. I THINK THAT'S WHY SHE WAS ABLE TO CREATE THIS WORLD.
I WAS TOLD TO PROMOTE MYSELF IF I WAS A PROFESSIONAL ARTIST, BUT I'M A PROFESSIONAL ASSISTANT... UMM, I USUALLY DO THINGS ON THE INTERNET WHEN I'M NOT WORKING... IT'S REALLY UNINTERESTING...
BY KAWASHIMA@KOTATSU

IN CHARGE OF SWEETS
I STARTED TO LOVE EATING SWEETS AND DRAWING THEM BECAUSE OF *OTOMEN*.

I ALSO DRAW COMICS, SO PLEASE TAKE A LOOK AT THEM IF YOU SEE ME. -KAINE AKITSUKI

THOSE WERE EIGHT OF MY ASSISTANTS. ONE OF THE OTHERS WHO WASN'T INTRODUCED BECAUSE SHE'S NOT A MANGA ARTIST IS SHIMADA-SAN. SHE'S BEEN MY FRIEND SINCE MIDDLE SCHOOL AND IS MY MANAGER AND FOOD ASSISTANT. THE OTHER IS SAYAKA-SAN (WHO DRAWS BEAUTIFUL LINES), WHO WAS MY ASSISTANT WHEN I FIRST BECAME A MANGA ARTIST.

PLEASE KEEP READING UNTIL THE END.

THE OTOMEN WORKPLACE IS VERY RELAXED. EVEN THOUGH THEY'RE MY ASSISTANTS, THEY'RE MORE LIKE MY FRIENDS. IT'S LIKE AN ALL-GIRLS SCHOOL. IT SOMETIMES BECOMES A SERIOUS 30-YEAR-OLD CHAT ROOM. I GET ALONG WITH THEM IN PUBLIC AND PRIVATE MATTERS. THEY ARE FUN FRIENDS.

I ALSO EXTEND MY THANKS TO THE MANY OTHER ASSISTANTS AND MANGA ARTISTS WHO HAVE HELPED ME OUT!

KANNO
☺

Confused by some of the terms, but too MANLY to ask for help?

Here are some **cultural notes** to assist you!

honorifics

Chan – an informal honorific used to address children and females. *Chan* can also be used toward animals, lovers, intimate friends and people whom one has known since childhood.

Kun – an informal honorific used primarily toward males; it can be used by people of more senior status addressing those junior to them or by anyone addressing male children.

San – the most common honorific title. It is used to address people outside one's immediate family and close circle of friends.

Senpai – used to address one's senior colleagues or mentor figures; it is used when students refer to or address more senior students in their school.

Sensei – honorific title used to address teachers as well as professionals such as doctors, lawyers and artists.

NOTES

Page 18, panel 5 | **Tsundere**
Tsundere describes someone who is cold or irritable (*tsuntsun*) and later becomes affectionate or sentimental (*deredere*).

Page 34, panel 1 | **Glass Mask**
Suzue Miuchi's *Glass Mask* (*Garasu no Kamen*) is a shojo manga series about acting.

Page 56, panel 4 | **Ono-no-Komachi**
Ono-no-Komachi is a Japanese female poet from the Heian period who was well known for her beauty.

Page 182, panel 4 | **Kokusensha**
Kokusensha is the fictional publisher of the *Love Chick* shojo manga series that Juta Tachibana draws secretly (under the pen name Jewel Sachihana).

Page 189, panel 1 | **Mori Girl**
"Mori Girl" is a Japanese fashion style that favors rustic, loose-fitting clothes that have earthy colors and are made from natural materials. The concept of the look is "a girl who lives in the forest."

Aya Kanno was born in Tokyo, Japan. She is the creator of *Soul Rescue* and *Blank Slate* (originally published as *Akusaga* in Japan's *BetsuHana* magazine).

OTOMEN

Vol. 16
Shojo Beat Edition

Story and Art by | **AYA KANNO**

Translation & Adaptation | **JN Productions**
Touch-up Art & Lettering | **Mark McMurray**
Design | **Fawn Lau**
Editor | **Amy Yu**

Otomen by Aya Kanno © Aya Kanno 2012
All rights reserved. First published in Japan in 2012 by HAKUSENSHA, Inc., Tokyo.
English language translation rights arranged with HAKUSENSHA, Inc., Tokyo.

The rights of the author(s) of the work(s) in this publication to be so identified
have been asserted in accordance with the Copyright, Designs and Patents Act 1988.
A CIP catalogue record for this book is available from the British Library.

Printed in the U.S.A.

Published by VIZ Media, LLC
P.O. Box 77010
San Francisco, CA 94107

10 9 8 7 6 5 4 3 2 1
First printing, September 2013

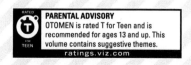

www.viz.com

www.shojobeat.com